Landmark Essays

Landmark
Essays
on
Basic Writing

Edited by Kay Halasek
and
Nels P. Highberg

 Hermagoras Press
An Imprint of Lawrence Erlbaum Associates, Publishers

Landmark Essays Volume Eighteen

Cover design by Kathi Zamminer

Lawrence Erlbaum Associates, Inc., Publishers
10 Industrial Avenue
Mahwah, New Jersey 07430

Library of Congress Cataloging-in-Publication Data

Landmark essays on basic writing / edited by Kay Halasek and Nels P. Highberg.
     p. cm. – (Landmark essays ; v. 18)
    Includes bibliographical references and index.
    ISBN 1-880393-29-8 (alk. Paper)
    1. English language–Rhetoric–Study and teaching. 2. English language–Grammar–Study and teaching. 3. Report writing–Study and teaching (Higher) 4. Basic English–Study and teaching (Higher) I. Halasek, Kay. II. Highberg, Nels Pearson. III. Series.
PE1404.L276 2001
808'.042'071–dc21   00-046130

Printed in the United States of America

10 9 8 7 6 5 4 3 2 1

In Memory of
Bob Conners

About the Editors

Kay Halasek is an Associate Professor of English at The Ohio State University where she also serves as the Director of First-Year Writing and teaches graduate and undergraduate courses in rhetoric and composition. She is author of *A Pedagogy of Possibility: Bakhtinian Perspectives on Composition Studies* (SIU Press, 1999) and *A Brief Guide to Basic Writing* (HarperCollins, 1993). Her current research project, *Literary Minds, Radical Lives* explores the teaching and social activism of Helen Grey Cone and others working at Hunter College in the late nineteenth and early twentieth centuries.

Nels P. Highberg is a PhD student in the Language, Literacy, and Rhetoric program in the Department of English at the University of Illinois at Chicago, where he has served as Assistant Director of Composition and as Production Editor for the journal, *Literature and Medicine*. He holds MAs in Women's Studies and Comparative Studies from The Ohio State University.

Acknowledgments

We are especially grateful to those who have assisted us in this project: Linda Bathgate, Tara Pauliny, Maureen Stanton, and Rebecca Greenberg Taylor. We also wish to acknowledge the Department of English at The Ohio State University for its financial support.

We are especially grateful to those who have assisted us in this project: Linda Bathgate, Tara Pauliny, Maureen Stanton, and Rebecca Greenberg Taylor. We also wish to acknowledge the Department of English at The Ohio State University for its financial support.

Table of Contents

Introduction:
Locality and Basic Writing
by Kay Halasek and Nels P. Highberg

Just when and where the first basic writing course was offered in an American college or university is a matter of ongoing debate among historians of composition. Most (e.g., Brereton, Connors, Lunsford) locate it in Harvard's English A and others (Cross, Levine) in Wellesley's "study habits" course or courses at Penn, Wisconsin, or Michigan (Wright). Mike Rose, on the other hand, argues against both the Harvard and Wellesley courses as the first remedial writing course in the United States, noting, for example, that the Wellesley course differed significantly from later remedial composition courses. Rather than identify origins at a particular location, Rose marks the appearance of basic writing at 1916 with the publication of Nila Banton Smith's *American Reading Instruction* ("Exclusion" 459). Despite differences of opinion on origins and location, historians generally agree that a quickly changing cultural and educational environment in the late 19th century was instrumental in the eventual development of basic writing courses. Most often cited by these historians as the first national attempt to address the perceived declining discursive skills among entering freshman are the Uniform Entrance Requirements and the Uniform Lists, two related initiatives of the National Education Association (NEA).

Responding to a "proliferation of entrance requirements" in American Colleges and Universities, the NEA established in 1892 The Committee of Ten, a group charged with "arrang[ing] a series of subject-area conferences to consider the whole problem of secondary school studies" (Applebee 32; see also Wright 9). Like the other conferences, the English conference met and submitted a report to Charles Eliot, chair of the Committee of Ten and then president of Harvard. Eliot collected the individual conference reports and compiled them into a final report in which he "attempted to create a consensus out of the often conflicting recommendations of the individual conferences" (Applebee 32–33). The report of the English conference, Arthur Applebee suggests, represented a summary and reconciliation of the contemporary points of view about the teaching of English. It began with a statement of the purpose of such studies:

The main objective of the teaching of English in schools seems to be two: (1) to enable the pupil to understand the expressed thoughts of others and to give expression to thoughts of his own; and (2) to cultivate a taste for reading, to give the pupil some acquaintance with good literature, and to furnish him with the means of extending that acquaintance. (33)

The report of the Committee of Ten appeared in 1894, the same year as the Uniform Entrance Requirements (UER), which came to dominate secondary school instruction. Not surprisingly, perhaps, Harvard had set the standard for college entrance requirements in 1873 when it tied the study of literature to composition courses, institutionalizing "the study of standard authors" in those courses (Applebee 30). Other colleges and universities adopted similar courses and initiated entrance examinations that included writing about literature. Because the texts upon which students were tested varied so greatly from college to college, schools were faced with the unenviable task of determining how to prepare students for the examinations. School educators soon insisted on uniformity (30–31). In 1894, the National Conference on Uniform Entrance Requirements in English met and established for the first time a Uniform List for the study of literature.

The UER were not, however, blindly or quietly accepted across the nation in colleges and universities. In the midwest, where the grip of the UER and its most problematic feature—the Uniform Lists—was weaker, resisters (like Fred Newton Scott of Michigan) called for abolition of the exams. In the east, where the UER were much more firmly entrenched, school and college faculty who saw little hope in abolishing the lists instead sought to "increase the freedom of the school within the general framework" (Applebee 50). Movements in New York City between 1907 and 1909 aimed to reorganize the secondary curricula and protested the Uniform Lists (51). The work of local and regional committees, like those in New York, and their concerns about English in the schools led, Applebee suggests, to the founding of the National Council of Teachers of English in 1911 (51).

The shifting focus in curricula at colleges had profound effect on secondary school instruction. Applebee reports that high school offerings of "'grammar'" in some schools "dropped from 60 to 35 percent," and "'rhetoric' from 90 to 63 percent" while "offerings in 'English literature'" rose from 30 percent to 70 percent between 1860 and 1890 as schools worked to prepare students for the study of literature (Applebee 37). A series of reports in 1907 showed that the curricula in 67 percent of midwestern high schools were determined by the UER. The percentages were much higher in schools along the eastern seaboard where the UER was even more dominant and "entrance lists were being elevated into a course of study" (49, 50).

One characteristic of most composition histories and their comments on the effects of the UER and Uniform List is a focus on particular locations: Ivy League, large land grant, or elite women's colleges. Notably absent from the discussion of the origins of basic writing are marginalized educational locations, the traditionally Black colleges and universities and female normal schools.[1] One such institution, the Female Normal School of New York City (later Hunter College), provides an interesting look into an alternative site for basic writing, one much more reflective of social and cultural change than Harvard, Penn, or Wellesley.[2] Unlike the more elite colleges, the Normal College (as an institution with an open admission policy for all female graduates of New York City high schools), saw come through its doors more immigrants, women of color, and first-generation college students than any Ivy league school at the turn of the century. Changes in school curricula as a result of the UER and Uniform Lists had an almost immediate effect on college curricula at schools like the Normal College, whose stated objective was the training of teachers for service in the public schools. Course offerings in both composition and literature at the College increased dramatically between 1893 (when students took only 6 points, or hours, of required or optional courses) and 1910, by which time the College had instituted a 22-hour minor in English and offered as many as 10 optionals in a given term.

Fast on the heels of the Report of the Committee of Ten, Professor Dundon, then chair of the Department of English and Classics at the Normal College, echoes in his 1894 Annual Report the same sentiments that led to the NEA initiatives:

> My assistants have almost succeeded in banishing slang from the conversation of students. They have done good work in the important matters of spelling, capitalizing, and punctuation, and have been diligent in enlarging the vocabularies of their pupils and in fixing the meaning of words. The business of our teachers did not, however, stop here. Our true objective point was the sentence, and the mastery of those principles that make or mar the expression of a complete thought.... That teaching may and does include with us other things, but there is sufficient in the sentence itself to call forth our best efforts.... (22)

These concerns, which reflect the statements of the Committee of Ten, remained entrenched at and guided the curricula of the Normal College well into the twentieth century and led in 1908 to the development of a "drill class" designed to make up "deficiencies" in elementary English and "defects" in oral English. Although a requirement for graduation, the drill class did not appear in college bulletins of information or programmes (published course offerings) and were never instituted officially as college offerings. Nevertheless, the drill class was an institutional response to a changing student body, entrance requirements, and secondary school curricula and illustrates shifts in the focus and intent of the writing program. What is more interesting, perhaps, than the drill course itself are Department Chair Helen Gray Cone's telling statements about the complicity of the Committee of Ten and UER themselves in bringing on the need for additional training in composition in the first year of study. Cone begins her Chair's report to the President of the Normal College in 1908 by noting the

> deficiency in elementary English of a small number of students in each of our college years, [which] greatly complicates the work of the department.... It appears that the deficiency is due rather to general conditions than to the defects of individual teachers or institutions. Personally I believe that the tendency of the College Entrance Requirements in English has been to place too much emphasis on the study of English

classics, at the expense of time needed for practice in the common forms of written and spoken English.

By emphasizing the study of literature, secondary schools teaching students under the mandates of the UER neglected—in Cone's estimation—necessary "preliminary" instruction in "elementary English." The UER, in effect, caused (or at least exacerbated) notable decline in the writing abilities of students enrolled in the Normal College.

Much of the scholarship between the early 1920s and early 1970s is dominated by complaints similar to those articulated by Dundon and Cone on two separate but related issues: (a) the pervasive and recurring perception that students' literacy skills were in significant decline and (b) the pedagogical and curricular difficulties caused by increasing numbers of immigrant, working-class, and non-White students attending college. In the minds of many educators, of course, the two events were intimately linked: The increased diversity of the student population was a direct cause of the decline in test scores, grades, and overall achievement among high school and college students. Deficiency became a recurring theme among those writing about their experiences in the "remedial" writing classroom. A reader needn't look far to find articles during this 50-year span that are informed by a deficiency model of the remedial writer. Carroll Towle's (1928) "The Awkward Squad at Yale," E. S. Noyes' (1929) "The Program of the Awkward Squad," John Kirby's (1931) "Make-Up English at Northwestern," Guy Diffenbaugh's (1932) "Teaching the Unteachables," Dorothy Dakin's (1934) "Sub-Freshman English," Frank McCloskey and Lillian Hornstein's (1950) "Subfreshman Composition—A New Solution," and Jeffrey Youdelman's (1978) "Limited Students: Remedial Writing and the Death of Open Admissions" all speak to the power of this characterization of basic writing students.[3]

The increasingly diverse student population between 1920 and 1970 was seen as problematic by many, whose suspicions were confirmed whenever working class and immigrant students and students of color did not perform as well as their privileged Anglo counterparts on entrance exams and in courses. The conflation of race and class and remediation in particular gained considerable speed in basic writing scholarship during the 1960s and 1970s with the advent of open admissions in many colleges and the return of veterans from Vietnam.[4] As Jacqueline Jones Royster and Jean Williams argue, this conflation of race and remediation simultaneously oversimplifies and deracinates the changing student popluation of this period and overlooks the significant history of students of color prior to open admissions.[5]

This very brief look into some of the early moments in the history of basic writing establishes for readers the context into which Mina Shaughnessy stepped with the publication in 1977 of *Errors and Expectations*, the first (and for over a decade the only) extensive and introspective look at the work of basic writing students. Although Shaughnessy's text does not mark the *beginning* of basic writing instruction, it stands as a crucial turn toward informed pedagogical and theoretical inquiry into the texts of basic writers, a relocation of the discipline, if you will. At the same time, it is also inaccurate to claim that Shaughnessy's work *alone* brought with it a paradigmatic shift in the scholarship, research, and teaching of basic writing. Her work stands alongside "The Students' Right to Their Own Language" (1974) and the work of Janet Emig, Andrea Lunsford, Sondra Perl, Geneva Smitherman, Lynn Troyka, Louise Yelin, and others whose contributions to the collective understanding of basic writing initiated in the 1970s a shift in the discipline's understanding of dialect, literacy skills, and basic writing instruction.

Scholarship on basic writing and basic writers that pre-dates "The Students' Rights" and Shaughnessy's earliest work was not entirely uninformed, but much of it, as we suggest above, defined and represented basic writing students as deficient, undisciplined, and illiterate. These early characterizations of basic writers as awkward, limited, and unteachable persist—if not in the scholarship appearing in the *Journal of Basic Writing, College English,* or *College Composition and Communication,* then in the public sphere. Not merely a matter of semantics, the notion of students as "unteachable" continues to carry with it significant capital in the university and in a U.S. consciousness that also equates remediation with race.

The essays selected for this volume of *Landmark Essays* speak directly to just those kinds of debilitating assumptions that place not only basic writing students but also teachers of basic writing and the discipline itself on the margins of educational, economic, and political localities of influence. The collection is designed to present readers with previously published essays that together depict the fundamental and shifting theoretical, methodological, and pedagogical assumptions of basic writing instruction over the past two decades. Arranged roughly chronologically, from Adrienne Rich's 1979 "Teaching Language in Open Admissions" to Jacqueline Jones Royster and Rebecca Greenberg Taylor's 1997 "Constructing Teacher Identity in the Basic Writing Classroom," the essays examine such issues as defining basic writers, the phenomenology of error, cognitivism and writing instruction, the social construction of remediation, and the politics of basic writing pedagogy in a postmodern world. That is, they collectively speak to what we perceive as some of the most enduring and important debates in the field of basic writing. At the same time, they collectively illustrate that neither the basic writing classroom nor recent scholarship need be *intellectually* marginalized locations. Here we valued scholars and teachers claiming the "margin"—the basic writing classroom—as a borderland, a site of contention and negotiation that allows for a cultural and pedagogical reflection and critique not available to them in more centrally located sites in English departments.

Landmark Essays on Basic Writing is not the first collection to bring together previously published essays on this subject. It joins Theresa Enos' (1987) comprehensive *Sourcebook for Basic Writing,* which in many ways set the terms for the essays included in this volume of *Landmark Essays.*[6] Enos' text encouraged us to limit ourselves either to seminal essays written before 1987 but not included in the *Sourcebook* or essays written after its publication. The goal in the *Landmark Essays on Basic Writing* is not, then, to provide a history of scholarship on basic writing or to retrace ground already covered by Enos. By including in the collection primarily essays published between 1987 and 1997, we bring together essays that historicize the preceding decades of scholarship and also anticipate the future of the field. The collection, for example, moves thematically from situating and defining basic writers and basic writing scholarship (Rich, Bizzell, Rose, Lu) to questions of the relationships among methodology, ideology, and race (Fiore and Elsasser, Delpit, Patthey-Chavez and Gergen, Lazere, and Lu). The volume closes with a series of essays (Harris, Bartholomae, Stygall, Scott, and Royster and Taylor) that collective move the field "Toward a Post-Critical Pedagogy of Basic Writing."

(Re)Defining Basic Writing and Basic Writers

This section of the collection begins and ends, as it were, with Mina Shaughnessy. It opens with Adrienne Rich's "Teaching Language in Open Admissions," which is dedicated to Shaughnessy's memory, and closes with Min-zhan Lu's "Redefining the Legacy of Mina Shaughnessy: A Critique of the Politics of Linguistic Innocence."

Rich's essay struck us as a fitting opening for this collection for it brings a narrative vision and quality rarely found in scholarship on basic writing. We see through Rich's experiences the "graffiti-sprayed walls of tenements" and "the uncollected garbage" on the streets of New York and witness the lives of students and teachers as they come together to make sense out of the circumstances of their collective educational endeavors in the SEEK program at the City College of New York in 1968. We encounter, in a way we do not in *Errors and Expectations*, the larger social, political, and human contexts for Shaughnessy's study. In the essay we also see Rich formulating many of the questions that continue to demand our attention in basic writing scholarship: What should be the materials for basic writing courses? Its goals? How can teachers of economic and educational privilege situate themselves in a basic writing classroom where many of the students are from the economic underclass? She articulates for us, as well, that condition of education that is most simply defined as institutional racism and classism. Rich relates Ellen Lurie's findings in *How to Change the Schools*, noting that "tracking begins at kindergarten (chiefly on the basis of skin color and language) and that nonwhite and working-class children are assumed to have a maximum potential which fits them only for the so-called general diploma" (59). From the opening pages of the collection, then, we have Rich introducing one of the most persistent, false, and problematic assumptions in education—what Royster and Williams refer to as a "conflation" of race and remediation (570). It is not surprising, perhaps, given her approach to the subject of basic writing, to see Rich citing Paulo Freire, insisting on the need for students to learn to use language for critical reflection, and calling on educators—as Shaughnessy did, as well—to reassess their methods and materials for teaching. At the same time, Rich's narrative demands of us a critical self-reflection of our own. To what degree, we might ask, have we managed to address the problematic state of affairs that she names?

Mina Shaughnessy's work enjoyed nearly universal acclaim from its publication.[7] Not until Min-zhan Lu's "redefinition" in 1991 is Shaughnessy's work subjected to sustained and powerful critique.[8] Lu turns to Shaughnessy's work to illustrate a larger disciplinary critique of basic writing pedagogy and theory, in part because of its significance in the field. *Errors and Expectations* illustrates for Lu the tendency among scholars to deemphasize or overlook altogether the "political dimensions of the linguistic choices students make in their writing" (27). Instead, studies like Shaughnessy's and the pedagogies that derive from them, Lu argues, focus almost exclusively on teaching students to master the conventions of academic discourse and develop a sense of personal authority and confidence in their writing. In redefining Shaughnessy's work, Lu points to the need for teachers to move beyond the grammatical and syntactic and toward the political and explain to students that as they become proficient in new languages (in this case, academic languages and discourses), they also develop new perspectives, new "points of view" on the subjects about which they're reading and writing (34). Adopting academic discourse, in other words, has political consequences, a fact not addressed by early pedagogies or theories of basic writing.

In her critique of *Errors and Expectations,* Lu identifies in Shaughnessy's work the presence of the long-standing debate taken up next by Patricia Bizzell in "What Happens When Basic Writers Come to College?" If one holds an essentialist view of language (as Lu claims Shaughnessy does), how does one address the conflicts that will naturally arise when students face the inevitable decisions between home and academic discourses? Bizzell, like Lu, denies essentialist notions of language and then extends the discussion to a question of epistemology. Basic writers' problems, Bizzell writes, "are best understood as stemming from the initial distance between their world-views and the academic world view, and perhaps also from the resistance to changing their own world views that is caused by this very distance" (297). We do not, in other words, gain anything by defining basic writers in terms of specific kinds of language practices or cognitive abilities. At the same time, we must pay particular attention to the very real consequences that basic writers face when entering the university.

In the late 1970s and well into the 1980s, Bizzell and other compositionists, including Mike Rose, felt the very real influence of cognitive science on research in the field, including basic writing. Rose's "Narrowing the Mind and Page: Remedial Writers and Cognitive Reductionism" stands as a critical moment in the developing scholarship in basic writing, for when it appeared in 1988, cognitive studies and cognitive understandings of student achievement still held significant sway. Rose, rather than simply dismiss cognitive studies out of hand (a move he was unlikely to make as he understood the value of insight provided by cognitive studies generally), argues that "we need to look closer at these claims and the theories used to support them, for both the theories and the claims lead to social distinctions that have important consequences, political as well as educational" (268). Like Lu and Bizzell, Rose situates his study as a means of identifying and critiquing those theories that relegate political and educational concerns to the background. He is methodical in his critique, examining the notions of field dependence–independence, hemisphericity, stages in cognitive development, and orality–literacy and drawing conclusions and implications for composition studies and basic writing. Most specifically, the study stands as a warning to those who would define basic writers too quickly as field dependent, situated at earlier levels of cognitive development, or bound to oral rather than literate discursive operations.

These first essays, collectively, articulate a series of related mandates for work in basic writing. Through either their own thick descriptions of cultural and educational scenes (Rich) or their explicit call for scholars to define both basic writers and their political contexts more fully (Bizzell, Rose, Lu), the essays in this section move basic writing from a reliance on essentialism and toward more politicized notions of basic writers, language, and epistemology.

Postmodernism and Literacy Education

If we see Bizzell, Rose, and Lu articulating the need for scholars and teachers to identify and focus upon the political and social as essential elements of basic writing theory, pedagogy, and research, then we find in Part II of *Landmark Essays on Basic Writing* scholars actively investigating the implications of the political on the basic writing classroom in a postmodern world. Here, we move into basic writing classrooms in a variety of locations—Albuquerque, the Bahamas, and Baltimore—in which students are encouraged to "bring their culture, their knowledge, into the classroom," and the curricula of basic writing classrooms change in response (Fiore and Elsasser 116). Gone are textbooks and workbooks that constrained and limited student writing experiences in the 1950s, 1960s, and 1970s. Textbooks and workbooks remain as alien and problematic here as they did for Rich and Shaughnessy in the SEEK program at CCNY. In fact, that very freedom from textbooks and a pedagogy informed by assumptions of student deficiency allows for the kind of change that makes the basic writing classrooms of Fiore and Elsasser and Patthey-Chavez possible.

Guided by Freire and Vygotsky and her conversations with colleagues in New Mexico, including Kyle Fiore, Nan Elsasser embarks on her teaching at the College of the Bahamas with a goal of moving the students from a position of accepting "passively received knowledge" and seeking it out and generating it (119). "'Strangers No More'" illustrates the ways that Elsasser worked to implement a student-generated pedagogy in which the women in her class shared responsibility for setting out the terms of the curriculum and course theme. The readings and assignments are challenging but rewarding, for the women invest a great deal (and have a great investment) in the subject and the eventual collaborative assignment they compose, an "Open Letter to Bahamian Men." This letter gives the women an opportunity to "use writing as a means of intervening in their own social environment" in a way no traditional curriculum could have (125). Fiore and Elsasser do, in fact, illustrate how Freire's pedagogy can work outside Brazilian peasant communities, but more than this, it illustrates the power of trusting students, their capabilities, their interests, their motivations, and their abilities to rise to the challenges put before them, individually and collectively, when they are given both the responsibility and opportunity to have a voice in the content of their writing courses.

Lisa Delpit's "'The Silenced Dialogue': Power and Pedagogy in Educating Other People's Children" is often read as a damning critique of process pedagogy, a statement of the problematic nature of a pedagogical method that often leaves unaddressed those discrete discursive skills that Black and poor students must master if their texts are to have the look of literacy. The essay is much more than this, in the same way that Lu's critique of Shaughnessy is much more. Here, Delpit uses the process vs. skills debate (as well as other examples) as a means of uncovering and critiquing larger societal and educational "'cultures of power'" that inform U.S. classrooms. Progressive and liberal educators, she argues, do significant and irreparable damage to students who are not participants in the culture of power (e.g., Black and poor students) by ignoring or denying that cultures of power exist and, in turn, by refusing or being unable to articulate for students the "rules of that culture" (282). Delpit, however, does not advocate a simple, unself-reflexive return to direct instruction. She clearly recognizes the necessity of allowing students to use their knowledge and to write for "real audiences and real purposes" (as Elsasser did) at the same time that the conventions and expectations of academic discourse are explicitly named, taught, and used (288). Delpit's narrative analysis, coupled with the chorus of teachers she quotes, constructs a rich look into the cultural divide that exists in classrooms in which (Anglo) teachers, even those with the best of intentions, do not recognize themselves as part of the institutional and cultural forces constructed to ensure the continued success of Anglo and middle class students at the further disenfranchisement of poor students and students of color. The pedagogical divide is articulated no stronger than in Delpit's contrastive descriptions of those classrooms many progressive educators would describe as democratic and those they would describe as authoritarian. The latter, she argues are, in fact, preferable for many students because the expectations and responsibilities are clearly defined. In the former, Delpit points out, directives are still sent; they're merely couched as invitations or suggestions, not as defined expectations.

G. Genevieve Patthey-Chavez and Constance Gergen's work illustrates the pedagogical value of a stance like Delpit's. The basic writing classroom, they argue, is a site ripe for exploring and bridging the kinds of cultural differences Delpit describes. Like Fiore and Elsasser, Patthey-Chavez and Gergen imagine the classroom as a place for bringing together for the benefit of students and teachers the variety of cultures represented in the classroom. In the case of Patthey-Chavez and Gergen's essay, the classroom described is one in which a variety of essayist traditions are studied and encouraged "*in concert with* rather than at the expense of student voices" (77). Here, we see Freirean and Vygotskian philosophies of critical pedagogy and language development used to produce a "problem-posing education" in basic writing. Like Fiore and Elsasser and Delpit, Patthey-Chavez and Gergen are centrally concerned with those basic writers who are not participants in the culture of power, namely "students from linguistic and ethnic minorities," including multilingual writers (83). Their assumptions, in many respects, read as glosses of Delpit:

> While it is necessary to have students explore their own beliefs about essay writing and other literacy events, it is equally important that they gain some insights into the values and beliefs of target discourses. They need "inside information" about future discourse communities that have not been too welcoming, and English teachers are an ideal source of such information. (85–86)

Teachers, as arbiters of the cultures of power, have both the ability and the responsibility to relay to students information that will lay bare those cultures. The cultural conversation in the classroom, they suggest, might well represent a Bakhtinian dialogue in which competing and colliding voices come together to construct a more complex and richer understanding of the subject at hand.

Daniel Lazere shakes the tree of "liberatory" pedagogy as it has come to be defined in the United States in generally Freirean terms, raising again the possibility of basic skills as a means of empowerment first articulated by Delpit:

> I have become convinced that leftists err greivously in rejecting, as dogmatically as conservatives endorse it, a restored emphasis on basic skills and knowledge which might be a force for liberation—not oppression—if administered with common sense, openness to cultural pluralism, and an application of basics toward critical thinking, particularly about sociopolitical issues, rather than rote memorizing. (9)

Where the other authors in this section depict classrooms and pedagogies, Lazere undertakes a marxist critique of both liberal and conservative motives for pedagogical choices. A leftist educator himself, Lazere nonetheless launches a critique of James Sledd, Andrew Sledd, and Richard Ohmann, among others, for their refusal to see beyond their own assumptions about the relative value of various approaches to literacy education. Here we have Delpit's argument abstracted, separated from the goings-on in the classroom and rearticulated as a manifesto encouraging leftist and progressive educators to reassess and perhaps redefine their understanding of pedagogical oppression and liberation.

Agonistic metaphors abound in Min-zhan Lu's "Conflict and Struggle: The Enemies or Preconditions of Basic Writing," just as they do in Lazere's "Back to Basics." Lu's work again provides a provocative culmination to a section of *Landmark Essays*. Although acknowledged in all of the essays in Part II, conflict and struggle present themselves in Lu's work as the central metaphors through which students outside the cultures of power—those about which Fiore, Elsasser, Delpit, Patthey-Chavez, Gergen, and Lazere write—negotiate the university classroom and its demands for certain kinds of literate behavior. The stories from the "borderlands," she writes, become increasingly important in an educational context in which multiculturalism, diversity, and postmodernism all speak to the value of imagining students as neither existing outside (and therefore entirely alienated from) nor "'comfortably inside'" (and therefore complacent about) the academy. Instead, she argues, writers might most productively situate themselves "at a site of conflict" (888). Taking Shaughnessy to task again, and also Kenneth Bruffee and Thomas Farrell, Lu uncovers and examines the tendency in basic writing scholarship to "treat the students' fear of acculturation and the accompanying sense of contradiction and ambiguity as a *deficit*" (889). She goes on to note, in terms that echo Delpit's, that on the one hand, "Bruffee and Farrell present students' acculturation as inevitable and beneficial" while "Shaughnessy promises them that learning academic discourse will not result in acculturation" (889). Lu argues, instead, that only through conflict and struggle will basic writers—again, particularly those outside the cultures of power—be able to locate themselves in the basic writing classroom and university.

Each of the essays defines as central to its study the relationships among methodology, ideology, and race and in so doing both Delpit and Lazere turn a critical eye toward the oftimes colonizing effects of good liberal and marxist intention and the classrooms that result. Fiore and Elsasser and Patthey-Chavez and Gergen, on the other hand illlustrate the kinds of classrooms that can rise from an informed, student-generated—not simply student-centered—classroom.

Toward A Post-Critical Pedagogy Of Basic Writing

If we were to cull the essays in this collection for a statement of what we refer to as a *post-critical pedagogy*, we would turn to Donald Lazere, who writes near the end of "Back to Basics" that teachers should use their pedagogy as an "opportunity to empower students ultimately to decide for themselves which end they should use their education for" (20). This same sentiment is implicit in the essays in part two and further informs the calls for change articulated in the essays in part three. Unlike the critical educators of the 1980s and 1990s who promoted marxist and leftist agendas in their classrooms (e.g., Giroux), theorists and teachers who advocate "post-critical" pedagogies encourage students to "decide for themselves" the ends to which they'll put their educations—regardless of those ends.

The essays in Part III provide new ways of reading and locating the discipline of basic writing, its classrooms, students, and teachers. Here, location stands as a primary concern. Harris writes of contact zones and the "hope of a more fluid and open culture in which we can *choose* the positions we want to speak from and for" (39). Bartholomae reads and rereads his own understanding of basic writing, reminding his readers of Shaughnessy's claim that we must "change the way the profession talked about the students who didn't fit" (21). What, we ask, does it mean (both for students and for the institution) if we imagine institutional and educational structures in which some students don't "fit"? The remaining essays in this part of *Landmark Essays on Basic Writing*—Stygall, Scott, and Royster and Taylor—take up and extend Harris' and Bartholomae's invitation to examine and critique the field and its representations of students.

Joseph Harris provides a useful introduction to part three, as he provides a retrospective on the history of basic writing through three central metaphors—growth, initiation, and conflict. By calling on Mary Louise Pratt's notion of "contact zones," Harris effectively situates and then critiques the practicality of enacting the conflict and struggle in the classroom for which Lu calls. He asks, for example, whether we can overcome the likely overpoliteness that we encounter. What, as well, might be the expected outcome of conflict, other than further factionalizing or "position-taking"? In the end, Harris does not dismiss conflict and struggle but instead desires something more than a site—he desires instead a new understanding of the notion of the contact zone that moves beyond those agonistic metaphors that inform both Lu's and Lazere's (and to some extent Delpit's) work.

David Bartholomae turns that same critical gaze on himself and, by extension, to the discipline of basic writing, looking at both through the eyes (and pens) of students. He tells a story about himself, recognizing and playing on both his own liberalism and the liberal tendencies in the field, asking that we "read against the grain of the narrative—to think about how and why and where it might profitably be questioned" (8). He reminds us of the constructed nature of the field of basic writing and the terms we now use to describe our work. We may no longer assume models of deficiency, but our terms—"basic" as an example—remain consequential. He not only encourages but also enacts the kind of self-reflection for which Delpit, Lazere, and Lu call.

Gail Stygall returns us to the importance of location at the same time she extends Bartholomae's commentary on our need to re-examine the terms by which we define basic writers and our (collective, institutional) motives for maintaining basic writing as a function of the university. As we construct basic writers in our classrooms, Stygall argues, we work from an assumption that values Author (in Foucauldian terms) and therefore implicitly supports power relations and privilege inherent in Author. By validating the notion of Author—a position defined not only by the work of those who occupy that space but also by the absence of those whose writing does not count—and allowing it to inscribe our pedagogies, basic writing instructors remain complicit (despite their good intentions) in the further disenfranchisement of students in their classes. At the same time, basic writing instructors (and compositionists generally) are well situated to resist the privilege of Author. "We do not," Stygall writes, "have to simply accept current practices, especially when those practices make it impossible for some student writers to escape the imposition of negative status" (339).

The issue for Jerrie Cobb Scott is problematic and simple: We have not moved beyond the deficit model of education. It lingers, barely below the surface—and many times on the surface—in discussions and understanding of basic writing. The reasons for this phenomenon, however, are not simple, for they go to the root of misguided and prejudiced institutional assumptions about literacy, basic writers, and teacher education. Where Stygall employs a Foucauldian analysis of the Author function to reveal the ways that institutional ideologies impose a "negative status" on basic writers, Scott turns to "technocratic definitions of literacy" and a resistance to change, calling on the notion of "uncritical dysconsciousness." On the one hand, because we define literacy so narrowly—as an inability to communicate using certain types of privileged discourses—we necessarily define those who cannot produce those kinds of discourses in negative, deficient terms. On the other hand, educators are impotent in efforts to evoke change because those efforts are informed by an uncritical dysconsciousness, an "acceptance, sometimes unconsciously of culturally sanctioned beliefs that . . . defend the advantages of insiders and the disadvantages of outsiders" (47).

Research and scholarship in basic writing can be characterized, throughout its history, as dominated by investigations into the students who populate our classrooms. Those student voices, however, are in nearly every case used in service of the teacher's or researcher's goal. Royster and Taylor challenge us to interrogate the place of teachers (something inherent in Lu) in the classroom, calling explicitly for a shift in the gaze that has been turned—nearly throughout the whole of basic writing scholarship—toward students. How are *teachers*, they ask, located in the basic writing classroom? This is a decided reading against the grain of basic writing scholarship, even that which precedes it in this volume, for here Royster and Taylor interrogate teacher identity and its absence as a focus of research in basic writing. They remark that they had "become impatient with the discussion of identity, most especially in basic writing classrooms, as the *students'* problem, rather than also as the *teacher's* problem" (28). Their call for additional research on teacher identity as an informing element of classrooms speaks to the tendency in composition studies at large to deny the power of teacher authority. The essay stands, as the concluding essay in the volume, as a call for new and vigorous inquiry into the location of teachers in the college writing classroom, into the ways our students see us and the implication of those constructs on the basic writing classroom.

Location and Subjectivity in Basic Writing

In many ways, the most recent scholarship in basic writing returns us to the place where such work began. The articles that make up Part III, "Toward a Post-Critical Pedagogy of Basic Writing," focus on issues that are strikingly similar to those raised in the pieces at the start of this collection. About whom are we talking when we talk about "basic writers"? What curriculum should basic writing programs institute? What do interrogations of teachers' political and pedagogical agendas tell us about the current state of basic writing scholarship?

At Ohio State, students interested in teaching basic writing courses address such questions when they enroll in English 881.02: Teaching Basic Composition. During the semester that he enrolled in this class (which Kay taught), Nels often thought of Virginia Woolf and her journey around Oxbridge that she chronicles in *A Room of One's Own*. He recalls:

> I taught portions of *A Room of One's Own* to students in my section of English 110: First-Year Composition course that quarter, which may explain why it remained so strongly etched in my mind. As I walked across the Oval towards University Hall where I checked messages related to the second course I was teaching that quarter, Women's Studies 367.01: US Women Writers, I remembered Woolf's description of a similar walk. In her case, she was forced to leave the grassy area where she had been walking and continue her tour on the gravel path. As she puts it, "Only the Fellows and Scholars are allowed here [on the grass]; the gravel is the place for me" (6). My students could not believe that Woolf was not allowed to walk in a certain area when the men could. After all, the university is for everyone, isn't it? Mike Rose wrangles with this very question in his work, particularly in *Lives on the Boundary*. Early on, Rose chronicles various shifts in education throughout American history of the last century or so. For example, he describes a variety of concerns about a perceived decline in Americans' proficiency in standard English, concerns that have existed since at least 1841. At the same time, he also describes how, since 1890, more and more Americans

have been earning high school diplomas and entering college (5-6). Rose's narrative works with the tension that exists between the belief that a college education should be for everyone and the concern that many students are not ready for college-level work. As Rose asks, "Is the educational system on the decline, or is it a system attempting to hone—through wrenching change—the many demands of a pluralistic democracy?" (7). What does it mean to earn a "place" within the university? How does a student earn the status of "belonging" in college?

I can't help but—like Woolf, Rose, and so many of the authors in this collection—to begin with myself. In my walks around campus, I sometimes wonder where I belong. During the quarter in which I enrolled in English 881.02, I taught classes in two separate departments—English and Women's Studies—and worked towards an MA in a third—Comparative Studies. When someone asked where they could leave notes for me, I thought of my three separate mailboxes in three separate buildings and wondered how to answer this question. My own shifting location in the university also reflects my shifting subjectivities. I move from student to teacher, to one building to another classroom, then to a separate meeting, as part of the process I need to undertake in order to meet my academic goals. But what about those like Woolf, who was told what buildings she could and could not enter? What about those like Rose, who was placed in a particular academic track without question until it was almost too late to change? What about all of these students we see every day, who are told what knowledge they can and cannot gain? These questions keep popping into my head. I wonder how my own teaching maintains the distinction between "good" students and "bad," "honors" and "remedial," underprepared, at-risk, gifted, typical, talented, bonehead, illiterate, undisciplined, normal students. Bartholomae address the academic constructions of these classifications in "The Tidy House," stating, that "basic writing programs have become expressions of our desire to produce basic writers to maintain the course, the argument, and the slot in the university community; to maintain the distinction (basic/normal) we have learned to think through and by" (8). When I say that certain students belong in the university, what am I saying? Where is this belonging taking place?

Donald McQuade presents a few points that relate to these issues in "Living In—and On—the Margins." McQuade delivered a version of this essay in his 1991 CCCC Chair's Address in Boston. He uses his essay to portray the story of one woman, Adelina Pisano. As the essay begins, Pisano, in her mid-to-late 80s, rests in a hospital bed having just suffered a stroke. It is not clear what the relationship is between Pisano and McQuade. She calls him "Da Professor!" (13), yet she appears to take on the role of mother, aunt, student, and friend of McQuade. When she suffers another stroke, Pisano stops talking and begins writing vociferously, describing what happened to her the night of her most recent stroke and asserting her desire that she hopes to live longer and leave the hospital. McQuade thinks about Pisano's use of language and lack of formal education. He wonders "where she is in relation to her own experience" (18), be it at the center where she would be able to articulate her position with skill and clarity or at the margins where her uses of language would require effort and struggle. However, his goal is not to resolve this issue. Instead, he uses his essay to question how the word "margin" is used in the first place. As he notes, "those who are 'marginal' or 'marginalized' lead lives determined—in fundamental ways—by others. Characteristically, they are reported to be viewed—and treated—by others as though they're inert, ignored, forgotten" (18). He continues by pointing out that traditional definitions of "margins" tend to focus "on some limitation of the place or the person described with this term" (19). Students believed to be on the margins are students who are believed to be limited.

> In my journey around campus, I cannot help but think of "marginal" students and their "marginal" status in a literal sense. Toward the northwest end of the Ohio State campus, past where classes are held and academic business is conducted, sits one of the most renowned campus locations: Ohio Stadium. The football stadium is a site of privilege and prestige, the home of Heisman trophy winners and Rose Bowl and national championship teams. Everyone knows the location of the stadium, but many do not know everything it contains. Nestled under the bleachers at Gate 16A is the Writing Workshop, home for those who administer and teach in the University's basic writing program. The program (designed to instruct students identified as those who will most benefit from specially designed, intensive courses in college-level writing) is given a space apart from almost all other academic programs, where it is greatly overshadowed by collegiate sports. What is the correlation between the location of this program and the status of the students that it serves?

Interestingly, and perhaps not coincidentally, Nels' statements on subjectivity and location took on a new relevance in the autumn of 1999 as we completed this introduction. The Writing Workshop, housed in the 1970s and early 1980s on "west" campus—at even further remove from "central" campus—and then at the stadium for nearly 12 years, moved once again. The workshop now resides (along with the ESL program, which also shared space in the stadium) in Arps Hall, which houses programs in the College of Education. The Writing Workshop may not yet have made it into Denney Hall, but its location, both physical and intellectual, has moved increasingly closer to the English Department of which it is a part. The shifting physical location, we contend, is not a coincidence. Neither is it a direct correlative to political change. That is, as basic writing instruction and scholarship has gained an intellectual location in the larger field of English studies, the Writing Workshop has moved increasingly closer to Denney Hall. This is not, of course, the case across the nation. In many states—New York and Texas, for example—basic writing finds no location, no place of its own, on 4-year college campuses.

If we return to Rich, who writes of "slashed budgets, enlarging class size, and national depression," we realize, in fact, that in many ways, the economic, and political cirumstances in which we teach basic writing in the 21st century do not differ dramatically from the circumstances in which Rich and Shaughnessy and their colleagues taught in 1970. We are, as Scott points out, still mired in the language of deficiency. Our desires and aspirations remain largely the same, as well, for like Rich, we no doubt believe that "language is power" and "can be a means of changing reality" (67). At the same time, we feel quite safe in claiming that the scholarship collected in this volume has had, and will continue to have, significant and meaningful effect on the educational experiences of the students and teachers located in the basic writing classroom.

Notes

1. Historians of composition, including Catherine Hobbs, Reginald Martin, and Jacqueline Jones Royster, are engaged in historical recovery at sites previously unexplored by disciplinary histories—traditionally Black colleges and universities and BIA schools.
2. In characterizing the Normal College English program, we exclusively rely on college materials—bulletins, programmes, college and departmental annual reports—housed in the Hunter College archives. We wish to acknowledge the invaluable contributions to this project of Dr. Julio Delgado, head archivist at Hunter. We also wish to recognize the financial support of The Ohio State University, The Elizabeth D. Gee Fund for Research on Women, and the Department of Women's Studies at The Ohio State University for research conducted at Hunter College.
3. For similar—but less explicitly offensive—characterizations of basic writers, see also Aldus, Clark, Farrell, and Key.
4. See, for examples of the conflation of race and remediation in composition scholarship during this period, see San-su Lin's (1965) "A Developmental English Program for the Culturally Disadvantaged," James Banks' (1968) "A Profile of the Black American: Implications for Teaching," Jacqueline Griffin's (1969) "Remedial Composition at an Open-Door College," and Vernon Lattin's (1978) "A Program for Basic Writing."
5. See also Jerrie Cobb Scott's (1993) "Literacies and Deficits Revisited" on the conflation of race and remediation.
6. Those interested in resources that address pedagogical issues, research and bureaucratic concerns in basic writing or provide citations for scholarship prior to 1990 might find helpful Lawrence W. Kasden and Daniel R Hoeber's *Basic Writing for Teachers, Researchers, and Administrators* or Michael G. Moran and Ronald F. Lunsford's 1984 *Research in Basic Writing: A Bibliographic Sourcebook* and Moran and Martin J. Jacobi's 1990 *Research in Basic Writing: A Bibliographic Sourcebook.*
7. John Rouse's 1979 "The Politics of Composition" is the exception to this rule.
8. Pamela Gay continues the critique of *Errors and Expectations* in 1993 with "Rereading Shaughnessy from a Postcolonial Perspective." Articles like those penned by Lu and Gay brought on Patricia Laurence's spirited defense of Shaughnessy in "The Vanishing Site of Mina Shaughnessy's *Errors and Expectations.*"

Works Cited

Aldus, P. J. "The Unprepared Student at Ripon College." *College Composition and Communication* 8 (1957): 127-128.

Annual Report, Female Normal College, 1894. New York City: Hunter College Archives.

Applebee, Arthur N. *Curriculum as Conversation: Transforming Traditions of Teaching and Learning.* Chicago: U of Chicago Press, 1996.

Banks, James A. "A Profile of the Black American: Implications for Teaching." *College Composition and Communication* 19 (1968): 288-296.

Bartholomae, David. "Inventing the University." *When A Writer Can't Write: Studies in Writer's Block and Other Composing Problems.* Ed. Mike Rose. New York: Guilford Press, 1985, 134-64.

_____. "The Study of Error." *College Composition and Communication* 31 (1980): 253-69.

_____. "The Tidy House: Basic Writing and the American Curriculum." *Journal of Basic Writing* 12.1 (1993): 4-21.

Berlin, James. *Rhetoric and Reality: Writing Instruction in American College, 1900-1985.* Studies in Writing and Rhetoric. Carbondale: Southern Illinois University Press, 1987.

_____. *Writing Instruction in Nineteenth-Century American Colleges.* Studies in Writing and Rhetoric. Carbondale: Southern Illinois University Press, 1984.

Bizzell, Patricia. "The Ethos of Academic Discourse." *College Composition and Communication* 29 (1978): 351-355.

_____. "What Happens When Basic Writers Come to College?" *College Composition and Communication* 37.3 (1986): 294-301.

_____. "William Perry and Liberal Education." *College English* 46 (1984): 447-54.

Brereton, John C., ed. *The Origins of Composition Studies in the American College, 1875-1925: A Documentary History*. Pittsburgh: University of Pittsburgh Press, 1995.

Butler, Melvin A., chair. *Students' Right to Their Own Language*. Urbana, IL: NCTE, 1974.

Clark, J. D. "A Four-Year Study of Freshman English." *English Journal* college ed. 24 (1935): 403-410.

Cone, Helen Gray. "1908 Chair's Report to the President of the Normal College." New York City: Hunter College Archives.

Connors, Robert. "Basic Writing Textbooks: History and Current Avatars." In Enos, 259-274.

Cross, Patricia K. *Accent on Learning: Improving Instruction and Shaping the Curriculum*. San Francisco: Jossey-Bass, 1976.

_____ . *Beyond the Open Door*. San Francisco: Jossey-Bass, 1971.

Dakin, Dorothy. "Sub-Freshman English: A 'Racket'?" *English Journal* college ed. 23 (1934): 502-503.

Delpit, Lisa D. "The Silenced Dialogue: Power and Pedagogy in Educating Other People's Children." *Harvard Educational Review* 58.3 (August 1988): 280-298.

Diffenbaugh, Guy Linton. "Teaching the Unteachables." *English Journal* college ed. (1932): 130-134.

DiPardo, Anne. *A Kind of Passport: A Basic Writing Adjunct Program and the Challenge of Student Diversity*. Urbana, IL: NCTE, 1993.

Edlund, John R. "Bakhtin and the Social Reality of Language Acquisition." *Writing Instructor* 7.2 (Winter 1988): 56-67.

Enos, Theresa, ed. *A Sourcebook for Basic Writing Teachers*. New York: Random House, 1987.

Emig, Janet. *The Composing Processes of Twelfth Graders*. Urbana: NCTE, 1971.

Farrell, Thomas J. "Developing Literacy: Walter J. Ong and Basic Writing." *Journal of Basic Writing* 2 (1978): 30-51.

Fiore, Kyle, and Nan Elsasser. "'Strangers No More': A Liberatory Literacy Curriculum." *College English* (February 1982): 115-28.

Gay, Pamela. "Rereading Shaughnessy from a Postcolonial Perspective." *Journal of Basic Writing* 12 (1993): 29-40.

Grego, Rhonda and Nancy Thompson. "Repositioning Remediation: Renegotiating Composition's Work in the Academy." *College Composition and Communication* 47 (1996): 62-84.

Griffin, Jacqueline. "Remedial Composition at an Open-Door College." *College Composition and Communication* 20 (1969): 360-363.

Halasek, Kay. *A Pedagogy of Possibility: Bakhtinian Perspectives on Composition Studies*. Urbana: Southern Illinois UP, 1999.

Harris, Joseph. "Negotiating the Contact Zone." Journal of Basic Writing 14.1 (1995): 27-42.

Hill, Carolyn Ericksen. *Writing From the Margins: Power and Pedagogy for Teachers of Composition*. New York: Oxford UP, 1990.

Hindman, Jane E. "Reinventing the University: Finding the Place for Basic Writers." *Journal of Basic Writing*. 12.2 (1993): 55-75.

Hobbs, Catherine. "'Invisible Colleges,' Domestic Rhetorics, and Colonizing Literacies: Writing the History of Women's Writing Instruction." Paper presented at the Modern Language Association Annual Meeting. San Diego, 1994.

Hull, Glenda, Mike Rose, *et al.* "Remediation as a Social Construct: Perspectives from an Analysis of Classroom Discourse." *College Composition and Communication* 42.3 (Oct. 1991): 299-329.

Hunter, Paul. "'Waiting for Aristotle' in the Basic Writing Movement." *College English* 54 (Dec. 1992): 914-27.

Jensen, George H. "The Reification of the Basic Writer." *Journal of Basic Writing* 5 (1986): 52-64.

Kasden, Lawrence W. and Daniel R Hoeber, eds. *Basic Writing for Teachers, Researchers, and Administrators* . Urbana, IL: NCTE, 1980.

Key, Howard C. "A Suggested Plan for Deficient Students." *College Composition and Communication* 8 (1957): 225-229.

Kirby, John Dillingham. "Make-Up English at Northwestern." *English Journal* college ed. 20 (1931): 829-831.

Kitzhaber, Alfred. "Freshman English: A Prognosis." *College English* 12 (1962): 476-483.

_____ . "A Time of Change." *College English* 28 (1966): 51-54.

_____ . *Rhetoric in American Colleges: 1850-1900*. Dallas: Southern Methodist UP, 1990.

_____ . *Themes, Theories, and Therapies: The Teaching of Writing in College*. New York: McGraw-Hill, 1963.

Kogen, Myra. "The Conventions of Expository Writing." *Journal of Basic Writing* 5 (1986): 24-37.

Lattin, Vernon E. "A Program for Basic Writing." *College English* 40 (1978): 312-317.

Laurence, Patricia. "The Vanishing Site of Mina Shaughnessy's *Errors and Expectations.*" *Journal of Basic Writing* 12 (1993): 18-28.

Lazere, Daniel. "Back to Basics: A Force for Oppression or Liberation?" *College English* 54 (1992): 7-21.

Levine, Arthur. *Handbook on Undergraduate Curriculum.* San Francisco: Jossey-Bass, 1981.

Lin, San-su. "A Developmental English Program for the Culturally Disadvantaged." *College Composition and Communication* 16 (1965): 273-276.

Lu, Min-zhan. "Conflict and Struggle: The Enemies or Preconditions of Basic Writing?" *College English* 54.8 (December 1992): 887-913.

_____. "Redefining the Legacy of Mina Shaughnessy: A Critique of the Politics of Linguistic Innocence." *Journal of Basic Writing* 10.1 (1991): 26-40.

Lunsford, Andrea. "Cognitive Development and the Basic Writer." *College English* 41 (1979): 38-6.

_____. "Politics and Practices in Basic Writing." In Enos, 246-258.

_____. "What We Know—and Don't Know—About Remedial Writing." *College Composition and Communication* 29 (1979): 47-52.

Martin, Reginald. "The 1611 King James Bible, William Shakespeare, Frederick Douglass, and Alain Locke: Writing and Rhetoric Instruction in the Historically Black College, 1930-1979." Paper presented at the Modern Language Association Annual Meeting. San Diego, 1994.

McCloskey, Frank H. and Lillian Herlands Hornstein. "Subfreshman Composition—A New Solution." *College English* 11 (1950): 331-339.

McQuade, Donald. "Living In—And On—The Margin." *College Composition and Communication* 43.1 (1992): 11-22.

Middendorf, Marilyn. "Bakhtin and the Dialogic Writing Class." *Journal of Basic Writing* 11.1 (Spring 1992): 34-46.

Moran, Michael G. and Ronald F. Lunsford, eds. *Research in Basic Writing: A Bibliographic Sourcebook.* Westport, CT: Greenwood Press, 1984.

Moran, Michael G. and Martin J. Jacobi, eds. *Research in Basic Writing: A Bibliographic Sourcebook.* Westport, CT: Greenwood Press, 1990.

Mutnick, Deborah. *Writing in an Alien World: Basic Writing and the Struggle for Equality in Higher Education.* CrossCurrents Series. Ed. Charles I. Schuster. Portsmouth, NH: Boynton/Cook Heinemann, 1996.

Noyes, E. S. "The Program of the Awkward Squad." *English Journal* college ed. 18 (1929): 678-680.

Patthey-Chavez, G. Genevieve and Constance Gergen. "Culture as Instructional Resource in the Multiethnic Composition Classroom." *Journal of Basic Writing* 11(1992): 75-91.

Perl, Sondra. "Basic Writing and the Process of Composing. In Kasden and Hoeber, 13-32.

Rich, Adrienne. "Teaching Language in Open Admissions." *On Lies, Secrets, and Silence: Selected Prose 1966-1978.* New York: W.W. Norton, 1979.

Ritchie, Joy S. "Beginning Writers: Diverse Voices and Individual Identities." *College Composition and Communication* 40 (1989): 152-74.

Rose, Mike. "The Language of Exclusion: Writing Instruction at the University." *College English* 47 (1985): 341-359.

_____. *Lives on the Boundaries: The Struggles and Achievements of America's Underprepared.* New York: The Free Press-Macmillan, Inc., 1989.

_____. "Narrowing the Mind and Page: Remedial Writers and Cognitive Reductionism." *College Composition and Communication* 39.3 (1988): 267-302.

Roueche, John E., George E. Baker, and Suanne D. Roueche. *College Responses to Low Achieving Students: A National Study.* Orlando, FL: HBJ Media Systems, 1984.

Rouse, John. "The Politics of Composition." *College English* 41 (Sept. 1979): 1-12.

Royster, Jacqueline Jones. "Life beyond the Veil: One View of Rhetoric and Composition in Historically African American Colleges and Universities." Paper presented at the Modern Language Association Annual Meeting. San Diego, 1994.

Royster, Jacqueline Jones, and Jean C. Williams. "History in the Spaces Left: African American Presence and Narratives of Composition Studies." *College Composition and Communication* (1999): 563-584.

Royster, Jacqueline Jones, and Rebecca Greenberg Taylor. "Constructing Teacher Identity in the Basic Writing Classroom." *Journal of Basic Writing* 16.1 (1997): 27-49.

Scott, Jerrie Cobb. "Literacies and Deficiencies Revisited." *Journal of Basic Writing* 12 (1993): 46-56.

Severino, Carol. "Where the Cultures of Basic Writers and Academia Intersect: Cultivating the Common Ground." *Journal of Basic Writing* 11.1 (1992): 4-15.

Shaughnessy, Mina P. "Basic Writing." *Teaching Composition: Ten Bibliographical Essays.* Fort Worth: Texas Christian UP, 1976. 137-68.

_____ . *Errors and Expectations*. New York: Oxford University Press, 1977.

Shor, Ira, ed. *Freire for the Classroom: A Sourcebook for Liberatory Teaching*. Portsmouth, NH: Boynton/Cook-Heinemann, 1987.

Smith, Nina Banton. *American Reading Instruction*. Newark, DE: International Reading Association, 1965.

Smitherman, Geneva. "'God Don't Never Change': Black English from a Black Perspective." *College English* 34 (1973): 828-33.

Stygall, Gail. "Resisting Privilege: Basic Writing and Foucault's Author Function." *College Composition and Communication* 45 (1994): 320-341.

Towle, Carroll S. "The Awkward Squad at Yale." *English Journal* college ed. 18 (1928): 672-677.

Troyka, Lynn Quitman. "Defining Basic Writers in Context." In Enos, 2-15.

_____ . "Perspectives on Legacies and Literacy in the 1980's." In Enos, 16-26.

Welch, Nancy. "One Student's Many Voices: Reading, Writing, and Responding with Bakhtin." *Journal of Advanced Composition* 494-501.

Williams, Jean. "Expanding the Field: Placing Students of Color in the Histories of Composition." Diss. Prospectus. Ohio State University, 1996.

_____ . "Portraits of the Field: Locating Color and Its Absence in Composition Studies." Paper delivered at the Conference on College Composition and Communication, Phoenix, AZ. March 1997.

Wozniak, John Michael. *English Composition in Eastern Colleges, 1850-1940*. Washington, D.C.: University Press of America, 1978.

Wright, Melinda. "Basic Writing Pedagogies in Context: A Multi-Dimensional Narrative." Diss. Ohio State University, 1996.

Yelin, Louise. "Deciphering the Academic Hieroglyph: Marxist Literacy Theory and the Practice of Basic Writing." *Journal of Basic Writing* 2 (1978): 13-29.

Youdelman, Jeffrey. "Limited Students: Remedial Writing and the Death of Open Admissions." *College English* 39 (1978): 562-572.

(Re)Defining Basic Writing and Basic Writers

Teaching Language
in Open Admissions
by Adrienne Rich

To the memory of Mina Shaughnessy, 1924-1978

I stand to this day behind the major ideas about literature, writing, and teaching that I expressed in this essay. Several things strike me in rereading it, however. Given the free rein allowed by the SEEK program (described in the text of the essay) when I first began teaching at the City College of New York, it is interesting to me to note the books I was choosing for classes: Orwell, Wright, LeRoi Jones, Lawrence, Baldwin, Plato's *Republic*. It is true that few books by black women writers were available; the bookstores of the late sixties were crowded with paperbacks by Frederick Douglass, Malcolm X, Frantz Fanon, Langston Hughes, Eldridge Cleaver, W. E. B. DuBois, and by anthologies of mostly male black writers. Ann Petry, Gwendolyn Brooks, June Jordan, Audre Lorde, I came to know and put on my reading lists or copied for classes; but the real crescendo of black women's writing was yet to come, and writers like Zora Neale Hurston and Margaret Walker were out of print. It is obvious now, as it was not yet then (except to black women writers, undoubtedly) that integral to the struggle against racism in the literary canon there was another, as yet unarticulated, struggle against the sexism of black and white male editors, anthologists, critics, and publishers.

For awhile I have thought of going back to City College to ask some of my former colleagues, still teaching there, what could be said of the past decade, what is left there of what was, for a brief time, a profound if often naively optimistic experiment in education. (Naively optimistic because I think the white faculty at least, those of us even who were most committed to the students, vastly underestimated the psychic depth and economic function of racism in the city and the nation, the power of the political machinery that could be "permissive" for a handful of years

Reprinted from Rich, Adrienne, "Teaching Language in Open Admissions," *Harvard English Studies*, Vol. 4: "Uses of Literature." Editor: Monroe Engel (1973): 257-273. Cambridge, MA: Harvard University Press.

only to retrench, break promises, and betray, pitting black youth against Puerto Rican and Asian, poor ethnic students against students of color, in an absurd and tragic competition for resources which should have been open to all.) But it has seemed to me that such interviews could be fragmentary at best. I lived through some of that history, the enlarging of classes, the heavy increase of teaching loads, the firing of junior faculty, and of many of the best and most dedicated teachers I had known, the efforts of City College to reclaim its "prestige" in the media; I know also that dedicated teachers still remain, who teach Basic Writing not as a white man's—or woman's—burden but because they choose to do so. And, on the corner of Broadway near where I live, I see young people whose like I knew ten years ago as college students "hanging out," brown-bagging, standing in short skirts and high-heeled boots in doorways waiting for a trick, or being dragged into the car of a plumed and sequined pimp.

Finally: in reprinting this essay I would like to acknowledge my debt to Mina Shaughnessy, who was director of the Basic Writing Program at City when I taught there, and from whom, in many direct and indirect ways, I learned—in a time and place where pedagogic romanticism and histrionics were not uncommon—a great deal about the ethics and integrity of teaching.

This essay was first published in *The Uses of Literature,* edited by Monroe Engel (Cambridge, Mass.: Harvard University, 1973).

My first romantic notion of teaching came, I think, from reading Emlyn Williams's play *The Corn Is Green,* sometime in my teens. As I reconstruct it now, a schoolteacher in a Welsh mining village is reading her pupils' essays one night and comes upon a paper which, for all its misspellings and dialect constructions, seems to be the work of a nascent poet. Turning up in the midst of the undistinguished efforts of her other pupils, this essay startles the teacher. She calls in the boy who wrote it, goes over it with him, talks with him about his life, his hopes, and offers to tutor him privately, without fees. Together, as the play goes on, they work their way through rhetoric, mathematics, Shakespeare, Latin, Greek. The boy gets turned on by the classics, is clearly intended to be, if not a poet, at least a scholar. Birth and family background had destined him for a life in the coal mines; but now another path opens up. Toward the end of the play we see him being coached for the entrance examinations for Oxford. I believe crisis strikes when it looks as if he has gotten one of the village girls pregnant and may have to marry her, thus cutting short a career of dazzling promise before it has begun. I don't recall the outcome, but I suspect that the unwed mother is hushed up and packed away (I would be more interested to see the play rewritten today as *her* story) and the boy goes off to Oxford, with every hope of making it to donhood within the decade.

Perhaps this represents a secret fantasy of many teachers: the ill-scrawled essay, turned up among so many others, which has the mark of genius. And looking at the first batch of freshman papers every semester can be like a trip to the mailbox—there is always the possibility of something turning up that will illuminate the weeks ahead. But behind the larger fantasy lie assumptions which I have only gradually come to recognize; and the recognition has to do with a profound change in my conceptions of teaching and learning.

Before I started teaching at City College I had known only elitist institutions: Harvard and Radcliffe as an undergraduate, Swarthmore as a visiting poet, Columbia as teacher in a graduate poetry workshop that included some of the best young poets in the city. I applied for the job at City in 1968 because Robert Cumming had described the SEEK program to me after Martin Luther King was shot, and my motivation was complex. It had to do with white liberal guilt, of course; and a political decision to use my energies in work with "disadvantaged" (black and Puerto Rican) students. But it also had to do with a need to involve myself with the real life of the city, which had arrested me from the first weeks I began living here.

In 1966 Mayor John Lindsay had been able, however obtusely, to coin the phrase "Fun City" without actually intending it as a sick joke. By 1968, the uncollected garbage lay bulging in plastic sacks on the north side of Washington Square, as it had lain longer north of 110th Street; the city had learned to endure subway strikes, sanitation strikes, cab strikes, power and water shortages; the policeman on the corner had become a threatening figure to many whites as he had long been to blacks; the public school teachers and the parents of their pupils had been in pitched battle. On the Upper West Side poor people were being evicted from tenements which were then tinned-up and left empty, awaiting unscheduled demolition to make room for middle-income housing, for which funds were as yet unavailable; and a squatter movement of considerable political consciousness was emerging in defiance of this uprooting.

There seemed to be three ways in which the white middle class could live in New York: the paranoiac, the solipsistic, and a third, which I am more hesitant to define. By the mid-sixties paranoia was visible and audible: streets of brownstones whose occupants had hired an armed guard for the block and posted notices accordingly; conversations on park benches in which public safety had replaced private health as a topic of concern; conversion of all personal anxieties into fear of the mugger (and the mugger was real, no doubt about it). Paranoia could become a life-style, a science, an art, with the active collaboration of reality. Solipsism I encountered first and most concretely in a conversation with an older European intellectual who told me he liked living in New York (on the East Side) because Madison Avenue reminded him of Paris. It was, and still is, possible to live, if you can afford it, on one of those small islands where the streets are kept clean and the pushers and nodders invisible, to travel by cab, deplore the state of the rest of the city, but remain essentially aloof from its causes and effects. It seems about as boring as most forms of solipsism, since to maintain itself it must remain thick-skinned and ignorant.

But there was, and is, another relationship with the city which I can only begin by calling love. The city as object of love, a love not unmixed with horror and anger, the city as Baudelaire and Rilke had previsioned it, or William Blake for that matter, death in life, but a death emblematic of the death that is epidemic in modern society, and a life more edged, more costly, more charged with knowledge, than life elsewhere. Love as one knows it sometimes with a person with whom one is locked in struggle, energy draining but also energy replenishing, as when one is fighting for life, in oneself or someone else. Here was this damaged, self-destructive organism, preying and preyed upon. The streets were rich with human possibility and vicious with human denial (it is breathtaking to walk through a street in East Harlem, passing among the lithe, alert, childish bodies and attuned, observant, childish faces, playing in the spray of a hydrant, and to know that addiction awaits every brain and body in that block as a potential killer). In all its historic, overcrowded, and sweated poverty, the Lower East Side at the turn of the century had never known this: the odds for the poor, today, are weighted by heroin, a fact which the middle classes ignored until it breathed on their own children's lives as well.

In order to live in the city, I needed to ally myself, in some concrete, practical, if limited way, with the possibilities. So I went up to Convent Avenue and 133rd Street and was interviewed for a teaching job, hired as a poet-teacher. At that time a number of writers, including Toni Cade Bambara, the late Paul Blackburn, Robert Cumming, David Henderson, June Jordan, were being hired to teach writing in the SEEK program to black and Puerto Rican freshmen entering from substandard ghetto high schools, where the prevailing assumption had been that they were of inferior intelligence. (More of these schools later.) Many dropped out (a lower percentage than the national college dropout rate, however); many stuck it out through several semesters of remedial English, math, reading, to enter the mainstream of the college. (As of 1972, 208 SEEK students—or 35 to 40 percent—have since graduated from City College; 24 are now in graduate school. *None* of these students would have come near higher education under the regular admissions programs of the City University; high-school guidance counselors have traditionally written off such students as incapable of academic work. Most could not survive economically in college without the stipends which the SEEK program provides.)

My job, that first year, was to "turn the students on" to writing by whatever means I wanted—poetry, free association, music, politics, drama, fiction—to acclimate them to the act of writing, while a grammar teacher, with whom I worked closely outside of class, taught sentence structure, the necessary mechanics. A year later this course was given up as too expensive, since it involved two teachers. My choice was to enlarge my scope to include grammar and mechanics or to find a niche elsewhere and teach verse writing. I stayed on to teach, and learn, grammar—among other things.

The early experience in SEEK was, as I look back on it, both unnerving and seductive. Even those who were (unlike me) experienced teachers of remedial English were working on new frontiers, trying new methods. Some of the most rudimentary questions we confronted were: How do you make standard English verb endings available to a dialect-speaker? How do you teach English prepositional forms to a Spanish-language student? What are the arguments for and against "Black English"? The English of academic papers and theses? Is standard English simply a weapon of colonization? Many of our students wrote in the vernacular with force and wit; others were unable to say what they wanted on paper in or out of the vernacular. We were dealing not simply with dialect and syntax but with the imagery of lives, the anger and flare of urban youth—how could this be *used*, strengthened, without the lies of artificial polish? How does one teach order, coherence, the structure of ideas while respecting the student's experience of his or her thinking and perceiving? Some students who could barely sweat out a paragraph delivered (and sometimes conned us with) dazzling raps in the classroom: How could we help this oral gift transfer itself onto paper? The classes were small—fifteen at most; the staff, at that time, likewise; we spent hours in conference with individual students, hours meeting together and with counselors, trying to teach ourselves how to teach and asking ourselves what we ought to be teaching.

So these were classes, not simply in writing, not simply in literature, certainly not just in the correction of sentence fragments or the redemptive power of the semicolon; though we did, and do, work on all these. One teacher gave a minicourse in genres; one in drama as literature; teachers have used their favorite books from *Alice in Wonderland* to Martin Buber's *The Knowledge of Man*; I myself have wandered all over the map of my own reading: D. H. Lawrence, W. E. B. DuBois, LeRoi Jones, Plato, Orwell, Ibsen, poets from W. C. Williams to Audre Lorde. Sometimes books are used as a way of learning to look at literature, sometimes as a provocation for the students' own writing, sometimes both. At City College all Basic Writing teachers have been free to choose the books they would assign (always keeping within the limits of the SEEK book allowance and considering the fact that non-SEEK students have no book allowance at all, though their financial need may be as acute). There has never been a set curriculum or a required reading list; we have poached off each others' booklists, methods, essay topics, grammar-teaching exercises, and anything else that we hoped would "work" for us.[1]

Most of us felt that students learn to write by discovering the validity and variety of their own experience; and in the late 1960s, as the black classics began to flood the bookstores, we drew on the black novelists, poets, and polemicists as the natural path to this discovery for SEEK students. Black teachers were, of course, a path; and there were some who combined the work of consciousness-raising with the study of Sophocles, Kafka, and other pillars of the discipline oddly enough known as "English." For many white teachers, the black writers were a relatively new discovery: the clear, translucent prose of Douglass, the sonorities of *The Souls of Black Folk*, the melancholy sensuousness of Toomer's poem-novel *Cane*. In this discovery of a previously submerged culture we were learning from and with our students as rarely happens in the university, though it is happening anew in the area of women's studies. We were not merely exploring a literature and a history which had gone virtually unmentioned in our white educations (particularly true for those over thirty); we were not merely having to confront in talk with our students and in their writings, as well as the books we read, the bitter reality of Western racism: we also found ourselves reading almost any piece of Western literature through our students' eyes, imagining how this voice, these assumptions, would sound to us if we were they. "We learned from the students"—banal cliché, one that sounds pious and patronizing by now; yet the fact remains that our white liberal assumptions *were* shaken, our vision of both the city and the university changed, our relationship to language itself made both deeper and more painful.

Of course the students responded to black literature; I heard searching and acute discussions of Jones's poem "The Liar" or Wright's "The Man Who Lived Underground" from young men and women who were in college on sufferance in the eyes of the educational establishment; I've heard similar discussions of *Sons and Lovers* or the *Republic*. Writing this, I am conscious of how obvious it all seems and how unnecessary it now might appear to demonstrate by little anecdotes that ghetto students can handle sophisticated literature and ideas. But in 1968, 1969, we were still trying to prove this—we and our students felt that the burden of proof was on us. When the Black and Puerto Rican Student Community seized the South Campus of C.C.N.Y. in April 1969, and a team of students sat down with the president of the college and a team of faculty members to negotiate, one heard much about the faculty group's surprised respect for the students' articulateness, reasoning power, and skill in handling statistics—for the students were negotiating in exchange for withdrawal from South Campus an admissions policy which would go far beyond SEEK in its inclusiveness.

Those of us who had been involved earlier with ghetto students felt that we had known their strength all along: an impatient cutting through of the phony, a capacity for tenacious struggle with language and syntax and difficult ideas, a growing capacity for political analysis which helped counter the low expectations their teachers had always had of them and which many had had of themselves; and more, their knowledge of the naked facts of society, which academia has always, even in its public urban form, managed to veil in ivy or fantasy. Some were indeed chronologically older than the average college student; many, though eighteen or twenty years old, had had responsibility for themselves and their families for years. They came to college with a greater insight into the actual workings of the city and of American racial oppression than most of their teachers or their elite contemporaries. They had held dirty jobs, borne children, negotiated for Spanish-speaking parents with an English-speaking world of clinics, agencies, lawyers, and landlords, had their sixth sense nurtured in the streets, or had made the transition from southern sharehold or Puerto Rican countryside to Bedford-Stuyvesant or the *barrio* and knew the ways of two worlds. And they were becoming, each new wave of them, more lucidly conscious of the politics of their situation, the context within which their lives were being led.

It is tempting to romanticize, at the distance of midsummer 1972, what the experience of SEEK—and by extension, of all remedial freshman programs under Open Admissions—was (and is) for the students themselves. The Coleman Report and the Moynihan Report have left echoes and vibrations of stereotypical thinking which perhaps only a first-hand knowledge of the New York City schools can really silence. Teaching at City I came to know the intellectual poverty and human waste of the public school system through the marks it had left on students—and not on black and Puerto Rican students only, as the advent of Open Admissions was to show. For a plain look at the politics and practices of this system, I recommend Ellen Lurie's *How to Change the Schools*, a handbook for parent activists which enumerates the conditions she and other parents, black, Puerto Rican, and white, came to know intimately in their struggles to secure their children's right to learn and to be treated with dignity. The book is a photograph of the decay, racism, and abusiveness they confronted, written not as muckraking journalism but as a practical tool for others like themselves. I have read little else, including the most lyrically indignant prose of radical educators, that gives so precise and devastating a picture of the life that New York's children are expected to lead in the name of schooling. She writes of "bewildered angry teen-agers, who have discovered that they are in classes for mentally retarded students, simply because they cannot speak English," of teachers and principals who "behaved as though every white middle-class child was gifted and was college material, and every black and Puerto Rican (and sometimes Irish and Italian) working-class child was slow, disadvantaged, and unable to learn anything but the most rudimentary facts." She notes that "81 elementary schools in the state (out of a total of 3,634) had more than 70 per cent of their students below minimum competence, and *65 of these were New York City public schools!*" Her findings and statistics make it clear that tracking begins at kindergarten (chiefly on the basis of skin color and language) and that nonwhite and working-class children are assumed to have a maximum potential which fits them only for the so-called general diploma, and hence are not taught, as are their middle-class contemporaries, the math or languages or writing skills needed to pass college entrance examinations or even to do academic-diploma high-school work.[2] I have singled out these particular points for citation because they have to do directly with our students' self-expectations and the enforced limitation of their horizons years before they come to college. But much else has colored their educational past: the drug pushers at the school gates, the obsolete texts, the punitive conception of the teacher's role, the ugliness, filth, and decay of the buildings, the demoralization even of good teachers working under such conditions. (Add to this the use of tranquilizing drugs on children who are considered hyperactive or who present "behavior problems" at an early age.)

To come out of scenes like these schools and be offered "a chance" to compete as an equal in the world of academic credentials, the white-collar world, the world beyond the minimum wage or welfare, is less romantic for the student than for those who view the process from a distance. The student who leaves the campus at three or four o'clock after a day of classes, goes to work as a waitress, or clerk, or hash-slinger, or guard, comes home at ten or eleven o'clock to a crowded apartment with TV audible in every corner—what does it feel like to this student to be reading, say, Byron's "Don Juan" or Jane Austen for a class the next day? Our students may spend two or three hours in the subway going to and from college and jobs, longer if the subway system is more deplorable than usual. To read in the New York subway at rush hour is impossible; it is virtually impossible to think.

How does one compare this experience of college with that of the Columbia students down at 116th Street in their quadrangle of gray stone dormitories, marble steps, flowered borders, wide spaces of time and architecture in which to talk and think? Or that of Berkeley students with their eucalyptus grove and tree-lined streets of bookstores and cafes? The Princeton or Vassar students devoting four years to the life of the mind in Gothic serenity? Do "motivation" and "intellectual competency" mean the same for those students as for City College undergraduates on that overcrowded campus where in winter there is often no place to sit between classes, with two inadequate bookstores largely filled with required texts, two cafeterias and a snack bar that are overpriced, dreary, and unconducive to lingering, with the incessant pressure of time and money driving at them to rush, to get through, to amass the needed credits somehow, to drop out, to stay on with gritted teeth? Out of a graduating class at Swarthmore or Oberlin and one at C.C.N.Y., which students have demonstrated their ability and commitment and how do we assume we can measure such things?

Sometimes as I walk up 133rd Street, past the glass-strewn doorways of P.S. 161, the graffiti-sprayed walls of tenements, the uncollected garbage, through the iron gates of South Campus and up the driveway to the prefab hut which houses the English department, I think wryly of John Donne's pronouncement that "the University is a Paradise; rivers of Knowledge are there; Arts and Sciences flow from thence." I think that few of our students have this Athenian notion of what college is going to be for them; their first introduction to it is a many hours' wait in line at registration, which only reveals that the courses they have been advised or wanted to take are filled, or conflict in hours with a needed job; then more hours at the cramped, heavily guarded bookstore; then perhaps, a semester in courses which they never chose, or in which the pace and allusions of a lecturer are daunting or which may meet at opposite ends of an elongated campus stretching for six city blocks and spilling over into a former warehouse on Broadway. Many have written of their first days at C.C.N.Y.: "I only knew it was different from high school." What was different, perhaps, was the green grass of early September with groups of young people in dashikis and gelés, jeans and tie-dye, moving about with the unquenchable animation of the first days of the fall semester; the encounter with some teachers who seem to respect them as individuals; something at any rate less bleak, less violent, less mean-spirited, than the halls of Benjamin Franklin or Evander Childs or some other school with the line painted down the center of the corridor and a penalty for taking the short-cut across that line. In all that my students have written about their high schools, I have found bitterness, resentment, satire, black humor; never any word of nostalgia for the school, though sometimes a word of affection for a teacher "who really tried."

The point is that, as Mina Shaughnessy, the director of the Basic Writing Program at City, has written: "the first stage of Open Admissions involves *openly admitting* that education has failed for too many students."[3] Professor Shaughnessy writes in her most recent report of the increase in remedial courses of white, ethnic students (about two-thirds of the Open Admissions freshmen who have below-80 high school averages) and of the discernible fact, a revelation to many, that these white students "have experienced the failure of the public schools in different ways from the black and Puerto Rican students." Another City College colleague, Leonard Kriegel, writes of this newest population: "Like most blue-collar children, they had lived within the confines of an educational system without ever having questioned that system. They were used to being stamped and categorized. Rating systems, grades, obligations to improve, these had beset them all their lives. . . . They had few expectations from the world-at-large. When they were depressed, they had no real idea of what was getting them down, and they would have dismissed as absurd the idea that they could make demands. They accepted the myths of America as those myths had been presented to them."[4]

Meeting some of the so-called ethnic students in class for the first time in September 1970, I began to realize that: there *are* still poor Jews in New York City; they teach English better to native speakers of Greek on the island of Cyprus than they do to native speakers of Spanish on the island of Manhattan; the Chinese student with acute English-language difficulties is stereotyped as "nonexpressive" and channeled into the physical sciences before anyone has a chance to find out whether he or she is a potential historian, political theorist, or psychologist; and (an intuition, more difficult to prove) white, ethnic working-class young women seem to have problems of self-reliance and of taking their lives seriously that young black women students as a group do not seem to share.

There is also a danger that, paradoxically or not, the white middle-class teacher may find it easier to identify with the strongly motivated, obviously oppressed, politically conscious black student than with the students of whom Kriegel has written. Perhaps a different set of prejudices exists: if you're white, why aren't you more hip, more achieving, why are you bored and alienated, why don't you *care* more? Again, one has to keep clearly in mind the real lessons of the schools—both public and parochial—which reward conformity, passivity, and correct answers and penalize, as Ellen Lurie says, the troublesome question "as trouble-making," the lively, independent, active child as "disruptive," curiosity as misbehavior. (Because of the reinforcement in passivity received all around them in society and at home, white women students seem particularly vulnerable to these judgments.) In many ways the damage is more insidious because the white students have as yet no real political analysis going for them; only the knowledge that they have not been as successful in school as white students are supposed to be.

Confronted with these individuals, this city, these life situations, these strengths, these damages, there are some harsh questions that have to be raised about the uses of literature. I think of myself as a teacher of language: that is, as someone for whom language has implied freedom, who is trying to aid others to free themselves through the written word, and above all through learning to write it for themselves. I cannot know for them what it is they need to free, or what words they need to write; I can only try with them to get an approximation of the story they want to tell. I have always assumed, and I do still assume, that people come into the freedom of language through reading, before writing; that the differences of tone, rhythm, vocabulary, intention, encountered over years of reading are, whatever else they may be, suggestive of many different possible of modes of being. But my daily life as a teacher confronts me with young men and women who have had language and literature *used against* them, to keep them in their place, to mystify, to bully, to make them feel powerless. Courses in great books or speed-reading are not an answer when it is the meaning of literature itself that is in question. Sartre says: "the literary object has no other substance than the reader's subjectivity; Raskolnikov's waiting is *my* waiting which I lend him. . . . His hatred of the police magistrate who questions him is my hatred, which has been solicited and wheedled out of me by signs. . . . Thus, the writer appeals to the reader's freedom to collaborate in the production of his work."[5] But what if it is these very signs, or ones like them, that have been used to limit the reader's freedom or to convince the reader of his or her unworthiness to "collaborate in the production of the work"?

I have no illuminating answers to such questions. I am sure we must revise, and are revising, our notion of the "classic," which has come to be used as a term of unquestioning idolatry instead of in the meaning which Sartre gives it: a book written by someone who "did not have to decide with each work what the meaning and value of literature were, since its meaning and value were fixed by tradition."[6] And I know that the action from the other side, of becoming that person who puts signs on paper and invokes the collaboration of a reader, encounters a corresponding check: in order to write I have to believe that there is someone willing to collaborate sub-jectively, as opposed to a grading "machine" out to get me for mistakes in spelling and grammar. (Perhaps for this reason, many students first show the writing they are actually capable of in an uncorrected journal rather than in a "theme" written "for class.") The whole question of *trust* as a basis for the act of reading or writing has only opened up since we began trying to educate those who have every reason to mistrust literary culture. For young adults trying to write seriously for the first time in their lives, the question "Whom can I trust?" must be an underlying boundary to be crossed before real writing can occur. We who are part of literary culture come up against such a question only when we find ourselves writing on some frontier of self-determination, as when writers from an oppressed group *within* literary cul-ture, such as black intellectuals, or, most recently, women, begin to describe and an-alyze themselves as they cease to identify with the dominant culture. Those who fall into this category ought to be able to draw on it in entering into the experience of the young adult for whom writing itself—as reading—has been part of the not-me rather than one of the natural activities of the self.

At this point the question of method legitimately arises: How to do it? How to de-velop a working situation in the classroom where trust becomes a reality, where the students are writing with belief in their own validity, and reading with belief that what they read has validity for them? The question is legitimate—How to do it?—but I am not sure that a description of strategies and exercises, readings, and writing topics can be, however successful they have proven for one teacher. When I read such material, I may find it stimulating and heartening as it indicates the variet-ies of concern and struggle going on in other classrooms, but I end by feeling it is useless to me. X is not myself and X's students are not my students, nor are my stu-dents of this fall the same as my students of last spring. A couple of years ago I de-cided to teach *Sons and Lovers,* because of my sense that the novel touched on facts of existence crucial to people in their late teens, and my belief that it dealt with cer-tain aspects of family life, sexuality, work, anger, and jealousy which carried over to many cultures. Before the students began to read, I started talking about the time and place of the novel, the life of the mines, the process of industrialization and pol-lution visible in the slag heaps; and I gave the students (this was an almost all-black class) a few examples of the dialect they would encounter in the early chapters. Sev-eral students challenged the novel sight unseen: it had nothing to do with them, it was about English people in another era, why should they expect to find it meaning-ful to them, and so forth. I told them I had asked them to read it because I believed it was meaningful for them; if it was not, we could talk and write about why not and how not. The following week I reached the classroom door to find several students already there, energetically arguing about the Morels, who was to blame in the mar-riage, Mrs. Morel's snobbery, Morel's drinking and violence—taking sides, justify-ing, attacking. The class never began; it simply continued as other students arrived. Many had not yet read the novel, or had barely looked at it; these became curious and interested in the conversation and did go back and read it because they felt it must have something to have generated so much heat. That time, I felt some essential connections had been made, which carried us through several weeks of talking and writing about and out of *Sons and Lovers*, trying to define our relationships to its people and theirs to each other. A year or so later I enthusiastically started working with *Sons and Lovers* again, with a class of largely ethnic students—Jewish, Greek, Chinese, Italian, German, with a few Puerto Ricans and blacks. No one initially challenged the novel, but no one was particularly interested—or, perhaps, as I told myself, it impinged too dangerously on materials that this group was not about to deal with, such as violence in the family, nascent sexual feelings, conflicting feelings about a parent. Was this really true? I don't know; it is easy to play sociologist and make generalizations. Perhaps, simply, a different chemistry was at work, in me and in the students. The point is that for the first class, or for many of them, I think a trust came to be established in the novel genre as a possible means of finding out more about themselves; for the second class, the novel was an assignment, to be done under duress, read superficially, its connections with themselves avoided wherever possible.

Finally, as to trust: I think that, simple as it may seem, it is worth saying: a fundamental belief in the students is more important than anything else. We all know of those studies in education where the teacher's previously induced expectations dramatically affect the reaming that goes on during the semester. This fundamental belief is not a sentimental matter: it is a very demanding matter of realistically conceiving the student where he or she is, and at the same time never losing sight of where he or she *can* be. Conditions at a huge, urban, overcrowded, noisy, and pollution-soaked institution can become almost physically overwhelming at times, for the students and for the staff: sometimes apathy, accidia, anomie seem to stare from the faces in an overheated basement classroom, like the faces in a subway car, and I sympathize with the rush to get out the moment the bell rings. This, too, is our context—not merely the students' past and my past, but this present moment we share. I (and I don't think I am alone in this) become angry with myself for my ineffectualness, angry at the students for their apparent resistance or their acceptance of mediocrity, angriest at the political conditions which dictate that we have to try to repair and extend the fabric of language under conditions which tend to coarsen our apprehensions of everything. Often, however, this anger, if not driven in on ourselves, or converted to despair, can become an illuminating force: the terms of the struggle for equal opportunity are chalked on the blackboard: this is what the students have been up against all their lives.

I wrote at the beginning of this article that my early assumptions about teaching had changed. I think that what has held me at City is not the one or two students in a class whose eyes meet mine with a look of knowing they were born for this struggle with words and meanings; not the poet who has fumed up more than once; though such encounters are a privilege in the classroom as anywhere. What has held me, and what I think holds many who teach basic writing, are the hidden veins of possibility running through students who don't know (and strongly doubt) that this is what they were born for, but who may find it out to their own amazement, students who, grim with self-depreciation and prophecies of their own failure or tight with a fear they cannot express, can be lured into sticking it out to some moment of break-through, when they discover that they have ideas that are valuable, even original, and can express those ideas on paper. What fascinates and gives hope in a time of slashed budgets, enlarging class size, and national depression is the possibility the many of these young men and women may be gaining the kind of critical perspective on their lives and the skill to bear witness that they have never before had in our country's history.

At the bedrock level of my thinking about this is the sense that language is power, and that, as Simone Weil says, those who suffer from injustice most are the least able to articulate their suffering; and that the silent majority, if released into language, would not be content with a perpetuation of the conditions which have betrayed them. But this notion hangs on a special conception of what it means to be released into language: not simply learning the jargon of an elite, fitting unexceptionably into the status quo, but learning that language can be used as a means of changing reality.[7] What interests me in teaching is less the emergence of the occasional genius than the overall finding of language by those who did not have it and by those who have been used and abused to the extent that they lacked it.

The question can be validly raised: Is the existing public (or private) educational system, school, or university the place where such a relationship to language can be developed? Aren't those structures already too determined, haven't they too great a stake in keeping things as they are? My response would be, yes, but this is where the *students* are. On the one hand, we need alternate education; on the other, we need to reach those students for whom unorthodox education simply means too much risk. In a disintegrating society, the orthodox educational system reflects disintegration. However, I believe it is more than simply reformist to try to use that system—while it still exists in all its flagrant deficiencies—to use it to provide essential tools and weapons for those who may live on into a new integration. Language is such a weapon, and what goes with language: reflection, criticism, renaming, creation. The fact that our language itself is tainted by the quality of our society means that in teaching we need to be acutely conscious of the kind of tool we want our students to have available, to understand how it has been used against them, and to do all we can to insure that language will not someday be used by them to keep others silent and powerless.

Notes

1. What I have found deadly and defeating is the anthology designed for multiethnic classes in freshman English. I once ordered one because the book stipends had been cut out and I was trying to save the students money. I ended up using one Allen Ginsberg poem, two by LeRoi Jones, and asking the students to write essays provoked by the photographs in the anthology. The college anthology, in general, as nonbook, with its exhaustive and painfully literal notes, directives, questions, and "guides for study," is like TV showing of a film—cut, chopped up, and interspersed with commercials: a flagrant mutilation by mass technological culture.
2. Ellen Lurie, *How to Change the Schools* (New York: Random House, 1970). See PP. 31, 32, 40–48.
3. Mina P. Shaughnessy, "Open Admissions—A Second Report," in *The City College Department of English Newsletter*, vol. 11, no. 1., January 1972. A. R., 1978: See also Shaughnessy's *Errors and Expecta-*

tions: A Guide for the Teacher of Basic Writing (New York: Oxford, 1977), a remarkable study in the methodology of teaching language.

4. "When Blue-Collar Students Go to College," in *Saturday Review*, July 22, 1972. The article is excerpted from the book, *Working Through: A Teachers Journal in the Urban University* (New York: Saturday Review Press, 1972). Kriegel is describing students at Long Island University of a decade ago; but much that he says is descriptive of students who are now entering colleges like C.C.N.Y. under Open Admissions.

5. Jean-Paul Sartre, *What Is Literature?* (New York: Harper Colophon Books, 1965), PP 39–40.

6. Ibid., p. 85.

7. Compare Paolo Freire: "Only beings who can reflect upon the fact that they are determined are capable of freeing themselves." *Cultural Action for Freedom,* Monograph Series No. I (Cambridge, Mass.: Harvard Educational Review and Center for the Study of Development and Social Change, 1970).

What Happens When Basic Writers Come to College?
by Patricia Bizzell

I wish to propose an hypothesis for researching an answer to this question. For the time being, let me suggest that "basic writers" are those who are least well prepared for college. They may be defined in absolute terms, by features of their writing, or in relative terms, by their placement in a given school's freshman composition sequence, but, either way, their salient characteristic is their "outlandishness"—their appearance to many teachers and to themselves as the students who are most alien in the college community. Currently there are three major ways to describe what happens to these outlanders when they enter college. Each approach tends to focus on one element of basic writers' complex experience. While each approach can give us a valuable partial view of basic writers' experience, I am seeking a more comprehensive approach to frame my research hypothesis.

One of these three current approaches says that basic writers entering college precipitate a clash among dialects. The basic writers are those students who experience the greatest distance between their home dialects and Standard English, the preferred dialect in school. These students feel that if only they could learn to write "grammatically," their problems would be solved. Some teachers agree, saying we should help—or require—these students to learn Standard English. This solution is institutionalized in the composition course requirements at most colleges. Once entangled in these requirements, however, basic writers may wish they could avoid the demands of Standard altogether—after all, it's only a matter of how they're saying it, not what they say, they feel. Scholars such as James Sledd have argued that the solution is to stop demanding that all school work be conducted in Standard English, and to give these students the option of either learning Standard English, if they so desire, or writing and speaking in school in their home dialects.

We know that all dialects of English, whether Standard or non-Standard, are capable of conveying complex thought. Given this consensus, students and teachers

Bizzell, Patricia. "What Happens When Basic Writers Come to College?" *College Composition and Communication, 37* (Oct. 1986): 294-301. Copyright (1986) by the National Council of Teachers of English. Reprinted with permission.

who wonder whether Standard English must be learned are assuming that the issue is whether thoughts, however complex, should be conveyed in Standard or in some other dialect. In other words, the thoughts are supposedly unchanged by the dialect in which they are conveyed. Advocates of requiring the Standard form often argue that although students can think complexly in their home dialects, unfortunately the larger society demands the Standard form and therefore if we wish to enable them to get ahead, we have to enable them to use it. Defenders of home dialects say that forcing students to abandon dialects, even if only occasionally or temporarily, presents such a barrier that students will learn very little while concentrating on the language problem. Hence James Britton, and his American followers such as Lil Brannon and C. H. Knoblauch, would provide many opportunities in school for "expressive" speaking and writing in the students' home dialects as important ways of learning prior to, or perhaps instead of, practice in "transactional" language using the Standard dialect.

A second approach says that basic writers' problem on entering college is that they face a clash, not of dialects, but of discourse forms. The focus here is not mainly on features of language, such as forms of the verb to be, but on features of texts, such as verbal devices used to achieve coherence. Basic writers discover that the ways of organizing information and convincing audiences with which they are most familiar are not the ways of winning arguments in academe, as Mina Shaughnessy has observed. These students do not know what Elaine Maimon calls the "genres" of academic writing, and, as David Bartholomae has shown, they will seek to shape their writing according to discourse conventions more familiar to them from other sources, such as soap operas or grammar-school history lessons on "great men." Basic writers will be puzzled at the unenthusiastic reception afforded such papers by their teachers, especially if they have managed to write them in Standard English!

To what extent are discourse conventions to be regarded as surface features of writing? If they are surface features only, then adherence to discourse conventions would be a matter of pouring thoughts into "formal shells," as Brannon and Knoblauch disparagingly call them. But what if following the conventions actually generates thoughts that would not be accessible without the conventions? If the conventions are seen as surface features, then we get a version of the debate over requiring Standard English: should all students be required to learn such conventional academic genres as the case study or the literature survey, or be allowed to pursue the "same" intellectual work in genres with which they feel more comfortable, such as the journal? Advocates of requiring students to practice academic genres argue that knowledge of them is necessary for success in college; advocates of other forms argue that the criteria for success in college must change.

If, however, the discourse conventions are seen as generating, and not merely conveying, certain kinds of complex thinking, then the "same" intellectual work is not possible in different genres. For example, the journal might be a genre that generates personal connections with classwork, such as expressing religious revulsion for generic research, but that discourages other kinds of thinking, such as surveying religiously-motivated resistance to scientific research through the ages. According to this line of argument, students would need to learn other, more "academic" genres in order to become able to perform more kinds of academic intellectual work. A corollary of this position is that whereas many genres, like the many dialects of English, are equally capable of generating complex thoughts, they are not capable of generating the same complex thoughts. Thus students will be thinking in different ways, depending upon the dialect and discourse forms with which they are familiar.

It is a short step, then, from seeing basic writers participating in a clash of discourse conventions to seeing them engaged in a clash of ways of thinking. Basic writers may begin to feel that their problem really is that they're too dumb for college, or that they just can't think the way the teacher wants. Suspecting that perhaps such students really are incapable of college-level thought, researchers such as Andrea Lunsford and Frank D'Angelo have turned to cognitive psychology for models to understand basic writers' intellectual development. In this third approach to understanding basic writers' problems, the developmental schemes of Jean Piaget or William Perry have been used to rank-order student writers, with basic writers placed at the least developed end of the scale. The teacher's task then becomes similar to the therapist's, in seeking ways to correct basic writers' cognitive dysfunctions. Other scholars argue that to use psychological models in this way is to stigmatize basic writers and to ignore the cultural bases of differences in thinking (see Bizzell, "Cognition, Convention, and Certainty").

I want to find an approach to the difficulties of basic writers entering college that can take into account these differences in dialects, discourse conventions, and ways of thinking. When students see their problem only as one of dialect, they're apt to say, "It's just that I can't talk right!" If they experience the problem as difficulty shaping a paper—what I've called a problem of unfamiliarity with academic discourse conventions—they may not see their problem as having to do with writing at all. They may just complain, "I don't know what the teacher wants." This kind of bewilderment increases if they begin to see their problem as a thinking problem—as I've suggested, this view often leads to a radical loss of self-confidence. When teachers see students' problems in only one of these ways—when they see it as only a dialect problem, or only a thinking problem—they risk similarly narrow views of basic writers' experiences.

We can correct this excessively narrow focus through the notion of a language community: that is, a community that coheres because of common language-using practices. Perhaps all communities are in some sense language communities, although social class or geographic proximity, for instance, may also play a part in their cohesion. But the academic community is a community united almost entirely by its language, I think; the academic community is not coterminous with any social class, though it is more closely allied to some than to others. Like any other language community, the academic community uses a preferred dialect (so-called "Standard" English) in a convention-bound discourse (academic discourse) that creates and organizes the knowledge that constitutes the community's world view. If we see the relation between dialect, discourse conventions, and ways of thinking as constituting a language community, then we can no longer see dialects or discourse conventions as mere conveyances of thoughts generated prior to their embodiment in language. Rather, dialect and discourse generate thoughts, constitute world view.

It would not be correct, however, to say that a language community's world view is *determined* by its language, because that would imply that the worldview could not change as a result of interaction by the community with the material world, and we know that such changes do occur. In order to participate in the community and its changes, however, one must first master its language-using practices. Thus basic writers, upon entering the academic community, are being asked to learn a new dialect and new discourse conventions, but the outcome of such learning is acquisition of a whole new world view. Their difficulties, then, are best understood as stemming from the initial distance between their world-views and the academic world view, and perhaps also from the resistance to changing their own world-views that is caused by this very distance.

To understand basic writers' problems in these terms, we need to ask three questions: what world views do basic writers bring to college? What is the new world view demanded in college? And do basic writers have to give up the world views they bring to college in order to learn the new world-view?

The first of these questions has not yet been answered, as far as I know. We do not know much about the world views basic writers bring to college. Demographic information, on race or income for example, cannot lead to a satisfactory answer because there is no widely accepted model of the American class structure to which world views could be linked. Assumptions about "working-class" world views help to explain the school difficulties of certain groups of students in the research of Basil Bernstein in England, for example, and Pierre Bourdieu and Jean-Claude Passeron in France. We cannot make similar assumptions because, unlike the European researchers, we cannot identify a working class securely enough to be able to form hypotheses about its world view and so to test whether basic writers belong to this group. Some American researchers have argued that we should see basic writers as the products of an oral culture, so that differences of world view become differences between "literacy" and "orality" (see Ong, Farrell). Such analyses seek to attend to what the European researchers call class differences, in that oral culture seems to occur more frequently in certain social groups. The orality/literacy dichotomy, however, eventually flattens out class differences on behalf of the two main categories. Hence the variety of basic writers' cultural backgrounds and the differences in world views arising from this variety are not taken into account.

We will find it hard to assess the difficulty of acquiring the academic world view until we know how different it is from basic writers' home world views. Even though we cannot now say how great the difference might be, since we do not know enough about basic writers' original world views, basic writers' "outlandishness" in college strongly suggests that the difference is great and that for them, to a much greater degree than for other students, acquiring the academic world view means becoming bicultural. We do not know how difficult it is to become bicultural, although evidence exists that this is possible (see Fishman). If with great effort students can acquire the academic world view without having to give up their original world views, we do not know what benefits might motivate the effort, although there is some evidence that such benefits exist (see Patterson, Hoggart).

Perhaps we could get a better idea of what benefits are to be derived from acquiring the academic world view if we knew just what that world view is. I think we do have a good start on an answer to the question of what world view the college demands, in the developmental scheme of William Perry. I have argued elsewhere that this scheme is culture-bound (see Bizzell, "William Perry and Liberal Education"). In other words, it anatomizes an "intellectual and ethical development" that results from four years in an American liberal arts college, not a genetically-determined growth process. Furthermore, Perry happened to perform his research at Harvard, a college of long-standing and far-reaching influence in American academic life. Hence the world view Perry describes can be taken as hegemonic, as the "target" world-view toward which basic writers are urged, to a greater or lesser degree, everywhere.

I do not wish to summarize Perry's entire scheme, partly because space is limited and partly because, since we cannot assume that basic writers are coming into the process from the same sort of cultural background as Perry's research subjects, we have no reason to assume they will go through the same stages on their way to the final developmental position. I will attempt, however, to summarize that final position as the one at which basic writers must eventually arrive, if they are to succeed in college, however they get there.

Perry finds that the young men who have completed the process he describes see the world as a place in which there are no "Absolutes," no standards of right and wrong that hold good for all times and places. They feel that anyone who still sees the world as governed by Absolutes is epistemologically provincial. The liberal arts college, instead of accepting such naive dependence on Absolutes, requires the comparative study of ideas as the only way to choose among competing standards, to arrive at an informed judgment. Perry states that the essential component in the world view of the "liberally educated man" is the willingness "to think about even his own thoughts, to examine the way he orders his data and the assumptions he is making, and to compare these with other thoughts that other men might have" (39). The outcome of his deliberations is that he chooses to make "Commitments" to certain ideas, projects, and people, Commitments which will order his adult life.

On what basis are these Commitments made? Perry implies that their content will be strongly influenced by the allegiances students bring with them to college, to a particular religion, for example. At the same time, however, their form will be influenced by academic standards of logic, evidence, and so on. Hence the adult Commitment to a religion is a decision to build an area of meaningfulness, through participation in a group that shares one's sense of what is important, in a world which Perry apparently sees as essentially without intrinsic meaning. While Perry certainly does not wish to suggest that liberal arts education is destructive of religious faith, he implies that that faith will never be the same again—that after one has fully entered into the academic world view, one cannot willfully return to a world view constituted by Absolutes when one worships. The young men who have completed the process Perry describes see themselves as having accepted the individual responsibility of constructing meaning in their world, while acknowledging that this responsibility can only be accomplished through participation in like-minded groups: religious, political, and so on.

If Perry is right, then the academic world view makes a strong bid to control all of a student's experience. The student is asked to take a certain distance on all of his or her Commitments, to weigh them against alternatives, and to give allegiance only as a result of a careful deliberative process. In this sense, the academic world view cannot coexist peacefully with another world view in which standards for commitment are different—for example, one in which a father is authorized to make his children's choices. Perry implies that if one's pre-college world view includes seeing one's father's decisions as law, then one should certainly take one's father's wishes into account when determining adult Commitments. But one cannot both follow one's father's decisions unquestioningly, and yet weigh them as only one factor, however important, in one's own decision-making process.

It seems, then, that biculturalism is likely to be very difficult when the academic world view is one of the world views involved, because the academic seeks to subsume other world views to which the students may retain allegiance. The privileged position of the academic world view in society makes it seem an even more domineering partner. In other words, basic writers may feel that they are being asked to abandon their less prestigious, less socially powerful world views in favor of the academic. Richard Rodriguez is one former basic writer who has written of the pain his conversion to the academic world view caused him, with its attendant estrangement from home.

It could be argued, however, that the home world view, especially if it is associated with a social group of relatively little power, has a better chance of surviving if some who hold allegiance to it are also sufficiently familiar with the academic world view to wield power in the larger society. They will be able to argue for the preservation of the language and culture of the home world view, for example, by making persuasive arguments to school administrators for bilingual education programs and by organizing political action to convince the larger society of these programs' value. But what is to prevent these academically successful students from going on simply to secure their own financial advantage, forgetting about their home communities? Although such aspirations are certainly legitimate, their pursuit will not necessarily foster preservation of the home language and world view.

According to Perry's understanding of the academic world view, true mastery of it is the preventative against simply self-serving behavior. The student seeking to make Commitments, in Perry's sense, cannot operate autonomously because to make a Commitment is to connect with other people, with like-minded groups. To put it another way, the student seeking to make Commitments comes to value his or her connections with like-minded groups precisely because the student realizes that only through such connections can Commitments be realized.

There is nothing in the Perry model to suggest that such a student must make a Commitment to the like-minded group of his or her own home community. This student will probably have other groups from which to choose in making Commitments, such as chose associated with his or her profession. But the Perry model does suggest an economy of Commitments, a desire not to sever connections with any group to which one might potentially make a Commitment and, moreover, a desire particularly to foster Commitments that preserve integrity—in both the senses of honor and of coherence—in the individual's life, such as to a religious faith, or to a home culture that differs from the dominant one of the larger society. Thus, if we believe Perry, there is grounds for hope that the student who masters the academic world view will for that very reason wish to preserve his or her ties to the home community, and so to preserve its language and world view, whatever estrangements may have occurred on the way to this mastery.

I would like to conclude by suggesting that we need a study of basic writers similar to that conducted by Perry—a series of interviews to tell us how they mediate between their home cultures and the academic culture as they move on through their college educations. Perry's scheme can suggest the kind of developmental process such research would seek, although we would have to be careful not to assume that this test group will go through the same positions as Perry's Harvard students. Such a study would help to answer the other two questions I raise above: we would get a better idea of what world views basic writers bring to college, and we would hear what they themselves think about the cost of acquiring a new one. I suspect that they will not find the comparative, deliberative stance of the academic world view as hard to accept as Perry's more sheltered students do. The basic writers already know that their home communities' standards are not the only ones possible; they learn this more immediately and forcefully when they come to college than do students whose home world views are closer to the academic, when they experience the distance between their home dialects and Standard English and the debilitating unfamiliarity they feel with academic ways of shaping thoughts in discourse. I also suspect that they will find the stakes for accepting this world view higher than the stakes were for Perry's student, given the greater difference between this world view and their pre-college world views, basic writers have more to lose in modifying their earlier world views. But precisely because of the hegemonic power of the academic world view, my hypothesis is that they will also find its acquisition well worth the risks.

Works Cited

Bartholomae, David. "Inventing the University." In *Writing Blocks*, Ed. Mike Rose, New York: Guilford Press, 1986.

Bernstein, Basil. *Class, Codes, and Control.* 1971 rpt. New York: Schocken Books, 1975.

Bizzell, Patricia. "Cognition, Convention, and Certainty: What We Need to Know about Writing." *Pre/Text*, 3 (Fall, 1982), 213–244.

_____. "William Perry and Liberal Education." *College English*, 46 (September, 1984), 447–454.

Bourdieu, Pierre, and Jean-Claude Passeron. *Reproduction in Education, Society, and Culture.* Beverly Hills, California: Sage, 1977.

Britton, James et al. *The Development of Writing Abilities (11–18).* London: Macmillan Education, 1975.

D'Angelo, Frank. "Literacy and Cognition: A Developmental Perspective." In *Literacy for Life: The Demand for Reading and Writing.* Eds. Richard W. Bailey and Robin Melanie Forsheim, New York: Modern Language Association, 1983.

Farrell, Thomas J. "IQ and Standard English." *College Composition and Communication,* 34 (December, 1983), 470–484.

Fishman, Joshua A. "Ethnocultural Dimensions in the Acquisition and Retention of Biliteracy." *Journal of Basic Writing,* 3 (Fall/Winter, 1980), 48–61.

Hoggart, Richard. "The Importance of Literacy." *Journal of Basic Writing,* 3 (Fall/Winter, 1980), 74–87.

Knoblauch, C. H. and Lil Brannon. "Writing as Learning through the Curriculum." *College English,* 45 (September, 1983), 465–474.

Lunsford, Andrea. "The Content of Basic Writers' Essays." *College Composition and Communication,* 31 (October, 1980), 278–290.

Maimon, Elaine. "Maps and Genres." In *Composition and Literature: Bridging the Gap.* Editor: Winifred Horner. Chicago: University of Chicago Press, 1983.

Ong, Walter J., S.J. *Interfaces of the Word.* Ithaca, New York: Cornell University Press, 1977.

Patterson, Orlando. "Language, Ethnicity, and Change." *Journal of Basic Writing,* 3 (Fall/Winter, 1980) 62–73.

Perry, William. *Forms of Intellectual and Ethical Development in the College Years: A Scheme.* New York: Holt, Rinehart and Winston, 1968.

Rodriguez, Richard. "The Achievement of Desire: Personal Reflection on Learning 'Basics." *College English,* 40 (November, 1978), 239–254.

Shaughnessy, Mina. "Some Needed Research on Writing." *College Composition and Communication,* 28 (December, 1977), 317–320.

Sledd, James. "In Defense of the Students' Right." *College English,* 45 (November, 1983), 667–675.

Narrowing the Mind and Page:
Remedial Writers
and Cognitive Reductionism
by Mike Rose

There has been a strong tendency in American education—one that took modern shape with the I.Q. movement—to seek singular, unitary cognitive explanations for broad ranges of poor school performance. And though this trend— I'll call it cognitive reductionism—has been challenged on many fronts (social and political as well as psychological and psychometric), it is surprisingly resilient. It re-emerges. We see it in our field in those discussions of basic and remedial writers that suggest that unsuccessful writers think in fundamentally different ways from successful writers. Writing that is limited to the concrete, that doesn't evidence abstraction or analysis, that seems illogical is seen, in this framework, as revealing basic differences in perception, reasoning, or language.[1] This speculation has been generated, shaped, and supported by one or more theories from psychology, neurology, and literary studies.

Studies of cognitive style suggest that people who can be characterized as "field-dependent" (vs. those who are "field-independent") might have trouble with analytical tasks. *Popular articles on brain research* claim a neurophysiological base for some humans to be verbal, logical, analytical thinkers and for others to be spatial, holistic, non-verbal thinkers. *Jean Piaget's work on the development of logical thought* seems pertinent as well: some students might not have completed their developmental ascent from concrete to abstract reasoning. And *orality-literacy theorists* make connections between literacy and logic and suggest that the thinking of some minority groups might be affected by the degree to which their culture has moved from oral to literate modes of behavior.

The applications of these theories to poor writers appear in composition journals and papers at English, composition, and remedial education conferences. This is by no means the only way people interested in college-age remedial writers talk about thinking-writing connections, but the posing of generalized differences in cognition and the invoking of Piaget, field dependence and the rest has developed into a way of talking about remediation. And though this approach has occasionally been challenged in journals, it maintains a popular currency and encourages a series of bold assertions: poor writers can't form abstractions; they are incapable of analysis; they perceive the world as an undifferentiated whole; the speech patterns they've acquired in their communities seriously limit their critical capacity.

I think we need to look closely at these claims and at the theories used to support them, for both the theories and the claims lead to social distinctions that have important consequences, political as well as educational. This is not to deny that the theories themselves have contributed in significant ways to our understanding of mental processes (and Piaget, of course, shaped an entire field of research), but their richness should not keep us from careful consideration of their limits, internal contradictions, and attendant critical discussions and counterstatements. Consideration of the theories leads us naturally to consideration of their applicability to areas beyond their original domain. Such application often overgeneralizes the theory: Ong's brilliant work on orality and literacy, for example, moves beyond its history-of-consciousness domain and becomes a diagnostic framework. A further problem—sometimes inherent in the theories themselves, sometimes a result of reductive application—is the tendency to diminish cognitive complexity and rely on simplified cognitive oppositions: independent vs. dependent, literate vs. oral, verbal vs. spatial, concrete vs. logical. These oppositions are textbook-neat, but, as much recent cognitive research demonstrates, they are narrow and misleading. Yet another problem is this: these distinctions are usually used in a way meant to be value-free (that is, they highlight differences rather than deficits in thinking), but, given our culture, they are anything but neutral. Social and political hierarchies end up encoded in sweeping cognitive dichotomies.

In this article I would like to reflect on the problems with and limitations of this particular discourse about remediation. To do this, I'll need to provide a summary of the critical discussion surrounding each of the theories in its own field, for that complexity is too often lost in discussions of thought and writing. As we move through the essay, I'll point out the problems in applying these theories to the thought processes of poor writers. And, finally, I'll conclude with some thoughts on studying cognition and writing in less reductive ways.

Cognitive Style: Field Dependence-Independence

Cognitive style, broadly defined, is an "individual's characteristic and consistent manner of processing and organizing what he [or she] sees and thinks about" (Harre and Lamb 98). In theory, cognitive style is separate from verbal, quantitative, or visual intelligence; it is not a measure of how much people know or how well they mentally perform a task, but the manner in which they perform, their way of going about solving a problem, their style. Cognitive style research emerges out of the study of individual differences, and there have been a number of theories of cognitive style proposed in American and British psychology since the late 40's. Varied though they are, all the theories discuss style in terms of a continuum existing between two polar opposites: for example, reflectivity vs. impulsivity, analytic vs. global, complexity vs. simplicity, levelling vs. sharpening, risk-taking vs. cautiousness, field-dependence vs. field-independence. Field dependence-independence, first described by Herman A. Witkin in 1949, is, by far, the most researched of the cognitive styles, and it is the style that seems to be most discussed in composition circles.

The origins of the construct are, as Witkin, Moore, Goodenough, and Cox note, central to its understanding. Witkin's first curiosity concerned the degree to which people use their surrounding visual environment to make judgments about the vertical position of objects in a field. Witkin devised several devices to study this issue, the best known being the Rod and Frame Test. A square frame on a dark background provides the surrounding visual field, and a rod that rotates within it is the (potentially) vertical object. Both the frame and the rod can separately be rotated clockwise or counter-clockwise, and "[t]he subject's task is to adjust the rod to a position where he perceives it as upright, while the frame around it remains in its initial position of tilt" ("Field-Dependent" 3). Witkin, et al.'s early findings revealed some interesting individual differences:

> For some, in order for the rod to be apprehended as properly upright, it must be fully aligned with the surrounding frame, wherever the position of the frame. If the frame is tilted 30 [degrees] to the right, for example, they will tilt the rod 30 [degrees] to the right, and say the rod is perfectly straight in that position. At the opposite extreme of the continuous performance range are people who adjust the rod more or less close to the upright in making it straight, regardless of the position of the surrounding frame. They evidently apprehend the rod as an entity discrete from the prevailing visual frame of reference and determine the uprightness of the rod according to the felt position of the body rather than according to the visual frame immediately surrounding it. ("Field-Dependent" 3-4)

A subject's score is simply the number of degrees of actual tilt of the rod when the subject claims it is straight.

Witkin and his associates later developed another measure—one that was much less cumbersome and could be given to many people at once—The Embedded Figures Test.[2] Witkin, et al. considered the Embedded Figures Test to be similar to the Rod and Frame Test in its "essential perceptual structure." The subject must locate a simple geometric design in a complex figure, and "once more what is at issue is the extent to which the surrounding visual framework dominates perception of the item within it" (6). A subject's score on the test is the number of such items he or she can disembed in a set time.

The "common denominator" between the two tests is "the extent to which the person perceives part of the field as discrete from the surrounding field as a whole, rather than embedded in the field; or the extent to which the organization of the prevailing field determines perception of its components" (7). Put simply, how strong is our cognitive predisposition to let surrounding context influence what we see?

Witkin soon began to talk of the differences between field dependence vs. independence as differences between articulated (or analytic) vs. global perception:

> At one extreme there is a consistent tendency for experience to be global and diffuse; the organization of the field as a whole dictates the manner in which its parts are experienced. At the other extreme there is a tendency for experience to be delineated and structured; parts of a field are experienced as discrete and the field as a whole organized. To these opposite poles of the cognitive styles we may apply the labels "global and articulated." ("Psychological Differentiation" 319)

Witkin's tests were tapping interesting individual differences in perception and cognition, but the really tantalizing findings emerged as Witkin and his colleagues began pursuing a wide-ranging research agenda that, essentially, sought correlations between performance on field dependence-independence tests and performance on a variety of other cognitive, behavioral, and personality tests, measures, and activities. Hundreds of these studies followed, ranging from the insightful (correlating cognitive style with the way teachers structure social science concepts) to the curious (correlating cognitive style with the shortness of women's skirts). Some of the studies yielded low correlations, and some were inconclusive or were contradictory—but, in general, the results, as summarized by educational psychologist Merlin Wittrock, resulted in the following two profiles:

- To the degree that people score high on field independence they tend to be: "relatively impersonal, individualistic, insensitive to others and their reinforcements, interested in abstract subject matter, and intrinsically motivated. They have internalized frames of reference, and experience themselves as separate or differentiated from others and the environment. They tend to use previously learned principles and rules to guide their behavior" (93).
- To the degree that people score low on field independence they are, by default, field-dependent, and they tend to be: "more socially oriented, more aware of social cues, better able to discern feelings of others from their facial expressions, more responsive to a myriad of information, more dependent on others for reinforcement and for defining their own beliefs and sentiments, and more in need of extrinsic motivation and externally defined objectives" (93).

The tendency of the field-independent person to perceive particular shapes and orientations despite context, and the tendency of the field-dependent person to let "the organization of the field as a whole dictate the manner in which its parts are experienced" seemed to be manifesting themselves in motivation, cognition, and personality. A few relatively simple tests were revealing wide-ranging differences in the way people think and interact.

The psychometric neatness of this work seems a little too good to be true, and, in fact, problems have been emerging for some time. My discussion of them will be oriented toward writing.

You'll recall that it is central to the theory that cognitive style is not a measure of ability, of how well people perform a task, but a measure of their manner of performance, their style. If we applied this notion to writing, then, we would theoretically expect to find interesting differences in the way discourse is produced, in the way a rhetorical act is conceived and executed: maybe the discourse of field independents would be more analytical and impersonal while field-dependent discourse would be richer in social detail. But these differences should not, theoretically, lead to gross differences in quality. By some general measure, papers written by field-dependent and field-independent students should have equal possibility of being acceptable discourse. They would just be different. However, the most detailed and comprehensive cognitive style study of college-level writers I've yet seen yields this: papers written by field-dependent students are simply poor papers, and along most dimensions—spelling, grammar, development (Williams). This doesn't fit. Conclusions emerge, but they don't jibe with what the theory predicts.

Such conceptual and testing perplexities are rooted, I believe, in the field dependence-independence work itself. My review of the psychological literature revealed seven problems with the construct, and they range from the technical to the conceptual level.

For cognitive style to be a legitimate construct, it has to be distinct from general intelligence or verbal ability or visual acuity, because cognitive style is not intended to be a measure of how "smart" someone is, but of the manner in which she or he engages in an intellectual task. Unfortunately, there are a number of studies which suggest that field dependence-independence significantly overlaps with measures of intelligence, which are, themselves, complex and controversial. As early as 1960, Lee J. Cronbach wrote in his authoritative *Essentials of Psychological Testing*. "General reasoning or spatial ability accounts for much of Embedded Figures performance as does difficulty in handling perceptual interference" (549). In 1972, Philip Vernon, also a prominent researcher of individual differences, reviewed studies that investigated relations between scores on field dependence-independence and various measures of "visual intelligence." He concluded that "the strong positive correlation with such a wide range of spatial tests is almost embarrassing" (368). And after conducting his own study, Vernon declaimed that Embedded Figures Tests "do not define a factor distinct from general intelligence . . . and spatial ability or visualization" (386). Things become more complicated. Vernon, and other researchers (see, for example, Linn and Kyllonen), present factor-analytic data that suggest that determining the position of the rod within the frame and disembedding the hidden figures tap *different* mental constructs, not the unitary construct Witkin had initially postulated.[3] It is possible, of course, that different aspects of field dependence-independence are being tapped by the different tests and that two of them should be administered together—as Witkin, in fact, recommended. But even if researchers used multiple measures (as few have—most use only the Embedded Figures Test because of its utility), the problem of overlap with measures of intelligence would remain. In short, it's not certain just what the field dependence-independence tests are measuring, and it's very possible that they are primarily tapping general or spatial intelligence.

There is a further testing problem. In theory, each pole of a cognitive style continuum "has adaptive value in certain circumstances . . . neither end of [a]cognitive style dimension is uniformly more adaptive . . . adaptiveness depends upon the nature of the situation and upon the cognitive requirements of the task at hand"

(Messick 9). Now, there have been studies which show that field-dependent people seem to attend more readily than field-independent people to social cues (though the effects of these studies tend to be small or inconsistent—see McKenna), but it is important to note that Witkin and his colleagues have never been able to develop a test that *positively* demonstrates field dependence. The Rod and Frame Test, the Embedded Figures Test—and all the other tests of field dependence-independence—assess how well a person displays field *in*dependence. Field dependence is essentially determined by default—the more a person fails at determining the true position of the rod or the slower he is at disembedding the figure, the more field dependent he is. This assessment-by-default would not be a problem if one were testing some level of skill or intellectual ability, say, mechanical aptitude. But where a bipolar and "value-free" continuum is being assessed—where one is not "deficient" or "maladaptive" regardless of score, but only different, where both field-independent and field-dependent people allegedly manifest cognitive strengths as well as limitations—then it becomes a problem if you can't devise a test on which field-dependent subjects would score well. Witkin, et al. admit that the development of such a test is "an urgent task" (16). It has not yet been developed.

But even if a successful test of field dependence could be created, problems with assessment would not be over. All existing tests of field dependence-independence are, as Paul L. Wachtel points out:

> in certain respects poorly suited for exploration of the very problem {they were} designed to deal with—that of style. It is difficult to organize ideas about different directions of development upon a framework which includes only one dimension, and only the possibility of "more" or "less." (186)

Consider the notion of style. It would seem that style is best assessed by the observation and recording of a range of behaviors over time. Yet the Rod and Frame and Embedded Figures Tests don't allow for the revelation of the cognitive processes in play as the person tries to figure them out. That is, there is no provision made for the subject to speak aloud her mental processes or offer a retrospective account of them or explain—as in Piagetian method—why she's doing what she's doing. We have here what Michael Cole and Barbara Means refer to as the problem of drawing process inferences from differences in task performance (65). It would be unfair to lay this criticism on Witkin's doorstep alone, for it is a general limitation with psychometric approaches to cognition. (See, for example, Hunt.) But Witkin's work, since it purports to measure style, is especially vulnerable to it.

Let us now rethink those composite profiles of field-independent vs. field-dependent people. You'll recall that the correlations of all sorts of measures suggest that field-dependent people are more socially oriented, more responsive to a myriad of information, etc., while field-independent people tend to be individualistic, interested in abstract subject matter, and so on. These profiles can be pretty daunting; they're built on hundreds of studies, and they complement our folk wisdom about certain kinds of personalities. But we must keep in mind that the correlations between tests of field independence and personality or cognitive measures are commonly .25 to .3 or .4; occasionally, correlations as high as .5 or .6 are recorded, but they are unusual. That means that, typically, 84% to 94% of the variance between one measure and the other remains to be accounted for by factors other than those posited by the cognitive style theorist. Such studies accrue, and eventually the theorist lays them all side by side, notes the seeming commonalities, and profiles emerge. You could consider these profiles telling and veridical, but you could also consider them webs of thin connection.

We in the West are drawn to the idea of consistency in personality (from Renaissance humors to Jungian types), and that attraction, I think, compels us to seek out similar, interrelated consistencies in cognition. Certainly there are regularities in the way human beings approach problems; we don't go at our cognitive tasks willy-nilly. But when cognitive researchers try to chart those consistencies by studying individual people solving multiple problems they uncover a good deal of variation, variation that is potentially efficient and adaptive. William F. Battig, for example, found in his studies of adult verbal learning that most subjects employed different strategies at different times, even when working on a single problem. At least in the cognitive dimension, then, it has proven difficult to demonstrate that people approach different problems, in different settings, over time in consistent ways. This difficulty, it seems to me, presents a challenge to the profiles provided by cognitive style theorists.

There are, finally, troubling conceptual-linguistic problems with field dependence-independence theory, and they emerge most dramatically for me when I try to rephrase some of Witkin's discussions of the two styles. Here is one example:

> Persons with a global style are more likely to go along with the field "as is," without using such mediational processes as analyzing and structuring. In many situations field-independent people tend to behave as if governed by general principles which they have actively abstracted from their experiences . . . In contrast, for field-dependent people information processing systems seem to make less use of such mediators. (Witkin, et al. 21)

Statements like this are common in Witkin, and they flow along and make sense in the discussion he offers us—but you stop cold if you consider for a minute what it might mean for people to have a tendency to operate in the world "without using such mediational processes as analyzing and structuring" or, by implication, to not "behave as if governed by general principles which they have actively abstracted from their experiences." These seem like pretty extreme claims, given the nature and limitations of tests of cognitive style. All current theories of cognition that I'm familiar with posit that human beings bring coherence to behavior by abstracting general principles from experiences, by interpreting and structuring what they see and do. When people can't do this sort of thing, or can only do it minimally, we assume that something is seriously wrong with them.

Witkin and his colleagues faced the dilemma that all theory builders face: how to find a language with which to express complex, abstract ideas. (For a Wittgensteinian analysis of Witkin's language, see Kurtz.) And given the nature of language, such expression is always slippery. I think, though, that Witkin and company get themselves into more than their fair share of trouble. The language they finally choose is often broad and general: it is hard to operationalize, and, at times, it seems applicable post hoc to explain almost any result (see Wachtel 184-85). It is metaphoric in troubling ways. And it implies things about cognition that, upon scrutiny, seem problematic. I would suggest that if we're going to apply Witkin's notions to the assessment of writing and cognition we'll need more focussed, less problematic definitions. Now, Witkin does, in fact, occasionally provide such definitions, but they raise problems of a different order. And here again we see the complications involved in connecting Witkin's theory to composing.

In an admirably precise statement, Witkin, et al. note:

> The individual who, in perception, cannot keep an item separate from the surrounding field—in other words, who is relatively field-dependent—is likely to have difficulty with that class of problems, and, we must emphasize, only with that class of problems, where the solution depends on taking some critical element out of the context in which it is presented and restructuring the problem material so that the item is now used in a different context. (9)

Consider rhetoric and the production of written language. For Witkin's formulation to apply, we would have to define rhetorical activity and written language production as *essentially* involving the disembedding of elements from contexts and concomitant restructuring of those contexts. It seems to me that such application doesn't hold. Even if there were a rhetorical-linguistic test of cognitive style—and there isn't; the tests are visual, perceptual-orientational—I think most of us would say that while we could think of linguistic-rhetorical problems that might fit Witkin's description, it would be hard to claim that it characterizes rhetorical activity and linguistic production in any broad and inclusive way.

Second of all, it's important to remember that Witkin is talking about a *general* disembedding skill, a skill that would be effective in a wide range of contexts: engineering, literature, social relations. A number of contemporary students of cognition, however, question the existence of such general cognitive skills and argue for more domain-specific strategies, skills, and abilities (see, for example, Carey; Fodor; Gardner, *Frames*; Glaser; Perkins). Given our experience in particular domains, we may be more or less proficient at disembedding and restructuring problem areas in literature but not in engineering. Our ability to disembed the hidden geometric figures in Witkin's test may be more related to our experience with such visual puzzles than to some broad cognitive skill at disembedding. If a student can't structure an essay or take a story apart in the way we've been trained to do, current trends in cognitive research would suggest that her difficulties have more to do with limited opportunity to build up a rich network of discourse knowledge and strategy than with some general difference or deficit in her ability to structure or analyze experience.

Hemisphericity

The French physician Paul Broca announced in 1865 that "we speak with the left hemisphere"; neurologists have had clinical evidence for some time that damage to certain areas of the left side of the brain could result in disruptions in production or comprehension of speech—aphasia—and that damage to certain areas of the right could result in space and body orientation problems; laboratory experiments with healthy people over the last 25 or so years have demonstrated that particular linguistic or spatial capacities seem to require the function of regions in the left or right brain respectively (though it is also becoming clear that there is some degree of right hemisphere involvement in language production and comprehension and left hemispheric involvement in spatial tasks); and radical neurosurgery on a dozen or so patients with intractable epilepsy—a severing of the complex band of neural fibers (the commissures) that connect the left and right cerebral hemispheres—has provided dramatic, if highly unusual, illustration of the anatomical specialization of the hemispheres. It is pretty much beyond question, then, that different areas of the brain contribute to different aspects of human cognition. As with any biological structure there is variation, but in 98% of right handers and 70% of "non-right" handers, certain areas of the left hemisphere are critical for the processing of phonology and syntax and for the execution of fine motor control, and certain areas of the right hemisphere are involved in various kinds of visual and spatial cognition.

These conclusions evolve from either clinical observation or experimental studies. Most studies fit the following paradigm: a set of tasks is presented to a subject, and the tasks are either isomorphic with the process under investigation (e.g., distinguishing nonsense syllables like "pa," "ta," "ka," "ba" as a test of phonetic discrimination) or can be assumed, in a common sense way, to tap the activity under investigation (e.g., mentally adding a list of numbers as a test of serial processing). The subject's speed or accuracy is recorded and, in some studies, other measures are taken that are hypothesized to be related to the mental processes being studied (e.g., recording the brain wave patterns or blood flow or glucose metabolism of the cerebral hemispheres while the subject performs the experimental task).

Studies of this type have enabled researchers to gain some remarkable insight into the fine neuropsychological processes involved in understanding language and, to a lesser degree, in making spatial-orientational discriminations. But it is also true that, ingenious as the work has been, the field is still at a relatively primitive state: many studies are difficult to duplicate (a disturbing number of them yield conflicting results), and the literature is filled with methodological quarrels, competing theories, and conceptual tangles. (For a recent, and very sympathetic, overview see Benson and Zaidel.)

In spite of the conflicts, there are various points of convergence in the data, and, in the yearning for parsimony that characterizes science, the areas of agreement have led some neuroscientists to seek simple and wide-ranging characterizations of brain function. They suggest that beneath all the particular findings about syntax and phonetics and spatial discrimination lie *fundamental* functional differences in the left and right cerebral hemispheres: each is best suited to process certain kinds of stimuli and/or each processes stimuli in distinct ways. A smaller number of neuroscientists—and many popularizers—go a step further and suggest that people tend toward reliance on one hemisphere or the other when they process information. This theory is commonly referred to as "hemisphericity" (Bogart, DeZure, TenHouton, and Marsh). And a few sociologically oriented theorists take another, truly giant, step and suggest that entire dominant and subdominant groups of people can be characterized by a reliance on left or right hemispheric processing (TenHouten). We have, then, the emergence of a number of cognitive dichotomies: the left hemisphere is characterized as being analytic while the right is holistic (or global or synthetic; the left is verbal, the right non-verbal (or spatial); the left a serial processor, the right a parallel processor—and the list continues: focal vs. diffuse, logical vs. intuitive, propositional vs. oppositional, and so on.

The positing of hemispheric dichotomies is understandable. Human beings are theory-makers, and parsimony is a fundamental criterion by which we judge the value of a theory: can it account for diverse data with a simple explanation? But, given the current state of brain research, such generalizations, to borrow Howard Gardner's phrase, leapfrog from the facts ("What We Know" 114). Gardner is by no means alone in his criticism. My reading of the neuroscientific literature reveals that the notion of dichotomous hemispheric function is very controversial, and the further notion of hemisphericity is downright dismissed by a broad range of neuroscientists, psychologists, psycholinguists, and research psychiatrists:

> [T]he concepts [analytic/synthetic, temporal/spatial, etc.] are currently so slippery that it sometimes proves impossible to maintain consistency throughout one paper. (John C. Marshall in Bradshaw and Nettleton 72)

> [M]uch of perception (certainly of visual perception) is very difficult to split up this way. The alleged dichotomy {between temporal-analytic and spatial-holistic} is, if it exists at all, more a feature of laboratory experiments than of the real world. (M.J. Morgan in Bradshaw and Nettleton 74)

> [T]he idea of hemisphericity lacks adequate foundation and . . . because of the assumptions implicit in the idea of hemisphericity, it will never be possible to provide such a foundation. The idea is a misleading one which should be abandoned. (Beaumont, Young, and McManus 191)

The above objections rise from concerns about method, subjects, and conceptualization. Let me survey each of these concerns.

A significant amount of the data used to support hemisphericity—and certainly the most dramatic—is obtained from people in whom accident or pathology has highlighted what particular sections of the brain can or can't do. The most unusual group among these (and they are much-studied) is the handful of people who have had severe and life-threatening epilepsy alleviated through a radical severing of the neural fibers that connect the right and left hemispheres. Such populations, however, present a range of problems: tumors and wounds can cause disruptions in other areas of the brain; stroke victims could have had previous "silent strokes" and could, as well, be arteriosclerotic; long disease histories (certainly a characteristic of the severe epileptics who underwent split-brain surgery) can lead to compensatory change in brain function (Bogart, "The Dual Brain"; Whitaker and Ojemann). Furthermore, extrapathological factors, such as education and motivation, can, as Bradshaw and Nettleton put it, also "mask or accentuate the apparent consequences of brain injury" (51). And, as a final caution, there is this: the whole enterprise of localizing linguistic function through pathological performance is not without its critics (see Caplan).

Studies with healthy subjects—and there are increasing numbers of these, remove one major difficulty with hemisphericity research, though here methodological problems of a different sort arise. Concern not with subjects but with instruments and measures now comes into focus. Space as well as my own technological shortcomings prohibit a full review of tools and methods, but it might prove valuable to briefly survey the problems with a representative approach: electroencephalographic methods. (Readers interested in critical review of procedures other than the one I cover can consult the following: Regional Cerebral Blood Flow: Beaumont; Lateral Eye Movements: Ehrlichman and Weinberger; Tachistoscopic Methods: Young; Dichotic Listening Tests: Efron.)

If you hypothesize that certain kinds of tasks (like discriminating between syllables or adding a list of numbers) are primarily left-brain tasks and that others (like mentally rotating blocks or recognizing faces) are primarily right-brain tasks, then neuroelectric activity in the target hemisphere should vary in predictable ways when the subject performs the respective tasks. And, in fact, such variation in brain wave activity has been empirically demonstrated for some time. Originally, such studies relied on the electroencephalogram (EEG)—the ongoing record of brain wave activity—but now it is possible to gain a more sophisticated record of what are called event-related potentials (ERP). ERP methods use the electroencephalographic machinery, but rely on computer averaging and formalization to more precisely relate brain wave activity to repeated presentations of specific stimuli (thus the waves are "event-related"). The advantage of EEG and ERP methods is that they offer a direct electrophysiological measurement of brain activity and, especially in the case of ERP, "can track rapid fluctuation in brain electrical fields related to cognitive processing . . ." (Brown, Marsh, and Ponsford 166). such tracking is important to hemisphericity theorists, for it can lend precision to their claims.

There are problems however. EEG/ERP methods are among the most technically demanding procedures in psychology, and that technical complexity gives rise to a number of difficulties involving variation in cortical anatomy, electrode placement, and data analysis (Beaumont; Gevins, Zeitlin, Doyle, Schaffer, and Callaway). And, when it comes to the study of language processing—certainly an area of concern to writing researchers—ERP procedures give rise to problems other than the technical. Most ERP studies must, for purposes of computer averaging, present each stimulus as many as 50 times, and such repetition creates highly artificial linguistic processing conditions. Even relatively natural language processing studies have trouble determining which perceptual, linguistic, or cognitive factors are responsible for results (see, e.g., Hillyard and Woods). So, though hemispheric differences in brain wave patterns can be demonstrated, the exceptional technical and procedural difficulties inherent in the EEG/ERP studies of language processing make it hard to interpret data with much precision. Cognitive psychophysiologists Emanual Donchin, Gregory McCarthy and Marta Kutas summarize the state of affairs:

[A]lthough a substantial amount of clinical data support the theory of left hemisphere superiority in language reception and production, the ERP data regarding this functional asymmetry are far from consistent. The methodological and statistical shortcomings which exist in some of the studies cited [in their review article] along with inconsistencies in the others render any decision about the efficacy of ERP's as indices of linguistic processing inconclusive. (239. For similar, more recent, assessments, see Rugg; Beaumont, Young, and McManus.)

In considering the claims of the hemisphericity theorists, we have reviewed problems with subjects, techniques, and procedures. There is yet a further challenge to the notion of hemisphericity. Some hemisphericity theorists believe that since people can be characterized by a tendency to rely on one hemisphere or the other, then such reliance should manifest itself in the way people lead their lives: in the way they solve problems, in the jobs they choose, and so on. Yet the few studies that have investigated this dimension of the theory yielded negative results. Hemisphericity advocates Robert Ornstein and David Galin failed to find overall systematic EEG differences between lawyers (assumed to be left hemispheric) and sculptors and ceramicists (assumed to be right hemispheric). In a similar study, Dumas and Morgan failed to find EEG differences between engineers and artists, leading the researchers to conclude that "the conjecture that there are 'left hemispheric' people and 'right hemispheric' people seems to be an oversimplification" (227). In a more ambitious study, Arndt and Berger gave graduate students in law, psychology, and sculpture batteries of tests to assess verbal analytic ability (for example, a vocabulary test) and spatial ability (for example, a figure recognition test), and, as well, tests to assess hemisphericity (letter and facial recognition tachistoscopic tasks). While they found—as one would expect—a significant correlation between verbal or spatial ability and occupation (e.g., sculptors scored better than lawyers on the spatial tests), they *did not* find significant correlations between the verbal or spatial tests and the hemisphericity task; nor did they find significant correlation between the hemisphericity task and occupation.

A postscript on the above. Failures to find hemispheric differences between individuals of various occupational groups—along with the methodological difficulties mentioned earlier—throw into serious doubt the neurosociological claim that entire *groups* of people can be characterized as being left or right hemispheric. The neurosociological literature makes some remarkable speculative leaps from the existence of left-right dualities in cultural myth and symbol to asymmetries in left-right brain function, and relies, for empirical support, on the results of individual verbal and spatial tests (like the sub-tests in I.Q. assessments)—precisely the kinds of tests that a number of psychologists and neurologists have shown to be limited in assessing left or right hemispheric performance (see, e.g., DeRenzi).

Let me try to draw a few conclusions for rhetoric and composition studies.

It is important to keep in mind that the experimental studies that do support hemispheric specialization suggest small differences in performance capacities, and the differences tend to be of degree more than kind: in the range of 6-12%. Researchers have to expose subjects to many trials to achieve these differences. (One hundred and fifty to two hundred is common; one facial recognition study ran subjects through 700 trials.) And the experiments deal with extremely specific—even atomistic—functions. (Researchers consider the distinguishing of homonyms in a sentence—"bear" v s. "bare"—to be a "complex verbal task.") It is difficult to generalize from results of this type and magnitude to broad statements about one hemisphere being the seat of logic and the other of metaphor. What happens, it seems, is that theorists bring to very particular (though, admittedly, very important) findings about phonology or syntax or pattern recognition a whole array of cultural beliefs about analytic vs. synthetic thinking and logic vs. creativity and apply them in blanket fashion. There is a related problem here, and it concerns the hemisphericity theorists' assumption that, say, distinguishing phonemes is an analytical or serial or propositional task while, say, facial recognition is synthetic or holistic or oppositional. These assumptions are sensible, but they are not proven. In fact, *one could argue the other way around:* e.g., that recognizing faces, for example, is not a holistic but a features analysis task. Unfortunately, neuroscientists don't know enough to resolve this very important issue. They work with indirect measures of information processing: differences in reaction time or variations in electrophysiological measures. They would need more direct access than they now have to the way information is being represented and problems are being solved.

Because the accounts of cerebral asymmetry can be so dramatic—particularly those from split-brain studies—it is easy to dwell on differences. But, in fact, there is wide-ranging similarity, overlap, and cooperation in the function of the right and left hemispheres:

> Complex psychological processes are not 'localized' in any one hemisphere but are the result of integration between hemispheres. (Alexander Luria cited in LeDoux 210)

If Luria's dictum applied anywhere, it would certainly be to the "complex psychological processes" involved in reading and writing. Under highly controlled laboratory conditions researchers can show that phoneme discrimination or word recognition can be relatively localizable to one hemisphere or the other. But attempts to comprehend or generate writing—that is perceived or produced as logical or metaphoric or coherent or textured—involve a stunning range of competencies: from letter recognition to syntactic fluency to an understanding of discourse structure and genre (see, e.g., Gardner and Winner 376-80). And such a range, according to everything we know, involves the whole brain in ways that defy the broad claims of the hemisphericity theorists. When students have trouble structuring an argument or providing imagistic detail, there is little neurophysiological evidence to support contentions that their difficulties originate in organic predisposition or social conditioning to rely on one hemisphere or the other.

Jean Piaget and Stages of Cognitive Development

Piaget's theory of cognitive development is generally held to be, even by its revisors and detractors, the modern West's most wide-ranging and significant account of the way children think. The theory, which Piaget began to articulate over 50 years ago, covers infancy to adolescence and addresses the development of scientific and mathematical reasoning, language, drawing, morality, and social perception; it has shaped the direction of inquiry into childhood cognition; and it has led to an incredible number of studies, a good many of which have been cross-cultural. In holding to the focus of this article, then, there's a lot I'll have to ignore—I'll be limiting myself to those aspects of Piaget's theory that have been most widely discussed in reference to college-age writers.

Though Piaget and his colleagues adjusted their theory to account for the wealth of data being generated by researchers around the world, there are several critical features that remain central to the theory. Piaget's theory is a stage theory. He posits four general stages (some with substages), and all children pass through them in the same order. A child's reasoning at each stage is *qualitatively* different from that at earlier or later stages, though the knowledge and strategies of earlier stages are incorporated into rarer ones. During any given stage, the child reasons in *similar* ways regardless of the kinds of problems she or he faces, and Piaget tended to rule out the possibility that, during a given stage, a child could be trained to reason in much more sophisticated ways. Passage, evolution really, from one stage to the next occurs over time, an interaction of genetic processes and engagement with the world. The child continually assimilates new information which both reshapes and is reshaped by the knowledge structures the child currently has—and, as the child continues to interact with the world, she or he experiences discontinuities between the known and the new, and these discontinuities lead to further development of knowledge of how things work. Thinking, then, gradually evolves to ever more complex levels, represented by each of the stages.

It is important to keep in mind that Piaget's perspective on cognition is fundamentally logical and mathematical. Late in his life he observed that he did not wish "to appear only as a child psychologist":

> My efforts, directed toward the psychogenesis of thought, were for me only a link between two dominant preoccupations: the search for the mechanisms of biological adaptation and the analysis of that higher form of adaptation which is scientific thought, the epistemological interpretation of which has always been my central aim. (in Gruber and Voneche xi)

With this perspective in mind, let us very briefly consider the stages of Piaget's theory that are appropriated to discussions of college-age remedial writers.

Concrete Operational (6-7 to 11-12 years). The cognitive milestone here is that children are freed from immediate perception and enter the realm of a logical—if concrete operations. They can use logic to solve everyday problems, can take other points of view, can simultaneously take into account more than one perspective. In many ways, though, the child's reasoning is still linked to the environment, to tasks that are concrete and well-specified: "Tasks that demand very abstract reasoning, long chains of deduction, or the recognition that the available evidence is insufficient to reach any conclusion are thought to be beyond the reach" of children at the concrete operational stage (Siegler 89). Children have trouble separating out and recombining variables, performing sophisticated conservation tasks, and solving proportionality problems. They also have trouble planning systematic experiments and understanding "purely hypothetical questions that are completely divorced from anything in their experience" (Siegler 90).

Formal Operational (11-15 years). During this stage, children develop into sophisticated logical thinkers—Piaget compared them to scientists—and can solve problems that throw concrete-operational children: like the pendulum task described below. Flavell summarizes the ability of the formal-operational child this way: "His thinking is *hypothetico-deductive* rather than *empirico-inductive*, because he creates hypotheses and then deduces the empirical states of affairs that should occur if his hypotheses are correct . . . The older individual's thinking can . . . be totally abstract, totally formal-logical in nature." (145. For a critical discussion of the notion of stages, see Brainerd.)

Piaget and his colleagues developed a number of tasks to distinguish concrete from formal operational thinking. The pendulum task is representative:

Children observed strings with metal balls at their ends swinging from a metal frame. The strings varied in length and the metal balls varied in how much they weighed; the task was to identify the factor or combination of factors that determined the pendulum's period. Plausible hypotheses included the weight of the metal balls, the length of the strings, the height from which the strings were dropped, and the force with which they were pushed. Although the length of the string is in fact the only relevant factor . . . 10- and 11- year olds almost always concluded that the metal ball's weight played a key role, either as the sole determining factor or in combination with the string's length. Thus the children failed to disentangle the influence of the different variables to determine which one caused the effect. (Siegler 89-90)

In the 1970's a number of studies appeared reporting that up to 50% of American college freshmen could not solve formal-operational problems like the pendulum task. The conclusion was that an alarming number of our 18-year-olds were locked at the level of concrete operations, a stage Piaget contends they should have begun evolving beyond by early and certainly by mid-adolescence. These data quickly found their way to a more general readership, and some people in composition understandably saw relevance in them and began to use them to explain the problems with the writing of remedial students. With support of the data, they wrote that up to 50% of college freshmen were locked into the level of the concrete, couldn't think abstractly, couldn't produce logical propositions, couldn't conceptualize—and, borrowing further from Piagetian terminology, they speculated that these students couldn't decenter, couldn't take another's point of view, were cognitively egocentric. The last two stages of the Piagetian framework became in application a kind of cognitive dichotomy unto themselves. If students couldn't produce coherent abstractions in writing, if they wrote about what was in front of them and couldn't express themselves on the conceptual level, if they described something in writing as though their reader shared their knowledge of it—then those limits in written expression suggested something broad and general about the state of their thinking: they might be unable to form abstractions . . . any abstractions; they couldn't decenter . . . at all.

There are problems with this line of reasoning, however, and they have to do with the application of the framework as well as with the framework itself.

As any developmental psychologist will point out, there are major conceptual problems involved in applying a *developmental model* to adults. Piaget's theory was derived from the close observation of infants, children, and early-to-mid-adolescents; it was intended as a description of the way thinking evolves in the growing human being. Applying it to college-age students and, particularly, to adult learners, is to generalize it to a population other than the one that yielded it. There are more specific problems to consider as well, and they have to do with testing.

It is important to underscore the fact that Piaget implies broad limitations in cognition from specific inadequacies on a circumscribed set of tasks. This is not an unreasonable induction—all sorts of general theories are built on the performance of specific tasks—but it must be pointed out that we are dealing with an inference of major consequence. As developmental psychologist Rochelle Gelman put it: "The child is said to lack cognitive principles of broad significance simply because he fails a particular task involving those principles" (326). It is, then, an inferential leap of some magnitude to say that because college students fail to separate out variables and formally test hypotheses in a few tasks typical of the physics lab, they cannot conceptualize or abstract or tease out variables in any other sphere of their lives. Piaget himself said as much in one of his late articles:

> In our investigation of formal structures we used rather specific types of experimental situations which were of a physical and logical-mathematical nature because these seemed to be understood by the school children we sampled. However, it is possible to question whether these situations are, fundamentally, very general and therefore applicable to any school or professional environment . . . It is highly likely that [people like apprentice carpenters, locksmiths, or mechanics] will know how to reason in a hypothetical manner in their specialty, that is to say, dissociating the variables involved, relating terms in a combinatorial manner and reasoning with propositions involving negations and reciprocities. (10)

Piaget's tests are clever and complex. To assist in replication, Piaget and his colleagues provided explicit instructions on how to set up the tests, what to say, and how to assess performance. This clarity contributed to the welter of Piagetian studies conducted over the years, many of which supported the theory. A significant body of recent research, however, has raised serious questions about the social conditions created when these tests are given. Most of this research has been done with younger children, and probably the best summary of it is Donaldson's. The thrust of this work is contained in one of Donaldson's chapter titles; when a child performs poorly on a Piagerian task, is it because of a "failure to reason or a failure to understand"? The tasks might be unfamiliar; the child might misunderstand the instructions; because psychological experiments are new to her, she might confuse the experimenter's intentions and "not see the experiment as the experimenter hopes [she] will" (Gelman 324). (See also philosopher Jonathan Adler's Grician critique of Piagetian testing.) What psychologists like Donaldson have done is keep the formal requirements of Piagetian tasks but change the particular elements to make them more familiar (e.g., substituting a toy policeman and a wall for a doll and a mountain), provide a chance for children to get familiar with the tasks, and rephrase instructions to make sure children understand what is being asked. Children in these conditions end up performing remarkably better on the tasks; significantly higher percentages of them can, for example, adopt other points of view, conserve quantity and number, and so on. What limited some children on Piaget's tasks, then, seems to be more related to experimental conditions rather than some absolute restriction in their ability to reason.

A somewhat related set of findings has do with training—one of the more controversial issues in Piagetian theory. This is not the place to recap the controversy; suffice it to say that a large number of studies has demonstrated that brief training sessions can have dramatic results on performance. One such study has direct bearing on our discussion. Kuhn, Ho, and Adams provided training to college freshman who failed at formal-operational tasks. After training, the students were once again presented with the tests, and "most of the college subjects showed immediate and substantial formal reasoning." The authors go on to speculate that the absence of formal-operational performance "may to a large extent reflect cognitive processing difficulties in dealing with the problem formats, rather than absence of underlying reasoning competencies" (1128).

I will conclude this brief critique by considering, once again, the mathematico-logical base of Piaget's theory. There is a tradition in the 20th century West—shaped by Russell, Whitehead, Carnap, and others—to study human reasoning within the framework of formal, mathematical logic, to see logic not only as a powerful tool, but as a representation of how people actually reason—at least when they're reasoning effectively. This tradition had a strong influence on Piaget's theory. In Toulmin's words, Piaget's "overall intellectual goal" was to:

> discover how growing children "come to *recognize the necessity of*" conforming to the intellectual structures of logic, Euclidean geometry, and the other basic Kantian forms. (256)

And as Inhelder and Piaget themselves said: "[R]easoning is nothing more than the propositional calculus itself" (305).

Mathematical logic is so privileged that we tend to forget that this assumption about logic being isomorphic with reasoning is highly controversial; it lies at the center of a number of current debates in cognitive psychology, artificial intelligence, and philosophy. Here is one of many counterstatements:

> Considerations of pure logic . . . may be useful for certain kinds of information under certain circumstances by certain individuals. But logic cannot serve as a valid model of how most individuals solve most problems most of the time. (Gardner, *Mind's New Science* 370)

Formal logic essentially strips away all specific connections to human affairs and things of the world; it allows us to represent relations and interactions within a wholly abstract system. Our elevation of this procedure blinds us to the overwhelming degree to which powerful and effective reasoning can be practical, non-formal, and concrete. As psychologist Barbara Rogoff puts it, "thinking is intricately interwoven with the context of the problem to be solved" (2). She continues:

> Evidence suggests that our ability to control and orchestrate cognitive skills is not an abstract context-free competence which may be easily transferred across widely diverse problem domains but consists rather of cognitive activity tied specifically to context. (3)

Much problem-solving and, I suspect, the reasoning involved in the production of most kinds of writing rely not only on abstract logical operations, but, as well, on the rich interplay of visual, auditory, and kinesthetic associations, feeling, metaphor, social perception, the matching of mental representations of past experience with new experience, and so on. And writing, as the whole span of rhetorical theory makes clear, is deeply embedded in the particulars of the human situation. It is a context-dependent activity that calls on many abilities. We may well need to engage in formal-logical reasoning when writing certain kinds of scientific or philosophical papers or when analyzing certain kinds of hypotheses and arguments, but we cannot assume that the ability or inability to demonstrate formal-operational thought on one or two Piagetian tasks has a necessary connection to our students' ability or inability to produce coherent, effective discourse.

Orality-Literacy

Orality-literacy theory draws on the studies of epic poetry by Milman Parry and Albert Lord, the classical-philological investigations of Eric Havelock, the wide-ranging theoretical work of Walter Ong, and, to a lesser degree, on the compelling, though dated, cross-cultural investigations of thought in primitive, non-literate cultures. The work is broad, rich, and diverse—ranging from studies of the structure of the epic line to the classification schemes of unlettered rural farmers—but as it comes to those of us in composition, its focus is on the interrelation of language and cognition. Various scholars say it in various ways, but the essential notion is that the introduction of literacy into a society affects the way the members of the society think. There seem to be strong and weak versions of this theory.

The strong version states that the acquisition of literacy brings with it not only changes in linguistic possibilities—e.g., subordinative and discursive rather than additive and repetitive styles, less reliance on epithets and maxims and other easily remembered expressions—but *necessarily* results in a wide variety of changes in thinking: only after the advent of literacy do humans possess the ability to engage in abstraction, generalization, systematic thinking, defining, logos rather than mythos, puzzlement over words as words, speculation on the features of language. And these abilities, depending on who you read, lead to even wider changes in culture, summarized, not without exasperation, by social historian Harvey Graff:

These characteristics include, in typical formulations or listings, attitudes ranging from empathy, innovativeness, achievement orientation, "cosmopoliteness," information and media awareness, national identification, technological acceptance, rationality, and commitment to democracy, to opportunism, linearity of thought and behavior, or urban residence. ("Reflections" 307)

The operative verb here is "transformed." Writing *transforms* human cognition.

The weak version of the oral-literate construct acknowledges the role literacy plays in developing modes of inquiry, building knowledge, etc., but tends to rely on verbs like "facilitate," "favor," "enable," "extend"—the potential of human cognition is extended more than transformed. Here's Jack Goody, an anthropologist who is often lumped in with those holding to the "strong version," but who, at least in his late work, takes issue with the oral-literate dichotomy. In discussing various differences between literate and oral expression, for example, he warns that such differences "do not relate primarily to differences of 'thought' or 'mind' (though there are consequences for these) but to differences in the nature of communicative acts" (26). So though Goody grants that writing "made it possible to scrutinize discourse in a different kind of way" and "increased the potentiality for cumulative knowledge" and freed participants from "the problem of memory storage" dominating "intellectual life," (37), he also insists that:

Even in non-literate societies there is no evidence that individuals were prisoners of pre-ordained schemes, of primitive classifications, of the structures of myth. Constrained, yes; imprisoned, no. Certain, at least, among them could and did use language in a generative way, elaborating metaphor, inventing songs and "myths," creating gods, looking for new solutions to recurring puzzles and problems, changing the conceptual universe. (33)

The theory is a sensible one: literacy must bring with it tremendous repercussions for the intellect. The problem is that when the theory, particularly the strong version, is applied to composition studies, it yields some troubling consequences. Late twentieth-century American inner-city adolescents and adults are thought to bear cognitive resemblance to (ethnocentric notions of) primitive tribesmen in remote third-world cultures (or these adolescents and adults think like children, and children think like primitives): they don't practice analytic thinking; they are embedded in the context of their lives and cannot analyze it; they see things only as wholes; they think that printed words are concrete things; they cannot think abstractly.

A little reflection on this application of orality-literacy theory—given its origins—reveals a serious problem of method. The theory emerges from anthropological work with primitive populations, from historical-philological study of Homeric texts, from folkloric investigations of non-literate taletellers, and from brilliant, though speculative, literary-theoretical reflection on what might have happened to the human mind as it appropriated the alphabet. It is, then, a tremendous conceptual leap to apply this theory to urban-industrial Americans entering school in the penultimate decade of the twentieth century. We have here a problem of generalizability.

Now one could admit these problems yet still see some analogic value in applying the oral-literate construct with a hedge—for it at least, as opposed to the other theories we've been exploring, is directly concerned with written language. Fair enough. Yet my reading has led me to doubt the strength and utility of the theory on its own terms. (My concern rests primarily with the strong version. The weak version makes less dramatic claims about cognition, though some of what I found would qualify weak versions as well.) There are problems with what the theory implies about the way written language emerges in society and the role it plays in determining how people lead their linguistic lives and conduct their cognitive affairs. This is not to deny the profound effects literacy can have on society; it is to question the strength of the orality-literacy construct in characterizing those effects. Let me briefly survey some of the difficulties.

Literacy and Society.   The historical record suggests that the technology and conventions of literacy work their way slowly through a society and have gradual—and not necessarily linearly progressive—influence on commerce, politics, bureaucracy, law, religion, education, the arts. (See, e.g., Marrou; Clanchy; Cressy.) Furthermore, it is hard to maintain, as the strong version does, that literacy is the primum mobile in social-cultural change. What emerges, instead, is a complex interaction of economic, political, and religious forces of which literacy is a part—and not necessarily the strongest element. Though there is no doubt that literacy shapes the way commerce, government, and religion are conducted, it, as John Oxenham puts it: "would have followed, not preceded, the formation of certain kinds of society (59). And Harvey Graff, pointing out all the "discontinuities" and "contradictions" in linear, evolutionary assumptions about the spread of literacy, emphasizes that "[n]either writing [n]or printing alone is an 'agent of change'; their impacts are determined by the manner in which human agency exploits them in a specific setting" ("Reflections" 307).[4]

Another way to view the problems with the transformational claims about literacy is to consider the fact that a number of societies have appropriated literacy to traditional, conservative purposes. In such societies literacy did not trigger various cultural-cognitive changes—changes in mores, attitudes, etc.—but reinforced patterns already in place. Again, John Oxenham:

> We have always to bear in mind that there have been literate social groups, who so far from being inventive and trusting, have been content merely to copy their ancient scriptures and pass them on virtually unaltered. It may be, then, that literate people can respond more readily to leadership for change in culture, technology, social mores, but that literacy by itself does not induce appetites for change, improvement or exploration. (52)

There are a number of illustrations of this; one specific case-study is provided by Kenneth Lockridge, whose inquiry into the social context of literacy in Colonial New England leads him to conclude:

> [T]here is no evidence that literacy ever entailed new attitudes among men, even in the decades when male literacy was spreading rapidly toward universality, and there

is positive evidence that the world view of literate New Englanders remained as traditional as that of their illiterate neighbors. (4)

It is even difficult to demonstrate causal links between reading and writing and
changes in the economic sphere an area that "modernization theorists" generally
thought to be particularly sensitive to gains in literacy. Harvey Graff's study of social mobility in three mid-19th century towns revealed that "systematic patterns of
inequality and stratification . . . were deep and pervasive and relatively unaltered by
the influence of literacy." He continues:

> Class, ethnicity, and sex were the major barriers of social inequality. The majority of
> Irish Catholic adults, for example, were literate . . . but they stood lowest in wealth and
> occupation, as did laborers and servants. Women and blacks fared little better, regard-
> less of literacy . . . social realities contradicted the promoted promises of literacy. (*The
> Literacy Myth* 320-21)

Similar assertions are made closer to home by Carman St. John Hunter and David
Harmon, whose overview of the research on contemporary adult illiteracy leads to
this conclusion:

> For most persons who lack literacy skills, illiteracy is simply one factor interacting
> with many others—class, race and sex discrimination, welfare dependency, unem-
> ployment, poor housing, and a general sense of powerlessness. The acquisition of
> reading and writing skills would eliminate conventional illiteracy among many but
> would have no appreciable effect on the other factors that perpetuate the poverty of
> their lives. (9-12. See also Ogbu.)

The oral-literate distinction can help us see differences in the communicative
technologies available to the members of a society, to get a sense of formats, means,
and forums through which communication occurs (Enos and Ackerman). But it appears to be historically, culturally, and economically reductive and politically naive
to view literacy as embodying an automatic transformational power. What is called
for is a contextual view of literacy: the ability to read or to write is a technology or a
method or a behavior, a set of conventions that interact in complex ways with a variety of social forces to shape society and culture. It is, to use Harvey Graff's phras-
ing, a "myth" to assume that literacy necessarily sparks social change.

Literacy and Cognition.   Let us move now from the social-cultural realm to
some of the claims made about cognition. These come from two highly diverse
sources: classical philological studies of epic poetry and anthropological studies of
thought and language. There are problems with both.
   The key work in the classicist vein is Eric Havelock's investigation of Greek culture before and after the advent of the alphabet. In books ranging from *Preface to
Plato* (published in 1963) to *The Muse Learns to Write* (1986) Havelock has made
the strong claim that pre-alphabetic Greeks, ingenious as they were, were barred
from philosophical thought because oral discourse could not generate abstract,

propositional language or self-conscious reflection on language as language. To be sure, there are times when Havelock's claims are less extreme, but even in *The Muse Learns to Write*, a tempered book, one finds questions and statements like these: "May not all logical thinking as commonly understood be a product of Greek alphabetic literacy?" (39) and "it is only as language is written down that it becomes possible to think about it" (112). And such theorizing quickly leads to a troublesome alphabetic determinism.

Havelock's work is compelling, but we must remember that when it comes to cognition, he is operating very much in the realm of speculation. That is, he infers things about cognitive processes and the limits of reasoning ability from the study of ancient texts, some of which represent genres that one would not expect to give rise to philosophic inquiry. Furthermore, even if we accepted his method, we could find powerful counterstatements to his thesis—and some of these are contained in a festschrift issued by the Monist Press. Examining the same texts from which Havelock built his case, University of Chicago classicist Arthur W. H. Adkins provides evidence of abstraction, verbal self-consciousness, and the linguistic resources to engage in systematic thinking. He concludes that:

> Havelock has not as yet demonstrated any *necessary* link between literacy and abstract thought . . . he has not as yet demonstrated that *in fact* the stimulus to abstract thought in early Greece was the invention of writing; [and] some features denied by Havelock to be available in oral speech are found in the Homeric poems. (220. See also Margolis.)

The other line of argument about literacy and cognition comes from twentieth-century anthropological studies of the reasoning of rural farmers and primitive tribesmen. These studies tend not to be of literacy-orality per se, but are appropriated by some orality-literacy theorists. A good deal of this cross-cultural research has involved classification tasks: a set of objects (or a set of pictures of the objects) is given to a tribesman, and the investigator asks the tribesman to group the objects/pictures. The key issue is the scheme by which the tribesman completes the grouping: does he, for example, place a hoe with a potato and offer the *concrete* reason that they go together because you need one to get the other, or does he place the hoe with a knife because he reasons *abstractly* that they are both tools? The Western anthropologist considers concrete reasoning to be less advanced than abstract reasoning, and orality-literacy theorists like to pose literacy as the crucial variable fostering abstract reasoning. It is because the tribesman lacks letters that he is locked into the concrete. This is an appealing conjecture, but, as I hope the previous discussion suggests, literacy is too intertwined with schooling and urbanization, with economics, politics, and religion to be able to isolate it and make such a claim. There are other problems too, not just with the causal linking of literacy and abstraction, but with traditional comparative research itself. Cole and Means put it this way:

> [D]epartures from the typical performance patterns of American adults are not necessarily deficits, but may indeed be excellent adaptions to the life circumstances of the people involved . . . Which type of classification is preferable will depend upon the

context, that is, the number of different types of objects to be grouped and the way in which the materials are going to be used . . . preference for one type of grouping over another is really no more than that—just a matter of preference. (161-62)

In line with the above, it must be kept in mind that because "primitive" subjects tend to classify objects in ways we label concrete does not necessarily mean that they can think in no other way. Consider, as we close this section, a wonderful anecdote from anthropologist Joseph Glick, as retold by Jacqueline Goodenow:

The investigators had gathered a set of 20 objects, 5 each from 4 categories: food, clothing, tools, and cooking utensils . . . [W]hen asked to put together the objects that belonged together, [many of the tribesmen produced] not 4 groups of 5 but 10 groups of 2. Moreover, the type of grouping and the type of reason given were frequently of the type we regard as extremely concrete, e.g., "the knife goes with the orange because it cuts it." Glick . . . notes, however, that subjects at times volunteered "'that a wise man would do things in the way this was done.' When an exasperated experimenter asked finally, 'How would a fool do it?' he was given back groupings of the type . . . initially expected—four neat piles with foods in one, tools in another." (170-71. For fuller cross-cultural discussions of concrete vs. abstract reasoning see Ginsburg; Lave; and Tulkin and Konner.)

Literacy and Language.   It is problematic, then, to claim that literacy necessarily causes a transformation of culture, society, or mind or that societies without high levels of literacy are barred from the mental activities that some theorists have come to associate with literacy: verbal self-consciousness, abstraction, etc. Perhaps, though, the orality-literacy construct does have value if one strips away the cultural-cognitive baggage; its real benefit might be its ability to help us understand the nature of the language experiences students received in their homes and communities and further help to distinguish between the oral and literate features in their writing. But even here there are problems, for the reality of speaking-writing relationships seems to be more complex than the oral-literate distinction suggests.

Certainly, there are bioanatomical and perceptual differences between speech and writing—differences in the way each is acquired, produced, and comprehended. And if you examine very different types of language (e.g., dinner-table conversation vs. academic prose), you will find significant grammatical and stylistic differences as well. (See, for example, Chafe.) But the oral-literate construct leads us to focus attention too narrowly on the channel, the mode of communication, in a way that can (a) imply a distinctive uniformity to oral modes vs. written modes and (b) downplay the complex interaction among human motive, language production, and social setting. Linguists currently working with oral narratives and written texts suggest that the notion of an oral narrative itself is problematic, for oral traditions can differ in major ways (Scollon and Scollon); that the narrative variations we see may have less to do with literateness than with cultural predispositions (Tannen, "A Comparative Analysis"); that features often defined as literate are frequently found in oral discourse and vice versa (Polanyi; Tannen, "Relative Focus"); that characteristics identified by some as a mark of preliterate discourse—e.g., formulaic expressions—are woven throughout the language of literate people (Fillmore); that while spoken sentences can be shown to differ from written sentences, they are not necessarily less complex grammatically (Halliday); and so on. Finally, it seems that many of the differences we can find between stretches of speech and writing might, as Karen Beamon suggests, depend on factors such as genre, context, register, topic, level of formality, and purpose as much as whether the passage is spoken or written.

These closer examinations of a wide variety of texts and utterances should make us wary of neat, bipolar characterizations—whether dichotomies or simple continua—of oral vs. written language. And it seems to me that this caution about the linguistic reality of the oral-literate distinction could lead to reservations about its contemporary social reality—that is, can we accurately and sensitively define, in late twentieth-century America, entire communities and subcultures as being oral and others as being literate? By what criteria, finally, will we be able to make such a distinction? In asking these questions, I am not trying to downplay the obvious: children enter school with widely different degrees of exposure to literacy activities and with significantly different experiences as to how those activities are woven into their lives. And these differences clearly have consequences for schooling.

What I do want to raise, though, is the possibility that the oral-literate continuum does not adequately characterize these differences. The continuum, because it moves primarily along the single dimension of speech-print, slights history and politics—remember, it weights literacy as *the* primary force in cognitive development and social change—and it encourages, because of its bipolarity, a dichotomizing of modes where complex interweaving seems to exist. Finally, the orality-literacy construct tends to reduce the very social-linguistic richness it is meant to describe. Here is Shirley Brice Heath on the language behaviors of two working-class communities in the Carolinas:

> The residents of each community are able to read printed and written materials in their daily lives and, on occasion, they produce written messages as part of the total pattern of communication in the community. In both communities, the residents turn from spoken to written uses of language and vice versa as the occasion demands, and the two modes of expression serve to supplement and reinforce each other. Yet, in terms of the usual distinctions made between oral and literate traditions, neither community may be simply classified as either "oral" or "literate." (*Ways with Words* 203)

Work like Heath's challenges the sociological and linguistic utility of the orality-literacy construct; in fact, elsewhere Heath directly criticizes "current tendencies to classify communities as being at one or another point along a hypothetical [oral-literate] continuum which has no societal reality" ("Protean Shapes" 116).

What is most troubling on this score is the way the orality-literacy construct is sometimes used to represent language use in the urban ghetto. What emerges is a stereotypic characterization of linguistic homogeneity—all the residents learn from the sermon but not the newspaper; they run the dozens but are ignorant of print. The literacy backgrounds of people who end up in remedial, developmental, or adult ed-

ucation classes are more complex than that: they represent varying degrees of distance from or involvement with printed material, various attitudes toward it and
skill with it, various degrees of embracement of or complicated rejection of traditions connected with their speech. Important here is what Mina Shaughnessy and
Glynda Hull so carefully demonstrate: some of the most vexing problems writing
teachers face are rooted in the past attempts of educationally marginalized people to
make sense of the uses of print. Print is splattered across the inner city, and, in effective and ineffective ways, people incorporate it into their lives.

There is a related problem. Some theorists link Piagetian notions of cognitive
egocentrism with generalizations about orality and conclude that without the language of high literacy, people will be limited in their ability to "decenter," to recognize the need to "decontextualize" what they are communicating, to perceive and
respond to the social and informational needs of the other. Certainly, people with
poor educations will have a great deal of trouble doing such things in writing, but
one must be very cautious about leaping from stunted and limited texts to inferences
about deficits in social cognition or linguistic flexibility. Developmentally and sociologically oriented linguists have demonstrated for some time that human beings
are not locked into one way of speaking, one register, and develop, at quite a young
age, the recognition that different settings call for different kinds of speech (Hudson). Poor writers are not as a population cognitively egocentric; they are aware of
the other, of "audience"—some disenfranchised people acutely so. What they lack
are the opportunities to develop both oral and written communicative facility in a
range of settings. Or they may resist developing that facility out of anger or fear or
as an act of identity. They may prefer one way of speaking, most of us do, and thus
haven't developed a fluency of voices. But rather than being cognitively locked out
of other registers, other linguistic roles, other points of view, they are more likely
emotionally and politically barred from them.

It is obvious that literacy enables us to do a great deal. It provides a powerful
solution to what Walter Ong calls "the problem of retaining and retrieving carefully
articulated thought" (34). It enables us to record discourse, scan and scrutinize it,
store it—and this has an effect on the way we educate, do business, and run the courts.
And as we further pursue intellectual work, reading and writing become integral parts
of inquiry, enable us to push certain kinds of analysis to very sophisticated levels. In
fact, as investigations of academic and research settings like Latour and Woolgar's
Laboratory Life suggest, it becomes virtually impossible to tease writing and reading
out of the conduct and progress of Western humanistic or scientific inquiry. One of the
values of the orality-literacy construct is that it makes us aware of how central literacy
is to such inquiry. But, finally, the bipolarity of the construct (as with the others we've
examined) urges a way of thinking about language, social change, and cognition that
easily becomes dichotomous and reductive. "The tyranny of conceptual dichotomies," Graff calls it ("Reflections" 313). If writing is thought to possess a given characteristic—say, decontextualization or abstraction—then the dichotomy requires you
to place the opposite characteristic—contextualization, concreteness—in the
non-writing category (cf. Elbow). We end up splitting cognition along linguistic
separations that exist more in theory than in social practice.

Conclusion

Witkin uncovered interesting perceptual differences and led us toward a deeper consideration of the interrelations of personality, problem solving, and social cognition. Hemisphericity theorists call our attention to the neurological substrate of information processing and language production. Piaget developed an insightful, non-behaviorist method to study cognitive growth and, more comprehensively than anyone in our time, attempted to articulate the changes in reasoning we see as children develop. And the orality-literacy theorists give us compelling reflection on spoken and written language and encourage us to consider the potential relations between modes of communication and modes of thought. My intention in this essay is not to dismiss these thinkers and theories but to present the difficulties in applying to remedial writers these models of mind. For there is a tendency to accept as fact condensed deductions from them—statements stripped away from the questions, contradictions, and complexities that are central to them. Let me summarize the problems I see with the theories we've been considering.

First, the theories end up levelling rather than elaborating individual differences in cognition. At best, people are placed along slots on a single continuum; at worst they are split into mutually exclusive camps—with one camp clearly having cognitive and social privilege over the other. The complexity of cognition—its astounding glides and its blunderous missteps as well—is narrowed, and the rich variability that exists in any social setting is ignored or reduced. This reductive labelling is going on in composition studies at a time when cognitive researchers in developmental and educational psychology, artificial intelligence, and philosophy are posing more elaborate and domain-specific models of cognition.

Second, and in line with the above, the four theories encourage a drift away from careful, rigorous focus on student writing and on the cognitive processes that seem directly related to it, that reveal themselves as students compose. That is, field dependence-independence, hemisphericity, etc., lead us from a close investigation of the production of written discourse and toward general, wide-ranging processes whose link to writing has, for the most part, been *assumed rather than demonstrated*. Even orality-literacy theory, which certainly concerns language, urges an antagonism between speech and writing that carries with it sweeping judgments about cognition.

The theories also avert or narrow our gaze from the immediate social and linguistic conditions in which the student composes: the rich interplay of purpose, genre, register, textual convention, and institutional expectation (Bartholomae; Bizzell; McCormick). When this textual-institutional context is addressed, it is usually in simplified terms: the faculty—and their discourse—are literate, left-hemispheric, field-independent, etc., and underprepared students are oral, right-hemispheric, and field dependent. I hope my critical surveys have demonstrated the conceptual limits of such labelling.

Third, the theories inadvertently reflect cultural stereotypes that should, themselves, be the subject of our investigation. At least since Plato, we in the West have separated heart from head, and in one powerful manifestation of that split we contrast rational thought with emotional sensibility, intellectual acuity with social awareness—and we often link the analytical vs. holistic opposition to these polarities. (I tried to reveal the confusion inherent in such talk when discussing cognitive style and hemisphericity.) These notions are further influenced by and play into other societal notions about independence and individuality vs. communal and tribal orientations and they domino quickly toward stereotypes about race, class, and gender.

Let me say now that I am not claiming that the research in cognitive style or hemisphericity or any of the other work we surveyed is of necessity racist, sexist, or elitist. The conclusions that can be drawn from the work, however, mesh with—and could have been subtly influenced by—cultural biases that are troubling. This is an important and, I realize, sensitive point. Some assert that student writers coming from particular communities can't reason logically or analytically, that the perceptual processes of these students are more dependent on context than the processes of white, middle-class students, that particular racial or social groups are right-hemispheric, that the student writers we teach from these groups are cognitively egocentric.

A number of recent books have amply demonstrated the way 19th and early 20th century scientific, social scientific, and humanistic assessments of mental capacity and orientation were shaped by that era's racial, gender, and class biases (see, for example, Gilman; Gould; Kamin; and Valenstein). We now find these assessments repellent, but it's important to remember that while some were made by reactionary social propagandistss, a number were made as well by thinkers operating with what they saw as rigorous method—and some of those thinkers espoused a liberal social philosophy. This is a powerful illustration of the hidden influences of culture on allegedly objective investigations of mind. We all try to make sense of problematic performance that's part of a teacher's or a researcher's job—but we must ask ourselves if speculation about cognitive egocentrism and concrete thinking and holistic perception embodies unexamined cultural biases about difference biases that would be revealed to us if we could adopt other historical and social perspectives.

These summary statements have a number of implications for research.

The leap to theory is a privileged move—it is revered in the academy and allows parsimonious interpretations of the baffling variability of behavior. But a theory, any theory, is no more than a best guess at a given time, simultaneously evocative and flawed. Especially when it comes to judging cognition, we need to be particularly aware of these flaws and limitations, for in our culture judgments about mind carry great weight. A good deal of careful, basic descriptive and definitional work must be done before we embrace a theory, regardless of how compelling it is.

A series of fundamental questions should precede the application of theory: Is the theory formulated in a way that allows application to writing; that is, can it be defined in terms of discourse? Given what we know about writing, how would the theory be expected to manifest itself—i.e., what would it mean textually and dynamically for someone to be a field-dependent writer? What will the theory allow us to explain about writing that we haven't explained before? What will it allow us to do pedagogically that we weren't able to do as well before? Will the theory strip and narrow experience and cognition, or does it promise to open up the histories of students' involvement with writing, their rules, strategies, and assumptions, the invitations and denials that characterized their encounters with print?

Beyond such general questions are more specific guidelines for those of us doing psychological research. Once we undertake an investigation of cognition we must be careful to discuss our findings in terms of the kinds of writing we investigate. Generalizing to other tasks, and particularly to broad cognitive processes, is not warranted without evidence from those other domains. If theories like the four we discussed, but others too (e.g., theories of moral development, social cognition, metacognition, etc.), are appropriated that are built on particular tests, then researchers must thoroughly familiarize themselves with the tests beneath the theories and consult with psychologists who use them. People who are going to administer such tests should take the tests themselves—see what they're like from the inside. My mentor Richard Shavelson also urges researchers to administer the tests to individual students and have them talk about what they're doing, get some sense of how students might interpret or misinterpret the instructions, the various ways they represent the task to themselves, what cognitive processes seem to come into play as the students work with the tests. Furthermore, it must be remembered that the results of testing will be influenced by the degree of familiarity the students have with the tests and by the social situation created in the administration of them. How will these conditions be adjusted for and acknowledged? Finally, the resulting data must be discussed as being specific to the students tested. Generalizing to others must be done with caution.

A special word needs to be said here about comparative studies. If we employ hi-lo designs, expert-novice studies, and the like—which can be powerfully revealing designs—we need to consider our design and our results from historical and sociopolitical perspectives as well as cognitive ones. That is, if class, gender, or race differences emerge—and they certainly could—they should not automatically be assumed to reflect "pure" cognitive differences, but rather effects that might well be conditioned by and interpreted in light of historical, socio-political realities. There is currently a lot of talk about the prospect of forging a social-cognitive orientation to composition research (see, for example, Freedman, Dyson, Flower, and Chafe; Bizzell and Herzberg). One of the exciting results of such an endeavor could be an increased sensitivity to the social forces that shape cognitive activity. I've argued elsewhere for a research framework that intersects the cognitive, affective, and situational dimensions of composing and that involves the systematic combination of multiple methods, particularly ones traditionally thought to be antagonistic. My assumption is that the careful integration of, say, cognitive process-tracing and naturalistic observation methods can both contribute to fresh and generative insight and provide a guard against reductive interpretation (Rose, "Complexity").

Much of this essay has concerned researchers and theoreticians, but at the heart of the discussion is a basic question for any of us working with poor writers: How do we go about judging the thought processes involved with reading and writing when performance is problematic, ineffective, or stunted? If I could compress this essay's investigation down to a single conceptual touchstone, it would be this: Human cognition—even at its most stymied, bungled moments—is rich and varied. It is against this assumption that we should test our theories and research methods and classroom assessments. Do our practices work against classification that encourages single, monolithic explanations of cognitive activity? Do they honor the complexity of interpretive efforts even when those efforts fall short of some desired goal? Do they foster investigation of interaction and protean manifestation rather than investigation of absence: abstraction is absent, consciousness of print is absent, logic is absent? Do they urge reflection on the cultural biases that might be shaping them? We must be vigilant that the systems of intellect we develop or adapt do not ground our students' difficulties in sweeping, essentially one-dimensional perceptual, neurophysiological, psychological, or linguistic processes, systems that drive broad cognitive wedges between those who do well in our schools and those who don't.[5]

Notes

1. For presentation, qualification, or rebuttal of this orientation see, for example: Ann E. Berthoff, "Is Teaching Still Possible?" *College English* 46 (1984): 743-55; Thomas J. Farrell, "I.Q. and Standard English," *CCC* 34 (1983): 470-85 and the replies to Farrell by Greenberg, Hartwell, Himley, and Stratton in *CCC* 35 (1984): 455-78; George H. Jensen, "The Reification of the Basic Writer," *Journal of Basic Writing 5* (1986): 52-64; Andrea Lunsford, "Conitive Development and the Basic Writer," *College English* 41 (1979): 38-46 and Lunsford, "Cognitive Studies and Teaching Writing," *Perspectives on Research and Scholarship in Composition*, Ed. Ben W. McClelland and Timothy R. Donovan, New York: MLA, (1986): 145-61; Walter J. Ong, "Literacy and Orality in Our Times," *Profession 79*, Ed. Jasper P. Neel, New York: MLA, 1979: 1-7; Lynn Quitman Troyka, "Perspectives on Legacies and Literacy in the 1980s," *CCC* 33 (1982): 252-62 and Troyka, "Defining Basic Writers in Context," *A Sourcebook for Basic Writing Teachers*, Ed. Theresa Enos, New York: Random House, 1987: 2-15; James D. Williams, "Coherence and Cognitive Style," *Written Communication* 2 (1985): 473-91. For illustration of the transfer of this issue to the broader media, see Ellen K. Coughlin, "Literacy: 'Excitement' of New Field Attracts Scholars of Literature," *The Chronicle of Higher Education* 29 (9 Jan. 1985): 1,10.
2. For a description of the other tests—the Body Adjustment Test and the rarely used auditory and tactile embedded figures tests—see Witkin, et al.
3. Witkin later revised his theory, suggesting that the rod and frame test and the embedded figures test were tapping different dimensions of the field dependence-independence construct. This revision, however, gives rise to further problems—see Linn and Kyllonen.
4. Educators and evaluators often seem locked into a 19th century linear progress conception of the way both societies and individuals appropriate literacy. Graff presents a provocative historical challenge to such notions; here's Vygotsky on individual development: "together with processes of development, forward motion, and appearance of new forms, we can discern processes of curtailment, disappearance, and reverse development of old forms at each step . . . only a naive view of development as a purely evolutionary process...can conceal from us the true nature of these processes" (106).
5. Particular sections of this paper were discussed with or reviewed by specialists who provided a great deal of expert help: Susan Curtiss (neurolinguistics), Richard Leo Enos (classical studies), Sari Gilman (research psychiatry), John R. Hayes, Richard Shavelson, and Catherine Stasz (cognitive and educational psychology), Thomas Huckin (linguistics), Robert Siegler (developmental psychology). David Bartholomae, Linda Flower, Glynda Hull, David Kaufer, and Stephen Witte commented generously on the entire manuscript. The project benefited as well from rich conversation with Mariolina Salvatori and Kathryn Flannery. Versions of the paper were read at Carnegie Mellon, Pitt, Indiana University of Pennsylvania, UCLA, Berkeley, CCCC (Atlanta), Penn State, and UCSD. My thanks for all the ideas generated at those conferences and colloquia. Finally, appreciation is due to Sally Magargee for her research assistance and the Carnegie Mellon Department of English and the Spencer Foundation for their support.

Works Cited

Adkins, Arthur W.H. "Orality and Philosophy." Robb 207-27.

Adler, Jonathan. "Abstraction is Uncooperative." *Journal for the Theory of Social Behavior* 14 (1984): 165-81.

Arndt, Stephen, and Dale E. Berger. "Cognitive Mode and Asymmetry in Cerebral Functioning." *Cortex* 14 (1978): 78-86.

Bartholomae, David. "Inventing the University." Rose, *When a Writer Can't Write* 134-65.

Battig, William F. "Within-Individual Differences in 'Cognitive' Processes." *Information Processing and Cognition*. Ed. Robert L. Solso. Hillsdale, NJ: Erlbaum, 1975. 195-228.

Beamon, Karen. "Coordination and Subordination Revisited: Syntactic Complexity in Spoken and Written Narrative Discourse." Tannen, *Coherence in Spoken and Written Discourse* 45-80.

Beaumont, J. Graham. "Methods for Studying Cerebral Hemispheric Function." *Functions of the Right Cerebral Hemisphere*. Ed. A.W. Young. London: Academic Press, 1983. 113-46.

Beaumont, J. Graham, A.W. Young, and l.C. McManus. "Hemisphericity: A Critical Review." *Cognitive Neuropsychology* 2 (1984): 191-212.

Benson, D. Frank, and Eran Zaidel, eds. *The Dual Brain. Hemispheric Specialization in Humans.* New York: Guilford, 1985.

Berthoff, Ann E. "Is Teaching Still Possible?" *College English* 46 (1984): 743-55.

Bizzell, Patricia. "Cognition, Convention, and Certainty: What We Need to Know about Writing." *Pre/Text* 3 (1982): 213-44.

Bizzell, Patricia, and Bruce Herzberg. *The Bedford Bibliography For Teachers of Writing*. Boston: Bedford Books, 1987.

Bogen, Joseph. "The Dual Brain: Some Historical and Methodological Aspects." Benson and Zaidel 27-43.

Bogen, Joseph, et al. "The Other Side of the Brain: The A/P Ratio." *Bulletin of Los Angeles Neurological Society* 37 (1972): 49-61.

Bradshaw, J.L., and N.C. Nettleton. "The Nature of Hemispheric Specialization in Man." *Behavioral and Brain Sciences* 4 (1981): 51-91.

Brainerd, Charles J. "The Stage Question in Cognitive-Developmental Theory." *The Behavioral and Brain Sciences* 2 (1978): 173-81.

Brown, Warren S., James T. Marsh, and Ronald E. Ponsford. "Hemispheric Differences in Event-Related Brain Potentials." Benson and Zaidel 163-79.

Caplan, David. "On the Cerebral Localization of Linguistic Functions: Logical and Empirical Issues Surrounding Deficit Analysis and Functional Localization." *Brain and Language* 14 (1981): 120-37.

Carey, Susan. *Conceptual Change in Childhood*. Cambridge: MIT P, 1985.

Chafe, Wallace L. "Linguistic Differences Produced by Differences in Speaking and Writing." Olson, Torrance, and Hildyard 105-23.

Clanchy, M.T. *From Memory to Written Record: England 1066-1307*. Cambridge: Harvard UP, 1979.

Cole, Michael, and Barbara Means. *Comparative Studies of How People Think*. Cambridge: Harvard UP, 1981.

Cressy, David. "The Environment for Literacy: Accomplishment and Context in Seventeenth-Century England and New England." *Literacy in Historical Perspective*. Ed. Daniel P. Resnick. Washington: Library of Congress, 1983. 23-42.

Cronbach, Lee J. *Essentials of Psychological Testing*. New York: Harper and Row, 1960.

DeRenzi, Ennio. *Disorders of Space Exploration and Cognition*. London: Wiley, 1982.

Donaldson, Margaret. *Children's Minds*. New York: Norton, 1979.

Donchin, Emanuel, Gregory McCarthy, and Marta Kutas. "Electroencephalographic Investigations of Hemispheric Specialization." *Language and Hemispheric Specialization in Man: Cerebral Event-Related Potentials*. Ed. John E. Desmedt. Basel, NY: Karger, 1977. 212-42.

Dumas, Roland and Arlene Morgan. "EEG Asymmetry as a Function of Occupation, Task and Task Difficulty. " *Neuropsychologia* 13 (1975): 214-28.

Efron, Robert. "The Central Auditory System and Issues Related to Hemispheric Specialization." *Assessment of Central Auditory Dysfunction: Foundations and Clinical Correlates*. Ed. Marilyn L. Pinheiro and Frank E. Musiek. Baltimore: Williams and Wilkins, 1985. 143-54.

Ehrlichman, Howard, and Arthur Weinberger. "Lateral Eye Movements and Hemispheric Asymmetry: A Critical Review." *Psychological Bulletin* 85 (1978): 1080-1101.

Elbow, Peter. "The Shifting Relationships Between Speech and Writing." *CCC* 34 (1985): 283-303.

Enos, Richard Leo, and John Ackerman, "*Letteraturizzazione* and Hellenic Rhetoric: An Analysis for Research with Extensions." *Proceedings of 1984 Rhetoric Society of America Conference*. Ed. Charles Kneupper, forthcoming.

Fillmore, Charles J. "On Fluency." *Individual Differences in Language Ability and Language Behavior*. Ed. Charles J. Fillmore, Daniel Kempler, and William S.Y. Wang. New York: Academic Press. 1979. 85-101.

Flavell, John H. *Cognitive Development*. Englewood Cliffs: Prentice-Hall, 1977.

Fodor, Jerry A. *The Modalarity of Mind*. Cambridge: MIT P, 1983.

Freedman, Sarah, et al. *Research in Writing: Past, Present, and Future*. Berkeley: Center for the Study of Writing, 1987.

Gardner, Howard. *Frames of Mind*. New York: Basic Books, 1983.

_____. *The Mind's New Science*. New York: Basic Books, 1985.

_____. "What We Know (and Don't Know) About the Two Halves of the Brain." *Journal of Aesthetic Education* 12 (197 8): 113-19.

Gardner, Howard, and Ellen Winner. "Artistry and Aphasia." *Acquired Aphasia*. Ed. Martha Taylor Sarno. New York: Academic Press, 1981. 361-84.

Gelman, Rochelle. "Cognitive Development." *Ann. Rev. Psychol* (1978): 297-332.

Gevins, A.S., et al. "EEG Patterns During 'Cognitive' Tasks." *Electroencephalography and Clinical Neurophysiology* 47 (1979): 704-10.

Gilman, Sander. *Difference and Pathology*. Ithaca, NY: Cornell UP, 1985.

Ginsburg, Herbert. "Poor Children, African Mathematics, and the Problem of Schooling." *Educational Research Quarterly* 2 (1978): 26-44.

Glaser, Robert. "Education and Thinking: The Role of Knowledge." *American Psychologist* 39 (1984): 93-104.

Goodenow, Jacqueline. "The Nature of Intelligent Behavior: Questions Raised by Cross-Cultural Studies." *The Nature of Intelligence*. Ed. Lauren B. Resnick. Hillsdale, NJ: Erlbaum, 1976. 168-88.

Goody, Jack. *The Domestication of the Savage Mind*. London: Cambridge UP, 1977.

Gould, Stephen Jay. *The Mismeasure of Man*. New York: Norton, 1981.

Graff, Harvey. *The Literacy Myth*. New York: Academic Press, 1979.

_____. "Reflections on the History of Literacy: Overview, Critique, and Proposals." *Humanities and Society* 4 (1981): 303-33.

Gruber, Howard E., and J. Jacques Voneche, eds. *The Essential Piaget*. New York: Basic Books, 1977.

Halliday, M.A.K. "Differences Between Spoken and Written Language." *Communication through Reading*. Vol. 2. Ed. Glenda Page, John Elkins, and Barrie O'Connor. Adelaide, SA: Australian Reading Association, 1979. 37-52.

Havelock, Eric. *The Muse Learns to Write*. Cambridge: Harvard UP, 1986.

_____. *Preface to Plato*. Cambridge: Harvard UP, 1963.

Harre, Rom, and Roger Lamb. *The Encyclopedic Dictionary of Psychology*. Cambridge: MIT P, 1983.

Heath, Shirley Brice. "Protean Shapes in Literacy Events: Ever-Shifting Oral and Literate Traditions." *Spoken and Written Language*. Ed. Deborah Tannen. Norwood, NJ: Ablex, 1982. 91-117

_____. *Ways With Words*. London: Cambridge UP, 1983.

Hillyard, Steve A., and David L. Woods. "Electrophysiological Analysis of Human Brain Function." *Handbook of Behavioral Neurobiology*. Vol. 2. Ed. Michael S. Gazzaniga. New York: Plenum, 1979. 343-78.

Hudson, R.A. *Sociolinguistics*. Cambridge: Cambridge UP, 1986.

Hull, Glynda. "The Editing Process in Writing: A Performance Study of Experts and Novices." Diss. U of Pittsburgh, 1983.

Hunt, Earl, "On the Nature of Intelligence." *Science* 219 (1983): 141 -46.

Hunter, Carman St. John, and David Harmon. *Adult Illiteracy in the United States*. New York: McGraw-Hill, 1985.

Inhelder, Barbel, and Jean Piaget. *The Growth of Logical Thinking from Childhood to Adolescence*. Trans. Anne Parsons and Stanley Milgram. New York: Basic Books, 1958.

Jensen, George H. "The Reification of the Basic Writer." *Journal of Basic Writing* 5 (1986): 52-64.

Kamin, Leon,. *The Science and Politics of I.Q.* Hillsdale, NJ: Erlbaum, 1974.

Kuhn, Deanna, Victoria Ho, and Catherine Adams. "Formal Reasoning Among Pre- and Late Adolescents." *Child Development* 50 (1979): 1128-35.

Kurtz, Richard M. "A Conceptual Investigation of Witkin's Notion of Perceptual Style." *Mind* 78 (1969): 522-33.

Latour, Bruno, and Steve Woolgar. *Laboratory Life*. Beverly Hills, CA: Sage, 1979.

Lave, Jean. "Cognitive Consequences of Traditional Apprenticeship Training in West Africa." *Anthropology and Education Quarterly* 8 (1977): 177-80.

LeDoux, Joseph E. "Cerebral Asymmetry and the Integrated Function of the Brain." *Function of the Right Cerebral Hemisphere*. Ed. Andrew W. Young. London: Academic Press, 1983. 203-16.

Linn, Marcia C., and Patrick Kyllonen. "The Field Dependence-Independence Construct: Some, One, or None." *Journal of Educational Psychology* 73 (1981): 261-73.

Lockridge, Kenneth. *Literacy in Colonial New England*. New York: Norton, 1974.

Margolis, Joseph. "The Emergence of Philosophy." Robb 229-43.

Marrou, H.I. *A History of Education in Antiquity*. Madison, WI: U of Wisconsin P, 1982.

McCormick, Kathleen. *The Cultural Imperatives Underlying Cognitive Acts*. Berkeley: Center for The Study of Writing, 1986.

McKenna, Frank P. "Field Dependence and Personality: A Re-examination." *Social Behavior and Personality* 11 (1983): 51-55.

Messick, Samuel. "Personality Consistencies in Cognition and Creativity." *Individuality in Learning*. Ed. Samuel Messick and Associates. San Francisco: Jossey-Bass, 1976. 4-22.

Ogbu, John U. *Minority Education and Caste*. New York: Academic Press, 1978.

Olson, David R., Nancy Torrance, and Angela Hildyard, eds. *Literacy, Language, and Learning*. New York: Cambridge UP, 1981.

Ong, Walter J. *Orality and Literacy: The Technologizing of the Word*. New York: Methuen, 1982.

Ornstein, Robert E., and David Galin. "Psychological Studies of Consciousness." *Symposium on Consciousness*. Ed. Philip R. Lee et al. New York: Viking, 1976. 53-66.

Oxenham, John. *Literacy: Writing, Reading, and Social Organisation*. London: Routledge and Kegan Paul, 1980.

Perkins, D.N. "General Cognitive Skills: Why Not?" *Thinking and Learning Skills*. Ed. Susan F. Chipman, Judith W. Segal, and Robert Glaser. Hillsdale, NJ: Erlbaum, 1985. 339-63.

Piaget, Jean. "Intellectual Evolution from Adolescence to Adulthood." *Human Development* 15 (1972): 1-12.

Polanyi, Livia. *Telling the American Story: A Structural and Cultural Analysis of Conversational Storytelling*. Norwood, NJ: Ablex, 1985.

Robb, Kevin, ed. *Language and Thought in Early Greek Philosophy*. LaSalle, IL: Monist Library of Philosophy, 1983.

Rogoff, Barbara. *Everyday Cognition*. Cambridge: Harvard UP, 1984.

Rose, Mike. "Complexity, Rigor, Evolving Method, and the Puzzle of Writer's Block: Thoughts on Composing Process Research." Rose, *When a Writer Can't Write* 227-60.

_____. ed. *When a Writer Can't Write. Studies in Writer's Block and Other Composing Process Problems*. New York: Guilford, 1985.

Rugg, Michael D. "Electrophysiological Studies." Divided Visual Field Studies of Cerebral Organisation. Ed. J. Graham Beaumont. New York: Academic Press, 1982. 129-46.

Scollon, Ron, and Suzanne B.K. Scollon. "Cooking It Up and Boiling It Down: Abstracts in Athabascan Children's Story Retellings." Tannen, *Coherence in Spoken and Written Discourse* 173-97.

Shaughnessy, Mina. *Errors and Expectations*. New York: Oxford UP, 1977.

Siegler, Robert S. "Children's Thinking: *The Search For Limits.*" *The Function of Language and Cognition*. Ed. G.J. Whitehurst and Barry J. Zimmerman. New York: Academic Press, 1979. 83-113.

Sperry, Roger W. "Consciousness, Personal Identity, and the Divided Brain." Benson and Zaidel 11-26.

Tannen, Deborah, ed. *Coherence in Spoken and Written Discourse*. Norwood, NJ: Ablex, 1984.

_____. "A Comparative Analysis of Oral Narrative Strategies: Athenian Greek and American English." *The Pear Stories*. Ed. Wallace Chafe. Norwood, NJ: Ablex, 1980. 51-87.

_____. "Relative Focus on Involvement in Oral and Written Discourse." Olson, Torrance, and Hildyard 124-47.

TenHouten, Warren D. "Social Dominance and Cerebral Hemisphericity: Discriminating Race, Socioeconomic Status, and Sex Groups by Performance on Two Lateralized Tests." *Intern J. Neuroscience* 10 (1980): 223-32.

Toulmin, Stephen. "Epistemology and Developmental Psychology." *Developmental Plasticity*. Ed. Eugene S. Gollin. New York: Academic Press, 1981. 253-67.

Tulkin, S.R., and M.J. Konner. "Alternative Conceptions of Intellectual Functioning." *Human Development* 16 (1973): 33-52.

Valenstein, Elliot S. *Great and Desperate Cures*. New York: Basic Books, 1986.

Vernon, Philip. "The Distinctiveness of Field Independence." *Journal of Personality,* 40 (1972): 366-91.

Vygotsky, L.S. *Mind in Society.* Cambridge: Harvard UP, 1978.

Wachtel, Paul L. "Field Dependence and Psychological Differentiation: Reexamination." *Perceptual and Motor Skills* 35 (1972): 174-89.

Whitaker, Harry A., and George A. Ojemann. "Lateralization of Higher Cortical Functions: A Critique." *Evolution and Lateralization of the Brain.* Ed. Stuart Dimond and David Blizard. New York: New York Academy of Science, 1977. 459-73.

Redefining the Legacy of Mina Shaughnessy: A Critique of the Politics of Linguistic Innocence
by Min-zhan Lu

The aim of this paper is to critique an essentialist assumption about language that is dominant in the teaching of basic writing. This assumption holds that the essence of meaning precedes and is independent of language, which serves merely as a vehicle to communicate that essence. According to this assumption, differences in discourse conventions have no effect on the essential meaning communicated. Using Mina Shaughnessy's *Errors and Expectations* as an example, I examine the ways in which such an assumption leads to pedagogies which promote what I call a politics of linguistic innocence: that is, a politics which preempts teachers' attention from the political dimensions of the linguistic choices students make in their writing.

My critique is motivated by my alignment with various Marxist and poststructuralist theories of language.[1] In one way or another, these theories have argued that language is best understood not as a neutral vehicle of communication but as a site of struggle among competing discourses. Each discourse puts specific constraints on the construction of one's stance—how one makes sense of oneself and gives meaning to the world. Through one's gender; family; work; religious, educational, or recreational life; each individual gains access to a range of competing discourses which offer competing views of oneself, the world, and one's relation with the world. Each time one writes, even and especially when one is attempting to use one of these discourses, one experiences the need to respond to the dissonance among the various discourses of one's daily life. Because different discourses do not enjoy equal political power in current-day America, decisions on how to respond to such dissonance are never politically innocent.

From the perspective of such a view of language, Shaughnessy's stated goal for her basic writers—the mastery of written English and the "ultimate freedom of deciding how and when and where" to use which language (11)—should involve at least three challenges for student writers. First, the students need to become familiar with the conventions or "the stock of words, routines, and rituals that make up" academic discourse (198). Second, they need to gain confidence as learners and writers. Third, they need to decide how to respond to the potential dissonance between academic discourse and their home discourses. These decisions involve changes in how they think and how they use language. Yet, most pedagogies informed by the kind of essentialist assumption I defined earlier, including the one Shaughnessy presents in *Errors and Expectations*, tend to focus attention on only the first two of these challenges.

I choose *Errors and Expectations* as an example of such pedagogies because, following Robert Lyons, I interpret the operative word in that book to be "tasks" rather than "achievements." As Lyons cogently points out, Shaughnessy's work "resists closure; instead, it looks to the future, emphasizing what needs to be learned and done" (186). The legacy of Shaughnessy, I believe, is the set of tasks she maps out for composition teachers. To honor this legacy, we need to examine the pedagogical advice she gives in *Errors and Expectations* as tasks which point to the future—to what needs to be learned and done—rather than as providing closure to our pedagogical inquiry. One of the first tasks Shaughnessy establishes for composition teachers is that of "remediating" ourselves ("Diving In" 238). She urges us to become "students" of our students and of new disciplines. Reading *Errors and Expectations* in light of current theories of language is one way of continuing that "remediation." Shaughnessy also argues that a good composition teacher should inculcate interest in and respect for linguistic variety and help students attain discursive option, freedom, and choice. She thus maps out one more task for us: to carry out some democratic aspirations in the teaching of basic writing.[2] Another task she maps out for composition teachers is the need to "sound the depths" of the students' difficulties as well as their intelligence ("Diving In" 236). If, as I will argue, some of her own pedagogical advice indicates that an essentialist view of language could impede rather than enhance one's effort to fulfill these tasks, then the only way we can fully benefit from the legacy of Shaughnessy is to take the essentialist view of language itself to task.

In *Errors and Expectations,* Shaughnessy argues that language "is variously shaped by situations and bound by conventions, none of which is inferior to the others but none of which, also, can substitute for the others" (121). Using such a view of language, she makes several arguments key to her pedagogy. For example, she uses such a view to argue for the "systematic nature" of her students' home discourses, the students' "quasi-foreign relationship" with academic discourse and, thus, the logic of some of their errors. She also uses this view of language to call attention to basic writers' existing mastery of at least one variety of English and thus, their "intelligence and linguistic aptitudes" (292). She is then able to increase the confidence of both teachers and students in the students' ability to master a new variety of English—academic English.

Shaughnessy's view of language indicates her willingness to "remediate" herself by studying and exploring the implications which contemporary linguistic theories have for the teaching of basic writing.[3] However, in looking to these fields for "fresh insights and new data," Shaughnessy seems to have also adopted an essentialist assumption which dominates these theories of language: that linguistic codes can be taught in isolation from the production of meaning and from the dynamic power struggle within and among diverse discourses.[4]

We see this assumption operating in Shaughnessy's description of a writer's "consciousness (or conviction) of what [he] means":

> It seems to exist at some subterranean level of language—but yet to need words to coax it to the surface, where it is communicable, not only to others but, in a different sense, to the writer himself. (80)

The image of someone using words to coax meaning "to the surface" suggests that meaning exists separately from and "at some subterranean level of language." Meaning is thus seen as a kind of essence which the writer carries in his or her mind prior to writing, although the writer might not always be fully conscious of it. Writing merely serves to make this essence communicable to oneself and others. As David Bartholomae puts it, Shaughnessy implies that "writing is in service of 'personal thoughts and styles' " (83). Shaughnessy does recognize that writing is "a deliberate process whereby meaning is crafted, stage by stage" (81), even that "the act of articulation refines and changes [thought]" (82). But the pedagogy she advocates seldom attends to the changes which occur in that act. Instead, it presents writing primarily as getting "as close a fit as possible between what [the writer] means and what he says on paper," or as "testing the words that come to mind against the thought one has in mind" (79, 204). That is, "meaning is crafted" only to match what is already in the writer's mind (81-82).

Such a view of the relationship between words and meaning overlooks the possibility that different ways of using words—different discourses—might exercise different constraints on how one "crafts" the meaning "one has in mind." This is probably why the pedagogical advice Shaughnessy offers in *Errors and Expectations* seldom considers the possibility that the meaning one "has in mind" might undergo substantial change as one tries to "coax" it and "communicate" it in different discourses. In the following section, I use Shaughnessy's responses to three student writings to examine this tendency in her pedagogy. I argue that such a tendency might keep her pedagogy from achieving all the goals it envisions. That is, it might teach students to "write something in formal English" and "have something to say" but can help students obtain only a very limited "freedom of deciding *how* and when and where" to "use which language" (11, emphasis mine).

The following is a sentence written by one of Shaughnessy's students:

> In my opinion I believe that you there is no field that cannot be effected some sort of advancement that one maybe need a college degree to make it. (62)

Shaughnessy approaches the sentence "grammatically," as an example of her students' tendency to use "fillers" such as "I think that . . ." and "It is my opinion that . . ."

(62). She argues that these "fillers" keep the writers from "making a strong start with a *real subject*" and make them lose their "*bearings*" (62, my emphasis). The distinction between a "real subject" and "fillers" suggests that in getting rid of the "fillers," the teacher is merely helping the writer to retrieve the real subject or bearings he has in mind. I believe Shaughnessy assumes this to be the case because she sees meaning as existing "at some subterranean level of language." Yet, in assuming that, her attention seems to have been occluded from the possibility that as the writer gets rid of the "fillers," he might also be qualifying the subject or bearing he originally has in mind.

For instance, Shaughnessy follows the student's original sentence with a consolidated sentence: "A person with a college degree has a better chance for advancement in any field" (63). Shaughnessy does not indicate whether this is the student's revised sentence or the model the teacher might pose for the student. In either case, the revised sentence articulates a much stronger confidence than the original in the belief that education entails advancement. For we might read some of the phrases in the original sentence, such as "in my opinion," "I believe that you," "some sort of," and "one maybe need," as indications not only of the writer's inability to produce a grammatically correct sentence but also of the writer's attempt to articulate his uncertainty or skepticism towards the belief that education entails advancement. In learning "consolidation," this student is also consolidating his attitude towards that belief. Furthermore, this consolidation could involve important changes in the writer's political alignment. For one can well imagine that people of different economic, racial, ethnic, or gender groups would have different feelings about the degree to which education entails one's advancement.

In a footnote to this passage, Shaughnessy acknowledges that "some would argue" that what she calls "fillers" are "indices of involvement" which convey a stance or point of view (62 n. 4). But her analysis in the main text suggests that the sentence is to be tackled "grammatically," without consideration to stance or point of view. I think the teacher should do both. The teacher should deliberately call the student's attention to the relationship between "grammar" and "stance" when teaching "consolidation." For example, the teacher might ask the student to consider if a change in meaning has occurred between the original sentence and the grammatically correct one. The advantage of such an approach is that the student would realize that decisions on what are "fillers" and what is one's "real subject" are not merely "grammatical" but also political: they could involve a change in one's social alignment. The writer would also perceive deliberation over one's stance or point of view as a normal aspect of learning to master grammatical conventions. Moreover, the writer would be given the opportunity to reach a self-conscious decision. Without practice in this type of decision making, the kind of discursive options, freedom, or choice the student could obtain through education is likely to be very limited.

Attention to this type of deliberation seems just as necessary if the teacher is to help the student who wrote the following paper achieve the style of "weav[ing] personal experience into analytical discourse" which Shaughnessy admires in "mature and gifted writers" (198):

It can be said that my parents have led useful live but that usefulness seems to deteriorate when they fond themselves constantly being manipulated for the benefit of one and not for the benefit of the community. If they were able to realize that were being manipulate successful advancements could of been gained but being that they had no strong political awareness their energies were consumed by the politicians who saw personal advancements at the expenses of dedicated community workers. And now that my parents have taken a leave of absence from community involvement, comes my term to participate on worthwhile community activities which well bring about positive results and to maintain a level of consciousness in the community so that they will know what policies affect them, and if they don't quite like the results of the policies I'll make sure, if its possible, to abolish the ones which hinder progress to ones which well present the correct shift in establishing correct legislation or enactments. In order to establish myself and my life to revolve around the community I must maintain a level of awareness to make sure that I can bring about positive actions and to keep an open mind to the problems of the community and to the possible manipulation machinery which is always on the watch when progressive leaders or members of the community try to build effective activities for the people to participate. (197)

Shaughnessy suggests that the reason this writer has not yet "mastered the style" is because he has just "begun to advance into the complexity of the new language" and "is almost certain to sound and feel alien with the stock of words, routines, and rituals that make up that language" (198). The "delicate task" of the teacher in such a situation, Shaughnessy points out, is to "encourag[e] the enterprise and confidence of the student" while "improving his judgment about both the forms and meanings of the words he chooses" (198).

I believe that there is another dimension to the teacher's task. As Shaughnessy points out, this writer might be "struggling to develop a language that will enable him to talk analytically, with strangers, about the oppression of his parents and his own resolve to work against that oppression" (197). If what Shaughnessy says of most of her basic writers is true of this writer—that he too has grown up in one of New York's ethnic or racial enclaves" (3)—then the "strangers" for whom he writes and whose analytical discourse he is struggling to use are "strangers" both in the political and linguistic sense. To this writer, these "strangers" are people who already belong to what Shaughnessy calls the world of "public transactions—educational, civic, and professional" (125), a world which has traditionally excluded people like the writer and his parents. These "strangers" enjoy power relationships with the very "politicians" and "manipulation machinery" against whom this writer is resolved to fight. In trying to "talk analytically," this writer is also learning the "strangers'" way of perceiving people like his parents, such as viewing the oppression of his parents and his resolution to work against that oppression with the "curiosity and sentimentality of strangers" (197-98). Thus, their "style" might put different constraints than the student's home discourse on how this writer re-views "the experiences he has in mind" (197). If all of this is so, the teacher ought to acknowledge that possibility to the students.

Let me use the writings of another of Shaughnessy's students to illustrate why attention to a potential change in point of view might benefit students. The following are two passages written by one of Shaughnessy's students at the beginning and the end of a semester:

Essay written at beginning of semester
Harlem taught me that light skin Black people was better look, the best to suceed, the best off fanicially etc this whole that I trying to say, that I was brainwashed and people aliked. I couldn't understand why people (Black and white) couldn't get alone. So as time went along I began learned more about myself and the establishment.

Essay written at end of semester
In the midst of this decay there are children between the ages of five and ten playing with plenty of vitality. As they toss the football around, their bodies full of energy, their clothes look like rainbows. The colors mix together and one is given the impression of being in a psychedelic dream, beautiful, active, and alive with unity. They yell to each other increasing their morale. They have the sound of an organized alto section. At the sidelines are the girls who are shy, with the shyness that belongs to the very young. They are embarrassed when their dresses are raised by the wind. As their feet rise above pavement, they cheer for their boy friends. In the midst of the decay, children will continue to play. (278)

In the first passage, the writer approaches the "people" through their racial and economic differences and the subject of childhood through racial rift and contention. In the second paper, he approaches the "children" through the differences in their age, sex, and the color of their clothes. And he approaches the subject of childhood through the "unity" among children. The second passage indicates a change in how this writer makes sense of the world around him: the writer has appeased his anger and rebellion against a world which "brainwashed" children with discriminatory perceptions of Blacks and Whites. Compared to the earlier and more labored struggle to puzzle out "why people (Black and white) couldn't get alone [sic], "the almost lyrical celebration of the children's ability to "continue to play" "in the midst of the decay" seems a much more "literary" and evasive form of confronting the world of "decay."

Shaughnessy characterizes this writer as a student who "discovered early in the semester that writing gave him access to thoughts and feelings he had not *reached* any other way" (278, my emphasis). She uses these essays to illustrate "the measure of his improvement in one semester." By that, I take Shaughnessy to have in mind the changes in length and style. By the end of the semester, the student is clearly not only finding more to say on the subject but also demonstrating better control over the formal English taught in the classroom. This change in length and style certainly illustrates the effectiveness of the kind of pedagogical advice Shaughnessy gives.

Yet, these two passages also indicate that the change in the length and style of the student's writing can be accompanied by a change in thinking—in the way one perceives the world around one and relates to it. This latter change is often political as well as stylistic. I think that Shaughnessy's responses to these student writings overlook this potential change in thinking because she believes that language will only help the writers "reach" but not change how they think and feel about a certain subject or experience. Thus, attention to a potential change in one's point of view or political stance seems superfluous.

If mastery of academic discourse is often accompanied by a change in one's point of view, as my reading of these three student writings suggests, then it ought to be the teacher's task to acknowledge to the students this aspect of their learning. However, teachers may hesitate to do so because they are worried that doing so might confirm the students' fear that education will distance them from their home discourses or communities and, as a result, slow down their learning. As Shaughnessy cogently points out, her students are already feeling overwhelmed by their sense of the competition between home and college:

> Neglected by the dominant society, [basic writers] have nonetheless had their own worlds to grow up in and they arrive on our campuses as young adults, with opinions and languages and plans already in their minds. College both beckons and threatens them, offering to teach them useful ways of thinking and talking about the world, promising even to improve the quality of their lives, but threatening at the same time to take from them their distinctive ways of interpreting the world, to assimilate them into the culture of academia without acknowledging their experience as outsiders. (292)

Again and again, Shaughnessy reminds us of her students' fear that college may distance them from "their own worlds" and take away from them the point of view they have developed through "their experience as outsiders." She argues that this fear causes her students to mistrust and psychologically resist learning to write (125). Accordingly, she suggests several methods which she believes will help students assuage that fear.

For example, when discussing her students' difficulty in developing an "academic vocabulary," Shaughnessy points out that they might resist a new meaning for a familiar word because accepting it would be like consenting to a "linguistic betrayal that threatens to wipe out not just a word but the reality that the word refers to" (212). She then goes on to suggest that "if we consider the formal (rather than the contextual) ways in which words can be made to shift meaning we are closer to the kind of practical information about words BW students need" (212). This seems to be her rationale: if a "formal" approach (in this case, teaching students to pay attention to prefixes and suffixes) can help students learn that words can be made to shift meaning, then why not avoid the "contextual" approach, especially since the "contextual" approach will only activate their sense of being pressured to "wipe out not just a word but the reality that the word refers to"?

But taking this "formal" approach only circumvents the students' attention to the potential change in their thinking and their relationship with home and school. It delays but cannot eliminate their need to deal with that possibility. As a result, students are likely to realize the change only after it has already become a fact. At the same time, because the classroom has suggested that learning academic discourse will not affect how they think, feel, or relate to home, students are also likely to perceive their "betrayal" of home in purely personal terms, the result of purely personal choices. The sense of guilt and confusion resulting from such a perception is best illustrated in Richard Rodriguez's narrative of his own educational experience, *Hun-*

ger of Memory. Rodriguez's narrative also suggests that the best way for students to cope constructively with their sense of having consented to a "betrayal" is to perceive it in relation to the politics of education and language. The long, lonely, and painful deliberation it takes for Rodriguez to contextualize that "betrayal" suggests that teachers might better help students anticipate and cope with their sense of "betrayal" if they take the "contextual" as well as the "formal" approach when teaching the conventions of academic discourse. In fact, doing both might even help students to minimize that "betrayal." When students are encouraged to pay attention to the ways in which diverse discourses constrain one's alignments with different points of view and social groups, they have a better chance to deliberate over how they might resist various pressures academic discourse exercises on their existing points of view. As Shaughnessy points out, "English has been robustly inventing itself for centuries—stretching and reshaping and enriching itself with every language and dialect it has encountered" (13). If the teacher acknowledges that all practitioners of academic discourse, including those who are learning to master it as well as those who have already mastered it, can participate in this process of reshaping, then students might be less passive in coping with the constraints that academic discourse puts on their alignments with their home discourses.

In preempting Shaughnessy's attention from the political decisions involved in her students' formal or linguistic decisions, the essentialist view of language also seems to have kept her from noticing her own privileging of academic discourse. Shaughnessy calls formal written English "the language of public transactions—educational, civic, and professional"—and the students' home discourse the language one uses with one's family and friends (125). Shaughnessy insists that no variety of English can "substitute for the others" (121). She reassures her students that their home discourses cannot be substituted by academic discourse, but neither can their home discourses substitute for academic discourse. Thus, she suggests that academic discourse is a "necessary" and "advantageous" language for *all* language users because it *is* the language of public transaction (125, 293). This insistence on the nonsubstitutive nature of language implies that academic discourse has been, is, and will inevitably be the language of public transaction. And it may very well lead students to see the function of formal English as a timeless linguistic law which they must respect, adapt to, and perpetuate rather than as a specific existing circumstance resulting from the historically unequal distribution of social power, and as a condition which they must recognize but can also call into question and change.

Further, she differentiates the function of academic discourse from that of the students' home discourses through the way she characterizes the degree to which each discourse mobilizes one's language learning faculty. She presents the students' efforts to seek patterns and to discriminate or apply rules "*self-sustaining* activities" (127, emphasis mine). She argues that the search for causes, like the ability to compare, is "a constant and deep urge among people of all cultures and ages" and "part of an *unfolding intellective power* that begins with infancy and continues, at least in the lives of some, until death" (263, emphasis mine). Academic discourse and the students' home discourses, Shaughnessy suggests, unfold their "intellective power" differently. The home discourses of basic writers are seen as allowing such power to remain "largely intuitive," "simplistic," and "unreasoned" (263), while the conventions of written English are seen as demanding that such power be "more thoroughly developed," "more consciously organized" (261). Thus, academic discourse is endowed with the power to bring the "native intelligence" or the "constant and deep urge" in *all* language learners to a higher and more self-conscious level.

This type of depiction suggests that learning academic discourse is not a violation but a cultivation of what basic writers or "people of all cultures and ages" have in and of themselves. Shaughnessy thus suggests basic writers are being asked to learn academic discourse because of its distinctive ability to utilize a "human" resource. Hence, her pedagogy provides the need to learn academic discourse with a "human," and hence with yet another seemingly politically innocent, justification. It teaches students to see discursive decisions made from the point of view of academic culture as "human" and therefore "innocent" decisions made absolutely free from the pressures of specific social and historical circumstances. If it is the student's concern to align himself or herself with minority economic and ethnic groups in the very act of learning academic discourse, the politics of "linguistic" innocence can only pacify rather than activate such a concern.

Shaughnessy's desire to propose a pedagogy which inculcates respect for discursive diversity and freedom of discursive choice articulates her dissatisfaction with and reaction to the unequal social power and prestige of diverse discourses in current day America. It also demonstrates her belief that education can and should attempt to change these prevailing unequal conditions. However, the essentialist view of language which underlies her pedagogy seems also to have led her to believe that a vision of language which insists on the equality and nonsubstitutive nature of linguistic variety, and an ideal writing classroom which promotes such a view, can stand in pure opposition to society, adjusting existing social inequality and the human costs of such inequality from somewhere "outside" the socio-historical space which it is trying to transform. As a result, her pedagogy enacts a systematic denial of the political context of students' linguistic decisions.

The need to critique the essentialist view of language and the politics of linguistic innocence is urgent when viewed in the context of the popular success of E. D. Hirsch, Jr.'s proposals for educational "reforms." Hirsch argues for the "validity" of his "vocabulary" by claiming its political neutrality. Hirsch argues that "it is used to support *all* conflicting values that arise in public discourse" and "to communicate any point of view effectively" or "in *whatever* direction one wishes to be effective" (*Cultural Literacy* 23, 102, 103; my emphasis). Hirsch thus implies that the "vocabulary" one uses is separate from one's "values," "point of view," or "direction." Like Shaughnessy, he assumes an essence in the individual—a body of values, points of view, a sense of direction—which exists prior to the act of "communication" and outside of the "means of communication" (*Cultural Literacy* 23).

Like Shaughnessy, Hirsch also argues for the need for everyone to learn the "literate" language by presenting it as existing "beyond the narrow spheres of family, neighborhood, and region" (*Cultural Literacy* 21). Furthermore, he assumes that there can be only one cause of one's failure to gain "literacy": one's unfamiliarity with "the background information and the linguistic conventions that are needed to read, write, speak effectively" in America (*Cultural Literacy* 22, "Primal Scene"

31). Thus, Hirsch also denies the students' need to deal with cultural differences and to negotiate the competing claims of multiple ways of using language when writing. He thereby both simplifies and depoliticizes the challenges facing the student writer.

Hirsch self-consciously invokes a continuity between Shaughnessy's pedagogy and his "educational reforms" ("Culture and Literacy" 27; *Cultural Literacy* 10). He legitimizes his New Right rhetoric by reminding us that Shaughnessy had approved of his work. For those of us concerned with examining writing in relation to the politics of gender, race, nationality, and class, the best way to forestall Hirsch's use of Shaughnessy is to point out that the continuity resides only in the essentialist view of language underlying both pedagogies and the politics of linguistic innocence it promotes. Critiquing the essentialist view of language and the politics of linguistic innocence in Shaughnessy's work contributes to existing criticism of Hirsch's New Right rhetoric (see Armstrong, Bizzell, Moglen, Scholes, and Sledd). It makes clear that if, as Hirsch self-consciously maintains, there is a continuity between Shaughnessy's work and Hirsch's ("Culture and Literacy" 27; *Cultural Literacy* 10); the continuity resides only in the most limiting aspect of Shaughnessy's pedagogy. Recognition of some of the limitations of Shaughnessy's pedagogy can also be politically constructive for the field of composition by helping us appreciate Shaughnessy's legacy. Most of the lessons she taught us in *Errors and Expectations,* such as students' "quasi-foreign relationship" with academic discourse, their lack of confidence as learners and writers, their desire to participate in academic work, and their intelligence and language-learning aptitudes, continue to be central to the teaching of basic writing. The tasks she delineates for us remain urgent for those of us concerned with the politics of the teaching of writing. Recognizing the negative effects that an essentialist view of language have on Shaughnessy's own efforts to execute these tasks can only help us identify issues that need to be addressed if we are to carry on her legacy: a fuller recognition of the social dimensions of students' linguistic decisions.[5]

Notes

1. My view of language has been informed by Louis Althusser's notion of ideology, Antonio Gramsci's analysis of hegemony, Jacques Derrida's critique of the metaphysics of presence, Michel Foucault's theory of discourse and power, and the distinction Raymond Williams makes between practical and official consciousness.
2. For discussion of Shaughnessy's pedagogy in relation to her democratic aspirations, see Robert Lyons and rebuttals to Rouse's "The Politics of Shaughnessy" by Michael Allen, Gerald Graff, and William Lawlor.
3. In arguing for the need to show "interest in and respect for language variety," Shaughnessy cites William Labov's analysis of the inner logic, grammar, and ritual forms in Black English Vernacular (17, 237, 304). Shaughnessy also cites theories in contrastive analysis (156), first-language interference (93), and transformational grammar (77-78) to support her speculations on the logic of basic writers' error.
4. For a critique of the way modern linguistics of language, code, and competence (such as Labov's study of Black English Vernacular) tend to treat discourses as discrete and autonomous entities, see Mary Louise Pratt's "Linguistic Utopias."

5. Material from this essay is drawn from my dissertation, directed by David Bartholomae at the University of Pittsburgh. I would like to thank my teachers and colleagues at the University of Pittsburgh and Drake University, especially David Bartholomae and Joseph Harris, for their criticism and support. I want to acknowledge particularly Bruce Horner's contributions to the conception and revisions of this essay.

Works Cited

Allen, Michael. "Writing Away from Fear: Mina Shaughnessy and the Uses of Authority." *College English* 41 (1980): 857–67.

Armstrong, Paul B. "Pluralistic Literacy." *Profession* 88: 29–32.

Bartholomae, David. "Released into Language: Errors, Expectations, and the Legacy of Mina Shaughnessy." *The Territory of Language: Linguistics, Stylistics, and the Teaching of Composition.* Ed. Donald A. McQuade. Carbondale, IL: U of Southern Illinois P, 1986. 65–88.

Bizzell, Patricia. "Arguing about Literacy." *College English* 50 (1988): 141–53.

Graff, Gerald. "The Politics of Composition: A Reply to John Rouse." *College English* 41 (1980): 851–56.

Hirsch, E. D., Jr. *Cultural Literacy: What Every American Needs to Know.* Boston: Houghton, 1987.

_____ . "Culture and Literacy." *Journal of Basic Writing* 3.1 (Fall/Winter 1980): 27–35.

_____ . "The Primal Scene of Education." *New York Review of Books* 2 Mar. 1989: 29–35.

Lawlor, William. "The Politics of Rouse." *College English* 42 (1980): 195–99.

Lyons, Robert. "Mina Shaughnessy." *Traditions of Inquiry.* Ed. John Brereton. New York: Oxford UP, 1985. 171–89.

Moglen, Helene. "Allen Bloom and E. D. Hirsch: Educational Reform as Tragedy and Farce." *Profession* 88: 59–64.

Pratt, Mary Louise. "Linguistic Utopias." *The Linguistics of Writing: Arguments between Language and Literature.* Ed. Nigel Fabb, Derek Attridge, Alan Durant, and Colin MacCabe. New York: Methuen, 1987. 48–66.

Williams, James Dale. "Coherence and Cognitive Style." Diss. U of Southern California, 1983.

Witkin, Herman A., "Psychological Differentiation and Forms of Pathology." *Journal of Abnormal Psychology* 70 (1965): 317–36.

Witkin, Herman A., et al. "Field-Dependent and Field-Independent Cognitive Styles and Their Educational Implications." *Review of Educational Research* 47 (1977): 1–64.

Wittrock, Merlin. "Education and the Cognitive Processes of the Brain." *Education and The Brain.* Ed. Jeanne S. Chall and Allen S. Mirsky. Chicago: U of Chicago P, 1978. 61–102.

Young, Andrew W. "Methodological and Theoretical Bases of Visual Hemifield Studies." *Divided Visual Field Studies of Cerebral Organisation.* Ed. J. Graham Beaumont. New York: Academic Press, 1982. 11–27.

*Postmodernism and
Literacy Education*

"Strangers No More":
A Liberatory Literacy Curriculum
by Kyle Fiore and Nan Elsasser

College of the Bahamas
November 17, 1979

Dear Kyle, Pat and Larry,

I think our basic writing curriculum works! After ten weeks of discussing reading and writing about the generative theme of marriage, students have actually begun to use their newly won knowledge and skills for their own purposes. Last night we were reviewing for the final—a test designed, administered and graded by the College English Department—when Louise, one of my students, broke in to say that no test could measure what she had learned over the semester! Another student nodded in agreement. She said, "We've learned about marriage, men, and women. We've learned to write. We've learned about ourselves." Perfect Freirian synthesis! As if that weren't reward enough for one night, Eurena suggested that the class—all women—summarize and publish their knowledge. Then everyone jumped in. Our review of dashes and semicolons was forgotten as the class designed its first publication. It's hard to believe that in September these women had difficulty thinking in terms of a paragraph—now they want a manifesto! I'll keep you posted.

Love, Nan

Nan Elsasser's letter elated us. That semester she had been experimenting with a remedial English program we had designed[1] in the spring of 1978. We had first come together just after Christmas, drawn to each other by the desire to share our classroom frustrations, our successes, our gripes, over a common pitcher of beer. Trading stories with one another, we discovered we were four teachers in search of a curriculum. Standard English textbooks and traditional curricula did not fit our students at the University of Albuquerque and the University of New Mexico. Chi-

Fiore, Kyle, and Nan Elsasser. "'Strangers No More': A Liberatory Literacy Curriculum." *College English* (February 1982): 115-28. Copyright (1982) by the National Council of Teachers of English. Reprinted with permission.

canos, Blacks, Anglos, and Native Americans, they had enrolled in our courses to gain writing skills which would help them succeed in college and carve a place for themselves in society. Once they arrived, however, our students found themselves strangers in a strange world. A wide gulf stretched between the classroom curriculum and their own knowledge gained in the barrios of Albuquerque and the rural towns and pueblos of New Mexico. Confronted by a course that negated their culture, many failed to master the skills they sought. Others succeeded by developing a second skin. Leaving their own customs, habits, and skills behind, they participated in school and in the world by adapting themselves to fit the existing order. Their acquisition of literacy left them not in control of their social context, but controlled by it.

We were troubled. We wanted our students to be able to bring their culture, their knowledge, into the classroom. We wanted them to understand and master the intricacies of the writing process. And we wanted them to be able to use writing as a means of intervening in their own social environment. Sparked by our common concerns, we decided to create a curriculum which would meet our goals. As we cast about for theories and pedagogies, we discovered the work of Lev Vygotsky and Paulo Freire. These scholars intrigued us because they believe writing involves both cognitive skills and social learnings. Their approaches parallel and complement each other. Vygotsky explores students' internal learning processes. Freire emphasizes the impact of external social reality.

Vygotsky's work clarifies the complex process of writing.[2] He postulates that learning to write involves the mastery of cognitive skills and the development of new social understandings. According to Vygotsky, we categorize and synthesize our lives through inner speech, the language of thought. In inner speech, a single word or phrase is embroidered with variegated threads of ideas, experiences, and emotions. The multileveled, personal nature of inner speech is illustrated by a woman student's response to a word association exercise: *sex*: home, time, never, rough, sleep.

Vygotsky explains that to transform the inner speech symbols to written text, this woman must consciously step outside the shorthand of her thoughts and mentally enter the social context she shares with her reader. Only from this common perspective can she begin to unfold the mystery of her thoughts to create written prose.

Focusing on the learner's environment, Freire discusses the social and political aspects of writing. A designer of liberatory or revolutionary literacy programs, Freire maintains that the goal of a literacy program is to help students become critically conscious of the connection between their own lives and the larger society and to empower them to use literacy as a means of changing their own environment. Like Vygotsky, Freire believes the transformation of thought to text requires the conscious consideration of one's social context. Often, Freire says, students unaware of the connections between their own lives and society personalize their problems. To encourage students to understand the impact of society on their lives, Freire proposes students and teachers talk about generative themes drawn from the students' everyday world. Investigating issues such as work or family life from an individual and a socio-historical perspective, students bring their own knowledge into the classroom and broaden their sense of social context.

For example, one woman beaten by her husband may think she has simply made a bad choice and must bear her lot with dignity. Another woman may think her husband would stop if she could live up to his expectations. When they talk with each other and other women, these two discover that brutality is a social phenomenon; it is widespread in the community. As they read, they learn that many aspects of their problem are rooted in the social realm and can best be attached by pressing for legal changes, battered women's shelters, more responsive attitudes on the part of the police. Through continued discussion, these women realize how they can use literacy to win those changes by swearing out complaints in court, sending petitions to public officials, or writing newspaper articles and letters to the editor.

We decided to base our curriculum on Vygotsky's theory and Freire's pedagogy. Vygotsky's theory of inner speech would enable students to understand the writing process. Freire's pedagogy would encourage them to bring their culture and personal knowledge into the classroom, help them understand the connections between their own lives and society, and empower them to use writing to control their environment.

As advanced literacy teachers in traditional universities, we realized we could not use a pure Freirian approach. Designed for teachers in revolutionary settings, Freire's basic literacy programs do not consider the time constraint of semesters or the academic pressure of preparing students to meet English department standards. However, we thought it would be possible to combine Freire's goal of increasing students' critical consciousness with the teaching of advanced literacy skills. As Freire wrote in *Pedagogy in Process* (New York: Seabury, 1978), "The best way to accomplish those things that are impossible today is to do today whatever is possible" (p. 64).

That spring we met every Saturday at each other's houses. Spurred on by coffee and raised glazed doughnuts, we talked about the advanced literacy techniques we were using and explored ways to link those techniques with Vygotsky's and Freire's work. We designed word association exercises to Vygotsky's theory of inner speech. We charted ways to fit rhetorical forms in a Freirian investigation. We finished in May. That same month Nan Elsasser won a Fulbright to teach advanced literacy at the College of the Bahamas. She would be the first to try our curriculum. The next fall Elsasser kept us abreast of her experiment by mail. In the pages that follow we have summarized her letters and combined them with copies of student papers to create a first-person account of our curriculum in process.

The College of the Bahamas:
An Experiment in Possibilities

Arriving in the Bahamas before the semester begins, I have a few days to learn about the college. Located on the island of New Providence, the College of the Bahamas is a two-year community college offering daytime and evening classes. Over ninety percent of the students at the College are black Bahamians. Many work by day, attend school by night. Two-thirds of these students are women.

The language skills class I am to teach is the first in a series of four English courses offered by the college prep program. All of these courses are taught along traditional lines. To practice grammar students change tenses, add punctuation, or fill in blank spaces in assigned sentences. To demonstrate reading ability they answer multiple choice or true-false questions on short paragraphs. A colleague tells me the year before forty-five to sixty percent of the students failed to meet English department standards. She also shows me a College of the Bahamas study demonstrating no significant correlation between grades in English and grades in other academic subjects. Her revelations strengthen my determination to try out our curriculum.

I get to class early on the first night, worried my students' traditional expectations will make them leery of a new approach. Checking my roster, I discover all my students are women (later, I learn women make up two-thirds of the college's student body). I start class by introducing myself and describing the problems I've encountered teaching English traditionally. Telling the women we'll be using an experimental approach, I stress this experiment will succeed only if we can pick topics, discuss material, and evaluate results together. I admit class will lack coherency at times, and one student asks if they will be able to pass the standardized English exam given at the end of the semester. I say I think so, but that she is free to transfer if she wants a more traditional approach. She leaves; but the rest stay.

To establish a sense of common ground, I ask my students about their work and former schooling. Half of them clerk in banks. The others type or run computers. Collectively, these women represent the first generation of Bahamian women to enter the business world and go to college. They have an average of six years of education behind them. Recalling her early school days, one woman speaks of days spent copying poems from a colonial primer. Another recounts the times she stayed home to care for the younger ones while her mother went to sell her wares at the straw market. They all remember problems with writing.

So they can begin to understand the cause of their problems, we spend the next three weeks investigating the complexities of going from inner speech to finished written product. We begin with a series of word association exercises designed to illustrate Vygotsky's theory. Comparing their responses to trigger words such as *sex, home, work*, the women start to see that even at this most basic level they categorize and store information in various ways. Some students list contrasting affective responses. Others jot down visual images. One woman divides the inner speech word into subtopics, like an outline: "job: where you would like to work, type boss, what specific field." Contrasting their different ways of organizing and listing thoughts, students gain a strong sense of why they need to elaborate their thoughts in writing. To end the session, we each transform our private lists to public prose.

To continue our study of the transformations involved in writing clear, explicit prose, I look for a topic which will stress the value of personal knowledge, break down the dichotomy between personal and classroom knowledge, and require explicit elaboration. As a newcomer to the island, I ask them to advise me "What You Need to Know to Live in the Bahamas." I introduce this assignment by talking about writing as an interaction between process and product, personal and social points of view, concrete and abstract knowledge. A student writing a recipe for conch salad needs concrete knowledge about preparing conch combined with the abstract knowledge of an audience as people with some shared assumptions as well as some lack of common ground.

The women have a number of problems with this assignment, evidencing what Freire calls the inability to step outside immediate contextual realities and incorporate broader points of view. Some students write very brief suggestions. Others write in the first person or list topics of interest, but don't include concrete information. Still others complain they are stymied trying to figure out what I'd like to do. Though she knows I am a stranger to the island, the woman writing me a recipe for conch salad assumes conch is a familiar food. Yet another woman constructs an imaginary audience to help herself focus on the assignment: "What You Need to Know to Live in the Bahamas. A Young married couple on Vacation. Leisure Activities. Whatever your taste in holiday diversion you'll never be at loss for something to do in the Bahamas. . . ."

This assignment extends over several sessions. Students write and rewrite their essays. During this time we develop the basic procedure we'll use to investigate a generative theme. First, we discuss the topic at hand (e.g., "What You Need to Know to Live in the Bahamas"). Then one student volunteers a thesis statement related to the topic. Other women help narrow and sharpen this statement and develop an essay outline. Students use these outlines as guidelines for their rough drafts. I reproduce the drafts, and we read and comment on them. After prolonged discussion, each woman rewrites her draft to meet the questions we've raised.

In moving from the discussion of inner speech to writing about the Bahamas, students take on more and more responsibility for the class. While in writing they are still trapped by their personal perspectives, in discussions they begin to critique and respond to one another's views. Gradually they start to investigate their environment. Before, they passively received knowledge. Now, they pursue it.

Freire states that students caught by their own subjectivity can break through personal walls and move to a collective social perspective through investigating generative themes. Such themes must be selected carefully so that they encourage students to write for a broader, more public audience and empower them to use writing to change their lives. Freire advises teachers searching for themes to involve themselves intimately in their students culture and minutely observe all the facets of their daily lives, recording "the way people talk, their style of life, their behavior at church and work" (*Pedagogy of the Oppressed* [New York: Seabury,1970], p. 103). Analyzing these observations with a team of other educators, the teacher will discern meaningful generative themes.

A stranger, unaccompanied by a "literacy team," I can't follow Freire's advice, and in my ignorance I turn to my students for help. We discuss generative themes, and they each select three issues from their daily lives that they would like to talk, read, and write about for the semester. When they bring in their suggestions, I list them on the board. We debate them briefly and they vote, picking marriage for their generative theme. This theme affects their lives economically, socially, and emotionally. Ninety percent of these women have been raised by two parents in traditional Bahamian homes. Seventy-five percent are now mothers. Two-thirds of these mothers are single parents totally responsible for their children's physical and emotional well-being.

Having chosen their theme, the women break into groups. They discuss the areas of marriage they want to investigate and construct an outline of subtopics, including *housework*, *divorce*, *sexuality*, an*d domestic violence*. With these subtopics in hand, I start to hunt for reading materials. I look for articles which bridge the distance between students' lives and society. We'll use these articles as a basis for dialogues about individual problems, common experiences, and the larger social world.

My search of the college library yields nothing on contemporary Bahamian marriage. Writing back to the United States for articles, culling my old *Ms.* magazines, and hounding the local newsstand, I collect a packet which fits our course outline. Initial reading assignments come from popular magazines: an article on wife beating from *New Woman,* one entitled "Why Bad Marriages Endure" from *Ebony.* As students' reading skills and knowledge increase, we will use more advanced texts, such as *Our Bodies Ourselves* (2nd ed., New York: Simon and Schuster, 1976), and *The Longest War: Sex Differences in Perspective* by Carol Tavris and Carole Offir (New York: Harcourt Brace Jovanovich, 1977). At the end of the semester we will read *Nectar in a Sieve* (New York: New American Library, 1971), a novel by Kamala Markandaya about peasant marriage in India.

For the rest of the semester we spend about one week co-investigating each subtopic of our marriage theme. I introduce each subject by handing out a related article. To help the women understand new information, I discuss the concepts I think unfamiliar, e.g., the historical concept of Victorian as a set of sexual attitudes. After reading and talking about the articles, we develop a thesis statement following the procedure we devised when writing essays on the Bahamas. When discussing articles and writing critiques students do not follow the traditional liberal arts criteria. Their criticism is not bound by the authors' intent or opinion, nor do they consider all articles equally valid. Rather, they judge the reading by whether or not it connects with their personal perspectives and tells them about marriage as a socioeconomic institution. They find much of value in *Our Bodies Ourselves*. They dismiss poet Judith Viorst as a spoiled middle-class housewife.

During our investigation students pass through three distinct phases as they hone their abilities to examine, critique, and write about marriage. They elaborate their own experience more skillfully, and they perceive stronger links between their own lives and the larger social context. They reach outside their own experience to seek new sources of knowledge. Finally, they become critically conscious of the way society affects their lives, and they begin to use writing as a means of intervening in their own social environment.

In the early weeks many women have trouble discerning the connections between their personal life and their social context. They analyze problems using concrete knowledge drawn from experience. They argue by anecdote. To encourage them to broaden their outlook, I ask for a definition of marriage as a social institution. In response, they describe what marriage should be ("communication," "love," "fidelity"), or they recite personal experiences ("men can come and go as they please, women cannot"; "men neglect their financial responsibilities"; "men have sweethearts"; "men are violent"). Posing questions targeting a social definition of marriage, I elicit broader, abstract responses: "legal procedure," "age requirements," "union between man and woman," "religious sanctioning of sex." Looking over this list, they ask me to throw out their earlier, more personal definitions.

Next, they construct lists of the positive and negative aspects of marriage as a social institution. These lists display a mixture of personal experiences, idealistic yearnings, and social traits.

Positive	*Negative*
Safe from rape and break-ins	Sex against our will
Not coming home to an empty house	Security sours relationships
Community approval of the relationship	Loss of freedom

Comparing these lists, the women start to talk about the social aspects of marriage. They conclude that the major benefit of marriage is security and social approval; its major shortcoming, a loss of freedom. Even after our extended dialogue, in their essays on "The Worst or Best Things about Marriage," women either write empty generalizations or briefly recount their own experience.

The Worst Thing About Marriage
By Rosetta Finlay

The worst thing about marriage is security, Whenever a couple is married they tend to become too sure of themselves. One would say, "All is well." I already have whom I want so I don't have to say I love you anymore; I don't have to show that I care as much. We don't have sex as often and you can go out with the boys while I go out with the girls.

This is where one would find time to go out of the home and look for the missing links in his marriage. That's when all the problem arises as soon as this happens, there's no end to problems.

The Best Thing About Marriage
By Eurena Clayton

I enjoyed being with my husband when we were dating and the things we did together drew us closer. After we got married my husband's business prevents us from doing as many things as we used to do together. Usually when we have a spare chance we take off on trips which we simply enjoy together. The feeling of not having to bother with the every day responsibilities is a great burden lifted for that period. We find ourselves taking in the movies, theatre, tennis, golfing or simply sightseeing.

There are special occasions such as anniversary or birthday which are always remembered. Sometimes for no reason you receive a beautiful gift which is always appreciated and thoughtful.

In order to achieve one's goal in life it is safe to pool both resources.

I suggest revisions for these essays, reproduce them, and pass them out. Students critique each other's papers, and each woman rewrites her piece. This time a number of students expand their essays through elaboration. However, at this stage no one goes beyond her own experience without writing platitudes, and few maintain a consistent focus throughout the entire paper. The woman writing this third draft has expanded and improved her mechanics and drawn clearer contrasts in her conclusion. She still reverts to an unrelated generality.

Draft III
By Rosetta Finlay

The worst thing about marriage is emotional security. When a couple is married, they tend to become too sure of themselves. One will say, "All is well I already have whom I want so I don't have to look nice anymore; I don't have to say I love you anymore; I don't have to show that I care as much; we don't have sex as often and you can go out with the boys while I go out with the girls."

Marriage shouldn't be taken so much for granted there's always improvement needed in every marriage. Marriage is like a job e.g.—one has a job everything is routine; you have a steady salary; steady hours nine o'clock in the morning to five o'clock in the evening; go to work every day and perform the duties your job position requires.

Marriage is very similar e.g.—one has a steady companion; cook every day; keep the house and laundry clean; have babies and bring them up. Apart from doing the house chores there's the chauffeuse part to be done and the office work.

I personally think that there is a lot more to be done if you want to have a successful marriage. Therefore if more interest is taken in these areas, marriage would be much better than what it is today.

In the sessions that follow, students evidence similar problems with the reading assignment. The article is about battered wives. Although they can read the words, the women have difficulty distinguishing major ideas from details. Where in writing they recounted personal experiences, now in reading they focus on anecdotes. They underline when, where, or how hard Frank hit Marlene, as opposed to the main concept this example illustrates.

To sharpen the contrast between a main idea and an illustration I ask them to list causes of domestic violence on the board. Then we start to talk about the difference between causes and anecdotes. It takes students several sessions to learn to select main points correctly on their own. During these sessions they also begin to gain a better grasp of the connections between their own lives and the forces of society.

I am reminded as I consider my students that teaching and learning are part of a single process. To present something in class is not to teach it. Learning happens when students make cognitive transformations, expanding and reorganizing the knowledge in their cerebral filing systems. Only then can they assimilate and act upon ideas.

By the end of Phase One the women have made several such transformations. They have an idea of their individual differences and a sense of the common ground they share. Although they still rely on personal experience as a source of knowledge, they are beginning to recognize how the outside society affects their lives. This awareness has improved their writing. They use more detail. They separate ideas and events into paragraphs. They sustain a third-person perspective with greater skill. They clarify generalizations with examples.

A "Typical" Bahamian Marriage
By Rosetta Finlay

"For richer, for poorer, for better, for worse, in sickness and in health, until death do us part." God has commanded his children to join in the holy matrimony and obey these rules. Unfortunately, the majority of the Bahamian marriages tend to focus more on the negative, than the positive aspects of marriage. A Typical Bahamian Marriage will begin with both, the male and female being in love with each other, so much in love that the husband will help with the house chores, such as washing the dishes, doing the laundry, taking out the garbage and making breakfast. It will even get to the point where the husband will stay up at night with their first child. Every Sunday the family will go to church and have dinner together. Later in the evening the husband and wife will go to the movies or a special function.

Week days, both the husband and wife will go out to work, usually they both work. After work the wife rushes home to prepare the dinner. The bills are paid by both the husband and wife's salary put together and if possible, a little is saved. For some period of time, the wife will satisfy her husband's need such as, sharing sex, understanding and the house chores. Then all of a sudden, for an unknown reason the husband changes.

He will start staying out X amount of hours and stop putting his share of monies towards the bills. Comes home and take out his frustration on his wife and children by, snapping at children and beating his wife. He does not even want to spend any time at home to help with the house chores or baby sit. He only comes home to change, if he is questioned about money it will end in a fight. Then he will leave home for another day or two.

The wife, is now in a situation where she does not have enough money to pay the bills and support the children, no husband to lean on and protect the family. She does not have any where to go, because he keeps telling her that she cannot go with out him. Getting a divorce in the Bahamas is completely out of the question. So she will have to, "grin and bear it" until death.

By mid-semester most women have entered Phase Two. We pause to take stock of our work. Looking back over their gains, women are sparked with pride. They begin seizing more control in class and start to generate their own theories on the writing mechanics. One night we tackle the problem of pronoun agreement. While aware they often switch back and forth in writing from *they* to *you, she/he,* and *I,* students have little success self-editing for pronouns because we don't know the cause of this problem. Then one woman comments she has no trouble writing general points in the third person. However, she says when she illustrates these points or gives advice, she starts mentally addressing a particular person and slips into a second-person referent. Examining several essays, classmates confirm her observation; as a result, they begin to catch and correct these errors.

Women also start to discover punctuation rules. Although I have not stressed punctuation as such, they observe patterns in the reading, and they hypothesize the rules themselves. While working on the use of logical connectors like *however* and *similarly*, a student asks if the first sentence always ends in a semicolon followed by the connector, a comma, and another sentence. After consulting with each other and essays, other students incorporate this rule in their writing.

During this phase students also break away from their total dependence on personal experience. They become more confident about gaining knowledge from class dialogues and reading. One night we debate whether or not women "ask for" rape. Remembering how reading about wife beating changed our stereotypes, one student asks for additional materials on rape. Others second her request. Spurred on by their own curiosity, they assail excerpts from Susan Brownmiller's *Against Our Will* and discuss how her theories and statistics destroy or reinforce their personal myths and beliefs.

Encouraged by their confidence and advancing skills, I begin to introduce the idea of rhetorical forms: cause and effect, definition, comparison and contrast. Rather than concentrating on these forms explicitly, we employ them as a means of pondering, exploring, and writing about various facets of marriage. When looking at the social forces that perpetuate wife beating, we cover cause and effect. To illustrate the relationships between wife beating and rape, we use comparison and contrast. The outline students construct for this topic clarifies the social similarities and differences between these two forms of violence.

Comparison and Contrast on Rape and Wife Beating

Comparison
    brutality to women
    —by men
    —at night
    —police take male side
    —society reluctant to believe women
    —female shame

Contrast
    —husband vs. stranger
    —predictability
    —sentence more severe for rape
    —provocation

In their essays comparing and contrasting rape and wife beating, the women bring together cognitive skills and social realizations. They now write from a unified perspective with more coherence, fewer sentence fragments, and more complex sentence structure. They combine information gained from discussions and reading with their personal knowledge to create a solid argument by crisp, focused examples.

Comparison and Contrast of Rape and Wife Beating
By Rosetta Finlay

In 1973 over half a million rapes were estimated by F.B.I. along with 14,000 wife abuse complaints in New York alone reached the family courts during a comparable period that same year. Rape and wife beating are common crimes done by men in our society.

Unfortunately, the women of our society have to turn to the law who are men for help. Very seldom a female will win a rape case to get protection from the law on a wife abuse complaint. Calling the police will not help, not when they ask you questions like, "Are there any witnesses to this assault?" "Look lady he pays the bills, doesn't he?" Only to conclude with "What he does in his house is his business." and "Why don't you two kiss and make up." They really don't act any different when called upon a rape assault not when they say things like, "well things certainly seem to be in order here now." "What was the problem?" "What were you wearing, were your pants tight?" On the other hand the female in wife abuse must think about her dependency upon her husband, when she thinks about taking her complaint to family court, eg:—who will pay the bills? In most cases the female doesn't work and what will she do without him, where will she turn after not working for years? This is where the female is trapped and cannot win.

Despite the trapping situation the women of our society have decided to fight against that to bring more rights and evidence for the female, for instance Judge Oneglia who as a lawyer specializes in marital problems, recommends that the female should get out of the house, go to a friend or neighbor, and cause as much disturbance as possible. The more witnesses the better. As in a rape case the victim must produce pictures or evidence of (bruises or semen) to corroborate the rape victim's testimony, another prohibits the introduction in court of evidence concerning a rape victim's previous sexual conduct.

The women in society have formed groups and organizations to fight and protect themselves from wife abuse and rape, for instance they have decided to get together with other women in their neighborhood or apartment building and establish a whistle signal. In cases where the female lives alone she should list only her first initial in the telephone directory and also keep all outside doors and windows dead bolt locked mostly used in a rape case. In a wife abuse case the women of our society have recommended to call a special meeting to discuss the problem inviting representatives from the police, clergy and social service agencies to participate. Hopefully, this would contribute to cut down on rape and wife abuse.

In Phase Three students begin to use writing as a means of intervening in their own social environment. A few weeks before the end of the semester the women decide to share the knowledge they have gained about marriage with the world outside classroom by publishing an open "Letter to Bahamian Men" in the island newspapers. Writing this manifesto takes four weeks. In addition to class time, we meet together on Sundays and put in hours of extra work. We start by writing individual letters. We discuss these letters in class, then outline a collective letter.

A. Introduction
    1. Role of women in Bahamian society
    2. Oppression of women in marriage
B. Women victims of men's inconsiderate actions
C. Men's financial neglect of the family
D. Men's lack of help at home
E. Men's lack of responsibility for their children
F. Men's failure to satisfy women sexually
G. Conclusion: recommendations for Bahamian men

After considering the concerns each woman mentioned in her first letter, I assign each one a particular topic to develop. I organize the topics into a text, leaving gaps where I think there is a need for further work. From this point on my role is limited to copying, cutting and pasting. Equipped with her own copy, each woman begins to edit her epistle. They go line by line, spending over an hour on each page. Students silent all semester defend their contributions vehemently. They argue over punctuation, style, and semantics. They debate whether to separate the list of men's inconsiderate actions with colons, semicolons, or full stops. One woman thinks a reference to *gambling* too colloquial. Another questions the use of *spend* vs. *squander*.

They consider their audience's viewpoint, calculating the effect of their words. They discuss whether to blame the issue of sweethearts on the men or the sweethearts themselves. One student observes that since the letter confronts the wrongs men perpetrate on women, it would be a tactical error to criticize other women. They finally compromise by using the term *extra-marital affairs*. Wanting to state their case clearly yet not run the risk of censorship, they rewrite the paragraph on sex several times. The final letter appears in both Nassau daily papers.

Bahamian Women Deserve a Change

Dear Bahamian Men:

The social, spiritual and economic growth of Bahamian society depends on men as well as women. For a very long time there has been a downward trend in male support of their wives and children. In the typical Bahamian marriage both the male and the female begin by thinking that they are in love, so much in love that the husband will help with the household chores. The husband will even stay up all night with their first child. Every Sunday the family will go to church and have dinner together. Later in the evening the husband and wife might go to a movie or a special function. Week days both the husband and wife will go to work. After work the wife rushes home to prepare dinner. The bills are paid by putting together both the husband and wife's salaries and if possible, a little is saved. For some time all will go very well in the home. Then all of a sudden, for some unknown reason, the husband begins to change.

We are a group of women who have all been victims of men's inconsiderate actions. We would like to focus on the punishment, deprivation, discourtesy, mental anguish and death of the soul for which Bahamian men are responsible: Punishment because some women are beaten by their husband; Deprivation because husbands give wives less and less to survive on each month; Discourtesy because extra-marital affairs disturb the home. Mental anguish is humiliation of the mind, for whose mind can be at ease in such a situation! Death of the soul deteriorates the whole body, for women are made to feel they serve no purpose.

These problems arise when the men begin to neglect their homes. The main problems between men and women in the Bahamas are: child raising, housekeeping, finances, and sex. Men are the root of most of these problems.

In most cases the male salary is more than the females. Despite this fact, the majority of Bahamian men neglect the financial upkeep of their families in some way or the other. Because of this, the greater part of the financial burden which includes savings, school fees, groceries, utilities, and even mortgages have been left to women. The male finds other things to do with his salary. Some men wait for the women to remind them about their bills. Others expect the women to pay all the bills. How can the female be expected to do all of this with a salary that is less than the males?

For centuries women have been solely responsible for housework. So men still think that a woman's place is in the home. Men expect women to work all day, come home and cook, wash dishes, clean house, wash clothes, prepare dinner and get the children ready for bed while they sit around and watch. It used to be that women did not work and were solely dependent on their husbands for support. Since women are now working and helping their husbands with most of the financial upkeep, there is no reason why the men can't be a part when it comes to housework. It is both the male's and the female's place to share the responsibilities of the home.

It takes two to produce a child and so it should be two to see to the upbringing of the child. Fathers do not spend sufficient time in the home. The most important stages in a child's life, the most cherished and once in a life time moments are when the child says his first word, makes his first step, and claps his hands for the first time. Fathers being around the home when moments like the above mentioned take place are important in children's lives. Here in the Bahamas fathers have failed to be real fathers, and children have been left totally dependent on their mothers. Having children and not supporting them is not a good way to prove one's manhood. A child should have both parents' care and attention. But before men see that their children are well taken care of they prefer to spend money on their own pleasure. Why be responsible for another life coming into the world if men don't care if the children are properly fed, have proper clothing to wear, and get a proper education?

Men tend not to realize the necessity in satisfying their partners when making love. Unfortunately, they are mainly concerned with the fulfillment of their desires. They come home at the most tiresome hours of the night, hop in bed and expect us to respond without any love or affection. Most Bahamian men don't take the time to caress women's bodies before having sex. Therefore, the instant they get into bed—if they're in the mood—women are expected to perform. However, when women are in the mood, they don't respond. This leaves women dissatisfied and angry.

Our recommendations to Bahamian men in relation to the above are as follows:

a) That men join in family worship at least twice a month.
b) That men stop putting most of the financial burden on women. 75% of the household responsibilities should be handled by men.
c) That men at least buy their children's groceries, pay school fees and buy clothes.
d) That men take their children out for recreation at least once a week.
e) That men do an equal share of the housework.

f) That men do not allow extra-marital affairs to damage or destroy their marriages.
g) That men make more effort to sexually satisfy their wives. Talk about the things that please them. Caress their women until they're ready for sex. Try not to climax until the women are ready.

Men, there is definitely room for improvement in love, affection and communication. Try it.

Sincerely,
English 016-06

Comparing this "Open Letter to Bahamian Men" with women's earlier essays on "Rape and Battered Wives," "The Worst Things in a Marriage," and life in the Bahamas demonstrates how, through the investigation of a generative theme, students can advance their reading and writing skills, recognize links between their own lives and the larger society, and develop ways of using their newfound writing skills to intervene in their own environment.

At the end of the semester all these women passed the College-administered English exam. Most received "B" grades on the essay component. Further, they decided to continue meeting throughout the next spring in order to read about women in other countries, broaden their understandings, and write a resource book for Bahamian women.

The success of this pedagogical experiment demonstrates that advanced literacy teachers can modify Freire's pedagogy to fit the needs of their students and the demands of the college. Through this approach students will achieve literacy in the truest, most profound sense: they will understand "their reality in such a way that they increase their power to transform it" (Darcy de Olivera and Rosiska de Olivera, *Guinea-Bissau Reinventing Education* [Geneva: Institute of Cultural Action, 1976], p. 48).

Notes

1. The curriculum described in this article was developed by Nan Elsasser, Kyle Fiore, Patricia Irvine, and Larry Smith.
2. See, especially, *Thought and Language* (Cambridge, Mass.: MIT Press, 1962). We would like to thank Vera John-Steiner for sharing with us her knowledge of and commitment to the theories of L. S. Vygotsky.

The Silenced Dialogue:
Power and Pedagogy in Educating
Other People's Children
by Lisa D. Delpit

A Black male graduate student who is also a special education teacher in a pre-dominantly Black community is talking about his experiences in predominantly White university classes:

> There comes a moment in every class where we have to discuss "The Black Issue" and what's appropriate education for Black children. I tell you, I'm tired of arguing with those White people, because they won't listen. Well, I don't know if they really don't listen or if they just don't believe you. It seems like if you can't quote Vygotsky or something, then you don't have any validity to speak about your *own* kids. Anyway, I'm not bothering with it anymore, now I'm just in it for a grade.

A Black woman teacher in a multicultural urban elementary school is talking about her experiences in discussions with her predominantly White fellow teachers about how they should organize reading instruction to best serve students of color:

> When you're talking to White people they still want it to be their way. You can try to talk to them and give them examples, but they're so headstrong, they think they know what's best for *everybody*, for *everybody's* children. They won't listen, White folks are going to do what they want to do *anyway*.

> It's really hard. They just don't listen well. No, they listen, but they don't hear—you know how your mama used to say you listen to the radio, but you hear your mother? Well they don't *hear* me.

> So I just try to shut them out so I can hold my temper. You can only beat your head against a brick wall for so long before you draw blood. If I try to stop arguing with them I can't help myself from getting angry. Then I end up walking around praying all

day "Please Lord, remove the bile I feel for these people so I can sleep tonight." It's funny, but it can become a cancer, a sore.

So, I shut them out. I go back to my own little cubby, my classroom, and I try to teach the way I know will work, no matter what those folk say. And when I get Black kids, I just try to undo the damage they did.

I'm not going to let any man, woman, or child drive me crazy—White folks will try to do that to you if you let them. You just have to stop talking to them, that's what I do. I just keep smiling, but I won't talk to them.

A soft-spoken Native Alaskan woman in her forties is a student in the Education Department of the University of Alaska. One day she storms into a Black professor's office and very uncharacteristically slams the door. She plops down in a chair and, still fuming, says, "Please tell those people, just don't help us anymore! I give up. I won't talk to them again!"

And finally, a Black woman principal who is also a doctoral student at a well-known university on the West Coast is talking about her university experiences, particularly about when a professor lectures on issues concerning educating Black children:

If you try to suggest that that's not quite the way it is, they get defensive, then you get defensive, then they'll start reciting research.

I try to give them my experiences, to explain. They just look and nod. The more I try to explain, they just look and nod, just keep looking and nodding. They don't really hear me.

Then, when it's time for class to be over, the professor tells me to come to his office to talk more.

So I go. He asks for more examples of what I'm talking about, and he looks and nods while I give them.

Then he says that that's just my experiences. It doesn't really apply to most Black people.

It becomes futile because they think they know everything about everybody. What you have to say about your life, your children, doesn't mean anything. They don't really want to hear what you have to say. They wear blinders and earplugs. They only want to go on research they've read that other White people have written.

It just doesn't make any sense to keep talking to them.

Thus was the first half of the title of this text born—"The Silenced Dialogue." One of the tragedies in the field of education is that scenarios such as these are enacted daily around the country. The saddest element is that the individuals that the Black and Native American educators speak of in these statements are seldom aware that the dialogue *has* been silenced. Most likely the White educators believe that their colleagues of color did, in the end, agree with their logic. After all, they stopped disagreeing, didn't they?

I have collected these statements since completing a recently published article (Delpit, 1986). In this somewhat autobiographical account, entitled "Skills and Other Dilemmas of a Progressive Black Educator," I discussed my perspective as a product of a skills-oriented approach to writing and as a teacher of process-oriented approaches. I described the estrangement that I and many teachers of color feel from the progressive movement when writing-process advocates dismiss us as too "skills oriented." I ended the article suggesting that it was incumbent upon writing-process advocates—or indeed, advocates of any progressive movement—to enter into dialogue with teachers of color, who may not share their enthusiasm about so-called new, liberal, or progressive ideas.

In response to this article, which presented no research data and did not even cite a reference, I received numerous calls and letters from teachers, professors, and even state school personnel from around the country, both Black and White. All of the White respondents, except one, have wished to talk more about the question of skills versus process approaches—to support or reject what they perceive to be my position. On the other hand, *all* of the non-White respondents have spoken passionately on being left out of the dialogue about how best to educate children of color.

How can such complete communication blocks exist when both parties truly believe they have the same aims? How can the bitterness and resentment expressed by the educators of color be drained so that the sores can heal? What can be done?

I believe the answer to these questions lies in ethnographic analysis, that is, in identifying and giving voice to alternative world views. Thus, I will attempt to address the concerns raised by White and Black respondents to my article "Skills and Other Dilemmas" (Delpit, 1986). My charge here is not to determine the best instructional methodology; I believe that the actual practice of good teachers of all colors typically incorporates a range of pedagogical orientations. Rather, I suggest that the differing perspectives on the debate over "skills" versus "process" approaches can lead to an understanding of the alienation and miscommunication, and thereby to an understanding of the "silenced dialogue."

In thinking through these issues, I have found what I believe to be a connecting and complex theme: what I have come to call "the culture of power." There are five aspects of power I would like to propose as given for this presentation:

1. Issues of power are enacted in classrooms.
2. There are codes or rules for participating in power; that is, there is a "culture of power."
3. The rules of the culture of power are a reflection of the rules of the culture of those who have power.
4. If you are not already a participant in the culture of power, being told explicitly the rules of that culture makes acquiring power easier.
5. Those with power are frequently least aware of—or least willing to acknowledge—its existence. Those with less power are often most aware of its existence.

The first three are by now basic tenets in the literature of the sociology of education, but the last two have seldom been addressed. The following discussion will explicate these aspects of power and their relevance to the schism between liberal educational movements and that of non-White, non-middle-class teachers and communities.[1]

1. *Issues of power are enacted in classrooms.*

These issues include: the power of the teacher over the students; the power of the publishers of textbooks and of the developers of the curriculum to determine the view of the world presented; the power of the state in enforcing compulsory schooling; and the power of an individual or group to determine another's intelligence or "normalcy." Finally, if schooling prepares people for jobs, and the kind of job a person has determines her or his economic status and, therefore, power, then schooling is intimately related to that power.

2. *There are codes or rules for participating in power; that is, there is a "culture of power."*

The codes or rules I'm speaking of relate to linguistic forms, communicative strategies, and presentation of self; that is, ways of talking, ways of writing, ways of dressing, and ways of interacting.

3. *The rules of the culture of power are a reflection of the rules of the culture of those who have power.*

This means that success in institutions—schools, workplaces, and so on—is predicated upon acquisition of the culture of those who are in power. Children from middle-class homes tend to do better in school than those from non-middle-class homes because the culture of the school is based on the culture of the upper and middle classes—of those in power. The upper and middle classes send their children to school with all the accoutrements of the culture of power; children from other kinds of families operate within perfectly wonderful and viable cultures but not cultures that carry the codes or rules of power.

4. *If you are not already a participant in the culture of power, being told explicitly thc rules of that culture makes acquiring power easier.*

In my work within and between diverse cultures, I have come to conclude that members of any culture transmit information implicitly to co-members. However, when implicit codes are attempted across cultures, communication frequently breaks down. Each cultural group is left saying, "Why don't those people say what they mean?" as well as, "What's wrong with them, why don't they understand?"

Anyone who has had to enter new cultures, especially to accomplish a specific task, will know of what I speak. When I lived in several Papua New Guinea villages for extended periods to collect data, and when I go to Alaskan villages for work with Alaskan Native communities, I have found it unquestionably easier—psychologically and pragmatically—when some kind soul has directly informed me about such matters as appropriate dress, interactional styles, embedded meanings, and taboo words or actions. I contend that it is much the same for anyone seeking to learn the rules of the culture of power. Unless one has the leisure of a lifetime of "immersion" to learn them, explicit presentation makes learning immeasurably easier.

And now, to the fifth and last premise:

5. *Those with power are frequently least aware of—or least willing to acknowledge—its existence. Those with less power are often most aware of its existence.*

For many who consider themselves members of liberal or radical camps, acknowledging personal power and admitting participation in the culture of power is distinctly uncomfortable. On the other hand, those who are less powerful in any situation are most likely to recognize the power variable most acutely. My guess is that the White colleagues and instructors of those previously quoted did not perceive themselves to have power over the non-White speakers. However, either by virtue of their position, their numbers, or their access to that particular code of power of calling upon research to validate one's position, the White educators had the authority to establish what was to be considered "truth" regardless of the opinions of the people of color, and the latter were well aware of that fact.

A related phenomenon is that liberals (and here I am using the term "liberal" to refer to those whose beliefs include striving for a society based upon maximum individual freedom and autonomy) seem to act under the assumption that to make any rules or expectations explicit is to act against liberal principles, to limit the freedom and autonomy of those subjected to the explicitness.

I thank Fred Erickson for a comment that led me to look again at a tape by John Gumperz[2] on cultural dissonance in cross-cultural interactions. One of the episodes showed an East Indian interviewing for a job with an all-White committee. The interview was a complete failure, even though several of the interviewers appeared to really want to help the applicant. As the interview rolled steadily downhill, these "helpers" became more and more indirect in their questioning, which exacerbated the problems the applicant had in performing appropriately. Operating from a different cultural perspective, he got fewer and fewer clear clues as to what was expected of him, which ultimately resulted in his failure to secure the position.

I contend that as the applicant showed less and less aptitude for handling the interview, the power differential became ever more evident to the interviewers. The "helpful" interviewers, unwilling to acknowledge themselves as having power over the applicant, became more and more uncomfortable. Their indirectness was an attempt to lessen the power differential and their discomfort by lessening the power-revealing explicitness of their questions and comments.

When acknowledging and expressing power, one tends towards explicitness (as in yelling to your 10-year-old, "Turn that radio down!"). When de-emphasizing power, there is a move toward indirect communication. Therefore, in the interview setting, those who sought to help, to express their egalitarianism with the East Indian applicant, became more and more indirect—and less and less helpful—in their questions and comments.

In literacy instruction, explicitness might be equated with direct instruction. Perhaps the ultimate expression of explicitness and direct instruction in the primary classroom is Distar. This reading program is based on a behaviorist model in which reading is taught through the direct instruction of phonics generalizations and blending. The teacher's role is to maintain the full attention of the group by continuous questioning, eye contact, finger snaps, hand claps, and other gestures, and by eliciting choral responses and initiating some sort of award system.

When the program was introduced, it arrived with a flurry of research data that "proved" that all children—even those who were "culturally deprived"—could learn to read using this method. Soon there was a strong response, first from academics and later from many classroom teachers, stating that the program was terrible. What I find particularly interesting, however, is that the primary issue of the conflict over Distar has not been over its instructional efficacy—usually the students did learn to read—but the expression of explicit power in the classroom. The liberal educators opposed the methods—the direct instruction, the explicit control exhibited by the teacher. As a matter of fact, it was not unusual (even now) to hear of the program spoken of as "fascist."

I am not an advocate of Distar, but I will return to some of the issues that the program—and direct instruction in general—raises in understanding the differences between progressive White educators and educators of color.

To explore those differences, I would like to present several statements typical of those made with the best of intentions by middle-class liberal educators. To the surprise of the speakers, it is not unusual for such content to be met by vocal opposition or stony silence from people of color. My attempt here is to examine the underlying assumptions of both camps.

"I want the same thing for everyone else's children as I want for mine."

To provide schooling for everyone's children that reflects liberal, middle-class values and aspirations is to ensure the maintenance of the status quo, to ensure that power, the culture of power, remains in the hands of those who already have it. Some children come to school with more accoutrements of the culture of power already in place—"cultural capital," as some critical theorists refer to it (for example, Apple, 1979)—some with less. Many liberal educators hold that the primary goal for education is for children to become autonomous, to develop fully who they are in the classroom setting without having arbitrary, outside standards forced upon them. This is a very reasonable goal for people whose children are already participants in the culture of power and who have already internalized its codes.

But parents who don't function within that culture often want something else. It's not that they disagree with the former aim, it's just that they want something more. They want to ensure that the school provides their children with discourse patterns, interactional styles, and spoken and written language codes that will allow them success in the larger society.

It was the lack of attention to this concern that created such a negative outcry in the Black community when well-intentioned White liberal educators introduced "dialect readers." These were seen as a plot to prevent the schools from teaching the linguistic aspects of the culture of power, thus dooming Black children to a permanent outsider caste. As one parent demanded, "My kids know how to be Black—you all teach them how to be successful in the White man's world."

Several Black teachers have said to me recently that as much as they'd like to believe otherwise, they cannot help but conclude that many of the "progressive" educational strategies imposed by liberals upon Black and poor children could only be based on a desire to ensure that the liberals' children get sole access to the dwindling pool of American jobs. Some have added that the liberal educators believe themselves to be operating with good intentions, but that these good intentions are only conscious delusions about their unconscious true motives. One of Black anthropologist John Gwaltney's (1980) informants reflects this perspective with her tongue-in-cheek observation that the biggest difference between Black folks and White folks is that Black folks *know* when they're lying!

Let me try to clarify how this might work in literacy instruction. A few years ago I worked on an analysis of two popular reading programs, Distar and a progressive program that focused on higher-level critical thinking skills. In one of the first lessons of the progressive program, the children are introduced to the names of the letter *m* and *e*. In the same lesson they are then taught the sound made by each of the letters, how to write each of the letters, and that when the two are blended together they produce the word *me*.

As an experienced first-grade teacher, I am convinced that a child needs to be familiar with a significant number of these concepts to be able to assimilate so much new knowledge in one sitting. By contrast, Distar presents the same information in about forty lessons.

I would not argue for the pace of the Distar lessons; such a slow pace would only bore most kids—but what happened in the other lesson is that it merely provided an opportunity for those who already knew the content to exhibit that they knew it, or at most perhaps to build one new concept onto what was already known. This meant that the child who did not come to school already primed with what was to be presented would be labeled as needing "remedial" instruction from day one; indeed, this determination would be made before he or she was ever taught. In fact, Distar was "successful" because it actually *taught* new information to children who had not already acquired it at home. Although the more progressive system was ideal for some children, for others it was a disaster.

I do not advocate a simplistic "basic skills" approach for children outside of the culture of power. It would be (and has been) tragic to operate as if these children were incapable of critical and higher-order thinking and reasoning. Rather, I suggest that schools must provide these children the content that other families from a different cultural orientation provide at home. This does not mean separating children according to family background, but instead, ensuring that each classroom incorporate strategies appropriate for all the children in its confines.

And I do not advocate that it is the school's job to attempt to change the homes of poor and non-White children to match the homes of those in the culture of power. That may indeed be a form of cultural genocide. I have frequently heard schools call poor parents "uncaring" when parents respond to the school's urging, that they change their home life in order to facilitate their children's learning, by saying, "But that's the school's job." What the school personnel fail to understand is that if the parents were members of the culture of power and lived by its rules and codes, then they would transmit those codes to their children. In fact, they transmit another culture that children must learn at home in order to survive in their communities.

"Child-centered, whole language, and process approaches are needed in order to allow a democratic state of free, autonomous, empowered adults, and because research has shown that children learn best through these methods."

People of color are, in general, skeptical of research as a determiner of our fates. Academic research has, after all, found us genetically inferior, culturally deprived, and verbally deficient. But beyond that general caveat, and despite my or others' personal preferences, there is little research data supporting the major tenets of process approaches over other forms of literacy instruction, and virtually no evidence that such approaches are more efficacious for children of color (Siddle 1986).

Although the problem is not necessarily inherent in the method, in some instances adherents of process approaches to writing create situations in which students ultimately find themselves held accountable for knowing a set of rules about which no one has ever directly informed them. Teachers do students no service to suggest, even implicitly, that "product" is not important. In this country, students will be judged on their product regardless of the process they utilized to achieve it. And that product, based as it is on the specific codes of a particular culture, is more readily produced when the directives of how to produce it are made explicit.

If such explicitness is not provided to students, what it feels like to people who are old enough to judge is that there are secrets being kept, that time is being wasted, that the teacher is abdicating his or her duty to teach. A doctoral student in my acquaintance was assigned to a writing class to hone his writing skills. The student was placed in the section led by a White professor who utilized a process approach, consisting primarily of having the students write essays and then assemble into groups to edit each others' papers. That procedure infuriated this particular student. He had many angry encounters with the teacher about what she was doing. In his words:

> I didn't feel she was teaching us anything. She wanted us to correct each others' papers and we were there to learn from her. She didn't teach anything, absolutely nothing.

> Maybe they're trying to learn what Black folks knew all the time. We understand how to improvise, how to express ourselves creatively. When I'm in a classroom, I'm not looking for that, I'm looking for structure, the more formal language.

> Now my buddy was in [a] Black teacher's class. And that lady was very good. She went through and explained and defined each part of the structure. This [White] teacher didn't get along with that Black teacher. She said that she didn't agree with her methods. But *I* don't think that White teacher *had* any methods.

When I told this gentleman that what the teacher was doing was called a process method of teaching writing, his response was, "Well, at least now I know that she *thought* she was doing *something*. I thought she was just a fool who couldn't teach and didn't want to try."

This sense of being cheated can be so strong that the student may be completely turned off to the educational system. Amanda Branscombe, an accomplished White teacher, recently wrote a letter discussing her work with working-class Black and White students at a community college in Alabama. She had given these students my "Skills and Other Dilemmas" article (Delpit, 1986) to read and discuss, and wrote that her students really understood and identified with what I was saying. To quote her letter:

> One young man said that he had dropped out of high school because he failed the exit exam. He noted that he had then passed the GED without a problem after three weeks of prep. He said that his high school English teacher claimed to use a process approach, but what she really did was hide behind fancy words to give herself permission to do nothing in the classroom.

The students I have spoken of seem to be saying that the teacher has denied them access to herself as the source of knowledge necessary to learn the forms they need to succeed. Again, I tentatively attribute the problem to teachers' resistance to exhibiting power in the classroom. Somehow, to exhibit one's personal power as expert source is viewed as disempowering one's students.

Two qualifiers are necessary, however. The teacher cannot be the only expert in the classroom. To deny students their own expert knowledge is to disempower them. Amanda Branscombe, when she was working with Black high school students classified as "slow learners" had the students analyze RAP songs to discover their underlying patterns. The students became the experts in explaining to the teacher the rules for creating a new RAP song. The teacher then used the patterns the students identified as a base to begin an explanation of the structure of grammar, and then of Shakespeare's plays. Both student and teacher are expert at what they know best.

The second qualifier is that merely adopting direct instruction is not the answer. Actual writing for real audiences and real purposes is a vital element in helping students to understand that they have an important voice in their own learning processes. Siddle (1988) examines the results of various kinds of interventions in a primarily process-oriented writing class for Black students. Based on readers' blind assessments, she found that the intervention that produced the most positive changes in the students' writing was a "mini-lesson" consisting of direct instruction about some standard writing convention. But what produced the *second* highest number of positive changes was a subsequent student-centered conference with the teacher. (Peer conferencing in this group of Black students who were not members of the culture of power produced the least number of changes in students' writing. However, the classroom teacher maintained—and I concur—that such activities are necessary to introduce the elements of "real audience" into the task, along with more teacher directed strategies.)

"It's really a shame but she (that Black teacher upstairs) seems to be so authoritarian, so focused on skills and so teacher directed. Those poor kids never seem to be allowed to really express their creativity. (And she even yells at them.)"

This statement directly concerns the display of power and authority in the classroom. One way to understand the difference in perspective between Black teachers and their progressive colleagues on this issue is to explore culturally influenced oral interactions.

In *Ways With Words,* Shirley Brice Heath (1983) quotes the verbal directives given by the middle-class "townspeople" teachers (p. 280):

—"Is this where the scissors belong?"

—"You want to do your best work today."

By contrast, many Black teachers are more likely to say:

—"Put those scissors on that shelf."

—"Put your name on the papers and make sure to get the right answer for each question."

Is one oral style more authoritarian than another?

Other researchers have identified differences in middle-class and working-class speech to children. Snow et al. (1976), for example, report that working-class mothers use more directives to their children than do middle- and upper-class parents. Middle-class parents are likely to give the directive to a child to take his bath as, "Isn't it time for your bath?" Even though the utterance is couched as a question, both child and adult understand it as a directive. The child may respond with "Aw Mom, can't I wait until . . . ," but whether or not negotiation is attempted, both conversants understand the intent of the utterance.

By contrast, a Black mother, in whose house I was recently a guest, said to her eight-year-old son, "Boy, get your rusty behind in that bathtub." Now I happen to know that this woman loves her son as much as any mother, but she would never have posed the directive to her son to take a bath in the form of a question. Were she to ask, "Would you like to take your bath now?" she would not have been issuing a directive but offering a true alternative. Consequently, as Heath suggests, upon entering school the child from such a family may not understand the indirect statement of the teacher as a direct command. Both White and Black working-class children in the communities Heath studied "had diffculty interpreting these indirect requests for adherence to an unstated set of rules" (p. 280).

But those veiled commands are commands nonetheless, representing true power, and with true consequences for disobedience. If veiled commands are ignored, the child will be labeled a behavior problem and possibly officially classified as behavior disordered. In other words, the attempt by the teacher to reduce an exhibition of power by expressing herself in indirect terms may remove the very explicitness that the child needs to understand the rules of the new classroom culture.

A Black elementary school principal in Fairbanks, Alaska, reported to me that she has a lot of difficulty with Black children who are placed in some White teachers' classrooms. The teachers often send the children to the office for disobeying teacher directives. Their parents are frequently called in for conferences. The parents' response to the teacher is usually the same: "They do what I say; if you just *tell* them what to do, they'll do it. I tell them at home that they have to listen to what you say." And so, does not the power still exist? Its veiled nature only makes it more diffcult for some children to respond appropriately, but that in no way mitigates its existence.

I don't mean to imply, however, that the only time the Black child disobeys the teacher is when he or she misunderstands the request for certain behavior. There are other factors that may produce such behavior. Black children expect an authority figure to act with authority. When the teacher instead acts as a "chum," the message sent is that this adult has no authority, and the children react accordingly. One reason this is so is that Black people often view issues of power and authority differently than people from mainstream middle-class backgrounds.[3] Many people of color expect authority to be earned by personal efforts and exhibited by personal characteristics. In other words, "the authoritative person gets to be a teacher because she is authoritative." Some members of middle-class cultures, by contrast, expect one to achieve authority by the acquisition of an authoritative role. That is, "the teacher is the authority because she is the teacher."

In the first instance, because authority is earned, the teacher must consistently prove the characteristics that give her authority. These characteristics may vary across cultures, but in the Black community they tend to cluster around several abilities. The authoritative teacher can control the class through exhibition of personal power; establishes meaningful interpersonal relationships that garner student respect; exhibits a strong belief that all students can learn; establishes a standard of achievement and "pushes" the students to achieve that standard; and holds the attention of the students by incorporating interactional features of Black communicative style in his or her teaching.

By contrast, the teacher whose authority is vested in the role has many more options of behavior at her disposal. For instance, she does not need to express any sense of personal power because her authority does not come from anything she herself does or says. Hence, the power she actually holds may be veiled in such questions/commands as "Would you like to sit down now?" If the children in her class understand authority as she does, it is mutually agreed upon that they are to obey her no matter how indirect, soft-spoken, or unassuming she may be. Her indirectness and soft-spokenness may indeed be, as I suggested earlier, an attempt to reduce the implication of overt power in order to establish a more egalitarian and nonauthoritarian classroom atmosphere.

If the children operate under another notion of authority, however, then there is trouble. The Black child may perceive the middle-class teacher as weak, ineffectual, and incapable of taking on the role of being the teacher; therefore, there is no need to follow her directives. In her dissertation, Michelle Foster (1987) quotes one young Black man describing such a teacher:

She is boring, bo::ring.* She could do something creative. Instead she just stands there. She can't control the class, doesn't know how to control the class. She asked me what she was doing wrong. I told her she just stands there like she's meditating. I told her she could be meditating for all I know. She says that we're supposed to know what to do. I told her I don't know nothin' unless she tells me. She just can't control the class. I hope we don't have her next semester. (pp. 67-68)

But of course the teacher may not view the problem as residing in herself but in the student, and the child may once again become the behavior-disordered Black boy in special education.

What characteristics do Black students attribute to the good teacher? Again, Foster's dissertation provides a quotation that supports my experience with Black students. A young Black man is discussing a former teacher with a group of friends:

---

*Editor's note: The colons [::] refer to elongated vowels.

We had f::un in her class, but she was mean. I can remember she used to say, "Tell me what's in the story, Wayne." She pushed, she used to get on me and push me to know. She made us learn. We had to get in the books. There was this tall guy and he tried to take her on, but she was in charge of that class and she didn't let anyone run her. I still have this book we used in her class. It's a bunch of stories in it. I just read one on Coca-Cola again the other day (p. 68).

To clarify, this student was *proud* of the teacher's "meanness," an attribute he seemed to describe as the ability to run the class and pushing and expecting students to learn. Now, does the liberal perspective of the negatively authoritarian Black teacher really hold up? I suggest that although all "explicit" Black teachers are not also good teachers, there are different attitudes in different cultural groups about which characteristics make for a good teacher. Thus, it is impossible to create a model for the good teacher without taking issues of culture and community context into account.

And now to the final comment I present for examination:

"Children have the right to their own language, their own culture. We must fight cultural hegemony and fight the system by insisting that children be allowed to express themselves in their own language style. It is not they, the children, who must change, but the schools. To push children to do anything else is repressive and reactionary."

A statement such as this originally inspired me to write the "Skills and Other Dilemmas" article. It was first written as a letter to a colleague in response to a situation that had developed in our department. I was teaching a senior-level teacher education course. Students were asked to prepare a written autobiographical document for the class that would also be shared with their placement school prior to their student teaching.

One student, a talented young Native American woman, submitted a paper in which the ideas were lost because of technical problems—from spelling to sentence structure to paragraph structure. Removing her name, I duplicated the paper for a discussion with some faculty members. I had hoped to initiate a discussion about what we could do to ensure that our students did not reach the senior level without getting assistance in technical writing skills when they needed them.

I was amazed at the response. Some faculty implied that the student should never have been allowed into the teacher education program. Others, some of the more progressive minded, suggested that I was attempting to function as gatekeeper by raising the issue and had internalized repressive and disempowering forces of the power elite to suggest that something was wrong with a Native American student just because she had another style of writing. With few exceptions, I found myself alone in arguing against both camps.

No, this student should not have been denied entry to the program. To deny her entry under the notion of upholding standards is to blame the victim for the crime. We cannot justifiably enlist exclusionary standards when the reason this student lacked the skills demanded was poor teaching at best and institutionalized racism at worst.

However, to bring this student into the program and pass her through without attending to obvious deficits in the codes needed for her to function effectively as a teacher is equally criminal—for though we may assuage our own consciences for not participating in victim blaming, she will surely be accused and convicted as soon as she leaves the university. As Native Alaskans were quick to tell me, and as I understood through my own experience in the Black community, not only would she not be hired as a teacher, but those who did not hire her would make the (false) assumption that the university was putting out only incompetent Natives and that they should stop looking seriously at any Native applicants. A White applicant who exhibits problems is an individual with problems. A person of color who exhibits problems immediately becomes a representative of her cultural group.

No, either stance is criminal. The answer is to *accept* students but also to take responsibility to *teach* them. I decided to talk to the student and found out she had recognized that she needed some assistance in the technical aspects of writing soon after she entered the university as a freshman. She had gone to various members of the education faculty and received the same two kinds of responses I met with four years later: faculty members told her either that she should not even attempt to be a teacher, or that it didn't matter and that she shouldn't worry about such trivial issues. In her desperation, she had found a helpful professor in the English Department, but he left the university when she was in her sophomore year.

We sat down together, worked out a plan for attending to specific areas of writing competence, and set up regular meetings. I stressed to her the need to use her own learning process as insight into how best to teach her future students those "skills" that her own schooling had failed to teach her. I gave her some explicit rules to follow in some areas; for others, we devised various kinds of journals that, along with readings about the structure of the language, allowed her to find her own insights into how the language worked. All that happened two years ago, and the young woman is now successfully teaching. What the experience led me to understand is that pretending that gatekeeping points don't exist is to ensure that many students will not pass through them.

Now you may have inferred that I believe that because there is a culture of power, everyone should learn the codes to participate in it, and that is how the world should be. Actually, nothing could be further from the truth. I believe in a diversity of style, and I believe the world will be diminished if cultural diversity is ever obliterated. Further, I believe strongly, as do my liberal colleagues, that each cultural group should have the right to maintain its own language style. When I speak, therefore, of the culture of power, I don't speak of how I wish things to be but of how they are.

I further believe that to act as if power does not exist is to ensure that the power status quo remains the same. To imply to children or adults (but of course the adults won't believe you anyway) that it doesn't matter how you talk or how you write is to ensure their ultimate failure. I prefer to be honest with my students. Tell them that their language and cultural style is unique and wonderful but that there is a political power game that is also being played, and if they want to be in on that game there are certain games that they too must play.

But don't think that I let the onus of change rest entirely with the students. I am also involved in political work both inside and outside of the educational system, and that political work demands that I place myself to influence as many gatekeeping points as possible. And it is there that I agitate for change—pushing gatekeepers to open their doors to a variety of styles and codes. What I'm saying, however, is that I do not believe that political change toward diversity can be effected from the bottom up, as do some of my colleagues. They seem to believe that if we accept and encourage diversity within classrooms of children, then diversity will automatically be accepted at gatekeeping points.

I believe that will never happen. What will happen is that the students who reach the gatekeeping points—like Amanda Branscombe's student who dropped out of high school because he failed his exit exam—will understand that they have been lied to and will react accordingly. No, I am certain that if we are truly to effect societal change, we cannot do so from the bottom up, but we must push and agitate from the top down. And in the meantime, we must take the responsibility to *teach*, to provide for students who do not already possess them, the additional codes of power.[4]

But I also do not believe that we should teach students to passively adopt an alternate code. They must be encouraged to understand the value of the code they already possess as well as to understand the power realities in this country. Otherwise they will be unable to work to change these realities. And how does one do that?

Martha Demientieff, a masterly Native Alaskan teacher of Athabaskan Indian students, tells me that her students, who live in a small, isolated, rural village of less than two hundred people, are not aware that there are different codes of English. She takes their writing and analyzes it for features of what has been referred to by Alaskan linguists as "Village English," and then covers half a bulletin board with words or phrases from the students' writing, which she labels "Our Heritage Language." On the other half of the bulletin board she puts the equivalent statements in "standard English," which she labels "Formal English."

She and the students spend a long time on the "Heritage English" section, savoring the words, discussing the nuances. She tells the students, "That's the way we say things. Doesn't it feel good? Isn't it the absolute best way of getting that idea across?" Then she turns to the other side of the board. She tells the students that there are people, not like those in their village, who judge others by the way they talk or write.

> We listen to the way people talk, not to judge them, but to tell what part of the river they come from. These other people are not like that. They think everybody needs to talk like them. Unlike us, they have a hard time hearing what people say if they don't talk exactly like them. Their way of talking and writing is called "Formal English."

> We have to feel a little sorry for them because they have only one way to talk. We're going to learn two ways to say things. Isn't that better? One way will be our Heritage way. The other will be Formal English. Then, when we go to get jobs, well be able to talk like those people who only know and can only really listen to one way. Maybe after we get the jobs we can help them to learn how it feels to have another language, like ours, that feels so good. We'll talk like them when we have to, but we'll always know our way is best.

Martha then does all sorts of activities with the notions of Formal and Heritage or informal English. She tells the students,

> In the village, everyone speaks informally most of the time unless there's a potlatch or something. You don't think about it, you don't worry about following any rules—it's sort of like how you eat food at a picnic—nobody pays attention to whether you use your fingers or a fork, and it feels so good. Now, Formal English is more like a formal dinner. There are rules to follow about where the knife and fork belong, about where people sit, about how you eat. That can be really nice, too, because it's nice to dress up sometimes.

The students then prepare a formal dinner in the class, for which they dress up and set a big table with fancy tablecloths, china, and silverware. They speak only Formal English at this meal. Then they prepare a picnic where only informal English is allowed.

She also contrasts the "wordy" academic way of saying things with the metaphoric style of Athabaskan. The students discuss how book language always uses more words, but in Heritage language, the shorter way of saying something is always better. Students then write papers in the academic way, discussing with Martha and with each other whether they believe they've said enough to sound like a book. Next, they take those papers and try to reduce the meaning to a few sentences. Finally, students further reduce the message to a "saying" brief enough to go on the front of a T-shirt, and the sayings are put on little paper T-shirts that the students cut out and hang throughout the room. Sometimes the students reduce other authors' wordy texts to their essential meanings as well.

The following transcript provides another example. It is from a conversation between a Black teacher and a Southern Black high school student named Joey, who is a speaker of Black English. The teacher believes it very important to discuss openly and honestly the issues of language diversity and power. She has begun the discussion by giving the student a children's book written in Black English to read.

Teacher: What do you think about that book?
    Joey: I think it's nice.
Teacher: Why?
    Joey: I don't know. It just told about a Black family, that's all.
Teacher: Was it difficult to read?
    Joey: No.
Teacher: Was the text different from what you have seen in other books?
    Joey: Yeah. The writing was.
Teacher: How?
    Joey: It use more of a southern-like accent in this book.
Teacher: Uhm-hmm. Do you think that's good or bad?
    Joey: Well, uh, I don't think it's good for people down this a way, cause that's the way they grow up talking anyway. They ought to get the right way to talk.
Teacher: Oh. So you think it's wrong to talk like that?
    Joey: Well . . . [*Laughs*]

> *Teacher:* Hard question, huh?
> *Joey:* Uhm-hmm, that's a hard question. But I think they shouldn't make books like that.
> *Teacher:* Why?
> *Joey:* Because they not using the right way to talk and in school they take off for that and li' l chirren grow up talking like that and reading like that so they might think that's right and all the time they getting bad grades in school, talking like that and writing like that.
> *Teacher:* Do you think they should be getting bad grades for talking like that?
> *Joey:* [*Pauses, answers very slowly*] No . . . No.
> *Teacher:* So you don't think that it matters whether you talk one way or another?
> *Joey:* No, not long as you understood.
> *Teacher:* Uhm-hmm. Well, that's a hard question for me to answer, too. It's, ah, that's a question that's come up in a lot of schools now as to whether they should correct children who speak the way we speak all the time. Cause when we're talking to each other we talk like that even though we might not talk like that when we get into other situations, and who's to say whether it's—
> *Joey:* [*Interrupting*] Right or wrong.
> *Teacher:* Yeah.
> *Joey:* Maybe they ought to come up with another kind of . . . maybe Black English or something. A course in Black English. Maybe Black folks would be good in that cause people talk, I mean Black people talk like that, so . . . but I guess there's a right way and wrong way to talk, you know, not regarding what race. I don't know.
> *Teacher:* But who decided what's right or wrong?
> *Joey:* Well that's true . . . I guess White people did.
> [*Laughter. End of tape.*]

Notice how throughout the conversation Joey's consciousness has been raised by thinking about codes of language. This teacher further advocates having students interview various personnel officers in actual workplaces about their attitudes toward divergent styles in oral and written language. Students begin to understand how arbitrary language standards are, but also how politically charged they are. They compare various pieces written in different styles, discuss the impact of different styles on the message by making translations and back translations across styles, and discuss the history, apparent purpose, and contextual appropriateness of each of the technical writing rules presented by their teacher. *And* they practice writing different forms to different audiences based on rules appropriate for each audience. Such a program not only "teaches" standard linguistic forms, but also explores aspects of power as exhibited through linguistic forms.

Tony Burgess, in a study of secondary writing in England by Britton, Burgess, Martin, McLeod, and Rosen (1975/1977), suggests that we should not teach "iron conventions . . . imposed without rationale or grounding in communicative intent," . . . but "critical and ultimately cultural awarenesses" (p. 54). Courtney Cazden (1987) calls for a two-pronged approach:

1. Continuous opportunities for writers to participate in some authentic bit of the un-ending conversation . . . thereby becoming part of a vital community of talkers and writers in a particular domain, and

2. Periodic, temporary focus on conventions of form, taught as cultural conventions expected in a particular community. (p. 20)

Just so that there is no confusion about what Cazden means by a focus on conven-tions of form, or about what I mean by "skills," let me stress that neither of us is speak-ing of page after page of "skill sheets" creating compound words or identifying nouns and adverbs, but rather about helping students gain a useful knowledge of the conven-tions of print while engaging in real and useful communicative activities. Kay Rowe Grubis, a junior high school teacher in a multicultural school, makes lists of certain technical rules for her eighth graders' review and then gives them papers from a third grade to "correct." The students not only have to correct other students' work, but also tell them why they have changed or questioned aspects of the writing.

A village teacher, Howard Cloud, teaches his high school students the conven-tions of formal letter writing and the formulation of careful questions in the context of issues surrounding the amendment of the Alaska Land Claims Settlement Act. Native Alaskan leaders hold differing views on this issue, critical to the future of lo-cal sovereignty and land rights. The students compose letters to leaders who reside in different areas of the state seeking their perspectives, set up audioconference calls for interview/debate sessions, and, finally, develop a videotape to present the differing views.

To summarize, I suggest that students must be *taught* the codes needed to partici-pate fully in the mainstream of American life, not by being forced to attend to hol-low, inane, decontextualized subskills, but rather within the context of meaningful communicative endeavors; that they must be allowed the resource of the teacher's expert knowledge, while being helped to acknowledge their own "expertness" as well; and that even while students are assisted in learning the culture of power, they must also be helped to learn about the arbitrariness of those codes and about the power relationships they represent.

I am also suggesting that appropriate education for poor children and children of color can only be devised in consultation with adults who share their culture. Black parents, teachers of color, and members of poor communities must be allowed to par-ticipate fully in the discussion of what kind of instruction is in their children's best in-terest. Good liberal intentions are not enough. In an insightful study entitled "Racism without Racists: Institutional Racism in Urban Schools," Massey, Scott, and Dornbusch (1975) found that under the pressures of teaching, and with all intentions of "being nice," teachers had essentially stopped attempting to teach Black children. In their words: "We have shown that oppression can arise out of warmth, friendliness, and concern. Paternalism and a lack of challenging standards are creating a distorted system of evaluation in the schools" (p. 10). Educators must open themselves to, and allow themselves to be affected by, these alternative voices.

In conclusion, I am proposing a resolution for the skills/process debate. In short, the debate is fallacious; the dichotomy is false. The issue is really an illusion created initially not by teachers but by academics whose world view demands the creation of categorical divisions—not for the purpose of better teaching, but for the goal of easier analysis. As I have been reminded by many teachers since the publication of my article, those who are most skillful at educating Black and poor children do not allow themselves to be placed in "skills" or "process" boxes. They understand the need for both approaches, the need to help students to establish their own voices, but to coach those voices to produce notes that will be heard clearly in the larger society.

The dilemma is not really in the debate over instructional methodology, but rather in communicating across cultures and in addressing the more fundamental issue of power, of whose voice gets to be heard in determining what is best for poor children and children of color. Will Black teachers and parents continue to be silenced by the very forces that claim to "give voice" to our children? Such an outcome would be tragic, for both groups truly have something to say to one another. As a result of careful listening to alternative points of view, I have myself come to a viable synthesis of perspectives. But both sides do need to be able to listen, and I contend that it is those with the most power, those in the majority, who must take the greater responsibility for initiating the process.

To do so takes a very special kind of listening, listening that requires not only open eyes and ears, but open hearts and minds. We do not really see through our eyes or hear through our ears, but through our beliefs. To put our beliefs on hold is to cease to exist as ourselves for a moment—and that is not easy. It is painful as well, because it means turning yourself inside out, giving up your own sense of who you are, and being willing to see yourself in the unflattering light of another's angry gaze. It is not easy, but it is the only way to learn what it might feel like to be someone else and the only way to start the dialogue.

There are several guidelines. We must keep the perspective that people are experts on their own lives. There are certainly aspects of the outside world of which they may not be aware, but they can be the only authentic chroniclers of their own experience. We must not be too quick to deny their interpretations, or accuse them of "false consciousness." We must believe that people are rational beings, and therefore always act rationally. We may not understand their rationales, but that in no way militates against the existence of these rationales or reduces our responsibility to attempt to apprehend them. And finally, we must learn to be vulnerable enough to allow our world to turn upside down in order to allow the realities of others to edge themselves into our consciousness. In other words, we must become ethnographers in the true sense.

Teachers are in an ideal position to play this role, to attempt to get all of the issues on the table in order to initiate true dialogue. This can only be done, however, by seeking out those whose perspectives may differ most, by learning to give their words complete attention, by understanding one's own power, even if that power stems merely from being in the majority, by being unafraid to raise questions about discrimination and voicelessness with people of color, and to listen, no, to *hear* what they say. I suggest that the results of such interactions may be the most powerful and empowering coalescence yet seen in the educational realm—for *all* teachers and for *all* the students they teach.

Notes

1. Such a discussion, limited as it is by space constraints, must treat the intersection of class and race some-what simplistically. For the sake of clarity, however, let me define a few terms: "Black" is used herein to refer to those who share some or all aspects of "core black culture" (Gwaltney, 1980, p. xxiii), that is, the mainstream of Black America—neither those who have entered the ranks of the bourgeoisie nor those who are participants in the disenfranchised underworld. "Middle-class" is used broadly to refer to the predominantly White American "mainstream." There are, of course, non-White people who also fit into this category; at issue is their cultural identification, not necessarily the color of their skin. (I must add that there are other non-White people, as well as poor White people, who have indicated to me that their perspectives are similar to those attributed herein to Black people.)
2. *Multicultural Britain: "Crosstalk,"* National Centre of Industrial Language Training, Commission for Racial Equality, London, England, John Twitchin, Producer.
3. I would like to thank Michelle Foster, who is presently planning a more in-depth treatment of the subject, for her astute clarification of the idea.
4. Bernstein (1975) makes a similar point when he proposes that different educational frames cannot be successfully institutionalized in the lower levels of education until there are fundamental changes at the post-secondary levels.

Works Cited

Apple, M. W. (1979). *Ideology and curriculum.* Boston: Routledge & Kegan Paul.

Bernstein, B. (1975). "Class and pedagogies: Visible and invisible." In B. Bernstein, *Class, codes, and control* (Vol. 3). Boston: Routledge & Kegan Paul.

Britton, J., Burgess, T., Martin, N., McLeod, A., & Rosen, H. (1975/1977). *The development of writing abilities.* London: Macmillan Education for the Schools Council, and Urbana, IL: National Council of Teachers of English.

Cazden, C. (1987, January). *The myth of autonomous text.* Paper presented at the Third International Conference on Thinking, Hawaii.

Delpit, L. D. (1986). "Skills and other dilemmas of a progressive Black educator." *Harvard Educational Review,* 56, (4), 379-385.

Foster, M. (1987). *"It's cookin' now": An ethnographic study of the teaching style of a successful Black teacher in an urban community college.* Unpublished doctoral dissertation, Harvard University.

Gwaltney, J. (1980). *Drylongso.* New York: Vintage Books.

Heath, S. B. (1983). *Ways with words.* Cambridge: Cambridge University Press.

Massey, G. C., Scott, M. V., & Dornbusch, S. M. (1975). "Racism without racists: Institutional racism in urban schools." *The Black Scholar,* 7(3), 2-11.

Siddle, E. V. (1986). *A critical assessment of the natural process approach to teaching writing.* Unpublished qualifying paper, Harvard University.

Siddle, E. V. (1988). *The effect of intervention strategies on thc revisions ninth graders make in a narrative essay.* Unpublished doctoral dissertation, Harvard University.

Snow, C. E., Arlman-Rup, A., Hassing, Y., Josbe, J., Joosten, J., & Vorster, J. (1976). Mother's speech in three social classes. *Journal of Psycholinguistic Research,* 5, 1-20.

Acknowledgments

I take full responsibility for all that appears herein; however, aside from those mentioned by name in this text, I would like to thank all of the educators and students around the country who have been so willing to contribute their perspectives to the formulation of these ideas, especially Susan Jones, Catherine Blunt, Dee Stickman, Sandra Gamble, Willard Taylor, Mickey Monteiro, Denise Burden, Evelyn Higbee, Joseph Delpit, Jr., Valerie Montoya, Richard Cohen, and Mary Denise Thompson.

Culture as an Instructional Resource in the Multiethnic Composition Classroom
by G. Genevieve Patthey-Chavez
and Constance Gergen

Introduction

Cultural difference can become the starting point for a rich and rewarding exchange between writing students and their teachers. Many of the basic writing courses into which budding college students are inducted are grappling with a growing influx of students from diverse ethnic and cultural backgrounds. The presence of different voices and visions of the world can be transformed into an instructional resource, a bridge between teachers and students. A careful, well-structured exploration of student and student-teacher differences can provide a curriculum that pulls in, validates, and ultimately builds on the divergent points of view about writing that need to converge to fulfill the basic writing course's mission. It is this curriculum we hope to describe here, a curriculum we have developed over the course of several years of teaching culturally and ethnically diverse basic college writing courses.

Because of the changing ethnic make-up of many basic college writing classes, their standardizing purpose is taking on a problematic character. Indeed, whether basic composition courses ought to teach only one particular essayist standard is increasingly being called into question on both practical and ethical grounds. In practical terms, it is hardly the case that only one essayist writing standard exists across disciplines. More difficult still are the potential ethical problems associated with the imposition of one such standard on students who may be unfamiliar with and/or marginalized by that standard. Yet the traditional function of basic college writing courses—establishing a hegemonic, dominant mainstream "discourse" (Gee 1991) at the expense of others—has not really changed. The essayist standard may be un-raveling empirically, but institutional writing curricula with well-defined perfor-mance criteria and exit exams spell out rather clearly that there still are standards to be met. Composition teachers are left facing a dilemma: On the one hand, a plethora of student-centered pedagogical approaches claim to provide a better instructional alternative because they validate student views and student writing. They are in fact so popular that they may be officially endorsed by writing programs.[1] On the other hand, students whose writing styles fall outside of the enduring canons of their in-stitutions are usually penalized for it. Teachers are to embrace diversity, but deliver conformity. This dilemma can be especially acute in a multiethnic composition classroom.

Old and deep-seated beliefs rooted in a racist and xenophobic ideology from the turn of the century decry cultural diversity as divisive and dangerous for both na-tions and individuals (Cummins 1981; Kloss 1977). These beliefs persist in spite of more recent protestations to the contrary.[2] Framed thusly, cultural difference be-comes a liability for students, who have to overcome language or cultural "barriers" in their educational quest (Sue and Padilla 1986; Suarez-Orosco 1989: 22-48); and it is a challenge for the instructional infrastructure in charge of "assisting" such stu-dents (Rumberger 1989). Cultural difference is said essentially to impede the work and eventual success of students and teachers alike.

To help instructors mediate between the contradictory requirements of their mul-tiethnic basic writing classes, we advocate a pedagogy that develops and encour-ages essayist literacy *in concert with* rather than at the expense of student voices. Drawing on the insights of educational critics like Freire (1982), the Vygotskyan school of psycholinguistics (1962; 1978; cf., Engeström 1986) and the Bakhtin cir-cle (1981; cf., Todorov 1985), we have attempted to implement a curriculum that capitalizes on cultural diversity. Ours is a curriculum for practitioners, an attempt to flesh out student centered principles that have been mulled over in the composition teaching community for quite some time, but that have not often been found rele-vant by teachers. Our experience in inner-city and ESL basic writing classes pro-vides the observational and testimonial support on which our findings are based. We want to stress that this experience informs our effort as much as the theoretical work from which we draw. Just as we propose to construct a bridge between stu-dents and teachers, so too do we hope to build an equally crucial bridge between practitioners and the body of research and theory meant to guide their efforts.[3]

Traditional Theoretical Approaches to Literacy Education

Several leading metaphors have greatly influenced how writing education is conceptualized and undertaken in North American education. The deconstruction of these metaphors unravels both misguided (but robust) theories about learning and the metaphors' disempowering impact on the work of both students and teachers.

Learning how to read and write, or how to do a better job of it, is commonly considered the acquisition of "skills" that are transmitted from teacher to student. In his 1988 book *Joining the Literacy Club*, Frank Smith argues against this view. The "skills acquisition" metaphor revolves around the notion of *information transfer* from one person to another (or others). Smith points out that this view, when applied to literacy instruction, overlooks the true nature of literacy activities:

> The danger in using the word skill in conjunction with reading and writing is that it can justify teaching blindly through instruction and drill. Literacy is a matter not of honing skills but of increasing confidence, familiarity, and understanding, all consequences of meaningful use. (103)

Moreover, when we let the metaphors of "information transfer" and "skills acquisition" inform our teaching, we, as teachers, are tacitly endorsing what Freire (1982) calls the "banking concept of education." Information and skills take on the characteristics of commodities. Teachers become the vendors of these commodities, and the academic success of students hinges on their consumption of such commodities.

In a dehumanizing cycle, students become "objects of assistance" within a system that denies that their own experiences and views have any value. In order to receive this assistance, they are frequently asked to repudiate their own ways of expression and are offered the controlled discourse of an elite as a replacement. That discourse reflects and privileges elite views, disparaging all others as simply not up to standard. Under these conditions, if students are to succeed, and become "good" readers and writers, they must learn the "correct" way to engage the world and the world of print; that is, the hegemonic discourse of the elite.

In the United States, the basic writing course often continues to focus on teaching remedial students the "skills" they are lacking, thus endorsing a "banking" view of education. This has not helped bilingual/bicultural students, who find themselves in remedial education in disproportionate numbers. Given the theory of literacy underlying "banking" education, this is an entirely predictable result. It is their difference which, after all, makes so many bicultural/bilingual students candidates for remediation. The liability represented by that difference is then often compounded: Encouraged to adopt elite views in order to conform to the writing norms of essayist literacy, students may come to disparage their own cultural origins while finding themselves simultaneously barred from elite membership. The banking view can become psychologically devastating.

To develop a different instructional approach, we have turned to Freire's alternative educational philosophy of "problem-posing" education. Working primarily in pre- and post-revolutionary Latin American contexts characterized by extreme class differences and explicit elite domination, Freire argues that the only way to deal with the literacy needs of oppressed populations is to create a form of education that would expose the elite-dominated values inherent in most available literacy materials and practices. To do so, he would ask his classes to ponder the origins of such problems as bad housing. While students might at first blame themselves or their neighbors for the dilapidated state of their own neighborhoods, theywould soon discuss bad services and their origins. Problem-posing literacy education takes as its starting point the learner's historicity, stimulating self-reflection and an awareness of the social production of history and oppression. It views the learner's own life and experiences as valuable resources with which to counter the elite view of the world. In this manner, elite values can be seen as the cultural practices they are and the "false consciousness" they engender can be confronted with a more critical one.

We propose to apply Freire's problem-posing philosophy to the teaching of basic college writing in a multiethnic setting. We aim to counter the prevailing view of cultural and linguistic difference as a liability by encouraging a new consciousness about cultural and linguistic variability. The Bakhtin circle, empirically supported by sociolinguistic research, provides an alternative view through which literacy practices can be redefined.

The Bakhtin circle contends that "language," and by extension "literacy," is a heterogeneous collection of "voices" from which language and literacy users continuously draw to engage with their worlds. If linguistic heterogeneity is the rule rather than the exception, cultural diversity cannot be a deviation from a homogeneous norm. Brought to the fore in the basic writing classroom, this view of language forces a reconsideration of the "norm" that can be highly beneficial. This norm is, in fact, nothing more or less than a set of writing *conventions* endorsed by a particular discourse community. Other communities, such as the bicultural students' communities of origin, endorse different sets of conventions that express different communicative preferences. Ideally, bilingual/bicultural students learn from unraveling the norm that "different" is not synonymous with "deficit," and that their language abilities are not deficient. Rather, they have a considerable store from which to draw in order to acquire new forms of expression, including the forms they will need as college students.

A Bakhtinian reading of the phenomenon of language allows one to (re)define literacy as the situated practices involving print of particular discourse communities. These communities use print for very specific, historically grounded communicative reasons. Essayist literacy is usually a benefit of membership in a distinct, definable discourse community, which socializes its members in its particular expressive tradition. Learning it, as well as other, even more specific discourse styles, is a function of that membership. All novices are socialized into literacy practices, regardless of their ethnic background, which does not affect the literacy learning process, but rather access to membership.

A growing body of sociolinguistic research into situated linguistic and literacy practices lends strong empirical evidence to both Freire's analysis of traditional literacy instruction and to the Bakhtin circle's conceptualization of language. Literacy research not only owes empirical debts to that research, but also some important conceptual ones. Recent literacy research aims to reach a socioculturally grounded understanding of the uses and purposes of literacy practices. To do so, it has adopted and adapted some key notions from sociolinguistic theory, foremost among them those of *speech communities and speech events* (Gumperz and Hymes 1964; 1972).

The first of these notions denotes the existence of a shared system of linguistic behaviors and beliefs amongst a group of people. For as many different sets of behaviors and beliefs as there are in the world, there are an equal number of such communities. According to Gumperz and Hymes (1972), speech events are "certain communicative routines" which members of a given speech community recognize on the basis of their "special rules of speech and nonverbal behavior." Thus, a given speech community will have many different speech events that help to define it as a particular community. One becomes a member of a speech community through meaningful apprenticeship, by participating in the speech practices of the community. There is an indexical relationship between speech practices and group membership so that to engage in the practices effectively signals affiliation.

Applied to the context of literacy, speech communities comprise a shared set of behaviors, values, and norms revolving around print. Like a speech event, a *literacy event* (Heath 1982) is characterized by socially organized communicative routines, but these are centered on print rather than oral discourse. The 1985 *Journal of Education* collection of literacy papers as well as the work of Heath (1983), Cook-Gumperz (1986), Scollon and Scollon (1981), and Gee (1991) are all exemplary of the recent merging of literacy research and sociolinguistic analysis. According to these researchers, learning to read and write requires socialization into a set of values, beliefs and ways of doing, in short into a *discourse style* that will in turn index group membership in a given literacy or discourse community. And literacy practices are just as multifaceted and cross-culturally variable as speech practices, requiring close, meaningful contact and eventual participation on the part of novices in order to become accessible.

These findings lend empirical weight to Freire's analysis of traditional literacy as a set of practices aimed to validate elite perceptions. A dominant discourse is as much a cultural product as other discourse styles, and it originates in its own discourse community. If students are to master that discourse, they need access to its community of origin, and such access is problematic, at best. As pointed out by Gee (1991), hegemonic discourses bode ill for nontraditional students, for there is an inherent contradiction in assuming the trappings of a group from which one is excluded *a priori*. It should not be surprising that such efforts result in feelings of inadequacy and alienation.

Sociolinguistic research offers argumentative and methodological models that can be adapted for problem-posing, and thus can become part of a potential solution to this dilemma. Just like sociolinguists, students can observe their own and their institution's literacy practices in order to see the correspondences between social setting and language choices. Our claim is that the acquisition of literacy practices is a function of membership. By encouraging our students to become participant-observers of the discourse communities' engendering practices they are supposed to master, we are trying to provide them with an alternative writing apprenticeship, in effect an alternative means to membership.

In addition, accumulated student observations will bear out the Bakhtin circle's finding that, with respect to speech and literacy practices, heterogeneity (and thus cultural diversity) is in fact the norm. This should unmask the fact that any norm represented by a hegemonic discourse is a false norm. And once the acquisition of schooled or essayist discourse styles is redefined as a specialized apprenticeship, the crucial factors leading to that acquisition is no longer linguistic or cultural homogeneity, but meaningful participation in an inclusive discourse community.

This is where the multiethnic classroom presents something of an advantage. That classroom is already heterogeneous, and the connection between community of origin and discourse styles is quite apparent to any serious observer. Our curriculum takes advantage of this linguistic wealth. It explores the voices of different student discourse communities, and juxtaposes them with voices from the academic discourse community. We hope that this double exploration brings about the kind of meaningful engagement with print that our students need to become members of the literacy club.

Theory into Practice

The criticism and research reviewed thus far provide insights into the roots of the discourse problems faced by a culturally diverse student body and yield some promising alternative starting points for instruction in the basic college writing classroom. Like most critical and investigative work, however, it has yet to engage in true dialogue with practitioners. Establishing such a dialogue is our project. Having drawn practical conclusions from research and criticism for three years, we have begun to flesh out an applied program for teachers. Our program, developed within the general spirit of problem-posing education, aims to establish a classroom "zone of proximal development." Following Vygotsky's pioneering framework, it is a curriculum that challenges all students to break beyond their actual level of performance to a more developed one with expert guidance (1978, 86). In addition, it challenges teachers to let students guide them to a better understanding of their needs and abilities.

Vygotsky concluded sixty years ago that "human learning presupposes a specific social nature and a process by which [novices] grow into the intellectual life of those around them" (1978, 88). He argued that instruction "must be aimed not so much at the ripe as at the ripening functions" of these novices (1962, 104). While one is learning to become literate, the key social process is meaningful participation in an inclusive discourse community. In a classroom, such a community can provide novice writers informed access to their target discourses. Our curriculum attempts to create one by examining and analyzing potential target discourses through a problem-posing frame, and by pulling the students into that analysis at every step. Culturally diverse students can become a true asset for such a project: They turn the classroom into a truly heteroglossic one, and thus help foreground the (seemingly transparent) cultural roots and interpretive processes at the basis of all discourse practices.

A number of principles have guided our adaptation of problem-posing education to basic writing instruction in the inner city. Three years of *field testing* in a number of inner-city composition classrooms have so far confirmed their usefulness. These *field-tested* principles can be summarized as follows:

1. Instructional activities are integrated around a central communicative or discourse problem that is analyzed through a problem-posing frame. In order to turn the classroom into a community of practice, direct instruction is balanced with repeated and intensive workshops, and the student voices need to be alternated with voices from the target academic discourse.

2. Integration and balance between student and teacher expertise is achieved with assignments that:
   a. focus on and take advantage of students' strengths: their knowledge of their own world and of their own beliefs;
   b. encourage the students to engage with their new college discourse community, especially through print;
   c. demonstrate to the students the functions of different essay writing conventions and styles. For example, the function of a cause and effect analysis is to find or argue about responsibilities for changes.
3. The analytical thrust of each unit is maintained through the use of two central questions about text. These foreground the fact that texts are human products and that their use entails shared values. They are:
   a. What is the author communicating to you? (What are you trying to communicate?)
   b. How do you know? (How would your audience know?)

When considering these two questions, students usually discover that authors often shape and manipulate language to appeal to their audiences, and that students can do the same.

Compared to Freire's original project, our work is a modest form of problem-posing education. Freire sought to give his students a better understanding of the historical and human origin of their circumstances. That understanding presumably included knowledge of how to effect changes. We seek to give our students a better understanding of the historical and human origin of various discourse practices, and hope to gain a better understanding about their ideas and forms of expression in return. The knowledge we offer includes information about essayist literacy as hegemonic discourse, and of the students' own position with respect to that discourse. In the knowledge we gain, we usually find the basis for joint educational activities. On the whole, we hope to give our students more power over their own or their second language.

Working in the Multiethnic Classroom

Students from linguistic and ethnic minorities are often considered *least likely to succeed* in mainstream institutions. As members of nondominant speech communities, they usually lack the kind of literacy experiences that would have socialized them into a mainstream, essayist discourse. In Gee's words, facility in mainstream discourse is "a product of acquisition, that is, it requires exposure to models in natural, meaningful, and functional settings and teaching is not liable to be very successful" (1991, 28). But essay writing may be neither natural nor meaningful in the lives of most minority students, whose classroom experiences have often not been terribly functional. Conversely, our own expectations about writing within our academic discourse communities have often been shaped by a lifetime's worth of professional experiences with text and literacy that few of our students have shared.

In order to start one functional cycle and to begin bridging the gap in experience at the start of a composition classroom, one can begin with what Gee calls "metaknowledge." New college writers are made conscious of what is expected of them as future members of academic discourse communities through joint consciousness-raising rooted in historical and contextual analysis. An important first step is to have students focus on themselves, their writing histories and beliefs about essay writing. This follows from Smith's (1988) contention that students, especially those marginalized by the dominant discourse, "need to find sense and relevance in the situation they are in" (54). As a way to start, the students can be asked to discuss what they think a "good essay" should be, and that discussion can form the basis for a first assignment and a first instructional unit.

Even if students are unfamiliar with essays, they often have their own (and sometimes their former teachers') folk theories about such texts. These folk theories can be elicited in a discussion format and/or in writing, the objective being to get students to be as explicit as possible. This exercise will yield a number of interesting but often vague and underelaborated theories of the good essay. For example, many students will say that a *good essay* has a strong beginning, and the instructor can press further by asking: "What do you mean by strong?" Ultimately, several rounds of questions like these produce an extensive dialogue through which a more fully elaborated theory—is constructed. The student also begins to explicate and perhaps even analyze his/her beliefs about literacy practices.

The analysis of the students' folk theories will eventually lead to their deconstruction, as can be documented by one of the present authors. Having been told that a *good essay* should "cover all possible sides of a given issue or topic," she pressed on and forced a more thorough analysis of both this belief and its origin. She asked the students if it were ever possible to cover "all sides" of an issue in a single essay, and started to list some of the sides to cover for a particular topic. Students soon realized that it was not possible, some with obvious relief. Through this questioning, they were also coming to realize that some of the ideas they had assimilated from past instructional practices were not written in stone. In fact, they began to sense that writing successfully had less to do with innate ability or deficit and more to do with working on and negotiating joint meaning through print.

A second way to raise consciousness about the relationship between writing and its origin and use is to have new college writers collect information about particular contexts. These student *mini-ethnographies* of print can start with a thorough accounting of the uses of writing at work or at home.[5] They then become the raw material with which to begin an analysis of the relationship between form and function. Students who often initially insist that "we don't read or write anything where I work" find an amazing array of print and almost universally conclude that "reading and writing is really important." They also come to understand *why* print may be important in a given context. A construction worker's account of written safety instructions, for example, drove that point home while at the same time leading to a more detailed and thorough discussion of the conventions of safety signs. Since the size and color of safety signs vary considerably cross-culturally, opening the discussion up to the whole class brought out their variability, and the local human conventions governing their makeup.

The articulation of local rules and standards, whether prompted by definitions of the *good essay* or descriptions of the uses of print in a variety of contexts, forms the basis for a reconsideration of essay writing in general. This reconsideration stresses the human origin of essay writing practices, and emphasizes active negotiation. Student participation in these activities serves to overcome the "student-as-objects-of-assistance" mindset common in banking forms of education. The articulation of the rules and standards of different essay writing traditions can also lead to a historical review for our students, and to an analysis of their present situation. If they are in remedial writing classes, for example, questions soon arise about the process and the criteria by which they came to be labeled "at risk." Students may also ask themselves why, in a world full of heterogeneity and "minority" peoples, they are considered the "minority" writers and the rather small community of English teachers represents the mainstream. Such students may even put the many labels that permeate their lives into perspective, and in deconstructing them, may gain some independence from their "institutional grip" (Douglas 1986).

The Teacher as Mediator

While it is necessary to have students explore their own beliefs about essay writing and other literacy events, it is equally important that they gain some insights into the values and beliefs of target discourses. They need "inside information" about future discourse communities that have not been too welcoming, and English teachers are an ideal source of such information. Teachers need to strike a delicate balance here. They have genuine authority over the subject matter, and they do know the standards to which their students will be held. But too much emphasis on standards and authority will quickly degenerate into a unidirectional, "banking" exchange. This conundrum can become especially acute when the teacher is responding to student work. How does one discuss difference when that difference is clearly stigmatized outside the classroom?

To achieve a balance of sorts, we have found it helpful first to discuss the values attached to accepted writing standards, and to follow up these discussions with informational lectures about the cultural values reflected in key college writing traditions. Essentially, either of the two initial units described above will, sooner or later, lead straight to values. Classroom discussions can touch on the historical basis of composition requirements in the United States (Heath 1981), or on the present testing rage that is sweeping higher education. But in order to lead an informed discussion, it is often helpful for the teacher again to begin by eliciting information about essay testing experiences from the students, and to probe student theories about successes or failures. While it is often true that students are mystified about why they might have aced one exam and failed another (an experience both present authors share!), they can usually recall whether or not an exam was "easy" or "hard," and they often have insight into what made it easy or hard for them.

Many new writers in multiethnic basic writing classes often come from communicative traditions that differ radically from those of their new discourse communities. The essayist tradition, for example, is one shaped by Anglo values requiring explicitness and decontextualization, both hallmarks of a "society of strangers" (Gee 1985). It requires a fictionalization of the self and of one's audience, but is otherwise marked by formality and restraint (Scollon and Scollon 1981). It strives for objectivity and a kind of cold passion that is uniquely North American and which, as Carlos Fuentes has observed, is obsessed with success and the realization of a utopian society. A second Anglo writing tradition, scientific report writing, embodies many of the same values, but it has been influenced by a greater need for conventions and cross-cultural transparency (Atkinson 1991).

To complicate matters further, marginalized groups in the United States have developed traditions of their own, emphasizing *the plain truth* in a society that wraps discriminatory and oppressive practices in legalistic language reminiscent of essayist literacy. This is why an information *exchange* between students and teacher is particularly important. In order to establish the right contrasts between the communicative epistemologies that guide academic and student writings, teachers need to generate a great deal of information. This enables them to calibrate lectures about alternative epistemologies and writing traditions and to introduce unfamiliar ones. The two processes, raising the students' consciousness about theories of writing and communication, and the introduction of essayist or other institutionally determined norms, work in concert to sensitize new college writers to the communicative forms they need to master.

As teachers and students exchange information about communicative styles, the instructor's feedback becomes increasingly important. In order for discussions and lectures to pay off, students have to start engaging in their own essayist practice. Frequently, "getting it right" requires coaching, and it is at this point that a good teacher is indispensable. Responding to student papers, orally and/or in writing, the instructor can relate the standards that students are expected to meet in their future work. For instance, when minority students were asked to write about their experiences with discrimination, they would start out with "discrimination hurts us" without specifying who "us" was. Another common feature in writings on the topic would be for ESL students to say "in my country" without ever specifying what their country was. They had a very hard time with the conventional fiction required in much essay writing, namely the pretense that their teacher who, after all, had given them the very assignment they were completing, would not know what they were writing about or who they meant. It is precisely at points like these that they could be reminded of their greater or potential audience, and that this notion could be made more real to them. The teacher could respond with something akin to, "You must pretend that your audience is a stranger and knows nothing about you," and thus lecture, discussion, and written practice dovetail.

Integrating Problem-Posing with Traditional Assignments

A final consideration in adapting a composition course to the needs of basic writers in the multiethnic classroom is how to tackle traditional rhetorical patterns. Often, composition teachers are constrained by their institution to adhere to certain instructional goals. They are expected to develop assignments that fit a particular curriculum and to use certain institutionally sanctioned materials. In such cases, the goal becomes once again to find a means to take advantage of student knowledge while introducing institutional requirements. This can be where a true meeting of mainstream expectations and student experiences takes place. The institution rarely dominates the day-to-day implementation of its material, and it is frequently possible to find the space for student experiences even in a prescribed curriculum.

During the Spring semester of 1990, one of the present authors was strongly encouraged by her institution to use literary texts chosen from a pre-established list of works. She was working with new writers from a number of Latin American and Asian countries in an ESL class for which George Orwell's *Animal Farm* was strongly recommended. It was read and discussed over the course of several weeks. It soon became clear that the book touched on a number of sensitive issues for most students. Many of them came from politically repressive systems, and they were reluctant to approach the political implications of Orwell's book. Instead of coercing them into a political analysis, the teacher chose to frame the discussion as one centered on the realizability of utopian systems. The discussion included family systems, college systems, or even economic systems. The assignment that was ultimately developed (see Appendix A) allowed the students to write about whether they thought utopian systems were possible. It asked point blank: "Can there be a perfect family, or a perfect school system, or a perfect economic system?" Only then were students asked to consider Orwell's text, and then in concert with their own experiences. We cannot really do justice to the many successful papers this assignment led to, but two cases were particularly gratifying: A student from Nicaragua (and former economist for the Sandinistas) chose to write about the impossibility of a "perfect economic system." Her paper discussed how the Sandinistas had tried to develop such a system and ultimately failed due to external pressures from the United States. Another Central American student chose to write about the inherent difficulties of trying to maintain "the perfect Latino family" in the United States. The following is his thesis:

> The ideal utopian family system is where the father, mother and children live together happy. But with the present American and Latino people these ideals are impossible to achieve because a lot of people have changed their beliefs about marriage, and education for their family.

He went on to discuss how North American social influences, such as a high divorce rate and the necessity of two parental incomes, tend to conflict with and sometimes supplant Latino family values of parents remaining married and someone staying home to care for the children.

It was interesting to note that few of the students actually discussed Orwell or his book in their papers. But instead of expecting such a discussion, the teacher felt it was more important for them to have absorbed the overarching theme of the text—an anti-utopian critique of communism—and to have applied it to their own lives and experiences. They were receiving the required exposure to a text privileged by the academic discourse community, yet they were not compelled to remain within its confines. Rather, they could draw on their own lives and experiences in relation to dominant themes within the text.

While not forced outright into this kind of creativity, the second author has struggled for a number of semesters to familiarize her students with such traditional essayist staples as the description, compare-and-contrast or cause-and-effect essay in remedial writing courses. An instructional unit centered on "neighborhood problems" was found to be particularly successful in teaching one of these forms, the cause-and-effect essay. Simply put, the students were asked to describe in detail a problem from their own lives or in their neighborhoods. They were then encouraged to provide as complete a list of causes for this problem as they could muster, and to relate the different causes to each other (see Appendix B).

The problems described and discussed by the mostly immigrant and African-American students in her class tended to fall into two types, which could be called "problems in the home country" and "problems in the new one." Central American students would write about the civil wars in Central America, while Mexican and Korean students would focus on corruption. Inner-city immigrants and their African-American peers would find a lot to say about the drug wars in their neighborhoods, or discuss the heavy MedFly Spraying schedule to which they had been subjected.[6]

In order for the assignment to lead to a successful conclusion, students were specifically asked to link causes and effects. They were also asked to identify responsible parties, if possible, at a later stage of their analyses. It was reasoned that some genuine insight into the problems under analysis might result from such a format. The two tasks turned out to be very challenging, requiring a mix of abstract thinking and real information that was new to the majority of students. The task also brought to light how little some of them valued their own knowledge. They were gunshy, meeting discussion questions and requests for elaboration with persistent silence, choosing not to divulge their own feelings on issues they themselves had chosen. They brought the instructor face to face with the "hidden injuries of class" Sennett and Cobb identified two decades ago (1973).

On a more positive note, the assignment also yielded some very successful papers by "new experts" who took to the investigative component in the assignment. A particularly memorable one examined the negative effects of year-round schooling[7] and offered this final analysis of the mode of instruction and its results:

> Students are treated as numbers not people. Year round school is at a much faster pace. The teacher has a series of books, programs and tests, they must conduct in a certain time frame. They have pressure. That pressure goes to the students. And the motif seems to be how many graduate not what grades did they graduate with? To develop this idea, I will quote my younger brother who graduated a year ago: "I can't believe 'Benny Martinez' made it. He couldn't read or write without messing up! He just got lucky, or they felt sorry for him too." I personally believe that the high school let go of students because it was afraid "Benny" would be there as long as they forced him to be there. They needed the room for new students, they decided to let him go. The problem is there are more than 1900 "Bennys" who graduate each year.

The student who wrote this had obviously pondered this problem, and had come to some conclusions about teaching that, we are sure, strike responsive chords in all of us.

Concluding Thoughts: Benefits and Limitation

Ultimately, the method advocated here should benefit teachers as well as students. No longer will teachers suffer the burden of being the sole providers of instructional resources, since multicultural diversity brought to the fore of the composition classroom ensures against this. Moreover, students and teachers alike, through a continual exchange of cultural values and beliefs on both sides, are opening a joint forum for much needed communication. This, in turn, narrows the gap between one of the dominant discourses of the academic community and more marginalized discourses. Finally, and perhaps most importantly, the gap between theory and practice is narrowed. Teachers begin to see for themselves how diverse, but connected, theories of learning, literacy, and sociolinguistics can work in concert with actual classroom practice.

Nevertheless, our approach is not without potential problems. Students may resist when asked to bring their own experiences with and theories about writing into the classroom. This can become especially troublesome when students wholeheartedly endorse a view of themselves as "objects" and teachers as "bankers," and dealing with this kind of resistance is not easy. However, teachers can at least begin to diverge from a disempowering educational model by asking students why they view their own education in this manner. Moreover, we have presented our method in a rather top-down fashion, starting with theories and beliefs and then shifting to specific literacy practices. Not all students or classes are ideally suited for such an approach, and some students may respond much more favorably to a bottom-up, exploratory classroom style. Working with the ideas we have outlined calls for *artful implementation* and sensitivity to the unique dynamics of each classroom. Each teacher ultimately needs to make his or her own decisions, based on his or her own understanding of the new writers' needs, implementing our suggestions in a manner most suitable for his/her particular population of students.

Appendix A

English 85

Assignment #5 (in class) and #6 (out of class)

Title: Perfection in a less than perfect world

Background

George Orwell's book, *Animal Farm* describes a situation where an attempt to create an ideal political and economic situation (a farm owned and run exclusively by animals) fails. Many felt that Orwell was right and that there can never be a successful revolution. For failed political and economic revolutions, people may point to the Soviet Union, certain countries in Central America or even the United States (where all men are created equal is an ideal, not a reality). What all of this implies is that *utopias* (systems that are perfect, i.e. no crime, no discrimination, equal rights for everybody, and the list goes on) are impossible to achieve in reality.

While Orwell's book focuses mainly on political and economic aspects, we could extend the notion of utopias to other systems beyond that of an entire country (or farm for that matter). For example, we could think of the educational system, in particular the community college system. What would the perfect community college system look like? We could even extend the idea of utopias to relationships and families. Is it possible to have the "perfect family"?

Assignment

What I would like for you to do in this assignment is to address the following question:

Are utopian systems possible in today's world? Why or why not?

In addressing this question I want you to focus on one particular system. In other words, you can answer this question with respect to education (community colleges perhaps?), family, national or economic systems. I do not want you to try and talk about all of these different systems, just choose *one*! You also will want to have specific examples to support your thesis.

Hints:

When you begin your paper, you might want to think about what a perfect family, school, political or economic system would be like. You ought to first write about this and then discuss whether or not this ideal is possible. Your answer to this will become your thesis. A good thesis will also be one that says *why* your answer is what it is.

Appendix B

English 31/86 Patthey-Chavez

Assignment #4: Cause and Effect Analysis

Now that you have heard how skillful descriptions can carry a convincing and powerful argument, I want you to apply your descriptive and organizational skills to your next assignment. This assignment will be a cause-and-effect analysis. I want you to use the second type of cause-and-effect organization we have discussed. Start with an effect, describe it, and then investigate the many causes that have led to it.

The topic of this essay is:

A problem in my neighborhood

Choose a problem *that you are really concerned about* (get as real as you can), and then follow these steps:

1. Describe the problem;

2. Identify as many *causes* of this problem as you can; this will probably involve assigning *responsibility* for the problem to various groups of people;

3. *Bank* the causes, and see if any of them are related;

4. Write a point sentence about the *main* cause(s); organize all the causes into superordinate and subordinate causes (big boss causes and contributing ones).

5. *Organize* all these causes into a rough outline and use roughly one to organize your paper. A good rule of thumb would be to devote paragraph to each subordinate cause.

6. Show us, through description and full elaboration, that your analysis is right, and that the cause(s) you identify as the main cause(s) do have the predicted effect(s), i.e. the problem you started out with.

You will see that even in an essay that is not meant to be descriptive, you can make use of both good organization *and* good descriptions to support your analysis. If readers become engrossed in your writing, they are much more likely to entertain the point you are trying to make than if they are bored. Your readers are much more likely to agree with you that something is a big problem if you show destructive effects than if you merely name it. For those of you with a creative spark, description is the one part of the essay where you can shine: Make your text come to life, make your readers understand the depth of your convictions by illustrating them vividly and skillfully.

I would like you to *refrain from developing or even suggesting any solutions*. Instead, I want you to convince your readers that the problem you are addressing is indeed a problem. Show them, clearly and vividly, the destructive effects of this problem. Show them, again clearly and vividly, how the problem you are describing effects different groups of people—the people concerned, yourselves, your kid brothers and sisters . . .

Notes

1. All three writing programs for which the authors have worked so far espoused a student-centered teaching philosophy.
2. Nothing exemplifies the persistence of this country's xenophobic legacy better than the current controversy about political correctness. Using "PC-excesses" like labeling the handicapped "differently abled" or setting up an Afrocentric curriculum of "questionable historical and scientific validity," the bitter polemics surrounding PC are setting up an irreconcilable conflict between inclusive curriculum efforts and "the American (educational) tradition." The conflict and the contrast it sets up perpetuates a view of "American" as homogeneously White, and a view of diversity as irreconcilably alien. One of the most comprehensive discussions of the phenomenon can be found in the July/August 1991 issue of the *Utne Reader.*
3. Another way to put this is that we are trying to reconcile two generally hostile constituencies, composition theorists/researchers, and composition teachers. The latter, faced with the immediate concerns of writing classes, find the work of the former overly abstract or obtuse. Teachers with whom we have worked, for example, have repeatedly asked for concrete, "hands on" ideas, while almost shrugging

aside the more general principles underlying these ideas. Researchers and theorists, meanwhile, find the teachers' repeated calls to "get real" insufficiently principled or orderly (i.e., unscientific), and dismiss classroom experience as "anecdotal." Perhaps because our experience spans both worlds, we feel the two groups have much to offer each other, and would like to see a *bidirectional* exchange replace this mutual hostility.

4. At the same time, it is important to let the students decide whether or not they accept the views we present about hegemonic discourse. It is very easy to turn our ideas into an alternate dogma, and simply to replace one set of views about literacy with another. One way to avoid this is to start with student-experiences with print and with schooling. These may bear out our views, or they may not. Many of our students have articulated analyses of language use by particular discourse communities that echo our own. For example, they see California's English-Only movement as a way to victimize them by excluding them from employment. Others tell us that they are grateful for past opportunities to learn "proper" English in order to get ahead. Unlike some proponents of problem-posing education, we do not advocate challenging such an opinion. Instead, we might encourage the student who holds it to try and investigate the English they think will help them.

5. The typical student at the site for which this assignment was developed is older, gainfully employed, and often has family responsibilities. No doubt the assignment would have to be adapted to a younger student population more exclusively dedicated to college studies.

6. In 1989 and 1990, parts of Los Angeles were subjected to monthly aerial sprayings of a toxic pesticide in response to an "agricultural emergency," an infestation by an agricultural pest known as the Mediterranean Fruit Fly. Most of the people on the receiving end of the sprayings were from immigrant or minority backgrounds. The disparity between the heavy sprayings of their neighborhoods and the light spraying ordered for richer neighborhoods (if any spraying was ordered at all) was not lost on them.

7. In the last decade, immigration has greatly swelled the enrollment of urban California school districts. Neither school funding nor teacher training has kept pace with this rising enrollment, and many school districts have found themselves in the position of having to do more with less. In order to relieve overcrowding, they have frequently opted for year-round schooling. In such a system, schools are kept open year-round, and students are divided into several tracks with rotating schedules. Since not all children are in school at the same time, more students can be accommodated by the same facilities. For the most part, these students have shorter school years and longer school days.

Works Cited

Atkinson, Dwight. "Discourse Analysis and Written Discourse Conventions." *Annual Review of Applied Linguistics* 11, R. B. Kaplan et al., eds. New York: Cambridge UP, 1991.

Bakhtin, Mikhail M. *The Dialogical Imagination*. M. Holquist, ed. Austin, TX: U of Texas P, 1981.

Cook-Gumperz, Jenny, ed. *The Social Construction of Literacy*. New York: Cambridge UP, 1986.

Cummins, James. "The Role of Primary Language Development in Promoting Success for Language Minority Students." *Schooling and Language Minority Students: A Theoretical Framework*. California State Department of Education. Division of Instructional Support and Bilingual Education. Office of Bilingual Bicultural Education, eds. Los Angeles: Evaluation, Dissemination and Assessment Center, California State U, Los Angeles, 1981.

Douglas, Mary. *How Institutions Think*. Syracuse, NY: Syracuse UP, 1981.

Engeström, Yrjo. "The Zone of Proximal Development as the Basic Category of Educational Psychology." *The Quarterly Newsletter of the Laboratory of Comparative Human Cognition* 8 (1986): 23-42.

Freire, Paulo. *Pedagogy of the Oppressed*. New York: Continuum, 1982.

Gee, James P., *Literacies and Discourses*. London: Falmer Press, 1991.

_____ , "The Narrativization of Experience in the Oral Style." *Journal of Education* 167.1 (1985): 9-35.

Gilmore, Perry. "'Gimme Room': School Resistance, Attitude, and Access to Literacy." *Journal of Education* 167.1 (1985): 11-28.

Gumperz, John J. and Dell Hymes, eds. *Directions in Sociolinguistics: The Ethnography of Communication*. New York: Holt, 1972.

_____ , eds. The Ethnography of Communication [Special Issue]. *American Anthropologist*. 66.6 (1964).

Heath, Shirley B. *Ways with Words: Language, Life and Work in Communities and Classrooms*. New York: Cambridge UP, 1983.

_____ , "Protean Shapes in Literacy Events: Ever-Shifting Oral and Literate Traditions." *Spoken and Written Language: Exploring Orality and Literacy.* D. Tannen, ed. Norwood, NJ: Ablex, 1982: 91-117.

_____ , "Toward an Ethnohistory of Writing in American Education." *Writing: The Nature, Development, and Teaching of Written Communication.* M. F. Whiteman, ed. Vol. 1: Variation in Writing: Functional and Linguistic-Cultural Differences. Hillsdale, NJ: Erlbaum, 1981.

Kloss, Heintz. *The American Bilingual Tradition.* Rowley, MA: Newbury, 1977.

Michaels, Sarah. "Hearing the Connections in Children's Oral and Written Discourse." *Journal of Education* 167.1 (1985): 36-56.

Rumberger, Russell W. "The Challenge and Opportunity of Educational Diversity." *Student Diversity.* California Public Schools Forum. J. H. Block, ed. Santa Barbara, CA: Graduate School of Education, U of California, Santa Barbara 3 (1989): 1-18.

Sennett, Richard and Jonathan Cobb. *The Hidden Injuries of Class.* New York: Vintage, 1973.

Scollon, Ron and Suzanne B. K. Scollon. *Narrative, Literacy and Pace in Interethnic Communication.* Norwood, NJ: Ablex, 1981.

Smith, Frank. *Joining the Literacy Club.* Portsmouth, NH: Heinemann, 1988.

Sola, Michele and Adrian T. Bennet. "The Struggle for Voice: Narrative Literacy and Consciousness in an East Harlem School." *Journal of Education* 167.1 (1985): 88-110.

Suarez-Orozco, Marcelo. *Central American Refugees and U. S. High Schools.* Stanford, CA: Stanford UP, 1989.

Sue, Stanley, and Amado Padilla. "Ethnic Minority Issues in the U. S.: Challenges for the Educational System." *Beyond Language: Social and Cultural Factors in Schooling Language Minority Students.* California State Department of Education. Division of Instructional Support and Bilingual Education. Office of Bilingual Bicultural Education, eds. Los Angeles: Evaluation, Dissemination and Assessment Center, California State U, Los Angeles, 1981.35-72.

Todorov, Tzvetan. *Mikhail Bakhtin. The Dialogical Principle.* W. Godzich, trans. Minneapolis, MN: U of Minnesota P, 1984.

Utne, Eric (Ed.). "Oh No! I'm PC!" [Special collection of articles on Political Correctness.] *Utne Reader. The Best of the Alternative Press.* (June/July 1991): 50-56.

Vygotsky, Lev S. *Mind in Society: The Development of Higher Psychological Processes.* M. Cole, V. John-Steiner, S. Scribner, and E. Souberman, eds. Cambridge, MA: Harvard UP, 1978.

_____ , *Thought and Language.* Cambridge, MA: Harvard UP, 1962.

Wolf, Dennie. "Ways of Telling: Text in Elementary School Children." *Journal of Education* 167.1 (1985): 71-87.

Back to Basics:
A Force for Opression or Liberation?
by Donald Lazere

From the 1960s to the present, leftist educational theorists in English have followed a persistent pattern of argument on a variety of current issues. Although I am myself a leftist and agree with much of the left analysis and position on these issues, I want to air some long-brewing critical questions about arguments expressed by leftists including James Sledd, Andrew Sledd, Richard Ohmann, Wayne O'Neil, and American followers of Paulo Freire. These critics have at various times opposed conventional college admission and course requirements; grading and notions of compensatory education; cultural or linguistic deficits; bidialectalism; the alleged "literacy crisis"; Hirschian cultural literacy; Bennett-Bloomian Eurocentric core curricula; and other manifestations of the "back to basics" movement on the grounds that these forces have intentionally or inadvertently served conservative hegemonic interests against aspirations to equality by minorities, women, and the working class. For similar reasons they have supported open admissions, the open classroom and Freirean liberatory literacy, *Students' Right to Their Own Language* (the controversial 1974 CCCC monograph), and particularly black and other nonstandard dialects versus the imposition of standard English. (I will not go at length into the recent disputes over multiculturalism, canon revision, and "political correctness" here, but I hope the applicability of my arguments to them is evident, as is my intense opposition to the current wave of malicious and often ill-informed right-wing attacks on the academic left, against which I have published many articles.)

In sum, leftists have for the most part claimed that, as Ohmann puts it, "The decline in literacy is a fiction, if not a hoax" (*Politics* 231). O'Neil identifies the devious motives behind this fabricated crisis: "It has become important for the ruling class to exclude the potentially radicalizing elements of higher education from the colleges. Thus everywhere along the scale of education there is a relentless march toward the basics" (15).

In a more recent expression of the same idea, "Readin' not Riotin': The Politics of Literacy," Andrew Sledd wrote:

> My first contention will be that there is no such crisis, that both the crisis and means to resolve it have been manufactured in order to serve purposes of which we should not be servants. . . . (495)

Retreat to the trivial, to rote learning and drill, will only retard intellectual development.

> If back to basics is a scheme to keep the great unwashed away from soap, functional literacy is another dirty trick. A trendy idea, it has all the flaws of the therapeutic goal of adjustment. Well-adjusted citizens are vulnerable to state propaganda, anxious to be consumed in the corporate economy, divorced from their deepest thoughts and emotions. (498)

On a more affirmative note, Ohmann, in his 1983 *College English* article, "Reflections on Class and Language" (reprinted in *Politics of Letters*), concluded:

> I think the educational moral is roughly that of the 1960s reform movements, now much condemned: students should have as much responsibility as possible for their own educations. The habits of expressive power come with actual shared power, not with computerized instruction in sentence-combining or with a back-to-basics movement that would freeze students' language into someone else's rules, imposed from without. Respect the linguistic resources students have; make language a vehicle for achievement of real political and personal aims. (293)

One can agree in large part with these and other points leftists have made while still taking issue with some overstatements and oversimplifications. I do not dispute the allegations that the publicizing over the past two decades of a literacy crisis and the course of the resultant back-to-basics movement have been turned to conservative political ends—for example, attempts, in an age of economic decline and Reaganite cuts in public services, to resort to the cheapest, most reactionary solutions, such as defunding innovative programs that favor the poor, minorities, and women (while excluding these groups from established schooling) or blaming educational problems on permissive leftist theories, "greedy" teachers' unions, and inept individual teachers (while suppressing the facts that teachers are overworked, underpaid, overly controlled by administrative bureaucracy, and often forced to work under dispiriting classroom conditions). Moreover, it seems likely that conservatives' concern has less to do with a decline in Americans' intellectual level than with a decline in the skills necessary for workers to do their jobs compliantly and efficiently. All of this does not prove, however, that there is *not* a literacy crisis. My own experience and that of most other teachers I know indicate there is, and that it has been detrimental to all social classes and ethnic groups except the most privileged. In defensive reaction against conservative preemption of the literacy crisis, leftists bend over so far backward that they sometimes seem to be endorsing illiteracy as politically progressive; at the very least, they facilely imply that conventional academic culture and language serve wholly reactionary ends, whereas their own radicalism, formed in many cases out of conventional education, is obvious evidence to the contrary. Does Andrew Sledd, for instance, believe that his own education has divorced him from his deepest thoughts and emotions?

Particularly in the new pool of college students in recent decades, preparation in basic reading, writing, and reasoning skills, as well as in what E. D. Hirsch calls cultural literacy, is often woefully inadequate for college level work. Nor do all of these new students consist, as leftists tend to assume, of minority and working-class students who are, in O'Neil's words, "potentially radicalizing elements." Most, at least in my twenty-five year teaching experience in the University of California and California State University systems, are middle-class whites, many of them quite conservative—indeed, potentially reactionary elements. Their secondary-school preparation for college, even in relatively affluent communities, has often been atrocious, partly because of the public's and legislators' stinginess toward public school funding, partly because of low standards in teacher qualification and training. Because conservatives tend to make teachers the scapegoat for all the faults of American education, and because conservative criticisms often appear to be aimed at minority teachers, many leftists seem compelled to reject any defense of accreditation standards and any criticism of teachers. But from what I have seen, the most poorly qualified teachers are, again, frequently middle-class, white, and relatively conservative.

For such students and teachers, then, the lack of basic skills and factual knowledge is an obstacle to autonomous critical thinking and to openness toward progressive politics; this is one of several areas I will discuss where leftist attitudes have inadvertently led to conservative results. Hence I have become convinced that leftists err grievously in rejecting, as dogmatically as conservatives endorse it, a restored emphasis on basic skills and knowledge which might be a force for liberation—not oppression—if administered with common sense, openness to cultural pluralism, and an application of basics toward critical thinking, particularly about sociopolitical issues, rather than rote memorizing.

In the November 1983 *College English*, against efforts within CCCC to revise *Students' Right to Their Own Language*, James Sledd published a defense of that document's criticism of the compulsory teaching of standard spoken and written English. (For an analysis of the confusion in *Students' Right* between the issues of standard versus nonstandard dialect and of oral versus literate language and culture—confusion that Sledd's defense perpetuates, see Lazere, "Orality.") Here as elsewhere, Sledd makes many compelling, eloquent criticisms of the complicity of English studies in the injustices of capitalist society; unfortunately, he also makes many questionable arguments. Thus he claims that standard English is a "bosses' language" and "essentially an instrument of domination" (669) whose imposition on the lower classes serves "simply to flatter the prejudices of the powers that be. . . . It does no good to argue that by coercing students now, we give them 'freedom to choose later.' However it may be concealed, the chief purpose of present coercion is to condition students to comply with later coercion, and two coercions do not make one freedom" (671).

Sledd does make clear that he believes "there is nobody who would not teach Standard English, spoken or written, to students who want to learn it (just as there is nobody who *can* teach it to students who *don't* want to learn)" (670) and that "since everybody agrees, then, that standard languages should indeed be taught to people who want to learn them, informed debate must concern the motives for that teaching, its methods, and the treatment of students who have either no desire to learn a standard dialect or no real chance to learn it" (671). Still, his position has troublesome implications. For example, how are teachers to determine which students want to learn standard written English and which don't? Should there be separate but equal classes in standard and each different nonstandard dialect so that nobody is coerced? (In some California public schools there are nearly as many different languages and dialects as there are students.) And if students who want to learn standard English are entitled to have teachers capable of teaching it, it would seem to follow that in order to get a credential, teacher candidates must be "coerced" into demonstrating that capability.

Perhaps another reason Sledd's line of argument so often provokes hostility or misunderstanding is that it seems to reduce all the problems of teaching standard English and basic cultural literacy in college to the student's volition and the teacher's benign motives, thereby glossing over the very substantial difficulties faced by both teachers and their students who, if they now so choose, have to make up for many lost years in which the needed pre-college level of literacy was not attained—difficulties that more conventionally oriented teachers and theorists like E. D. Hirsch and Thomas J. Farrell, who are belittled by radicals, have at least tried to deal with realistically.

If the major issues turn out to be only matters of motives, methods, and priorities of instruction, as Sledd claims, there may be less distance than it seems between Sledd, or other leftists who make similar arguments, and those in the English profession they criticize, since in recent decades few influential composition theorists, at least at the college level, have claimed that "correctness" in mechanics or usage is of primary importance; most theorists and textbook writers have moved toward more student-centered approaches in writing instruction, emphasizing the composing process and invention, revision, sense of audience, and collaborative learning, and most have also stressed the need for a respectful approach to the dialect and culture of nonstandard speakers. It is true, though, that practice has not always been consistent with theory; excessive class sizes and courseloads in writing courses—which do not seem to be prime concerns of many left critics, with the admirable exception of the Sledds—often force teachers to fall back on mechanical standards of grading.

As for Sledd's claim that standard English is a "bosses' language," if this was unequivocally true, wouldn't it be in the bosses' interests to *deny* the lower classes access to that language rather than forcing it on them, which would seem to provide them with the possibility (however restricted by other socioeconomic forces) of either *attaining* the upper classes or gaining valuable weapons for cracking upper-class codes so as to more effectively combat the class structure? There appears to be the same kind of self-contradiction in Andrew Sledd first saying that "back to basics is a scheme to keep the great unwashed away from soap [apparently meaning functional literacy]," then in the same sentence saying that "functional literacy is another dirty trick."

The closest that James Sledd comes to addressing this question is in the following passage:

> It is a simple fact that many students, regardless of their intelligence, cannot learn what the school asks them to do—cannot learn because of hunger, fear, grief, disease, or other circumstances beyond their control. The obverse of that truth is that circumstances beyond control by teachers often make it impossible to teach the prescribed subjects; teachers cannot do what an unjust society at once requires and forbids them to do. (671)

This is a powerful argument, and Sledd is surely right that the tendency to blame the victim, both lower-class students and schools or teachers themselves, "diverts attention from the deep social causes which are the roots of the trouble and which ought to be dug up and removed" (671); the only problem I have with the argument is that it is not only minorities and the poor who are having difficulties in reading and writing at the college level, but many whites of the middle and upper-middle class who have never gone hungry or suffered other social or educational deprivation. If Sledd's position can validly be applied to these students, he gives no indication of how it might be done.

Sledd's essay goes in quite a different direction when he asserts that "upward mobility would be an evil goal even if it were a possible goal" (672), because of the irremediable inequities and destructiveness of American capitalist society. The only authentic response to the problems of American society and education, Sledd concludes, is commitment to revolutionary action by teachers and students: "[I]f working within the System to right the System's wrongs ends constantly in failure, why should one not at last say 'Smash it all!'" (675). Whether or not one agrees with Sledd's general condemnation of capitalist society (I happen to agree with it in large measure), the conclusions he draws from it for English pedagogy are questionable, both in relation to the role of English teachers and to their students' attitudes. Conservatives are correct in insisting that it is illegitimate for teachers to advocate a revolutionary or any other ideological position in a one-sided way and to force that position on students—and despite the tendentious exaggerations of conservative critics about the tyranny of left political correctness, this sometimes does occur. To do so is only to replace the coercion that Sledd condemns in mainstream education with coercion into accord with an opposing ideology.

As for students' political attitudes, Sledd and other radical educators still seem, like many recent conservative polemicists, to be fixated in the realities of the sixties, when there was a substantial body of rebellious students, black and white, rather than in the nineties, when the prevalent mood among students of most races and classes is at least relatively conservative, the prevalent goal not revolution but getting a job. Statements like the following from *Students' Right* now sound a bit bizarre: "English teachers who feel they are bound to accommodate the linguistic prejudices of current employers perpetuate a system that is unfair to both students who have job skills and to the employers who need them" (14). If there are jobs available that require aptitude in spoken or written standard English, are we supposed to tell our students, "You'd be better off unemployed than having to work for that nasty employer with his linguistic prejudices"? To be sure, we can, as even Sledd agrees, try to explain to students what we perceive to be linguistic prejudices or the fallacies in the goal of upward mobility, while leaving to them the option of taking or leaving our arguments, but in my experience, making this effort is apt to meet with a great deal of resistance built up from a lifetime of conditioning in the possibility and desirability of success in the present social order.

When Sledd asserts, "If working within the System to right the System's wrongs ends constantly in failure, why should one not at last say 'Smash it all!'," the students he is concerned about might well answer, "What you mean 'one,' Paleface?" Without belittling either the sincerity of radical teachers or the validity of their political analyses in the abstract, one must—*especially* from a Marxist perspective—take account of the anomaly involved in the advocacy of revolutionary politics (or linguistic revolution against standard English) to working-class students desperate to get jobs, by professors of upper-middle-class status with Ivy League educations and tenured positions (in many cases in elite universities). Radical teachers too, no less than the liberals or conservatives they criticize, are captives of the cultural contradictions of capitalism. This is not to suggest that there is an easy way out of their situation; if they voluntarily drop out of teaching to become full-time revolutionaries, or push radical ideas in their classes so far that they are fired, that will simply leave education to be dominated by those who uncritically perpetuate the status quo.

About educational coercion in general, particularly in the form of academic requirements, the question can be raised—not only from a conservative political position but equally well from a leftist, anti-authoritarian one—doesn't education unavoidably involve some degree of coerciveness? Doesn't cognitive development, like emotional development, involve a gradual progression from dependency on authority to autonomy? The issue of coercion is a difficult one in elementary and secondary education because going to school itself is compulsory at those levels—a policy whose basic soundness is certainly debatable. But students in college have chosen to come there—economic, parental, and peer pressures notwithstanding—and it seems legitimate to make clear to them that this choice and their enrollment in each particular course, whether required or elective, is a contractual agreement binding them to a reasonable amount of externally imposed requirements and internal discipline. For these and other reasons that follow, I have decided in my own teaching that admission and course requirements, quizzes, letter grades, and grading down for written errors in standard English (without making these the primary focus of instruction or evaluation) are necessary evils.

In wanting to give college-age or younger students complete free choice of courses or of standard versus nonstandard English, leftists make the debatable assumption that most young people are sufficiently mature, well-informed, and resistant to peer pressure to make these choices in their best interests. If, before coming to college, students have lost precious years in the development of language proficiency and background reading—whether through deprivation, their own earlier choice, their own or teachers' indifference, or other causes—the undeniable difficulties of the remedial effort necessary for handling college-level work are often so discouraging that they are apt just to give up. For this reason, the enforcement of demanding academic requirements prior to and in the first years of college is likely to save many students from regrets in later years—with the proviso that such requirements must be tied to a larger political program for eliminating the socioeconomic discrimination in education at all levels that turns requirements into a form of *de facto* segregation.

To be sure, teachers face the dilemma that their role as authority in the classroom is bound to be identified by students with all the authoritarian forces in American society, although we *can* try to explain, and prove by our actions, that there is a difference between wholly-constricting forms of authority and the provisional authority of teachers helping students ultimately to attain autonomy. But this is only one side of the problem; the other involves the paradox that, as Herbert Marcuse argues, in twentieth-century capitalist society, social conformity and control have not been perpetuated solely through authoritarian repression but increasingly through "repressive desublimation" and tolerance–apparent permissiveness and indulgence of hedonistic individualism as a means of distracting people from the hidden realities of social regimentation and constriction of personal choice. This hedonistic individualism—termed by Christopher Lasch the culture of narcissism—is inimical to the external and internal discipline essential to critical education. Students today grow up in a society that lulls them with the "freedom to choose" in the marketplace and the promise of instant, easy gratification through passive consumption of commodities, entertainment and recreation, glib political rhetoric and news reporting.

Such conditioning is almost sure to prejudice students' responses against the kind of noncoercive choices leftists say we should offer them. If nonstandard English is easier than standard English, that's what most will choose. If requirements of difficult liberal arts courses are dropped, most will take the Mickey Mouse vocational and recreational courses. (The latter courses, of course, invariably have a conservative political identity, while liberal arts courses are more apt to promote liberal or radical attitudes; the fact that leftist-inspired reforms of the sixties have resulted in students flocking to the conservative curriculum can only be regarded as a case of chickens coming home to roost.) If taking courses on a credit/Noncredit basis requires less work than on a letter-grade basis or enables students to avoid lowering their GPAs in a difficult course, that's what many will do. Around 1971 a group of us graduate and undergraduate students at Berkeley, the mecca of educational radicalism' put together a student-initiated course on Marxist theory, to be taken credit/Noncredit and with everyone enrolled automatically receiving credit without any specific requirements. As I recall, about a hundred registered; a couple dozen attended class more than a few times, and somewhat fewer than that actively contributed to the class. I don't mean to be overly hard on students here; social pressures make most of us take the easiest route. These would simply seem to be elementary lessons in the Marxist principle that attempts at reform in the cultural superstructure are likely to be bent to the shape of the dominant economic system and its ideology. The irony, again, is that when leftist teachers, including myself, try to present students with an honest account of the necessity—and difficulty—of critical education, students perceive *us* as the coercive authority figures, in contrast to the liberally permissive mainstream culture.

Further confusion on the issue of coercion results from many leftists' apparent belief that compulsory standard English and all of the other established features of American education serve entirely regressive purposes. In a society whose information environment is immensely sophisticated, ability to gain access to, understand, and critically evaluate the dominant modes of discourse (of which academic English is a key component) is an essential survival skill—not only for conforming to the dominant culture, but for resisting or opposing its manipulations of information and rhetoric. (A similar argument can be made against separatist versions of multiculturalism: no subculture in isolation can provide a substitute for attaining the culture of academic discourse, if only to be able to use it in challenging the dominant culture.) This is what I take to be the main point of Hirsch's *Cultural Literacy*, which for all its faults is not the reactionary tract painted by its liberal and leftist critics; as Hirsch says, cultural literacy can lead to "radicalism in politics, but conservatism in literate knowledge" (35).

Many leftist educators seem perversely blind to the radicalizing potential of traditional education and culture. Their standard response is to point to instances of highly educated and cultured people who nonetheless act in a conformist or malicious manner, and to uneducated people who act in an oppositional or noble manner. There seems to me to be a "necessary and sufficient" fallacy in both of these arguments. I can assert that a sophisticated level of literacy is virtually necessary, or at least highly advantageous, for effective opposition to the dominant culture in today's society, even though it is not sufficient in itself to lead anyone to an oppositional attitude and can equally well be turned to bolster a conformist attitude. Conversely, oppositional behavior by formally uneducated people in today's society might occur in spite of their lack of education, not because of it; such people are more likely to respect conventional higher education than pseudo-revolutionary middle-class intellectuals do.

At this point, I must put the discussion on a personal level. I and most of my closest schoolmates in Des Moines and later in college, who are now middle-aged, are children or grandchildren of working-class or petit bourgeois immigrants; few of our parents went to college, and those who did mostly followed a vocational curriculum, without acquiring the traits of intellectuals or the liberally educated. For me and many other "scholarship boys," in Richard Hoggart's term, higher education and upward mobility did not take the form of socialization into conservative conformity. Quite the opposite: it meant liberation from an uncritically conservative Middle American upbringing into what Alvin Gouldner calls "the culture of critical discourse." It also meant initiation into left-liberal or radical politics, not through the kind of personal oppression experienced by proletarian masses, but through reading, in English and other humanities and social science courses, those particular "great books" that constitute their own canon of rebellion and skepticism. It meant an entree to the world of leftist faculty and other political intellectuals—their scholarship and journalism, political organizations and social circles.

Certainly, a sizeable component of the sixties New Left and counterculture was formed from people with similar petit bourgeois backgrounds. Another sizeable component, especially prominent in leadership roles, was formed from people with upper-class backgrounds acting out of either moral principles or guilty consciences—a type that appears in every age and that Seymour Martin Lipset approvingly identifies as "Tory radicals." (Earlier examples in American history include the Revolutionary leaders and the Ivy League graduates and faculty who opposed slavery, the Mexican-American and Spanish-American wars, and World War I.) These upper-class radicals were in the sixties, and still are, frequently the most vocal in denouncing higher education and high culture as class privileges, modes either of suppressing working-class radicalism or of co-opting it into corporate liberalism. There may be much truth in these denunciations, but they certainly have come as a rude shock to those of us for whom higher education has been a radicalizing experience, and for whom entering the academic world entailed alienation from the ties of family and early friendships, renunciation of prospects for better money or higher social status in business or the lucrative professions. When radicals with the security of family wealth and social connections to fallback on in case they lose a job or go to jail for left causes start sounding more-radical-than-thou, I'm inclined to respond, "That's easy for *you* to say."

My radical friends kid me about my weakness for Brooks Brothers clothes, which they identify with conservatism, or at least professional-managerial-class liberalism. What they do not understand is that for one who grew up in a small midwestern city in the fifties, the Ivy League and its dress codes symbolized a rebellion against provincial, philistine conservatism and its Chamber-of-Commerce, polyester-and-patent-leather style—an espousal of cosmopolitan culture, academic-left politics, and the relatively monastic lifestyle of intellectuals compared to that of the business people most of my youthful peers would become. These perceptions from my formative years are obviously still shared by the provincial conservatives of today who regard the "Eastern establishment" of the Ivy League, mass media, and highbrow culture as an iniquitous hotbed of leftism.

Marxists may reply that the pseudo-radicalism of middle- or upper-class intellectuals lacks sufficient grounding in personal oppression and ties with the proletariat to make it an effective revolutionary force. They may point to the prevalence of such voluntaristic radicalism as a symptom of the shaky state of the American left, and they may further argue that the oppositional tendencies in intellectual culture have been far outweighed by the conformist ones. All of this may well be true; and yet, wouldn't the American left probably be even weaker than it is if it were not for the influence of liberal and radical intellectuals? Haven't they contributed significantly since the fifties to the movements for civil rights and black power, feminism, environmentalism, and educational reform, and to opposition to the nuclear arms race, the Vietnam war and more recent American foreign interventions? And isn't the alarm of neoconservatives over the growing influence of "new class," intellectuals and their "adversary culture" testimony that, from a left viewpoint, intellectuals must be doing something right (or left)?

Academic radicals who insist that "the laying on of culture" is against the interests of proletarian students are in the anomalous position of denouncing a class and culture in which they and their radicalism play a not insignificant role. And with apologies for an ad hominem argument, isn't the anomaly compounded by the fact that many of them teach at the same "elite" universities they denounce as bastions of the ruling class (even though in some cases they are regarded as pariahs by administrators and colleagues)? Thus academic radicals almost inevitably must appear to be denigrating the value of their own cultural codes (including scrupulous adherence to standard English)—codes which *they* can afford to take for granted—in the eyes of students or of teachers in less prestigious schools, for whom these codes are far less accessible. For such students and teachers, radical teachers' belittling of academic English is bound again not only to appear as patronizing but, in effect, as a denial of access to the radical possibilities in academic culture.

This is only one of several points on which many leftists' positions reflect a most unmarxian fuzziness about the class relations of faculties and students in differing social positions. Another such point involves attempts to apply Paulo Freire's theories to American classroom situations with students whose class situations and political attitudes differ sharply from the Third World peasants with whom Freire originally worked. Freire's pedagogy for the oppressed is grounded on the premise that their alienation and acute awareness of their socioeconomic powerlessness will serve as a strong motivating factor for acquiring the literacy skills and knowledge that can help liberate them. There appear to have been some effective applications of Freire's theories in the United States among poor people, mainly nonwhite, in slums, ghettos, and depressed rural areas—applications recounted by teachers like Jonathan Kozol in *Death at an Early Age* and Ira Shor *In Critical Teaching and Everyday Life*. Where such applications are apt to run into trouble in the United States is with students who are neither poor nor ostensibly oppressed and alienated, or with students who *are*, but who have decided on pursuing upward mobility and integration rather than rebellion or separatism. In terms of teachers' own class relations to the latter group, or to black and other minority and white lower-working-class students who have opted for upward mobility, Freirean pedagogy becomes much more problematic (even though, aside from specific political aims, it can be a powerful method of teaching with students of most social classes and in nearly any academic subject).

One complicating factor here involves Basil Bernstein's correlation of class with elaborated versus restricted linguistic-cognitive codes. Freirean dialogue and other left pedagogical concepts, such as the open classroom, elimination of requirements, exams, and grades, generally aim at fostering elaborated-code thought in working-class students. But, as Myron Tuman has argued, following Bernstein's later work, in the American context most leftist methods of nonauthoritarian teaching designed to liberate the working class are likely to be met with most resistance by working-class students and to be best received by middle-and upper-class students already socialized in the elaborated codes implicit in such methods. (This point is confirmed by Lisa Delpit, who says she has concluded from her experience teaching black inner-city children that they are far less receptive to open-classroom and other progressive pedagogy than middle-class whites, that they dislike the current emphasis on encouraging students' natural expression in writing to the neglect of standard form and mechanics because they want instruction in the formal skills they need to progress in schooling; in other words, it is the teachers bending over backwards to avoid patronizing such children who are in fact patronizing them.) It is probably no accident that the American educators who have formulated these liberatory theories have mostly had upper-middle-class or academic parents and elite educations themselves: Richard Ohmann's father was a teacher, and he attended Oberlin and Harvard; Jonathan Kozol was the son of a Harvard professor and in turn studied at Harvard.

Ohmann, in "Reflections on Class and Language," denies "that we should teach elaborated codes to working-class kids, within the customary [middle-class] social relations of the school," and advocates instead Freirean pedagogy for empowerment keyed to working-class culture. Now, I venerate Ohmann as the most astute contemporary analyst of the politics of literacy, and my own work is immeasurably indebted to him, but I think a weakness of that essay (and the rest of both *English in America* and *Politics of Letters)* is that he never really thinks through the implications of the class situation he himself is writing from. If he and other left theorists are correct about the class structure of American education, it would seem to follow that teaching at schools like his, Wesleyan, serves mainly to empower the scions of the ruling class and recruits into the professional-managerial class to oppress the working class more effectively. Why, then, should leftists continue to teach at elite colleges rather than seeking jobs at working-class ones? I can see little justification in their own arguments for their remaining where they are, although *I* happen to believe that they serve the valuable functions of maintaining an oppositional presence in the higher circles of American culture and politics through their scholarship, and of perpetuating a leftist intelligentsia through their teaching, even if only a minority of their students end up as leftists.

Moreover, students from upper-class backgrounds and attending elite colleges are more likely than those at working-class or non-elite middle-class colleges to have been socialized in academic English and the culture of critical discourse and to have acquired a sense of social power—that is, they are already adept in elaborated codes. They can better afford to devote their college years to critical, liberal education, and they have the financial and emotional security to be open to progressive pedagogy and even radical politics. Likewise for the minority, working-class, and provincial scholarship boys and girls who gain admission to elite colleges. Ohmann aptly criticizes the capacity of the capitalist system to avert large-scale challenges to class inequities by allowing selected lower-class students to gain upward mobility via elite higher education; but he does not acknowledge that such students are in many cases more receptive to leftist critical pedagogy than their counterparts in nonelite schools, for many reasons including the facts that elite colleges select from among the brightest of them and have more resources than nonelite schools for recruiting, financial aid, tutoring, and counseling.

By contrast, the majority of my students at Cal Poly come from families that are middle-class economically but lacking in what Pierre Bourdieu calls cultural capital—including proficiency in standard English, cultural literacy, and critical understanding of social forces; in other words, their cognitive and linguistic codes are the restricted ones Bernstein associates with the working class, and their political attitudes reflect the reflex conservatism of uncritical subordination to established social order and authority. They are typically being tracked for skilled-labor or middle-managerial positions at best, in high-tech industry, or for careers like sales and accounting.

The pressure toward conservatism among students in such colleges is compounded by other factors; for example, these colleges usually have fewer writing and general education course requirements, and place less importance on them, than elite ones. At Cal Poly, the English faculty had to fight for years to increase writing courses from three hours a quarter to four and to require three one-quarter courses rather than one for all students, along with augmented literature and other general education requirements, against the fierce opposition of faculty *and* students in technical majors who resent any requirements outside their majors. So much for leftist arguments against "coercive" requirements! The fact that students at nonelite colleges generally have to take heavier courseloads and work more at part-time jobs to get through school than those at elite schools creates a further barrier to critical education, since the inclination of those who are overburdened with busy work is to shut out all sources causing cognitive dissonance and competing for the energy needed just to get through school and get a job; this is doubly true for the minority and working-class students struggling to survive in middle-class colleges. Moreover, excessive class sizes and teaching loads make the kind of personal interaction among students and between teacher and students that is necessary for Freirean pedagogy much harder at nonelite schools. Ohmann's analysis simply does not take adequate account of these particular kinds of hierarchical relations in teaching and learning that reproduce the conservative social order and make critical education in the lower sectors far more difficult than in more privileged sectors. (For development of these points in the context of the stratification of teachers and students of English in California's three-tiered system of higher education, see Lazere, "Stratification.")

What should be the goals of liberatory pedagogy for students in middle-class, nonelite colleges? In my experience, the best starting point is to challenge their conditioned belief in their freedom of choice and mobility within American society by bringing them to a critical awareness of the constrictions in their own class position—constrictions that include their lack of control of academic language and cultural codes. Explicit discussion of the problems addressed in this article is one means of raising these issues. Many are contemptuous of the working class, the poor, minorities, and feminists, and they have little awareness at all of the Third World. Conversely, they idolize the wealthy, whose ranks they dream of joining. Their own biases can be critically examined, under the rhetorical topic of prejudice, through studies of the poor, minorities, women's socioeconomic situation, and the Third World peoples on whose exploitation their own comforts depend. Under the rhetorical topic of learning to examine issues from viewpoints differing from their own ethnocentric one, they can be exposed to sources delineating the gross inequities between the upper class and themselves; the odds against their attaining room at the top; the way their education (particularly in its vocational emphasis at the expense of liberal education and verbal skills) has channeled them toward a mid-level professional and social slot and conditioned them into authoritarian conformity: and their manipulation by the elites controlling big business, mass politics, media and consumership, in large part through the rhetoric of public doublespeak. These issues impinging on their own class situation can be connected to a more general questioning of the purposes of much American economic and educational activity, most particularly in the jobs most Americans are slated for—the kind of critique developed in the early sixties by Paul Goodman in *Growing Up Absurd*, Students for a Democratic Society, and the Berkeley Free Speech Movement, which voiced the theretofore suppressed alienation of serious middle-class youths; documents like SDS's "Port Huron Statement" and Mario Savio's "An End to History" remain timely sources for classroom study here. A literary dimension can be added with readings from authors like Thoreau, Emerson, Fuller, and Melville expressing similar ideas a century earlier. My experience has been that after varying degrees of initial defensiveness, most students end up affirming the validity of these critical views and start to question their prior educational and vocational choices. (For more detailed exposition of my teaching approach, see Lazere, *Composition and American Media*—especially the introduction to critical pedagogy in mass culture and the readings in the section "Alternatives and Cultural Activism" in the latter.)

For such students, then, a curriculum for liberatory literacy needs to include the kind of factual knowledge, mechanical and analytic skills (including remedial instruction in reading and writing standard English) that can help empower them both in gaining access to academic sources expressing oppositional ideas, and in mastering the culture of critical discourse themselves. Democratic learning methods of the kind Ohmann advocates—collaborative research, classroom dialogue, peer editing, community activism, media production, and so forth—can be applied to students' development of critical reading skills, their use of research resources, persuasive writing, and speaking. At the same time, however, it must be kept in mind that these students are at a disadvantage compared to those at elite universities in their level of pertinent cultural literacy and familiarity with academic codes, so that compensatory time must be spent in these realms that unfortunately conflicts with the time available for Freirean pedagogy. Dealing with these priorities and other external restrictions, as well as with students who in many cases are far from receptive to oppositional education, is a complex and often enervating task for which most leftist theory heretofore has provided little help.

In summary, teachers may unavoidably have to "coerce" students and "lay on" academic culture and standard English in the cause of showing that they contain the potential to be a force for *either* conformity or nonconformity. For teachers to use this opportunity to empower students ultimately to decide for themselves which ends they should use their education for would seem to be a pedagogical endeavor that is legitimate from any political viewpoint, as well as a personal endeavor that justifies an academic career, freeing us in some measure from the kind of self-laceration that we leftists are prone to indulge in.

Works Cited

Bernstein, Basil. *Class, Codes, and Control: Theoretical Studies Toward a Sociology of Language.* New York: Schocken, 1975.

Bourdieu, Pierre, and Jean-Claude Passeron. *Reproduction in Education, Society, and Culture.* Trans. Richard Nice. London: Sage, 1977.

Delpit, Lisa D. "Skills and Other Dilemmas of a Black Educator." *Harvard Educational Review* 56 (1986): 379–85.

Farrell, Thomas J. "IQ and Standard English." *College Composition and Communication* 34 (1983): 470–84.

Freire, Paulo. *Education for Critical Consciousness*. New York: Seabury, 1974.

_____ . *Pedagogy of the Oppressed*. New York: Seabury, 1970.

Goodman, Paul. *Growing Up Absurd*. New York: Random, 1960.

Gouldner, Alvin. "The New Class as a Speech Community." *The Future of Intellectuals and the Rise of the New Class*. New York: Seabury, 1979. 28–42.

Hirsch, E. D. *Cultural Literacy*. Boston: Houghton-Mifflin, 1987.

Hoggart, Richard. *The Uses of Literacy*. New York: Oxford UP, 1957.

Kozol, Jonathan. *Death at an Early Age*. New York: Bantam, 1965.

Lasch, Christopher. *The Culture of Narcissism*. New York: Norton, 1978.

Lazere, Donald, ed. *American Media and Mass Culture: Left Perspectives*. Berkeley: U of California P, 1987.

_____ . *Composition for Critical Thinking: A Course Description*. ERIC Database Network, 1986.

_____ . "Orality, Literacy, and Standard English." *Journal of Basic Writing* 10 (1991): 87–98.

_____ . "Stratification in the Academic Profession and in the Teaching of Composition." *Humanities in Society* 4 (1981): 379–94.

Lipset, Seymour Martin. *Political Man*. New York: Doubleday, 1963.

Marcuse, Herbert. *One Dimensional Man*. Boston: Beacon, 1964.

Ohmann, Richard. *English in America: A Radical View of the Profession*. New York: Oxford UP, 1976.

_____ . *Politics of Letters*. Middletown, CT: Wesleyan UP, 1987.

O'Neil, Wayne. "Why Newsweek Can't Explain Things." *Radical Teacher*, 2 (1977): 15–17.

Shor, Ira. *Critical Teaching and Everyday Life*. Boston: South End, 1980.

_____ . ed. *Freire for the Classroom*. Portsmouth, NH: Boynton. 1987.

Sledd, Andrew. "Readin' not Riotin': The Politics of Literacy." *College English* 50 (1988): 495–508.

Sledd, James. "In Defense of the Students' Right." *College English* 45 (1983): 667–75.

Students' Right to Their Own Language. College Composition and Communication 25.3 (1974).

Tuman, Myron. "Class, Codes, and Composition: Basil Bernstein and the Critique of Pedagogy." *College Composition and Communication* 39 (1988): 42–51.

Conflict and Struggle: The Enemies
or Preconditions of Basic Writing?
by Min-zhan Lu

Harlem taught me that light skin Black people was better look, the best to suceed, the best off fiaincially etc this whole that I trying to say, that I was brainwashed and people aliked.

I couldn't understand why people (Black and white) couldn't get alone. So as time went along I began learned more about myself and the establishment.

> —Sample student paper, *Errors and Expectations*, 278.

. . . Szasz was throwing her. She couldn't get through the twelve-and-a-half pages of introduction. . . .

One powerful reason Lucia had decided to major in psychology was that she wanted to help people like her brother, who had a psychotic break in his teens and had been in and out of hospitals since. She had lived with mental illness, had seen that look in her brother's eyes. . . . The assertion that there was no such thing as mental illness, that it was a myth, seemed incomprehensible to her. She had trouble even entertaining it as a hypothesis. . . . Szasz's bold claim was a bone sticking in her assumptive craw.

> —Mike Rose, *Lives on the Boundary* 183-84.

In perceiving conflicting information and points of view, she is subjected to a swamping of her psychological borders.

> —Gloria Anzaldua, *Borderlands/La Frontera: The New Mestiza* 79.

In the Preface to *Borderlands*, Gloria Anzaldua uses her own struggle "living . . . on borders and in margins" to discuss the trials and triumphs in the lives of "border residents." The image of "border residents" captures the conflict and struggle of students like those appearing in the epigraphs. In perceiving conflicting information and points of view, a writer like Anzaldua is "subjected to a swamping of her psy-

Lu, Min-zhan. "Conflict and Struggle: The Enemies or Preconditions of Basic Writing." *College English 54* (1992): 887-913. Copyright (1992) by the National Council of Teachers of English. Reprinted with permission.

chological borders (79). But attempts to cope with conflicts also bring "compensa-tions," "joys," and "exhilaration" (Anzaldua, Preface). The border resident develops a tolerance for contradiction and ambivalence, learning to sustain contra-diction and turn ambivalences into a new consciousness— "a *third* element which is *grea*ter than the sum of its *severed parts*": "a mestiza consciousness" (79-80; em-phasis mine). Experience taught Anzaldua that this developing consciousness is a source of intense pain. For development involves struggle which is "inner" and is played out in the outer terrains (87). But this new consciousness draws energy from the "continual creative motion that keeps breaking down the unitary aspect of each new paradigm" (80). It enables a border resident to act on rather than merely react to the conditions of her or his life, turning awareness of the situation into "inner changes" which in turn bring about "changes in society" (87).

Education as Repositioning

Anzaldua's account gathers some of the issues on which a whole range of recent composition research focuses, research on how readers and writers necessarily struggle with conflicting information and points of view as they reposition them-selves in the process of reading and writing. This research recognizes that reading and writing take place at sites of political as well as linguistic conflict. It acknowl-edges that such a process of conflict and struggle is a source of pain but constructive as well: a new consciousness emerges from the creative motion of breaking down the rigid boundaries of social and linguistic paradigms.

Compositionists are becoming increasingly aware of the need to tell and listen to stories of life in the borderlands. The CCCC Best Book Award given Mike Rose's *Lives on the Boundary* and the Braddock Award given to Glynda Hull and Mike Rose for their research on students like Lucia attest to this increasing awareness. *College Composition and Communication* recently devoted a whole issue (Febru-ary 1992) to essays which use images of "boundary," "margin," or "voice" to re-view the experience of reading and writing and teaching reading and writing within the academy (see also Lu, "From Silence to Words"; Bartholomae, "Writing on the Margins"' and Mellix). These publications and their reception indicate that the field is taking seriously two notions of writing underlying these narratives: the sense that the writer writes at a site of conflict rather than "comfortably inside or powerlessly outside of the academy" (Lu, "Writing as Repositioning" 20) and a def-inition of "innovative writing" as cutting across rather than confining itself within boundaries of race, class, gender, and disciplinary differences.

In articulating the issues explored by these narratives from the borderlands, compositionists have found two assumptions underlying various feminist, marxist, and poststructuralist theories of language useful: first, that learning a new discourse has an effect on the re-forming of individual consciousness; and second, that indi-vidual consciousness is necessarily heterogeneous, contradictory, and in process (Bizzell; Flynn; Harris; Lunsford, Moglen, and Slevin; Trimbur). The need to repo-sition oneself and the positive use of conflict and struggle are also explored in a range of research devoted to the learning difficulties of Basic Writers (Bartholomae, "Inventing"; Fox; Horner; Hull and Rose; Lu, "Redefining"; Ritchie; Spellmeyer; Stanley). Nevertheless, such research has had limited influence on Basic Writing instruction, which continues to emphasize skills (Gould and Heyda) and to view conflict as the enemy (Schilb, Brown). I believe that this view of conflict can be traced in the work of three pioneers in Basic Writing: Kenneth Bruffee, Thomas Farrell, and Mina Shaughnessy. In what follows, I examine why this view of conflict had rhetorical power in the historical context in which these pioneers worked and in relation to two popular views of education: education as acculturation and education as accommodation. I also explore how and why this view persists among Basic Writing teachers in the 1990s.

Although Bruffee, Farrell, and Shaughnessy hold different views on the goal of education, they all treat the students' fear of acculturation and the accompanying sense of contradiction and ambiguity as a *deficit*. Even though stories of the borderlands like Anzaldua's suggest that teachers can and should draw upon students' perception of conflict as a constructive resource, these three pioneers of Basic Writing view evidence of conflict and struggle as something to be dissolved and so propose "cures" aimed at *releasing* students from their fear of acculturation. Bruffee and Farrell present students' acculturation as inevitable and beneficial. Shaughnessy promises them that learning academic discourse will not result in acculturation. Teachers influenced by the work of these pioneers tend to view all signs of conflict and struggle as the *enemy* of Basic Writing instruction. In perpetuation this view, these teachers also tend to adopt two assumptions about language: 1) an "essentialist" view of language holding that the essence of meaning precedes and is independent of language (see Lu, "redefining" 26); 2) a view of "discourse communities" as "discursive utopias," in each of which a single, unified, and stable voice directly and completely determines the writings of all community members (Harris 12).

In the 1970s, the era of open admissions at CUNY, heated debate over the "educability" of Basic Writers gave these views of language and of conflict exceptional rhetorical power. The new field of Basic Writing was struggling to establish the legitimacy of its knowledge and expertise, and it was doing so in the context of arguments made by a group of writers—including Lionel Trilling, Irving Howe, and W.E.B. DuBois—who could be viewed as exemplary because of their ethnic or racial backgrounds, their academic success, and the popular view that all Basic Writers entering CUNY through the open admissions movement were "minority" students. The writings of Bruffee, Farrell, and Trilling concur that the goal of education is to acculturate students to the kind of academic "community" they posit. Shaughnessy, on the other hand, attempts to eliminate students' conflicting feelings towards academic discourse by reassuring them that her teaching will only "accommodate" but not weaken their existing relationship with their home cultures. Shaughnessy's approach is aligned with the arguments of Irving Howe and W E. B. DuBois, who urge teachers to honor students' resistance to deracination. Acculturation and accommodation were the dominant models of open admissions education for teachers who recognized teaching academic discourse as a way of empowering students, and in both models conflict and struggle were seen as the enemies of Basic Writing instruction.

This belief persists in several recent works by a new generation of compositionists and "minority" writers. I will read these writings from the point of view of the border resident and through a view of education as a process of repositioning. In doing so, I will also map out some directions for further demystifying conflict and struggle in Basic Writing instruction and for seeing them as the preconditions of all discursive acts.

Education as Acculturation

In *Errors and Expectations*, Mina Shaughnessy offers us one way of imagining the social and historical contexts of her work: she calls herself a trailblazer trying to survive in a "pedagogical West" (4). This metaphor captures the peripheral position of Basic Writing in English. To other members of the profession, Shaughnessy notes, Basic Writing is not one of their "'real' subjects"; nor are books on Basic Writing "important enough" either to be reviewed or to argue about ("English Professor's Malady" 92). Kenneth Bruffee also testifies to feeling peripheral. Recalling the "collaborative learning" which took place among the directors of CUNY writing programs—a group which included Bruffee himself, Donald McQuade, Mina Shaughnessy, and Harvey Wiener—he points out that the group was brought together not only by their "difficult new task" but also by their sense of having more in common with one another than with many of their "colleagues on [their] own campuses" ("On Not Listening" 4-5).

These frontier images speak powerfully of a sense of being *in* but not *of* the English profession. The questionable academic status of not only their students (seen as "ill-prepared") but also themselves (Basic Writing was mostly assigned to beginning teachers, graduate students, women, minorities, and the underemployed but tenured members of other departments) would pressure teachers like Shaughnessy and Bruffee to find legitimacy for their subject. At the same time, they had to do so by persuading both college administrators who felt "hesitation and discomfort" towards open admissions policies and "senior and tenured professorial staff" who either resisted or did not share their commitment (Lyons 175). Directly or indirectly, these pioneers had to respond to, argue with, and persuade the "gatekeepers" and "converters" Shaughnessy describes in "Diving In." It is in the context of such challenges that we must understand the key terms the pioneers use and the questions they consider—and overlook—in establishing the problematics of Basic Writing.

One of the most vehement gatekeepers at CUNY during the initial period of open admissions was Geoffrey Wagner (Professor of English at City College). In *The End of Education*, Wagner posits a kind of "university" in which everyone supposedly pursues learning for its own sake, free of all "worldly"—social, economic, and political—interests. To Wagner, open admissions students are the inhabitants of the "world" outside the sort of scholarly "community" which he claims existed at Oxford and City College. They are dunces (43), misfits (129), hostile mental children (247), and the most sluggish of animals (163). He describes a group of Panamanian "girls" taking a Basic Writing course as "abusive, stupid, and hostile" (128). Another student is described as sitting "in a half-lotus pose in back of class with a transistor strapped to his Afro, and nodding off every two minutes" (134). Wagner calls the Basic Writing program at City a form of political psychotherapy (145), a welfare agency, and an entertainment center (173). And he calls Shaughnessy "the Circe of CCNY's remedial English program" (129). To Wagner, Basic Writers would cause "the end of education" because they have intellects comparable to those of beasts, the retarded, the psychotic, or children, and because they are consumed by non-"academic"—i.e., racial, economic, and political—interests and are indifferent to "learning."

Unlike the "gatekeepers," Louis Heller (Classics Professor, City College) represents educators who seemed willing to shoulder the burden of converting the heathens but disapproved of the ways in which CUNY was handling the conversion. Nonetheless, in *The Death of the American University* Heller approaches the "problems" of open admissions students in ways similar to Wagner's. He contrasts the attitudes of open admissions students and of old Jewish City College students like himself:

> In those days ["decades ago"] there was genuine hunger, and deprivation, and discrimination too, but when a child received failing marks no militant parent group assailed the teacher. Instead parent and child agonized over the subject, placing the responsibility squarely on the child who was given to know that he had to measure up to par, not that *he* was the victim of society, a wicked school system, teachers who didn't understand him, or any of the other pseudosociological nonsense now handed out. (138)

According to Heller, the parents of open admissions students are too "militant." As a result, the students' minds are stuffed with "pseudosociological nonsense" about their victimization by the educational system. The "problem" of open admissions students, Heller suggests, is their militant attitude, which keeps them from trying to "agonize over the subject" and "measure up to par."

Wagner predicts the "end of education" because of the "*arrival* in urban academe of *large,* indeed *overwhelming, numbers of hostile* mental children" (247; emphasis mine). As the titles of Heller's chapters suggest, Heller too believes that a "Death of the American University" would inevitably result from the "Administrative Failure of Nerve" or "Capitulation Under Force" to "Violence on Campus" which he claims to have taken place at City College. The images of education's end or death suggest that both Wagner and Heller assume that the goal of education is the acculturation of students into an "educated community." They question the "educability" of open admissions students because they fear that these students would not only be hostile to the education they promote but also take it over—that is, change it. The apocalyptic tone of their book titles suggests their fear that the students' "hostile" or "militant" feelings towards the existing educational system would weaken the ability of the "American University" to realize its primary goal—to acculturate. Their writings show that their view of the "problems" of open admissions students and their view of the goal of education sustain one another.

This view of education as a process of acculturation is shared by Lionel Trilling, another authority often cited as an exemplary minority student (see, for example,

Howe, "Living" 108). In a paper titled "The Uncertain Future of the Humanistic Educational Ideal" delivered in 1974, Trilling claims that the view of higher education "as the process of initiation into membership" in a "new, larger, and more complex community" is "surely" not a "mistaken conception" (*The Last Decade* 170). The word "initiation," Trilling points out, designates the "ritually prescribed stages by which a person is brought into a community" (170-71). "Initiation" requires "submission," demanding that one "shape" and "limit" oneself to "a self, a life" and "preclude any other kind of selfhood remaining available" to one (171, 175; emphasis mine). Trilling doubts that contemporary American culture will find "congenial" the kind of "initiation" required by the "humanistic educational ideal" (171). For contemporary "American culture" too often encourages one to resist any doctrine that does not sustain aa multiplicity of options" (175). And Trilling admits to feeling "saddened" by the likelihood that "an ideal of education closely and positively related to the humanistic educational traditions of the past" will be called into being in contemporary America (161).

The trials of "initiation" are the subject of Trilling's short story "Notes on a Departure." The main character, a young college professor about to leave a university town, is portrayed as being forced to wrestle with an apparition which he sometimes refers to as the "angel of Jewish solitude" and, by the end of the story, as "a red-haired comedian" whose "face remained blank and idiot" (*Of This Time* 53, 55). The apparition hounds the professor, often reminding him of the question "'What for?' Jews did not do such things" (54). Towards the end of the story, the professor succeeds in freeing himself from the apparition. Arriving at a state of "readiness," he realizes that he would soon have to "find his *own* weapon, his *own* adversary, his *own* things to do"—findings in which "this red-haired figure . . . would have *no* part" (55; emphasis mine).

This story suggests—particularly in view of Trilling's concern for the "uncertain future" of the "humanistic educational ideal" in the 1970s—that contemporary Americans, especially those from minority cultural groups, face a dilemma: the need to combat voices which remind them of the "multiplicity of options." The professor needs to "wrestle with" two options of "selfhood." First, he must free himself from the authority of the "angel"/"comedian." Then, as the title "Notes on a Departure" emphasizes, he must free himself from the "town." Trilling's representation of the professor's need to "depart" from the voice of his "race" and of the "town" indirectly converges with the belief held by Wagner and Heller that the attitudes "parents" and "society" transmit to open admissions students would pull them away from the "university" and hinder their full initiation—acculturation—into the "educated" community.

Read in the 1990s, these intersecting approaches to the "problems" of "minority" students might seem less imposing, since except perhaps for Trilling, the academic prestige of these writers has largely receded. Yet we should not underestimate the authority these writers had within the academy. As both the publisher and the author of *The End of Education* (1976) remind us within the first few pages of the book, Wagner is not only a graduate of Oxford but a full professor at City College and author of a total of twenty-nine books of poetry, fiction, literary criticism, and sociology. Heller's *The Death of the American University* (1973) indicates that he has ten years' work at the doctoral or postdoctoral level in three fields, a long list of publications, and years of experience as both a full professor of classics and an administrator at City College (12). Furthermore, their fear of militancy accorded with prevalent reactions to the often violent conflict in American cities and college campuses during the 1960s and 70s. It was in the context of such powerful discourse that composition teachers argued for not only the "educability" of open admissions students but also the ability of the "pioneer" educators to "educate" them. Bruffee's and Farrell's eventual success in establishing the legitimacy of their knowledge and expertise as Basic Writing teachers, I believe, comes in part from a conjuncture in the arguments of the two Basic Writing pioneers and those of Wagner, Heller, and Trilling.

For example, Thomas Farrell presents the primary goal of Basic Writing instruction as acculturation—a move from "orality" to "literacy." He treats open admissions students as existing in a "residual orality": "literate patterns of thought have not been interiorized, have not displaced oral patterns, in them" ("Open Admissions" 248). Referring to Piaget, Ong, and Bernstein, he offers environmental rather than biological reasons for Basic Writers' "orality"—their membership in "communities" where "orality" is the dominant mode of communication. To Farrell, the emigration from "orality" to "literacy" is unequivocally beneficial for everyone, since it mirrors the progression of history. At the same time, Farrell recognizes that such a move will inevitably be accompanied by "anxiety": "The *psychic strain* entailed in moving from a highly oral frame of mind to a more literate frame of mind is *too great* to allow rapid movement" (252; emphasis mine). Accordingly, he promotes teaching strategies aimed at "reducing anxiety" and establishing "a supportive environment." For example, he urges teachers to use the kind of "collaborative learning" Bruffee proposes so that they can use "oral discourse to improve written discourse" ("Open Admissions" 252-53; "Literacy" 456-57). He reminds teachers that "highly oral students" won't engage in the "literate" modes of reasoning "unless they are shown how and reminded to do so often," and even then will do so only "gradually" ("Literacy" 456).

Kenneth Bruffee also defines the goal of Basic Writing in terms of the students' acculturation into a new "community." According to Bruffee, Basic Writers have already been acculturated within "local communities" which have prepared them for only "the narrowest and most limited" political and economic relations ("On Not Listening" 7). The purpose of education is to "reacculturate" the students—to help them "gain membership in another such community" by learning its "language, mores, and values" (8). However, Bruffee believes that the "trials of changing allegiance from one cultural community to another" demand that teachers use "collaborative learning" in small peer groups. This method will "create a *temporary transition* or 'support' group that [one] can join *on the way*" (8; emphasis mine). This "transition group," he maintains, will offer Basic Writers an arena for sharing their "trials," such as the "uncertain, nebulous, and protean thinking that occurs in the process of change" and the "painful process" of gaining new awareness ("On Not Listening" 11; "Collaborative Learning" 640).

Two points bind Bruffee's argument to Farrell's and enhance the rhetorical power of their arguments for the Wagners, Hellers, and Trillings. First, both arguments assume that the goal of education is acculturation into a "literate" community. The image of students who are "changing allegiance from one cultural community to another" (Bruffee), like the image of students "moving" from "orality" to "literacy" (Farrell), posits that "discourse communities" are discrete and autonomous entities rather than interactive cultural forces. When discussing the differences between "orality" and "literacy," Farrell tends to treat these "discourses" as creating coherent but distinct modes of thinking: "speaking" vs. "reading," "cliches" vs. "explained and supported generalizations," "additive" vs. "inductive or deductive" reasoning. Bruffee likewise sets "*coherent* but *entirely* local communities" against a community which is "broader, highly diverse, *integrated*" ("On Not Listening" 7; emphasis mine). Both Farrell and Bruffee use existing analyses of "discourse communities" to set up a seemingly nonpolitical hierarchy between academic and non-academic "communities." They then use the hierarchy to justify implicitly the students' need to be acculturated by the more advanced or broader "community." Thus, they can be construed as promising "effective" ways of appeasing the kind of "hostility" or "militancy" feared in open admissions students. The appeal of this line of thinking is that it protects the autonomy of the "literate community" while also professing a solution to the "threat" the open admissions students seem to pose to the university. Farrell and Bruffee provide methods aimed at keeping students like Anzaldua, Lucia, and the writer of Shaughnessy's sample paper from moving the points of view and discursive forms they have developed in their home "communities" into the "literate community" and also at persuading such students to willingly "move" into that "literate community."

Second, both Bruffee and Farrell explicitly look for teaching methods aimed at reducing the feelings of "anxiety" or "psychic strain" accompanying the process of acculturation. They thus present these feelings as signs of the students' still being "on the way" from one community to another, i.e., as signs of their failure to complete their acculturation or education. They suggest that the students are experiencing these trials only because they are still in "transition," bearing ties to both the old and new communities but not fully "departed" from one nor comfortably "inside" the other. They also suggest that these experiences, like the transition or support groups, are "temporary" (Bruffee, "On Not Listening" 8). In short, they sustain the impression that these experiences ought to and will disappear once the students get comfortably settled in the new community and sever or diminish their ties with the old. Any sign of heterogeneity, uncertainty, or instability is viewed as problematic; hence conflict and struggle are the enemies of Basic Writing instruction.

This linkage between students' painful conflicts and the teacher's effort to assuage them had rhetorical power in America during the 1970s because it could be perceived as accepting rather than challenging the gatekeepers' and converters' arguments that the pull of non-"academic" forces—"society" (Wagner), "militant parents" (Heller), and minority "race" or "American culture" at large (Trilling)—would render the open admissions students less "educable" and so create a "problem" in their education. It feeds the fear that the pulls of conflicting "options," "selfhoods," or "lives" promoted by antagonistic "communities" would threaten the university's ability to acculturate the Basic Writers. At the same time, this linkage also offers a "support system" aimed at releasing the gatekeepers and converters from their fear. For example, the teaching strategies Farrell promotes, which explicitly aim to support students through their "psychic strain," are also aimed at gradually easing them into "interiorizing" modes of thinking privileged by the "literate community," such as "inductive or deductive" reasoning or "detached, analytic forms of thinking" ("Literacy" 455, 456). Such strategies thus provide a support system for not only the students but also the kind of discursive utopia posited by Trilling's description of the "humanistic educational ideal," Heller's "American University," and Wagner's "education." Directly and indirectly, the pedagogies aimed at "moving" students from one culture to another support and are supported by gatekeepers' and converters' positions towards open admissions students.

The pedagogies of Bruffee and Farrell recognize the "psychic strain" or the "trials" experienced by those reading and writing at sites of contradiction, experiences which are depicted by writers like Trilling ("Notes on a Departure"), Anzaldua, and Rose and witnessed by teachers in their encounters with students like Lucia and the writer of Shaughnessy's sample paper. Yet, for two reasons, the approaches of Bruffee and Farrell are unlikely to help such students cope with the conflicts "swamping" their "psychological borders." First, these approaches suggest that the students' primary task is to change allegiance, to "learn" and "master" the "language, mores, and values" of the academic community presented in the classroom by passively internalizing them and actively rejecting all points of view or information which run counter to them (Bruffee, "On Not Listening" 8). For the author of Shaughnessy's sample student paper, this could mean learning to identify completely with the point of view of authorities like the Heller of *The Death of the American University* and thus rejecting "militant" thoughts about the "establishment" in order to "agonize over the subject." For Lucia, this could mean learning to identify with the Trilling of "Notes on a Departure," viewing her ability to forget the look in her brother's eyes as a precondition of becoming a psychologist like Szasz. Yet students like Lucia might resist what the classroom seems to indicate they must do in order to achieve academic "success." As Rose reminds us, one of the reasons Lucia decided to major in psychology was to help people like her brother. Students like these are likely to get very little help or guidance from teachers like Bruffee or Farrell.

Secondly, though Bruffee and Farrell suggest that the need to cope with conflicts is a temporary experience for students unfamiliar with and lacking mastery of dominant academic values and forms, Rose's account of his own education indicates that similar experiences of "confusion, anger, and fear" are not at all temporary (Rose 235-36). During Rose's high school years, his teacher Jack MacFarland had successfully helped him cope with his "sense of linguistic exclusion" complicated by "various cultural differences" by engaging him in a sustained examination of "points of conflict and points of possible convergence" between home and academic canons (193). Nevertheless, during Rose's first year at Loyola and then during his graduate school days, he continued to experience similar feelings when encountering texts and settings which reminded him of the conflict between home and school. If students like Rose, Lucia, or the writer of Shaughnessy's sample paper learn to view experiences of conflict exclusion, confusion, uncertainty, psychic pain or strain—as "temporary," they are also likely to view the recurrence of those experiences as a reason to discontinue their education. Rather than viewing their developing ability to sustain contradictions as heralding the sort of "new mestiza consciousness" Anzaldua calls for (80), they may take it as signaling their failure to "enter" the academy, since they have been led to view the academy as a place free of contradictions.

Education as Accommodation

Whereas the gatekeepers and converters want students to be either barred from or acculturated into academic culture, Irving Howe (Distinguished Professor of English, Graduate Center of CUNY and Hunter College), another City graduate often cited by the public media as an authority on the education of open admissions students (see Fiske), takes a somewhat different approach. He believes that "the host culture, resting as it does on the English language and the literary traditions associated with it, has . . . every reason to be *sympathetic* to the *problems* of those who, from choice or necessity, may *live with* the *tension of biculturalis*m" ("Living" 110; emphasis mine).

The best way to understand what Howe might mean by this statement and why he promotes such a position is to put it in the context of two types of educational stories Howe writes. The first type appears in his *World of Our Fathers*, in which he recounts the "cultural bleaching" required of Jewish immigrants attending classes at the Educational Alliance in New York City around the turn of this century. As Eugene Lyons, one immigrant whom Howe quotes, puts it, "We were 'Americanized' about as gently as horses are broken in." Students who went through this "crude" process, Lyons admits, often came to view their home traditions as "alien" and to "unconsciously resent and despise those traditions" (234). Howe points out that education in this type of "Americanization" exacted a price, leaving the students with a "nagging problem in self-perception, a crisis of identity" (642). Read in the context of Howe's statement on the open admissions students cited above, this type of story points to the kind of "problems" facing students who have to live with the tension between the "minority subcultures" in which they grow up and a "dominant" "Western" "host culture" with which they are trying to establish deep contact through education ("Living" 110). It also points to the limitations of an educational system which is not sympathetic to their problems.

The "Americanization" required of students like Eugene Lyons, Howe points out, often led Jewish students to seek either "a full return to religious faith or a complete abandonment of Jewish identification" (642). But Howe rejects both such choices. He offers instead an alternative story—the struggle of writers like himself to live with rather than escape from "the tension of biculturalism." In *A Margin of Hope*, he recounts his long journey in search of a way to "achieve some equilibrium with that earlier self which had started with childhood Yiddish, my language of naming, and then turned away in adolescent shame" (269). In "Strangers," Howe praises Jewish writers like Saul Bellow and the contributors to *Partisan Review* for their attitudes towards their "partial deracination" (*Selected Writings* 335). He argues that these writers demonstrated that being a "loose-fish" (with "roots loosened in Jewish soil but still not torn out, roots lowered into American soil but still not fixed") is "a badge" to be carried "with pride" (335). Doing so can open up a whole "range of possibilities" (335), such as the "forced yoking of opposites: gutter vividness and university refinement, street energy and high-culture rhetoric" Howe sees these writers achieving (338). This suggests what Howe might mean by "*living with* the tension of biculturalism*." The story he tells of the struggle of these Jewish writers also proves that several claims made in the academy of the earlier 1970s, as Howe points out, are "true and urgent": 1) students who grow up in "subcultures" can feel "pain and dislocation" when trying to "connect with the larger, cosmopolitan culture"; 2) for these students, "there must always be some sense of 'difference,' even alienation"; 3) this sense of difference can "yield moral correction and emotional enrichment" ("Living" 110). The story of these writers also suggests that when dealing with students from "subcultures," the dominant culture and its educational system need, as Howe argues, to be more "sympathetic to" the pain and alienation indicated by the first two claims, and at the same time should value more highly the "infusion of vitality and diversity from subcultures" that the third claim suggests these students can bring (110).

Howe believes that the need for reform became especially urgent in the context of the open admissions movement, when a large number of "later immigrants, newer Americans" from racial as well as ethnic "subcultures" arrived at CUNY ("A Foot"). He also believes that, although the dominant culture needs to be more "responsive" and "sympathetic" towards this body of students, it would be "a dreadful form of intellectual condescension—and social cheating" for members of the "host culture" to dissuade students from establishing a "deep connection" with it. The only possible and defensible "educational ideal" is one which brings together commitments to "the widespread diffusion of learning" and to the "preservation of the highest standards of learning" ("Living" 109).

However, as Howe himself seems aware throughout his essay, he is more convinced of the need to live up to this ideal than certain about how to implement it in the day-to-day life of teaching, especially with "the presence of large numbers of ill-prepared students in our classroom" ("Living" 110, 112). For example, the values of "traditionalism" mean that teachers like Howe should try to "preserve" the "English language and the literary traditions" associated with "the dominant culture we call Western" (109, 110). Yet, when Howe tries to teach *Clarissa* to his students, he finds out that he has to help students to "transpose" and "translate" Clarissa's belief in the sanctity of her virginity into their "terms." And he recognizes that the process of transposing would "necessarily distort and weaken" the original belief (112). This makes him realize that there is "reason to take seriously the claim" that "a qualitative transformation of Western culture threatens the survival of literature as we have known it" (112).

Although Howe promotes the images of "loose-fish" and "partial deracination" when discussing the work of Jewish writers, in his discussion of the education of "ill-prepared" students, he considers the possibility of change from only one end of the "tension of bi-culturalism"—that of "Western culture." His essay overlooks the possibility that the process of establishing a deep connection with "Western culture," such as teaching students to "transpose" their "subcultural" beliefs into the terms of "Western culture," might also "distort and weaken"— *transform*—the positions students take towards these beliefs, especially if these beliefs conflict with those privileged in "Western culture." In fact, teachers interested in actively honoring the students' decisions and needs to "live with the tension of biculturalism" must take this possibility seriously (see Lu, "Redefining" 33).

In helping students to establish deep connections with "Western culture," teachers who overlook the possibility of students' changing their identification with "subcultural" views are likely to turn education into an accommodation—or mere tolerance—of the students' choice or need to live with conflicts. This accommodation could hardly help students explore, formulate, reflect on, and enact strategies for coping actively with conflicts as the residents of borderlands do: developing a "tolerance for" and an ability to "sustain" contradictions and ambiguity (Anzaldua 79). Even if teachers explicitly promote the image of "partial deracination," they are likely to be more successful in helping students unconsciously "lower" and "fix" their roots into "Western culture" than in also helping them keep their roots from being completely "torn out" of "subcultures."

Two recurring words in Howe's essay, "preserve" and "survival," suggest a further problematic, for they represent the students as "preservers" of conflicting but unitary paradigms—a canonical "literary tradition" and "subcultures" with "attractive elements that merit study and preservation" ("Living" 110). This view of their role might encourage students to envision themselves as living at a focal point where "severed or separated pieces merely come together" (Anzaldua 79). Such perceptions might also lead students to focus their energy on "accommodating" their thoughts and actions to rigid boundaries rather than on actively engaging themselves in what to Anzaldua is the resource of life in the borderlands: a "continual creative motion" which breaks entrenched habits and patterns of behavior (Anzaldua 79). The residents of the borderlands act on rather than react to the "borders" cutting across society and their psyches, "borders" which become visible as they encounter conflicting ideas and actions. In perceiving these "borders," the mestizas refuse to let these seemingly rigid boundaries confine and compartmentalize their thoughts and actions. Rather, they use these "borders" to identify the unitary aspects of "official" paradigms which "set" and "separate" cultures and which they can then work to break down. That is, for the mestizas, "borders" serve to delineate aspects of their psyches and the world requiring change. Words such as "preserve" and "survival," in focusing the students' attention on accommodation rather than change, could not help students become active residents of the borderlands.

The problematics surfacing from Howe's writings the kind of "claims" about students from "subcultures" that he considers "true and urgent," the kind of "problems" he associates with students living with the tension of conflicting cultural forces, and the questions he raises as well as those he overlooks when discussing his "educational ideal"—map the general conceptual framework of a group of educators to whose writings I now turn. The writings of Leonard Kriegel, another member of the CUNY English faculty, seem to address precisely the question of how a teacher might implement in the day-to-day teaching of "remedial" students at City College, the educational ideal posited by Howe.

In *Working Through: A Teacher's Journey in the Urban University*, Kriegel bases his authority on his personal experience as first a City undergraduate and then a City professor before and during the open admissions movement. Kriegel describes himself as a "working-class Jewish youth"—part of a generation not only eager to "get past [its] backgrounds, to deodorize all smells out of existence, especially the smells of immigrant kitchens and beer-sloppy tables," but also anxious to emulate the "aggressive intellectualism" of City students (32, 123). Kriegel maintains that in his days as a student, there existed a mutual trust between teachers and students: "My teachers could assume a certain intelligence on my part; I, in turn, could assume a certain good will on theirs" (29).

When he was assigned to teach in the SEEK program, Kriegel's first impression was that such a mutual trust was no longer possible. For example, when he asked students to describe Canova's *Perseus Holding the Head of Medusa*, a student opened his paper, "When I see this statue it is of the white man and he is holding the head of the Negro" (176). Such papers led Kriegel to conclude that these students had not only "elementary" problems with writing but also a "racial consciousness [which] seemed to obscure everything else" (176). Yet working among the SEEK students gradually convinced Kriegel that the kind of mutual trust he had previously enjoyed with his teachers and students was not only possible but necessary. He discovered that his black and Puerto Rican students "weren't very different from their white peers": they did not lack opinions and they did want in to the American establishment (175, 178). They can and do trust the "good will" of the teacher who can honestly admit that he is a product of academic culture and believes in it, who rids himself of the "inevitable white guilt" and the fear of being accused of "cultural colonialism," and who permits the students to define their needs in relation to the culture rather than rejecting it for them (180). Kriegel thus urges teachers to "leave students alone" to make their own choices (182).

Kriegel's approach to his journey falls within the framework Howe establishes. The university ought to be "*responsive* to the needs and points of view of students who are *of two minds* about what Western culture offers them" ("Playing It Black" 11; emphasis mine). Yet, when summarizing the lessons he learned through SEEK, Kriegel implies that being "responsive" does not require anything of the teacher other than "*permit[ting]* the student *freedom of choice*, to let him take what he felt he needed and let go of what was not important to him" (*Working Through* 207; emphasis mine). Kriegel ultimately finds himself "mak[ing] decisions based on old values" and "placing greater and greater reliance on the traditional cultural orientation to which [he] had been exposed as an undergraduate" (201-2). The question he does not consider throughout his book is the extent to which his reliance on "old values" and "traditional cultural orientation" might affect his promise to accommodate the students' freedom of choice, especially if they are of "two minds" about what Western culture offers them. That is, he never considers whether his teaching practice might implicitly disable his students' ability to exercise the "freedom" he explicitly "permits" them.

Kriegel's story suggests that business in the classroom could go on as usual so long as teachers openly promise students their "freedom of choice." His story implies that the kind of teaching traditionally used to disseminate the conventions of the "English language or literary tradition" is politically and culturally neutral. It takes a two-pronged approach to educational reform: 1) explicitly stating the teacher's willingness to accommodate—i.e., understand, sympathize with, accept, and respect—the students' choice or need to resist total acculturation; 2) implicitly dismissing the ways in which particular teaching practices "choose" for students—i.e., set pressures on the ways in which students formulate, modify, or even dismiss—their position towards conflicting cultures (for comparable positions by other City faculty, see Volpe and Quinn). This approach has rhetorical currency because it both aspires to and promises to deliver the kind of education envisioned by another group of minority writers with established authority in 1970s America, a group which included black intellectuals W. E. B. DuBois and James Baldwin. Using personal and communal accounts, these writers also argue for educational systems which acknowledge students' resistance to cultural deracination. Yet, because their arguments for such an educational reform are seldom directly linked to discussion of specific pedagogical issues, teachers who share Kriegel's position could read DuBois and Baldwin as authorizing accommodation.

For example, in *The Education of Black People*, DuBois critiques the underlying principle of earlier educational models for black students, such as the "Hampton Idea" or the Fisk program, which do not help students deal with what he elsewhere calls their double-consciousness (12, 51). Instead, such models pressure students to "escape their cultural heritage and the body of experience which they themselves have built-up." As a result, these students may "meet *peculiar frustration* and in the end be unable to achieve success in the new environment or fit into the old" (144; emphasis mine).

DuBois's portrayal of the "peculiar frustration" of black students, like Howe's account of the "problems" of Jewish students, speaks powerfully of the need to consider seriously Howe's list of the "claims" made during the open admissions movement ("Living" 110). It also supports Howe's argument that the dominant culture needs to be more "sympathetic" to the "problems" of students from black and other ethnic cultures. DuBois's writings offer teachers a set of powerful narratives to counter the belief that students' interests in racial politics will impede their learning. In fact, DuBois's life suggests that being knowledgeable of and concerned with racial politics is a precondition to one's eventual ability to "force" oneself "in" and to "share" the world with "the owners" (*Education* 77).

At the same time, DuBois's autobiography can also be read as supporting the idea that once the teacher accepts the students' need to be interested in racial politics and becomes "sympathetic to"—acknowledges—their "peculiar frustration," business in the writing classroom can go on as usual. For example, when recalling his arrival at Harvard "in the midst of a violent controversy about poor English among students," DuBois describes his experiences in a compulsory Freshman English class as follows:

> I was at the point in my intellectual development when the content rather than the form of my writing was to me of prime importance. Words and ideas surged in my mind and spilled out with disregard of exact accuracy in grammar, taste in word or restraint in style. I knew the Negro problem and this was more important to me than literary form. I knew grammar fairly well, and I had a pretty wide vocabulary; but I was bitter, angry and intemperate in my first thesis.... Senator Morgan of Alabama had just published a scathing attack on "niggers," in a leading magazine, when my first Harvard thesis was due. I let go at him with no holds barred. My long and blazing effort came back marked "E"—not passed. (*Autobiography* 144)

Consequently, DuBois "went to work at" his English and raised the grade to a "C." Then, he "*elected* the best course on the campus for English composition," one which was taught by Barrett Wendell, "then the great pundit of Harvard English" (144-45; emphasis mine).

DuBois depicts his teacher as "fair" in judging his writing "technically" but as having neither any idea of nor any interest in the ways in which racism "scratch[ed] [DuBois] on the raw flesh" (144). DuBois presents his own interest in the "Negro problem" as a positive force, enabling him to produce "solid content" and "worthy" thoughts. At the same time, he also presents his racial/political interest as making him "bitter, angry, and intemperate." The politics of style would suggest that his "disregard of exact accuracy in grammar, taste in word or restraint in style" when writing the thesis might have stemmed not only from his failure to recognize the importance of *form* but also from the particular constraints this "literary form" placed on his effort to "spill out" bitter and angry contents against the establishment. Regard for "*accuracy* in grammar, *taste* in word or *restraint* in style" would have constrained his effort to "let go at [Senator Morgan] with no holds barred" (emphasis mine). But statements such as "style is subordinate to content" but "*carries* a message further" suggest that DuBois accepts wholeheartedly the view that the production of "something to say" takes place before and independent of the effort to "say it well" (144; emphasis mine). Nor does DuBois fault his teachers for failing to help him recognize and then practice ways of dealing with the politics of a "style" which privileges "restraint." Rather, his account suggests only that writing teachers need to become more understanding of the students' racial/political interests and their tendency to view "the Negro problem" as more important than "literary form." Thus, his account allows teachers to read it as endorsing the idea that once the teachers learn to show more interest in what the students "have to say" about racism, they can continue to teach "literary form" in the way DuBois's composition teachers did.

Neither do the writings of James Baldwin, whom Shaughnessy cites as the kind of "mature and gifted writer" her Basic Writers could aspire to become (*Errors* 197), provide much direct opposition to this two-pronged approach to reform. In "A Talk to Teachers" (originally published in the *Saturday Review,* 21 December 1963), Baldwin argues that "any Negro who is born in this country and undergoes the American educational system runs the risk of becoming schizophrenic" (Price 326; see also *Conversations* 183), thus providing powerful support for Howe's call for sympathy from the dominant culture. Baldwin does offer some very sharp and explicit critiques of the view of literary style as politically innocent. In "If Black

English Isn't a Language, Then Tell Me, What Is" Baldwin points out that "the rules of the language are dictated by what the language must convey" (*Price* 651). He later explains that standard English "was not designed to carry those spirits and patterns" he has observed in his relatives and among the people from the streets and churches of Harlem, so he "had to find a way to bend it [English]" when writing about them in his first book (*Conversations* 162). These descriptions suggest that Baldwin is aware of the ways in which the style of one particular discourse mediates one's effort to generate content or a point of view alien to that discourse. Yet, since he is referring to his writing experience *after* he has become what Shaughnessy calls a "mature and gifted writer" rather than to experience as a student in a writing classroom, he does not directly challenge the problematics surfacing in discussions of educational reform aimed at accommodation without change.

The seeming resemblances between minority educators and Basic Writers—their "subculture" backgrounds, the "psychic woe" they experience as a result of the dissonance within or among cultures, their "ambivalence" towards cultural bleaching, and their interest in racial/class politics—make these educators powerful allies for composition teachers like Shaughnessy who are not only committed to the educational rights and capacity of Basic Writers but also determined to grant students the freedom of choosing their alignments among conflicting cultures. We should not underestimate the support these narratives could provide for the field of Basic Writing as it struggled in the 1970s to establish legitimacy for its knowledge and expertise. I call attention to this support because of the intersection I see between Shaughnessy's approach to the function of conflict and struggle in Basic Writing instruction and the problematics I have sketched out in discussing the writings of Howe, Kriegel, DuBois, and Baldwin.

Like Howe and DuBois, Shaughnessy tends to approach the problems of Basic Writers in terms of their ambivalence toward academic culture:

> College both beckons and threatens them, offering to teach them useful ways of thinking and talking about the world, promising even to improve the quality of their lives, but threatening at the same time to take from them their distinctive ways of interpreting the world, to assimilate them into the culture of academia without acknowledging their experience as outsiders. (*Errors* 292)

Again and again, Shaughnessy reminds us of her students' fear that mastery of a new discourse could wipe out, cancel, or take from them the points of view resulting from "their experience as outsiders." This fear, she argues, causes her students to mistrust and psychologically resist learning to write. And she reasons that "if students understand why they are being asked to learn something and if the reasons given *do not conflict* with deeper needs for self-respect and loyalty to their group (whether that be an economic, racial, or ethnic group), they *are disposed* to learn it" (Errors 125; emphasis mine).

Shaughnessy proposes some teaching methods towards that end. For example, when discussing her students' difficulty developing an "academic vocabulary," she suggests that students might resist associating a new meaning with a familiar word because accepting that association might seem like consenting to a "linguistic betrayal that threatens to wipe out not just a word but the reality that the word refers to" (*Errors* 212). She then goes on to suggest that "if we consider the formal (rather than the contextual) ways in which words can be made to shift meaning we are closer to the kind of practical information about words BW students need" (212). Shaughnessy's rationale seems to be that the "formal" approach (in this case teaching students to pay attention to prefixes and suffixes) is more "practical" because it will help students master the academic meaning of a word *without* reminding them that doing so might "wipe out" the familiar "reality"—the world, people, and meanings—previously associated with that word. However, as I have argued elsewhere, the "formal" approach can be taken as "practical" only if teachers view the students' awareness of the conflict between the home meaning and the school meaning of a word as something to be "dissolved" at all costs because it will make them less "disposed to learn" academic discourse, as Shaughnessy seems to believe (Lu, "Redefining" 35). However, the experiences of Anzaldua and Rose suggest that the best way to help students cope with the "pain," "strain," "guilt," "fear," or "confusions" resulting from this type of conflict is not to find ways of "releasing" the students from these experiences or to avoid situations which might activate them. Rather, the "contextual" approach would have been more "practical," since it could help students deal self-consciously with the threat of "betrayal," especially if they fear and want to resist it. The "formal approach" recommended by Shaughnessy, however, is likely to be only a more "practical" way of preserving "academic vocabulary" and of speeding the students' internalization of it. As Rose's experiences working with students like Lucia indicate, it is exactly because teachers like him took the "contextual" approach—"encouraging her to talk through opinions of her own that ran counter to these discussions" (Rose 184-85)—that Lucia was able to get beyond the first twelve pages of Szasz's text and learn the "academic" meaning of "mental illness" posited by Szasz, a meaning which literally threatens to wipe out the "reality" of her brother's illness and her feelings about it.

Shaughnessy's tendency to overlook the political dimensions of the linguistic choices students make when reading and writing also points to the ways in which her "essentialist" view of language and her view of conflict and struggle as the enemies of Basic Writing instruction feed on one another (Lu, "Redefining" 26, 28-29). The supposed separation between language, thinking, and living reduces language into discrete and autonomous linguistic varieties or sets of conventions, rules, standards, and codes rather than treating language as a site of cultural conflict and struggle. From the former perspective, it is possible to believe, as Shaughnessy seems to suggest when opting for the "formal" approach to teaching vocabulary, that learning the rules of a new "language variety"—"the language of public transactions"—will give the student the "ultimate freedom of deciding how and when and where he will use which language" (*Errors* 11, 125). And it makes it possible for teachers like Shaughnessy to separate a "freedom" of choice in "linguistic variety" from one's social being one's need to deliberate over and decide how to reposition oneself in relationship to conflicting cultures and powers. Thus, it might lead teachers to overlook the ways in which one's "freedom" of cultural alignment might impinge on one's freedom in choosing "linguistic variety."

Shaughnessy's approach to Basic Writing instruction has rhetorical power because of its seeming alignment with positions taken by "minority" writers. Her portrayal of the "ambivalent feelings" of Basic Writers matches the experiences of "wrestling" (Trilling) and "partial deracination" (Howe), "the distinctive frustration" (DuBois), and "schizophrenia" (Baldwin) portrayed in the writings of the more established members of the academy. All thus lend validity to each other's understanding of the "problems" of students from minority cultures and to their critiques of educational systems which mandate total acculturation. Shaughnessy's methods of teaching demonstrate acceptance of and compassion towards students' experience of the kind of "dislocation," "alienation," or "difference" which minority writers like Howe, DuBois, and Baldwin argue will always accompany those trying by choice or need to "live with" the tensions of conflicting cultures. Her methods of teaching also demonstrate an effort to accommodate these feelings and points of view. That is, because of her essentialist assumption that words can express but will not change the essence of one's thoughts, her pedagogy promises to help students master academic discourse without forcing them to reposition themselves—i.e., to reform their relation—towards conflicting cultural beliefs. In that sense, her teaching promises to accommodate the students' need to establish deep contact with a "wider," more "public" culture by "releasing" them from their fear that learning academic discourse will cancel out points of view meaningful to their non "academic" activities. At the same time, it also promises to accommodate their existing ambivalence towards and differences from academic culture by assuming that "expressing" this ambivalence and these differences in academic "forms" will not change the "essence" of these points of view. The lessons she learns from her journey in the "pedagogical West" thus converge with those of Kriegel, who dedicates his book to "Mina Shaughnessy, who knows that nothing is learned simply." That is, when discussing her teaching methods, she too tends to overlook the ways in which her methods of teaching "linguistic codes" might weaken her concern to permit the students freedom of choice in their points of view. Ultimately, as I have argued, the teaching of both Shaughnessy and Kriegel might prove to be more successful in preserving the traditions of "English language and literature" than in helping students reach a self-conscious choice on their position towards conflicting cultural values and forces.

Contesting the Residual Power of Viewing Conflict and Struggles as the Enemies of Basic Writing Instruction: Present and Future

The view that all signs of conflict and struggle are the enemies of Basic Writing instruction emerged partly from a set of specific historical conditions surrounding the open admissions movement. Open admissions at CUNY was itself an attempt to deal with immediate, intense, sometimes violent social, political, and racial confrontations. Such a context seemed to provide a logic for shifting students' attention *away* from conflict and struggle and *towards* calm. However, the academic status which pioneers like Bruffee, Farrell, and Shaughnessy have achieved and the practical, effective *cures* their pedagogies seem to offer have combined to perpetuate the rhetorical power of such a view for Basic Writing instruction through the 1970s to the present. The consensus among the gatekeepers, converters, and accommodationists furnishes some Basic Writing teachers with a complacent sense that they already know all about the "problems" Basic Writers have with conflict and struggle. This complacency makes teachers hesitant to consider the possible uses of conflict and struggle, even when these possibilities are indicated by later developments in language theories and substantiated both by accounts of alternative educational experiences by writers like Anzaldua and Rose and by research on the constructive use of conflict and struggle, such as the research discussed in the first section of this essay.

Such complacency is evident in the works of compositionists like Mary Epes and Ann Murphy. Epes's work suggests that she is aware of recent arguments against the essentialist view of language underlying some composition theories and practices. For example, she admits that error analysis is complex because there is "a crucial area of overlap" between "*encoding*" (defined by Epes as "controlling the visual symbols which represent meaning on the page") and "*composing* (controlling meaning in writing)" (6). She also observes that students are most likely to experience the "conflict between composing and decoding" when the "norms of the written code" are "in conflict" with "the language of one's nurture" (31). Given Epes's recognition of the conflict between encoding and composing, she should have little disagreement with compositionists who argue that learning to use the "codes" of academic discourse would constrain certain types of meanings, such as the formulation of feelings and thoughts towards cultures drastically dissonant from academic culture. Yet, when Epes moves from her theory to pedagogy, she argues that teachers of Basic Writers can and ought to treat "encoding" and "composition" as two separate areas of instruction (31). Her rationale is simple: separating the two could avoid "exacerbating" the students' experience of the "conflict" between these activities (31). The key terms here (for me, at any rate) are "exacerbating" and "conflict." They illustrate Epes's concern to eliminate conflict, disagreement, tension, and complexity from the Basic Writing classroom (cf. Horner).

Ann Murphy's essay "Transference and Resistance" likewise demonstrates the residual power of the earlier view of conflict and struggle as the enemies of Basic Writing instruction. Her essay draws on her knowledge of the Lacanian notion of the decentered and destabilized subject. Yet Murphy argues against the applicability of such a theory to the teaching of Basic Writing on the ground that Basic Writers are not like other students. Basic Writers, Murphy argues, "may need centering rather than decentering, and cognitive skills rather than (or as compellingly as) self-exploration" (180). She depicts Basic Writers as "shattered and destabilized by the social and political system" (180). She claims that "being taken seriously as *adults* with something of value to say can, for many Basic Writing students, be a *traumatic* and *disorienting* experience" (180; emphasis mine). Murphy's argument demonstrates her desire to eliminate any sense of uncertainty or instability in Basic Writing classrooms. Even though Murphy is willing to consider the implications of the Lacanian notion of individual subjectivity for the teaching of other types of students (180), her readiness to separate Basic Writing classrooms from other classrooms demonstrates the residual power of earlier views of conflict and struggle.

Such a residual view is all the more difficult to contest because it is supported by a new generation of minority educators. For example, in "Teacher Background and Student Needs" (1991), Peter Rondinone uses his personal experiences as an open admissions student taking Basic Writing 1 at CCNY during the early 70s and his Russian immigrant family background in the Bronx to argue for the need to help Basic Writers understand that "in deciding to become educated there will be times when [basic writers] will be forced to . . . reject or *betray* their family and friends in order to succeed" ("Teacher" 42). Rondinone's view of how students might best deal with the conflict between home and school does not seem to have changed much since his 1977 essay describing his experience as a senior at City College (see Rondinone, "Open Admissions"). In his 1991 essay, this time writing from the point of view of an experienced teacher, Rondinone follows Bruffee in maintaining that "learning involves shifting social allegiances" ("Teacher" 49). My quarrel with Rondinone is not so much over his having opted for complete deracination (for I honor his right to choose his allegiance even though I disagree with his choice). I am, however, alarmed by his unequivocal belief that his choice is the *a priori* condition of his academic success, which reveals his conviction that conflict can only impede one's learning.

Shelby Steele's recent and popular *The Content of Our Character* suggests similar assumptions about experiences of cultural conflict. Using personal experiences, Steele portrays the dilemma of an African-American college student and professor in terms of being caught in the familiar "trap": bound by "two equally powerful elements" which are "at odds with each other" (95). Steele's solution to the problem of "opposing thrusts" is simple: find a way to "unburden" the student from one of the thrusts (160). Thus, Steele promotes a new, "peacetime" black identity which could "release" black Americans from a racial identity which regards their "middle-class" values, aspirations, and success as suspect (109).

To someone like Steele, the pedagogies of Bruffee, Farrell, and Rondinone would make sense. In such a classroom, the black student who told Steele that "he was not sure he should master standard English because then he "wouldn't be black no more"" (70) would have the comfort of knowing that he is not alone in wanting to pursue things "all individuals" want or in wishing to be drawn "into the American mainstream" (71). Furthermore, he would find support systems to ease him through the momentary pain, dislocation, and anxiety accompanying his effort to "unburden" himself of one of the "opposing thrusts." The popular success of Steele's book attests to the power of this type of thinking on the contemporary scene. Sections of his book originally appeared in such journals as *Harper's, Commentary,* the *New York Times Magazine,* and *The American Scholar.* Since publication of the book, Steele has been touted as an expert on problems facing African-American students in higher education, and his views have been aired on PBS specials, *Nightline,* and *The MacNeil/Lehrer News Hour,* and in *Time* magazine. The popularity of his book should call our attention to the direct and indirect ways in which the distrust of conflict and struggle continues to be recycled and disseminated both within and outside the academy. At the same time, the weight of the authority of the Wagners and Hellers should caution us to take more seriously the pressures the Rondinones and Steeles can exert on Basic Writing teachers, a majority of us still occupying peripheral positions in a culture repeatedly swept by waves of new conservatism.

But investigating the particular directions taken by Basic Writing pioneers when establishing authority for their expertise and the historical contexts of those directions should also enable us to perceive alternative ways of conversing with the Rondinones and Steeles in the 1990s. Because of the contributions of pioneers like Bruffee, Farrell, and Shaughnessy, we can now mobilize the authority they have gained for the field, for our knowledge as well as our expertise as Basic Writing teachers. While we can continue to benefit from the insights into students' experiences of conflict and struggle offered in the writings of all those I have discussed, we need not let their view of the cause and function of such experiences restrict how we view and use the stories and pedagogies they provide. Rather, we need to read them against the grain, filling in the silences left in these accounts by re-reading their experiences from the perspective of alternative accounts from the borderlands and from the perspective of new language and pedagogical theories. For many of these authors are themselves products of classrooms which promoted uncritical faith in either an essentialist view of language or various forms of discursive utopia that these writers aspired to preserve. Therefore, we should use our knowledge and expertise as compositionists to do what they did not or could not do: re-read their accounts in the context of current debates on the nature of language, individual consciousness, and the politics of basic skills. At the same time, we also need to gather more oppositional and alternative accounts from a new generation of students, those who can speak about the successes and challenges of classrooms which recognize the positive uses of conflict and struggle and which teach the process of repositioning. The writings of the pioneers and their more established contempo raries indicate that the residual distrust of conflict and struggle in the field of Basic Writing is sustained by a fascination with cures for psychic woes, by two views of education—as acculturation and as accommodation—and by two views of language—essentialist and utopian. We need more research which critiques portrayals of Basic Writers as belonging to an abnormal—traumatized or underdeveloped—mental state and which simultaneously provides accounts of the "creative motion" and "compensation," "joy," or "exhilaration" resulting from Basic Writers' efforts to grapple with the conflict within and among diverse discourses. We need more research analyzing and contesting the assumptions about language underlying teaching methods which offer to "cure" all signs of conflict and struggle, research which explores ways to help students recover the latent conflict and struggle in their lives which the dominant conservative ideology of the 1990s seeks to contain. Most of all, we need to find ways of foregrounding conflict and struggle not only in the generation of meaning or authority, but also in the teaching of conventions of "correctness" in syntax, spelling, and punctuation, traditionally considered the primary focus of Basic Writing instruction.

Author's Note: Material for sections of this essay comes from my dissertation, directed by David Bartholomae at the University of Pittsburgh. This essay is part of a joint project conducted with Bruce Homer which has been supported by the Drake University Provost Research Fund, the Drake University Center for the Humanities, and the University of Iowa Center for Advanced Studies. I gratefully acknowledge Bruce Horner's contributions to the conception and revisions of this essay.

Works Cited

Anzaldua, Gloria. *Borderlands/La Frontera: The New Mestiza.* San Francisco: spinsters/aunt lute, 1987.

Baldwin, James. *Conversations with James Baldwin.* Ed. Fred L. Standley and Louis H. Pratt. Jackson: UP of Mississippi, 1989.

_____ . *The Price of the Ticket.* New York: St. Martin's, 1985.

Bartholomae, David. "Inventing the University." *When a Writer Can't Write: Studies in Writer's Block and Other Composing Process Problems.* Ed. Mike Rose. New York: Guildford, 1985. 134–65.

_____ . "Writing on the Margins: The Concept of Literacy in Higher Education." *A Sourcebook for Basic Writing Teachers.* Ed. Theresa Enos. New York: Random, 1987. 66–83.

Bizzell, Patricia. "Beyond Anti-Foundationalism to Rhetorical Authority: Problems Defining 'Cultural Literacy.'" *College English* 52 (Oct. 1990): 661–75.

Brown, Rexford G. "Schooling and Thoughtfulness." *Journal of Basic Writing* 10.1 (Spring 1991): 3–15.

Bruffee, Kenneth A. "On Not Listening in Order to Hear: Collaborative Learning and the Rewards of Classroom Research." *Journal of Basic Writing* 7.1 (Spring 1988): 3–12.

_____ . "Collaborative Learning: Some Practical Models." *College English* 34 (Feb. 1973): 634–43.

DuBois, W. E. B. *The Autobiography of W. E. B. DuBois: A Soliloquy on Viewing My Life from the Last Decade of Its First Century.* New York: International, 1968.

_____ . *The Education of Black People: Ten Critiques 1906-1960.* Ed. Herbert Aptheker. Amherst: U of Massachusetts P, 1973.

Epes, Mary. "Tracing Errors to Their Sources: A Study of the Encoding Processes of Adult Basic Writers." *Journal of Basic Writing* 4.1 (Spring 1985): 4–33.

Farrell, Thomas J. "Developing Literacy: Walter J. Ong and Basic Writing." *Journal of Basic Writing* 2.1 (Fall/Winter 1978): 30–51.

_____ . "Literacy, the Basics, and All That Jazz." *College English* 38 Jan. 1977): 443–59.

_____ . "Open Admissions, Orality, and Literacy." *Journal of Youth and Adolescence* 3 (1974): 247–60.

Fiske, Edward B. ''City College Quality Still Debated after Eight Years of Open Admission." *New York Times* 19 June 1978: A1.

Flynn, Elizabeth. "Composing as a Woman." *College Composition and Communication* 39 (Dec. 1988): 423–35.

Fox, Tom. "Basic Writing as Cultural Conflict." *Journal of Education* 172.1 (1990): 65–83.

Gould, Christopher, and John Heyda. "Literacy Education and the Basic Writer: A Survey of College Composition Courses." *Journal of Basic Writing* 5.2 (Fall 1986): 8–27.

Harris, Joseph. "The Idea of Community in the Study of Writing." *College Composition and Communication* 40 (Feb. 1989): 11–22.

Heller, Louis G. *The Death of the American University: With Special Reference to the Collapse of City College of New York.* New Rochelle, NY: Arlington House, 1973.

Horner, Bruce. "Re-Thinking the 'Sociality' of Error: Teaching Editing as Negotiation." Forthcoming, *Rhetoric Review.*

Howe, Irving. "A Foot in the Door." *New York Times* 27 June 1975: 35.

_____ . "Living with Kampf and Schlaff: Literary Tradition and Mass Education." *The American Scholar* 43 (1973-74): 107–12.

_____ . *A Margin of Hope: An Intellectual Autobiography.* New York: Harcourt, 1982.

_____ . *Selected Writings 1950-1990.* New York: Harcourt, 1990.

_____ . *World of Our Fathers.* New York: Harcourt, 1976.

Hull, Glynda, and Mike Rose. "'This Wooden Shack Place': The Logic of an Unconventional Reading." *College Composition and Communication* 41 (Oct. 1990): 287–98.

Kriegel, Leonard. "Playing It Black." *Change* (Mar./Apr. 1969): 7–11.

_____ . *Working Through: A Teacher's Journey in the Urban University.* New York: Saturday Review, 1972.

Lu, Min-Zhan. "From Silence to Words: Writing as Struggle." *College English* 49 (Apr. 1987): 433–48
_____ . "Redefining the Legacy of Mina Shaughnessy: A Critique of the Politics of Linguisitic Innocence."
       Journal of Basic Writing 10.1 (Spring 1991): 26–40.
_____ . "Writing as Repositioning." *Journal of Education* 172.1 (1990): 18–21.
Lunsford, Andrea A., Helene Moglen, and James Slevin, eds. *The Right to Literacy.* New York: MLA, 1990.
Lyons, Robert. "Mina Shaughnessy." *Traditions of Inquiry.* Ed. John Brereton. New York: Oxford UP, 1985.
       171–89.
Mellix, Barbara. "From Outside, In." *Georgia Review* 41 (1987): 258–67.
Murphy, Ann. "Transference and Resistance in the Basic Writing Classroom: Problematics and Praxis."
       College Composition and Communication 40 (May 1989): 175–87.
Quinn, Edward. "We're Holding Our Own." Change (June 1973): 30–35.
Ritchie, Joy S. "Beginning Writers: Diverse Voices and Individual Identity." *College Composition and
       Communication* 40 (May 1989): 152–74.
Rondinone, Peter. "Teacher Background and Student Needs." *Journal of Basic Writing* 10.1 (Spring 1991):
       41–53.
_____ . "Open Admissions and the Inward 'I'." *Change* (May 1977): 43–47.
Rose, Mike. *Lives on the Boundary.* New York: Penguin, 1989.
Schilb, John. "Composition and Poststructuralism: A Tale of Two Conferences." *College Composition and
       Communication* 40 (Dec. 1989): 422–43.
Shaughnessy, Mina. "Diving In: An Introduction to Basic Writing." *College Composition and Communica-
       tion* 27 (Oct. 1976): 234–39.
_____ . "The English Professor's Malady." *Journal of Basic Writing* 3.1 (Fall/Winter 1980): 91–97.
_____ . *Errors and Expectations: A Guide for the Teacher of Basic Writing.* New York: Oxford UP, 1977.
Spellmeyer, Kurt. "Foucault and the Freshman Writer: Considering the Self in Discourse." *College English*
       51 (Nov. 1989): 715–29.
Stanley, Linda C. "'Misreading' Students' Journals for Their Views of Self and Society." *Journal of Basic
       Writing* 8.1 (Spring 1989): 21–31.
Steele, Shelby. *The Content of Our Character: A New Vision of Race in America.* New York: Harcourt, 1979.
Trilling, Lionel. *The Last Decade: Essays and Reviews, 1965-75.* Ed. Diana Trilling. New York: Harcourt,
       1979.
_____ . *Of This Time, Of That Place, and Other Stories.* Selected by Diana Trilling. New York: Harcourt,
       1979.
Trimbur, John. "Beyond Cognition: The Voices in Inner Speech." *Rhetoric Review* 5 (1987): 211–21.
Volpe, Edmond L. "The Confession of a Fallen Man: Ascent to the DA." *College English* 33 (1972):
       765–79.
Wagner, Geoffrey. *The End of Education.* New York: Barnes, 1976.

Toward a Post-Critical Pedagogy
of Basic Writing

Negotiating the Contact Zone[1]
by Joseph Harris

> What I want is less multiculturalism, which suggests the equal right of each group to police its boundaries, than a polyglot, cosmopolitan culture in which boundaries break down and individuals are free to reinvent themselves, not just affirm what they've inherited.
>
> —Ellen Willis, "Sex, Hope, and Madonna" (xxxii)

This article stems from a paper that I wrote several years ago and that went nowhere at the time—that was in fact rejected for publication, and I now think quite justly so, by reviewers for the *Journal of Basic Writing*. That paper was called "Growth, Initiation, and Struggle: Three Metaphors for Basic Writing," and in it I tried to delineate three stages of thinking about the teaching of composition—the first centering on metaphors of individual growth, the second on metaphors of initiation into academic discourse communities, and a third and evolving view emphasizing the need for students to name, confront, and struggle with a whole range of discourses of which they are part (home, school, work, religion, the media, and so on). The problem with my argument, as the readers for *JBW* were quick enough to point out, was that I treated my three central terms quite differently. While I offered a strenuous critique of the metaphors of growth and initiation, I glamorized notions of struggle and conflict, talking about them as though they were somehow the final answer to the difficulties of teaching writing. For a long while I didn't know how to respond to this criticism. It seemed fair; I just wasn't sure of how to gain a critical edge on a view of teaching that I found exciting and was only then beginning to formulate. So the paper sat there. In the meantime, quite a number of people have begun to talk about things like contact zones and conflict and struggle—enough to make the terms seem a little more accessible to critique. And so I'd like to pick up here where I left off in that paper, to point out some of the limits of the new vocabulary we have begun to use in talking about the aims, practices, and politics of teaching writing.

But first let me cover a bit of old ground. I'll do so quickly.[2] I'd argue that most serious approaches to teaching writing in the last twenty years have been framed by the competing metaphors of *growth* and *initiation*. Talk about learning has of course long been suffused by metaphors of growth. The strong effect these metaphors have had on the current teaching of writing in American colleges, though, stems in large part from the work of the 1966 Dartmouth Seminar, where many Americans were introduced to a "growth model" of teaching and learning that centered on the attempts of students to find increasingly rich and complex ways of putting experience into words. Many early studies of basic writing in the 1970s and 80s drew on the metaphor of growth in order to talk about the difficulties faced by basic writers, encouraging teachers to view such students as inexperienced or immature users of language and defining their task as one of helping students develop their nascent skills in writing. A continuum was set up between what inexperienced writers could already do and what they would be asked to do at a university. Academic discourse was presented not as something different from the sorts of writing and speech students were already familiar with, but as simply a more complex and powerful way of using words. The task set for student writers, then, was not so much to learn something new as to get better at what they could already do, to grow as users of language. The growth model pulled attention away from the forms of academic discourse and towards what students could or could not do with language. It also encouraged teachers to respect and work with the skills students brought to the classroom. Implicit in this view, though, was the notion that many students, and especially less successful or "basic" writers, were somehow stuck in an early stage of language development, their growth as language users stalled. Their writing was seen as "concrete-operational" rather than "formal," or "egocentric" rather than "reader-based," or "dualistic" rather than "relativistic."[3] However it was phrased, such writers ended up at the low end of some scale of conceptual or linguistic development—children in a world of adult discourse.

Yet this conclusion, pretty much forced by the metaphor of growth, ran counter to what many teachers felt they knew about their students—many of whom were returning to school after years at work, most of whom were voluble and bright in conversation, and almost all of whom seemed at least as adept as their teachers in dealing with the ordinary vicissitudes of life. What sense did it make to call these young adults "egocentric"? What if the trouble they were having with writing at college was less a sign of some general failing in their thought or language than evidence of their unfamiliarity with the workings of a specific sort of (academic) discourse? In a recent *JBW* article, Min-zhan Lu shows how this tension between the metaphors of growth and initiation ran through the work of Mina Shaughnessy—as can be seen especially in her 1977 *Errors and Expectations*, where Shaughnessy wavers between a respect for the diverse ways with words students bring with them to the university, and an insistence that, once there, they put them aside in order to take on a supposedly neutral and "adult language of public transactions" (Shaughnessy 125, Lu 35).

But if she was unable to resolve such conflicts, Shaughnessy did succeed in bringing questions of social context back into a discussion that had long been preoccupied with the thought and language of the writer viewed as an isolated individual, and it was this social bent in her thought that many of her most influential followers were to pick up on. In 1978, for instance, Patricia Bizzell invoked Shaughnessy in arguing that what basic writers most needed to learn was the "ethos of academic discourse," the characteristic ways in which university writers represented not only their work but themselves to their readers. From there, her next step was to argue that the academy formed a kind of "discourse community" with its own distinctive ways of using language. If this were so, then the task of teachers was not to help students grow into more complex uses of language but to "initiate" them into the peculiar ways in which texts get read and written at a university—an argument Bizzell was to make throughout the 1980s along with others like Mike Rose, Myra Kogen, and David Bartholomae.[4]

These theorists argued that in coming to the university students confront discourses that draw on and make use of rules, conventions, commonplaces, values, and beliefs that can be quite separate from (and sometimes in conflict with) those they already know or hold. These new forms of speech and writing are not only often more complex and refined than their own, they are *different* from their own. What student writers need to learn, then, is how to *shift* from using one form of discourse to another, which in turn means that many of the issues they face are not only intellectual but political and ethical as well. But if metaphors of growth tended to gloss over such conflicts and differences, metaphors of initiation have often seemed to exaggerate them. It soon became commonplace to argue that one masters a discourse by entering into the community that uses it, by accepting the practices and values of that community as one's own. But this seemed to lead to yet another transmission metaphor for learning in which experts initiate novices into the beliefs and practices of the community. In acquiring a new discourse the student was pictured as moving from one community to another, leaving behind old ways of interpreting in order to take on new forms of organizing experience. Learning was equated with assimilation, acculturation, conversion: You need to get inside to get heard, but to get in you may have to give up much of who you used to be. As Bizzell put it in her 1986 essay on "What Happens When Basic Writers Come to College," "Upon entering the academic community, [students are] asked to learn a new dialect and new discourse conventions, but the outcome of such learning is the acquisition of a whole new world view" (297).

And so by the late 1980s, a number of teachers and theorists, myself included, had started to argue that this is not the case, that the metaphor of initiation—with its split between insiders and outsiders—misrepresents not only the task faced by student writers but the conditions that give rise to much good writing. For both the metaphors of growth and initiation view the student writer as a kind of special case: The first sees her as an adult whose uses of language are mysteriously immature, the second as someone who has found her way into the university and yet somehow remained an outsider to it. But what if students were viewed instead as dramatizing a problem that all of us face—that of finding a place to speak within a discourse that does not seem to ignore or leave behind the person you are outside of it? If this is so, then the job of a student writer is not to leave one discourse in order to enter another, but to take things that are usually kept apart and bring them together, to negotiate the gaps and conflicts between several competing discourses. The goal of courses in writing would thus become less the nurturing of individual student voices, or the building of collaborative learning communities, but the creation of a space where the conflicts between our own discourses, those of the university, and those which our students bring with them to class are made visible.

Such spaces have been named "contact zones" by the theorist and critic Mary Louise Pratt, who in coining the term borrowed from the sociolinguistic notion of a "contact language"—that is, a sort of creole or pidgin that speakers of differing languages develop when forced into communication with one another. In an influential article that she wrote for *Profession 91*, Pratt defines contact zones as "spaces where cultures meet, clash, and grapple with each other, often in contexts of highly asymmetrical relations of power, such as colonialism, slavery or their aftermaths as they are lived out in the world today" (34), and then puts the term to use in theorizing a teaching practice which seeks not to erase linguistic and cultural differences but to examine them. Her ideas have held strong appeal for many teachers of basic writing, perhaps since our classrooms seem so often a point of contact for various and competing languages and perspectives, and in the last few years a growing number of theorists have cited Pratt in arguing for pedagogies that are open to conflict and controversy.[5]

In her *Profession* article, Pratt draws on her experiences both as the parent of a school-age child and as the teacher of a large introductory course in "Culture, Ideas, Values" at Stanford University in order to sketch out what a classroom might look like if thought of as contact zone rather than as a unified community. She analyzes moments where teachers fail not only to deal with dissent but even to acknowledge it. For instance, she tells of how when told to write about "a helpful invention" he would like to have for his own use, her fourth-grade son came up with an idea for a vaccine that would inoculate him with answers for stupid homework assignments (like this one, presumably). What did he get in response? "The usual star to indicate the task had been fulfilled in an acceptable way" (3839). In a similar vein, Pratt tells of a conversation she had with her son when he switched from a traditional to a more progressive school:

> "Well," he said, "they're a lot nicer, and they have a lot less rules. But know *why* they're nicer?"
> "Why?" I asked. "So you'll obey all the rules they don't have," he replied. (38)

In both cases conflict and difference get dealt with by not being noticed—much as the views, experiences, and writings of minority cultures have been studiously ignored in most American classrooms, even in schools where many students are African American, Asian, Hispanic, or working class. This leads Pratt to call for classrooms where such voices do get heard, even if at the cost of some conflict or confusion—for pedagogical contact zones rather than communities.

This is an appealing idea. Pratt is vague, though, about how one might actually go about making sure such dissenting voices get their say. What she seems to be doing is *importing* difference into her classroom through assigning her students a number of readings from diverse cultures. Students are thus brought "in contact" with writings from various cultures, but Pratt never explains the kinds of talk about these texts that occur among and across the various groupings of *students* that make up the class. That is, at no point does Pratt speak of how she tries to get students to articulate or negotiate the differences they perceive among themselves. How, for instance, might white students speak with black classmates about a text written by an African author? What forms of evasion, overpoliteness, resistance, hostility, or boredom might be expected to interfere with their talk? And how might these be lessened or acknowledged so something more like conversation and less like a simple trading of positions can take place? Or what happens when a student finds that—due to the accidents of race or class or gender—he or she has somehow become the "representative" of a text (and by implication, culture) that the class is reading? In what ways is this student free to criticize or resist as well as to celebrate or identify with the claims that the text may be making? Or, conversely, how do students who are not members of the same culture as the author of a text gain the authority to speak critically about it?

Pratt has little to say about such questions. Part of the problem no doubt has to do with the logistics of teaching a large lecture course. But I think her silence about practical issues in teaching also points to a real difficulty with how she has conceptualized the idea of a contact zone. Pratt's phrasings evoke images of war and oppression, of "grappling and clashing" in contexts of "colonialism, slavery or their aftermaths." And yet many students whom I have asked to read and write about Pratt's article have chosen instead to view the contact zone as a kind of multicultural bazaar, where they are not so much brought into conflict with opposing views as placed in a kind of harmless connection with a series of exotic others. While I think this is a misreading of Pratt, it is one encouraged by her examples, which tend to be either innocuous or esoteric—a clever dodge on a homework assignment, an odd Peruvian text (more on this later). Taken either way, as hinting at conflict or at connection, what is missing from such descriptions of the contact zone is a sense of how competing perspectives can be made to intersect with and inform each other. The very metaphor of *contact* suggests a kind of superficiality: The image is one of cultures banging or sliding or bouncing off each other. Pratt offers little sense of how more tolerant or cosmopolitan cultures might be created out of the collisions of such local groupings, or of how (or why) individuals might decide to change or revise their own positions (rather than simply to defend them) when brought into contact with differing views.

So far as I can determine, contact languages do not often seem to hold the sort of symbolic or personal value for their users that native languages do; they are rather born out of expediency, as a way of getting by. It is thus a little hard to see who (except perhaps for a teacher) would have much at stake in preserving the contact zone, since it is not a space to which anyone owes much allegiance. And, indeed, in her descriptions of her own teaching, Pratt quickly retreats to talk about the importance of what she calls "safe houses," which she describes as places for "healing and mutual recognition... in which to construct shared understandings, knowledges, claims on the world" (40). Pratt thus fails to do away with the idea of a unified and utopian community; she simply makes it smaller, reduces it to the level of an affinity group. And so while her aim is to offer a view of intellectual life in which difference and controversy figure more strongly than in descriptions of seemingly homogenous discourse communities, she is left in the end with no real answer to the question of how one constructs a public space in which the members of various "safe houses" or affinity groups are brought into negotiation (not just conflict or contact) with other competing views and factions. Or, to put the question in terms of classroom practice, Pratt never makes it clear how a teacher might help students move between the exhilaration and danger of contact zones and the nurturance of safe houses.

Much of this issue was recently the subject of intense debate in the pages of *College English*, sparked by Min-zhan Lu's 1992 piece on "Conflict and Struggle: The Enemies or Preconditions of Basic Writing?" Lu argues that in seeking to make their classrooms more comfortable and less threatening, many basic writing teachers end up disallowing the very expression of conflict and difference that could lend real interest to the writings of their students. Such teachers thus enforce a kind of stylistic and intellectual blandness by in effect making sure that students never get to draw on their strengths as writers—since doing so would surface the very sort of conflicts in culture, language, and politics that many teachers hope to contain and assuage. Lu's piece attracted a number of vehement responses which appeared in a "Symposium on Basic Writing" the following year in *College English*. Her critics argued variously that she romanticized the underclass, didn't work with "real" basic writers, was too hard on her students, and was intent on imposing her own political program upon them. Lu replied that she had been misunderstood, and that it was not she but her respondents who were acting as if they had sure knowledge of what the needs, abilities, and concerns of basic writers were. And thus it was they, not she, who were verging on intellectual and political dogmatism.

Basically, I agree with Lu on all counts. But I found myself troubled by the form the debate had taken, which reminded me of several difficult and polarizing arguments that had recently occurred in the department where I work over issues in personnel and required course offerings. For while there was plenty of conflict and struggle in these arguments, very little if any of it seemed to result in a useful negotiation of views or perspectives. Instead the exchanges quickly devolved into a kind of position-taking, as the competing factions on both sides of the issue soon retreated back to and defended the very arguments they had entered the debate with. As it happens, I was on the losing side of one of those departmental arguments and on the winning side of the other, and I can say that I felt equally miserable after both. For neither argument produced anything but a victory or a loss; no refinement of ideas, no negotiation of perspectives, no real surprises (at least of an intellectual sort) came out of either. And I felt much the same way reading the arguments in *College English*: I knew what side I was on, but that was pretty much it; I didn't feel as though I had learned much from the encounter. Such experiences have helped to convince me that there is something missing from a view of teaching that suggests that we simply need to bring people out of their various "safe houses" and into a "contact zone"—and that is a sense of how to make such a meeting of differences less like a battle and more like a negotiation. We need, that is, to learn not only how to articulate our differences but how to bring them into useful relation with each other.

Pratt tends to downplay the importance of such negotiation and to romanticize the expression of dissent. "What is the place of unsolicited oppositional discourse" in the classroom? (39), she asks, but her few examples of resistance are all suspiciously sympathetic. Her son is clearly a smart and likeable kid, and we appreciate his parodies of schooling even if his actual teachers do not. And the only other example Pratt offers of a writer in the contact zone is rather exotic: Guaman Poma, a seventeenth-century Peruvian cleric who wrote a long and slightly mad letter to the King of Spain, explaining and defending his home culture to its new colonial ruler. Pratt praises Poma for his blurring of western and indigenous discourses, dominant and oppositional ideologies, but his writing could just as readily be seen as a negative example of two cultures brought into contact but not meaningful interaction—since the letter Poma wrote quite literally made nothing happen: The King of Spain never read it and it lay unnoticed in an Amsterdam archive for the next three centuries. Tellingly, much of the current appeal of Poma's text has to do with how it voices the very sort of "opposition" to the status quo that, as liberal academics, we now most tend to value. Poma's letter is a hypererudite version of the sort of writing we wish we *would* get from students but rarely do. In particular, Poma says just the right sort of thing for advocates (like both Pratt and myself) of a more culturally diverse reading list for undergraduates in the current debate over the canon. His unsolicited oppositional discourse has made it to *our* mailboxes if not to the King of Spain's. We have read it and we agree.

But what about discourse we don't agree with? What about students or writings that oppose our own views or authority? The "Culture, Ideas, Values" course that Pratt taught was the focus of a highly publicized debate over political correctness at Stanford a few years ago.[6] While I don't side with its detractors, I do think we have to see how the inability of Pratt (and many others) to articulate how the competing views of students in their courses are acknowledged, criticized, and negotiated points to a legitimate worry about the micropolitics of teaching—about whose voices get heard in what classrooms and why. This is not a concern that can be answered with new theories or new reading lists; it calls instead for attention to the details of classroom work, to how teachers set up and respond to what students have to say.

And this is precisely where teachers of writing can powerfully extend and revise the agenda of recent cultural criticism. For instance, in his recent "Fault Lines in the Contact Zone," Richard E. Miller contrasts two differing and actual forms of response to what was, in both cases, truly unsolicited and unwanted discourse. In the first instance, the chairman of a large corporation responded to a racist illustration in a company magazine by firing several of the people involved with its production and writing a letter to his employees calling the cartoon a "deplorable mistake" and urging them to "tear that page out and throw it in the trash where it belongs" (389-90). In the second case, an openly gay teacher responded to a homophobic student narrative by treating it as a work of fiction and commenting on its effectiveness as a story—a strategy which, while in some ways dodging the politics of the piece, did not totally avoid or dismiss its troubling content and also kept student and teacher on good working terms. Miller notes that when this teaching situation was discussed at a recent meeting of CCCC, most of the teachers present argued for a response much closer to that of the corporate chairman's—namely, "that the student be removed from the classroom and turned over either to a professional counselor or to the police" (392), while others insisted on ignoring the content of the piece altogether and commenting on its formal surface features alone. Though Miller admits that the teacher's decision to treat the essay as fiction was in many ways a problematic one, he argues that:

> [The chairman] did not address the roots of the problem that produced the offensive cartoon; he merely tried to make it more difficult for another "deplorable mistake" of this kind to further tarnish the image of multicultural harmony the company has been at such pains to construct. [The teacher], on the other hand, achieved the kind of partial, imperfect, negotiated, microvictory available to those who work in the contact zone when he found a way to respond to his student's essay that... kept the student in his course. (407)

The lesson to be learned here, then, is not that treating troubling student writings as fiction is always or even usually a good idea, but that if we hope to get students to re-think (rather than merely repress) what strike us as disturbing positions—if we want, that is, to work with students who voice beliefs that are not so much "oppositional" as they are simply opposed to our own—then we need first to find ways of keeping them an active part of the conversation of the class. Miller deepens the idea of the contact zone by imagining it not as a space which one can form simply through bringing differing groups and views together, but as a forum which one can only keep going through a constant series of local negotiations, interventions, and compromises. The contact zone thus becomes something more like a process or event than a physical space—and it thus needs to be theorized, as Miller does, as a local and shifting series of interactions among perspectives and individuals.

A similar interest in how differences get negotiated (or not) in varying situations by particular teachers and students now characterizes some of the best work being done in composition. Tom Fox, for instance, has explored how African-American students can learn to use writing not only to enter into the university but also (and at the same time) to criticize some of its characteristic values ("Repositioning"). Similarly, Geoff Chase and Bruce Herzberg have described writing courses that have helped students from comfortable backgrounds (white, suburban, upper-middle-class) take on a much more critical stance towards mainstream American culture than might have been expected while, conversely, Cy Knoblauch and James Berlin have noted how students can often resist or tune out teachers who seem to push a particular political line too openly or aggressively. And Bruce Horner and Min-zhan Lu ("Professing") have both written on ways of teaching students to edit their writing that problematize easy distinctions between "error" and "style," and thus point to very specific and local ways in which a writer's phrasings can be linked to a set of political choices and affiliations. Such work does more than take the concerns of recent cultural criticism with conflict and diversity and apply them to the classroom. It redefines those concerns by looking for signs of difference not only in the revered texts of a culture (whether these are seen as authored by Guaman Poma or William Shakespeare, Alice Walker or Saul Bellow, Emily Dickinson or Janet Jackson) but also in the views and writings of ordinary people. Rather than representing life in the contact zone through a set of ideal texts or suggestive yet brief classroom anecdotes, such work populates it with the differing and sometimes disturbing writings of actual students. The contact zone thus becomes less of a neomarxist utopia and more of a description of what we now often actually confront in our classrooms: a wrangle of competing interests and views. And the goals of pedagogies of the contact zone, of conflict, become not the forcing of a certain "multicultural" agenda through an assigned set of readings or lectures but the creating of a forum where students themselves can articulate (and thus perhaps also become more responsive to) differences among themselves.

Still I worry about the view of intellectual life that the idea of the contact zone seems to promote. One of the central aims of public education in America—at least when viewed from a certain liberal or Deweyite perspective—is that of working towards the forming of a nation state that is not tied to any single ethnicity, of helping to create a public culture open to all individuals regardless of race, gender, or social rank. To invoke this sort of democratic culture is *not* to call for a return to a set of shared and communal values; rather, it is to call for a forum in which issues and concerns that go *beyond* the borders of particular communities or interest groups can be worked through collectively, debated, negotiated. It is to call for a sort of public discourse, that is, that dialogue about contact zones and safe houses often seems to work against. Look, for instance, at this brief glimpse Pratt offers us of her Stanford course:

> All the students in the class had the experience, for example, of hearing *their culture* discussed and objectified in ways that horrified them; all the students saw *their roots* traced back to legacies of both glory and shame; all the students experienced face-to-face the ignorance and incomprehension, and occasionally the hostility, of others. (39, my italics)

"Their culture" and "their roots" subjected to the uncomprehending gaze of "others." There is no hint here that, despite the differences in their backgrounds, these students might also hold some experiences in common as members of contemporary American culture, or even that they might share a certain set of concerns and issues as U.S. citizens. Instead we are offered an image of a balkanized classroom: a collection of different "cultures" with separate "roots" clustered in their various "safe houses." Who could blame students in such a class if they chose not to venture into the "contact zone" that sprawls dangerously beyond? What reason, beyond the thrill of the exotic, have they been offered for doing so? Why should they care about what goes on in the contact zone if they already have their safe houses to live in?

I don't mean in any way to suggest that we should step back from a valuing of difference or a willingness to work through the conflicts that may result from doing so. But I am growing less inclined to valorize notions of conflict or struggle in and of themselves. I want instead to argue for a more expansive view of intellectual life than I now think theories of the contact zone have to offer—one that admits to the ways in which we are positioned by gender, race, and class, but that also holds out the hope of a more fluid and open culture in which we can *choose* the positions we want to speak from and for. To work as teachers towards such a culture, we need to move beyond thinking in terms of fixed affinities or positions and the possible conflicts between them. We instead need to imagine a different sort of social space where people have *reason* to come into contact with each other because they have claims and interests that extend beyond the borders of their own safe houses, neigh-borhoods, disciplines, or communities. We need to find ways of urging writers not simply to defend the cultures into which they were born but to imagine new public spheres which they would like to have a hand in making.

Notes

1. I have had the opportunity to present various versions of this article at a number of conferences—CCCC, the National Conference on Basic Writing, Penn State—and thus owe thanks to the many colleagues who have talked with me about these issues. But I would particularly like to thank Tom Fox, Richard Miller, and Phil Smith for the advice they offered me in refining this piece for publication.
2. I have criticized each of these metaphors at some length in "After Dartmouth: Growth and Conflict in English" and "The Idea of Community in the Study of Writing."
3. These terms come from three pioneering works on basic writing: Lunsford's "Content of Basic Writers' Essays," Flower's "Revising Writer-Based Prose," and Hays' "Development of Discursive Maturity in College Writers."
4. See Bizzell's "College Composition" and "What Happens," Rose's "Remedial Writing" and "Language of Exclusion," Kogen's "Conventions," and Bartholomae's "Inventing."
5. See Lu's "Conflict and Struggle," Fox's "Basic Writing as Cultural Conflict," Bartholomae's "Tidy House," and Bizzell's "Contact Zone."
6. Pratt herself offers an account of this debate in "Humanities for the Future."

Works Cited

Bartholomae, David. "Inventing the University." *Journal of Basic Writing* 5.1 (1986): 4-23.

_____ . "The Tidy House: Basic Writing in the American Curriculum." *Journal of Basic Writing* 12.1 (1993): 4-21.

Berlin, James. "Composition and Cultural Studies." *Composition and Resistance.* Ed. C. Mark Hurlbert and Michael Blitz. Portsmouth, NH: Boynton, 1991. 47-55.

Bizzell, Patricia. "College Composition: Initiation into the Academic Discourse Community." *Curriculum Inquiry* 12.2 (1982): 191 -207.

_____ . "Contact Zones and English Studies." *College English* 56 (1994): 163-69.

_____ . "The Ethos of Academic Discourse." *College Composition and Communication* 29 (1978): 351-55.

_____ . "What Happens When Basic Writers Come to College?" *College Composition and Communication* 37 (1986): 294-301.

Chase, Geoffrey. "Accommodation, Resistance, and the Politics of Student Writing." *College Composition and Communication* 39 (1988): 13-22.

_____ . "Perhaps We Just Need to Say Yes." *Journal of Education* 172 (1990): 29-37.

Flower, Linda. "Revising Writer-Based Prose." *Journal of Basic Writing* 3.3 (1981): 62-74.

Fox, Tom. "Basic Writing as Cultural Conflict." *Journal of Education* 172 (1990): 65-83.

_____ . "Repositioning the Profession: Teaching Writing to African American Students." *Journal of Advanced Composition* 12 (1992): 291-304.

Harris, Joseph. "After Dartmouth: Growth and Conflict in English." *College English* 53 (1991): 631-46.

_____ . "The Idea of Community in the Study of Writing." *College Composition and Communication* 40 (1989): 11-22.

Hays, Janice. "The Development of Discursive Maturity in College Writers." *The Writer's Mind: Writing as a Mode of Thinking.* Ed. Janice Hays, Phyllis A. Roth, Jon R. Ramsey, and Robert D. Foulke. Urbana, IL: NCTE, 1983. 127-44.

Herzberg, Bruce. "Community Service and Critical Literacy." *College Composition and Communication* 45 (1994): 307-19.

Horner, Bruce. "Rethinking the 'Sociality' of Error: Teaching Editing as Negotiation." *Rhetoric Review* 11 (1992): 172-99.

Knoblauch, C. H. "Critical Teaching and Dominant Culture." *Composition and Resistance.* Ed. C. Mark Hurlbert and Michael Blitz. Portsmouth, NH: Boynton, 1991. 12-21.

Kogen, Myra. "The Conventions of Expository Writing." *Journal of Basic Writing* 5.1 (1986): 24-37.

Lu, Min-zhan. "Conflict and Struggle: The Enemies or Preconditions of Basic Writing?" *College English* 54 (1992): 887-913.

_____. "Professing Multiculturalism: The Politics of Style in the Contact Zone." *College Composition and Communication* 45 (1994): 442-58.

_____. "Redefining the Legacy of Mina Shaughnessy: A Critique of the Politics of Linguistic Innocence." *Journal of Basic Writing* 10.1 (1991): 26-40.

Lunsford, Andrea. "The Content of Basic Writers' Essays." *College Composition and Communication* 31 (1980): 278-90.

Miller, Richard E. "Fault Lines in the Contact Zone." *College English* 56 (1994): 389-408.

Pratt, Mary Louise. "Arts of the Contact Zone." *Profession 91* (1991): 33-40.

_____. "Humanities for the Future: Reflections on the Western Culture Debate at Stanford." *South Atlantic Quarterly* 89 (1990): 7-26.

Rose, Mike. "The Language of Exclusion: Writing Instruction at the University." *College English* 47 (1985): 341-59.

_____. "Remedial Writing Courses: A Critique and a Proposal." *College English* 45 (1983): 109.

Shaughnessy, Mina P. *Errors and Expectations.* New York: Oxford UP, 1977.

"Symposium on Basic Writing." Patricia Laurence, Peter Rondinone, Barbara Gleason, Thomas J. Farrell, Paul Hunter, and Min-Zhan Lu. *College English* 55 (1993): 879-903.

Willis, Ellen. "Sex, Hope, and Madonna." Introduction to the 2nd ed. *Beginning to See the Light.* Hanover, NH: Wesleyan UP, 1992. xxiii-xxxvi.

The Tidy House: Basic Writing in the American Curriculum
by David Bartholomae

The unrecognized contradiction within a position that valorizes the concrete experience of the oppressed, while being so uncritical about the historical role of the intellectual, is maintained by a verbal slippage.

—Gayatri Spivak, "Can the Subaltern Speak?"

Remember, in Foucault's passage in his *History of Sexuality*: "One must be a nominalist." *Power* is not this, *power* is not that. *Power* is the name one must lend to a complex structure of relationships. To that extent, the subaltern is the name of the place which is so displaced from what made me and the organized resister, that to have it speak is like Godot arriving on a bus. We want it to disappear as a name so that we can all speak.

—Gayatri Spivak, in an interview with Howard Winant,
"Gayatri Spivak on the Politics of the Subaltern."

1.

I found my career in basic writing. I got my start there and, to a degree, helped to construct and protect a way of speaking about the undergraduate curriculum that has made "basic writing" an important and necessary, even an inevitable, term. This is a story I love to tell.

I went to graduate school in 1969 under an NDEA fellowship (NDEA stands for National Defense Education Act). The country had been panicked by Sputnik; the Congress had voted funds to help America's schools and children become more competitive. The money was directed toward math and science, but NCTE wisely got its foot in the door and saw that at least a token sum was directed toward the humanities, and English in particular, and so NDEA helped send me to Rutgers to graduate school. You could think of it this way—I went to graduate school to save the world from communism.

Because I was an NDEA fellow, I went to graduate school but I never had to teach, at least not until I was well into my dissertation. And so, in 1973, when the money ran out and in order to see what the job might be like, I asked my chair if I could teach a course. He agreed and I found myself teaching Freshman English for the first time.

I did what I was prepared to do. I taught a course where we asked students, all lumped into a single group, "Freshmen," to read an essay by Jean Paul Sartre, and I gave them a question to prompt their writing: "If existence precedes essence, what is man." This was my opening move. By some poor luck of the draw, about half of my students were students who we would now call "basic writers." I knew from the first week that I was going to fail them; in fact, I knew that I was going to preside over a curriculum that spent 14 weeks slowly and inevitably demonstrating their failures. This is what I (and my school) were prepared (by "English") to do. I want to cast this moment, in other words, as more than an isolated incident. I want it to be representative.

One student wrote the following essay (you can visualize the page—the handwriting is labored and there is much scratching out). The writer's name is Quentin Pierce:

If existence precedes essence main is responsible for what he is.

This is what stinger is trying to explain to us that man is a bastard without conscience I don't believe in good or evil they or meanless words or phase. Survive is the words for today and survive is the essence of man.

To elaborate on the subject matter. the principle of existentialism is logic, but stupid in it self.

Then there is a string of scratched out sentences, and the words "stop" and "lose" written in caps.

Then there is this:

Let go back to survive, to survive it is neccessary to kill or be kill, this what existentialism is all about.

Man will not survive, he is a asshole.

STOP

The stories in the books or meanless stories and I will not elaborate on them This paper is meanless, just like the book, But, I know the paper will not make it.

STOP.

Then there are crossed out sentences. At the end, in what now begins to look like a page from *Leaves of Grass* or *Howl*, there is this:

I don't care.

I don't care

about man and good and evil I don't care about this shit fuck this shit, trash and should
be put in the trash can with this shit

Thank you very much

I lose again.

I was not prepared for this paper. In a sense, I did not know how to read it. I could
only ignore it. I didn't know what to write on it, how to bring it into the class I was
teaching, although, in a sense, it was the only memorable paper I received from that
class and I have kept it in my file drawer for 18 years, long after I've thrown away all
my other papers from graduate school.

I knew enough to know that the paper was, in a sense, a very skillful performance
in words. I knew that it was written for me; I knew that it was probably wrong to
read it as simply expressive (an expression of who Quentin Pierce "really was"); I
think I knew that it was not sufficient to read the essay simply as evidence that I had
made the man a loser—since the document was also a dramatic and skillful way of
saying "Fuck you—I'm not the loser, you are." I saw that the essay had an idea, "existentialism is logical but stupid," and that the writer called forth the moves that
could enable its elaboration: "To elaborate on the subject," he said, "let's go back to
survive."

The "Fuck You" paper was a written document of some considerable skill and
force—more skill and force, for example, than I saw in many of the "normal" and
acceptable papers I read: "In this fast-paced modern world, when one considers the
problems facing mankind. . . . " I know you know how to imagine and finish that essay. It has none of the surprises of the fuck you essay. It would still, I think, be used
to classify its student as a "normal" writer; the other would identify a "basic" writer.

I could see features in the fuck you essay that spoke to me in my classroom. I did
not, as I said earlier, know how to read it. I didn't know how to make it part of the
work of my class. I failed the "basic writers" in my Freshman English class and I
went to my chairman, Dan Howard, a man whom I admired greatly, and I told him I
would never do this again. I would never teach a course where I would meet a group
of students, know that some would fail, watch those students work to the best of
their ability and my preparation and then fail them. It was not the job for me. I would
rather be a lawyer. (This is true, not just a joke; I took the law boards.) He said,
"Why don't you set up a basic writing program" and gave me my first full-time job.
A year later I went to Pitt, again to work with a basic writing program. The one decision I made was that I was not going to get rid of Jean Paul Sartre. I wanted to imagine a course where students worked with the materials valued in the college
curriculum. I did not want to take those materials away from them. I wanted, rather,
to think about ways of preparing unprepared students to work with the kinds of materials that I (and the profession) would say were ours, not theirs, materials that
were inappropriate, too advanced. And so we set up a seminar, with readings and a
subject or theme to study (so that basic writing students, we said, could work first-

hand with the values and methods of the academy); we did this rather than teach a "skills" course that could lead, later, to "real" work.

I felt then, as I feel now, that the skills course, the course that postponed "real" reading and writing, was a way of enforcing the very cultural divisions that stood as the defining markers of the problem education and its teachers, like me, had to address. In its later versions, and with my friend and colleague Tony Petrosky, the course became the course reported in *Facts, Artifacts and Counterfacts*. I am thrilled to see that there will be talk about this kind of course here at the conference today. There are versions of the course being taught in the most remarkable variety of settings—city schools, rural schools, Indian reservations, high schools, colleges for the deaf. The course is still being taught at Pitt, with wonderful revisions. The two features of the course that have remained constant are these: difficulty is confronted and negotiated, not erased (the Jean Paul Sartre slot remains); students' work is turned into a book (the fuck you paper becomes an authored work, a text in the course).

Now—as I said, this is a story I love to tell. It is convenient. It is easy to understand. Like basic writing, it (the story) and I are produced by the grand narrative of liberal sympathy and liberal reform. The story is inscribed in a master narrative of outreach, of equal rights, of empowerment, of new alliances and new understandings, of the transformation of the social text, the American university, the English department. I would like, in the remainder of my talk, to read against the grain of that narrative to think about how and why and where it might profitably be questioned. I am not, let me say quickly, interested in critique for the sake of critique; I think we have begun to rest too comfortably on terms that should make us nervous, terms like "basic writing." Basic writing has begun to seem like something naturally, inevitably, transparently there in the curriculum, in the stories we tell ourselves about English in America. It was once a provisional, contested term, marking an uneasy accommodation between the institution and its desires and a student body that did not or would not fit. I think it should continue to mark an area of contest, of struggle, including a struggle against its stability or inevitability.

Let me put this more strongly. I think basic writing programs have become expressions of our desire to produce basic writers, to maintain the course, the argument, and the slot in the university community; to maintain the distinction (basic/normal) we have learned to think through and by. The basic writing program, then, can be seen simultaneously as an attempt to bridge AND preserve cultural difference, to enable students to enter the "normal" curriculum but to insure, at the same time, that there are basic writers.

2.

Nothing has been more surprising to a liberal (to me) than the vehement (and convincing) critique of the discourse of liberalism, a discourse that, as I've said, shaped my sense of myself as a professional. I have been trying to think about how to think outside the terms of my own professional formation, outside of the story of

Quentin Pierce and my work in basic writing. I am trying to think outside of the ways of thinking that have governed my understanding of basic writers, of their identity as it is produced by our work and within the college curriculum.

To do this counterintuitive thinking, the critique of liberalism has been useful to me. Let me provide two examples as a form of demonstration.

Here is Shelby Steele, in the preface to *The Content of Our Character*, talking about how he writes. I like to read this as an account of the composing process, the composing process NOT as an internal psychological drama (issue trees, short-term memory, problem-solving, satisficing) but as an accommodation of the discursive positions (the roles or identifications) that can produce a writer and writing. It is also a program for a liberal rhetoric, a way of writing designed to produce or enforce the ideology of liberalism (in this case, the argument that differences of race and class don't matter):

> In the writing, I have had to both remember and forget that I am black. The forgetting was to see the human universals within the memory of the racial specifics. One of the least noted facts in this era when racial, ethnic, and gender differences are often embraced as sacred is that being black in no way spares one from being human. Whatever I do or think as a black can never be more than a variant of what all people do and think. Some of my life experiences may be different from those of other races, but there is nothing different or special in the psychological processes that drive my mind. So in this book I have tried to search out the human universals that explain the racial specifics. I suppose this was a sort of technique, though I was not conscious of it as I worked. Only in hindsight can I see that it protected me from being overwhelmed by the compelling specifics—and the politics—or racial difference. Now I know that if there was a secret to writing this book, it was simply to start from the painfully obvious premise that all races are composed of human beings. (xi)

It is a remarkable statement and enacts, in the paragraph, the link between an attitude (a recognition of common humanity, looking beneath surfaces) and the discursive trick, the "sleight of word," to steal a phrase from Gayatri Spivak, the displacement this position requires/enables in the act of writing. The attitude that all men are equal produces a text where the overwhelming specifics—and the politics of racial difference—disappear. It is a figuration that enables a certain kind of writing. It is, I think, a writing we teach in basic writing (the control of the overwhelming details, the specifics; the erasure or oversight of the problems— personal, social, historic—that produce basic writing), just as it is a writing we perform, in a sense, in the administration of basic writing programs, making certain "overwhelming specifics" disappear. When I first came upon this book, I knew that I was supposed to be critical of Steele (that he was a conservative, an old-fashioned humanist); I knew I was supposed to be critical before I could perform or feel the critique. Actually, I'll confess, I loved his book and what it stood for. It evokes sympathies and identifications I have learned to mistrust.

Here is a different statement about writing, one that is harder to read (or it was for me), this time by Patricia Williams, from her remarkable book, *The Alchemy of Race and Rights*. It is not, directly, a critique of Steele, but it speaks a version of writing and the writer that stands opposed to his. It is not, I should say quickly, what we would have once called a "Black power" statement on race and writing—that is, it does not simply reverse Steele's position (Steele argues that he must forget he is Black) to argue that a writer must remember, discover her Blackness, to let race define who, as a writer, she essentially is. Williams' argument is not produced by the same discourse.

Williams' position is different; it sees subject positions as produced, not essential, and as strategic. Williams' book thinks through what it is like to write, think, live, and practice law as a Black woman—that is, to occupy positions that are White and Black, male and female, all at once.

She recalls a time when, back to back, a White man and a Black woman wondered aloud if she "really identified as black." She says:

> I heard the same/different words addressed to me, a perceived white-male-socialized black woman, as a challenge to mutually exclusive categorization, as an overlapping of black and female and right and male and private and wrong and white and public, and so on and so forth. That life is complicated is a fact of great analytic importance. Law too often seeks to avoid this truth by making up its own breed of narrower, simpler, but hypnotically powerful rhetorical truths.

> Acknowledging, challenging, playing with these as rhetorical gestures is, it seems to me, necessary for any conception of justice. Such acknowledgment complicates the supposed purity of gender, race, voice, boundary; it allows us to acknowledge the utility of such categorizations for certain purposes and the necessity of their breakdown on other occasions. It complicates definitions in its shift, in its expansion and contraction according to circumstance, in its room for the possibility of creatively mated taxonomies and their wildly unpredictable offspring. (1-10)

And over and over again in her book, she offers this as the figure of the writer:

> But I haven't been able to straighten things out for them [her students] because I'm confused too. I have arrived at a point where everything I have ever learned is running around and around in my head; and little bits of law and pieces of everyday life fly out of my mouth in weird combinations. (14)

There is a double edge to this comparison. On the one hand, Williams represents the critique of liberalism and its easy assumptions, say, about the identify of African Americans and White Americans, or Workers and Owners, or Men and Women. It defines sympathy as something other than the easy understanding of someone else's position; it makes that sympathy, rather, a version of imperial occupation, the act of the taking possession of someone else's subjectivity. The pairing also represents how writing and the writer might be said to be figured differently when one reconfigures the relationship of the individual to convention, the writer to writing, including the conventions of order and control. Williams' writing is disunified; it mixes genres; it willfully forgets the distinction between formal and colloquial, public and private; it makes unseemly comparisons. In many ways, her prose has the features we associate with basic writing, although here those features mark her achievement as a writer, not her failure.

Here is a simple equation, but one that will sum up the thoughts this leads me to: to the degree to which the rhetoric of the American classroom has been dominated by the topic sentence, the controlling idea, gathering together ideas that fit while excluding, outlawing those that don't (the overwhelming, compelling specifics); to the degree that the American classroom has been a place where we *cannot* talk about race or class or the history of the American classroom, it has taught both the formal properties and the controlling ideas that produce, justify, and value the humanism of Shelby Steele, that produce Patricia Williams' text as confusing, unreadable (which, in a classroom sense, it is—our students are prepared to find her writing hard to read and his easy), and it produces basic writing as the necessary institutional response to the (again) overwhelming politics and specifics of difference. It is a way of preserving the terms of difference rooted in, justified by the liberal project, one that has learned to rest easy with the tidy distinction between basic and mainstream. In this sense, basic writers are produced by our desires to be liberals—to enforce a commonness among our students by making the differences superficial, surface-level, and by designing a curriculum to both insure them and erase them in 14 weeks.

In her recent work, Mary Louise Pratt has argued against the easy, utopian versions of community that have governed the ways we think about language and the classroom. In linguistics, for example:

> The prototypical manifestation of language is generally taken to be the speech of individual adult native speakers face-to-face (as in Saussure's famous diagram) in monolingual, even monodialectal situations—in short, the most homogeneous case linguistically and socially. The same goes for written communication. Now one could certainly imagine a theory that assumed different things—that argued, for instance, that the most revealing speech situation for understanding language was one involving a gathering of people each of whom spoke two languages and understood a third and held only one language in common with any of the others. It depends on what working of language you want to see or want to see first, on what you choose to define as normative. (38)

If you want to eliminate difference, there are programs available to think this through. In the classroom, similarly, she argues, teachers are prepared to feel most successful when they have eliminated "unsolicited oppositional discourse"—that is, the writing they are not prepared to read—along with parody, resistance, and critique, when they have unified the social world in the image of community offered by the professions. Who wins when we do that, she asks? And who loses? Or, to put it another way, if our programs produce a top and bottom that reproduces the top and bottom in the social text, insiders and outsiders, haves and have nots, who wins and who loses?

This is not abstract politics, not in the classroom. Pratt acknowledges this. In place of a utopian figure of community, she poses what she calls the "contact zone." I use this term, she says,

> to refer to social spaces where cultures meet, clash, and grapple with each other, often in contexts of highly asymmetrical relations of power, such as colonialism, slavery, or their aftermaths as they are lived out in many parts of the world today. (34)

She extends this term to classrooms and proposes a list of both the compositional and pedagogical arts of the contact zone. Imagine, in other words, a curricular program designed not to hide differences (by sorting bodies) but to highlight them, to make them not only the subject of the writing curriculum, but the source of its goals and values (at least one of the versions of writing one can learn at the university). Pratt lists the various arts of the contact zone. These are wonderful lists to hear as lists, since they make surprising sense and come out of no order we have been prepared to imagine or, for that matter, value.

These are, according to Pratt, some of the literate arts of the contact zone: autoethnography (representing one's identity and experience in the terms of a dominant other, with the purpose of engaging the other), transculturation (the selection of and improvisation on the materials derived from the dominant culture), critique, collaboration, bilingualism, mediation, parody, denunciation, imaginary dialogue, vernacular expression. (Imagine these as the stated goals of a course.) And these are some of the pedagogical arts: exercises in storytelling and in identifying with the ideas, interests, histories, and attitudes of others; experiments in transculturation and collaborative work and in the arts of critique, parody, and comparison (including unseemly comparisons between elite and vernacular cultural forms); the redemption of the oral; ways for people to engage with suppressed aspects of history (including their own histories); ways to move *into and out of* rhetorics of authenticity; ground rules for communication across lines of difference and hierarchy that go beyond politeness but maintain mutual respect; a systematic approach to the all-important concept of *cultural mediation*. (Imagine these as exercises.)

Now—the voice of common sense says, basic writers aren't ready for this, they can't handle it, they need a place to begin. But this sense makes sense only under the sway of a developmental view of language use and language growth (and "developmentalism"—cherishing and preserving an interested version of the "child" and the "adult"—this, too, is inscribed in the discourse of liberalism). Thinking of development allows one to reproduce existing hierarchies but as evidence of natural patterns—basic writers are just like other writers, but not quite so mature. One could imagine that oppositional discourse, parody, unseemly comparisons, if defined as "skills," are the equal possession of students in *both* basic writing and mainstream composition courses. In fact, one could argue that "basic writers" are better prepared to produce and think through unseemly comparisons than their counterparts in the "mainstream" class. Pratt rejects the utopian notion of a classroom where everyone speaks the same language to the same ends; she imagines, rather, a classroom where difference is both the subject and the environment. She gives us a way of seeing existing programs as designed to hide or suppress "contact" between cultural groups rather than to organize and highlight that contact.

Now of course education needs to be staged, and of course tracking makes strategic sense; of course one needs a place to begin and a place to end or to mark beginnings and endings, but it is not impossible to think beyond our current sense of beginnings and endings (of basic writing and the courses that follow), beyond placement exams that measure the ability to produce or recognize the conventionally correct and unified text.

There is caricature here, I know, but one could imagine the current proportion of students in basic writing courses and mainstream courses redistributed by an exam that looked for willingness to work, for a commitment to language and its uses, for an ability to produce a text that commands notice, or (in Pratt's terms) for the ability to produce opposition, parody, unseemly comparisons, to work outside of the rhetoric of authenticity, to produce the autoethnographic text. Or we could imagine not tracking students at all. We could offer classes with a variety of supports for those who need them. These might be composition courses where the differences in students' writing becomes the subject of the course. The differences would be what the course investigates. We would have, then, a course in "multiculturalism" that worked with the various cultures represented in the practice of its students. There would be no need to buy an anthology to find evidence of the cultural mix in America, no need to import "multiple cultures." They are there, in the classroom, once the institution becomes willing to pay that kind of attention to student writing.

There is caricature here, but so is there caricature in our current accounts of *the* basic writer and his or her essential characteristics. There is a great danger in losing a sense of our names as names—in Patricia Williams' terms, as rhetorical gestures, useful for certain purposes but also necessarily breaking down at the very moment that we need them.

Or—to put it another way. Basic writers may be ready for a different curriculum, for the contact zone and the writing it will produce, but the institution is not. And it is not, I would argue, because of those of us who work in basic writing, who preserve rather than question the existing order of things.

3.

Developmentalism.   Certainly the most influential conduit for this discourse in American composition is James Britton. He has been given the kind of saintly status given Mina Shaughnessy. He seems to represent (in his sympathy for the other, for children, for diversity, for growth and empowerment) a position beyond positions. This is, of course, a sleight of hand, and a problem, one we share in producing when we read Britton generously. (And let me be quick to say, I understand all the good reasons why we might read him generously.)

As a way of thinking outside of Britton, both about writing and about children, but also about professional work and about the consequences of such thinking, I want to turn to a comparatively unknown book, *The Tidy House*, one that could be thought of as a countertext to *The Development of Writing Abilities*. It is written in a similar time and place, in the late 60s and early 70s in Britain. It looks at the same subject: writing and schooling.

In Steedman's words, this is what *The Tidy House* is about:

> In the summer of 1976, three working-class eight-year-old girls, Melissa, Carla and
> Lindie, wrote a story about romantic love, marriage and sexual relations, the desire of

mothers for children and their resentment of them, and the means by which those children are brought up to inhabit a social world.

This book, which takes its title from the children's narrative, offers an account of their story, and suggests what interpretations we, as adults, can make of it. Their story, which is structured around two opposing views of childcare held by their two central female characters, served the children as an investigation of the ideas and beliefs by which they themselves were being brought up, and their text can serve us too in this way. (1)

I'll confess that I have been very much taken by this book. It is beautifully written, sensible, evocative, surprising. And it powerfully suggests the roads not taken by composition studies and its professionals.

The book begins with the girls' story, called "The Tidy House." It is written all in dialogue. Here, for example, is the children's account of what adults say to each other in bed at night when they are making babies:

What time is it?

Eleven o'clock at night.

Oh no! Let's get to bed.

Ok.

'Night, sweetheart, See you in the morning.

Turn the light off, Mark.

I'm going to.

Sorry.

All right.

I want to get asleep.

Don't worry, you'll get to sleep in time.

Don't let us, really, this time of the night.

Shall I wait till the morning?

Oh stop it.

Morning.

Don't speak.

No, you.

No. Why don't you?

Look, it's all over.

Thank you, Mark.

Mark kissed Jo, Jo kissed Mark. (43-44)

Steedman's work on this story leads her to women's accounts of their lives in the working-class neighborhood of the girls, to Henry Mayhew and the words of girls from the streets of London in the 19th century, to domestic education and the historical uses of children's writing. And, in Steedman's career, it has led to interests in history and autobiography, in the production of "the child" in England.

Steedman saw in the student's story a history of social practices, practices that not only argue about educability and appropriateness but about how girls become women and what it means to live within one's class. Teachers are not prepared, she argues, to see history and culture in the classroom or in the work of its children.

> It is almost impossible for a teacher to look at a room full of children and not see them in some way as being stretched out along some curve of ability, some measuring up to and exceeding the average, some falling behind. This is the historical inheritance we operate with, whether we do so consciously or not, and it has been a matter of "common sense" and common observation rather than a matter of theory to know as a teacher that children of class IV and V parents are going to perform relatively badly compared with children of higher socioeconomic groups. (5)

And, "What teachers know as a result of this history, and as a matter of 'common sense,' is that, in general, ability groupings turn out in practice to make rough and comprehensible matches with social class divisions."

For Steedman, as both a teacher and a social historian, the fundamental question is how these young writers, given their positions as girls and as working-class girls, can negotiate, understand, and critically confront those versions of themselves that are written into the social text. An uncritical schooling, an education in language divorced from its social and political contexts, would effectively preserve the narratives of class and gender within which these children find themselves (within which they write "their" story). For Steedman, the writing done in school gives both the professional and the student access to a history and attitudes and feelings shaping their particular moment. Writing is the way history, class, and culture become manifest in the classroom, in an environment that pretends to stand outside of time.

What Steedman suggests is not just a direction for research but a different version of professional responsibility, where as professionals who manage writing in institutional settings we might see that writing as material for an ongoing study of American life and culture. It is a telling irony that on my campus, where young working-class women write, scholars go to archives to "discover" working-class writing by women.

To learn to read her students' story, Steedman went to a record of children's voices from the eighteenth century to the twentieth. To learn to read her students' stories, Mina Shaughnessy went to her heart—to the remarkable sympathy which would allow her to understand the work of students distinctly different from her in culture and sensibility. Shaughnessy's text, in a sense, is the quintessential liberal reflex; it demonstrates that beneath the surface we are all the same person; it writes her students' lives, needs, desires into a master text that she commands. Basic writing, as an extension of that moment, preserves that project: fitting students into a version of who they are as writers that we tend to take for granted, that seems to stand beyond our powers of revision and inquiry, because it is an expression of our founding desires to find, know, and help (to construct, theorize, and preserve) basic writers.

4.

So what in the world have I done here? I find myself characterizing basic writing as a reiteration of the liberal project of the late 60s early 70s, where in the name of sympathy and empowerment, we have once again produced the "other" who is the incomplete version of ourselves, confirming existing patterns of power and authority, reproducing the hierarchies we had meant to question and overthrow, way back then in the 1970s.

We have constructed a course to teach and enact a rhetoric of exclusion and made it the center of a curriculum designed to hide or erase cultural difference, all the while carving out and preserving an "area" in English within which we can do our work. Goodness.

Now, at the end of my talk, it seems important to ask, "Do I believe what I have said?" If this has been an exercise in reading against the grain of the discourse that has produced basic writing (and, I said, my work as a professional), do I believe this negative, unyielding rereading?

The answer is yes and no, and sometimes yes and no at the same moment. Let me conclude, then, with a series of second thoughts (or "third thoughts" as the case may be).

If you look back over the issues of the *Journal of Basic Writing* (or at programs and courses), there is a record of good and careful work. I couldn't begin to turn my back on all that or to dismiss it as inconsequential. We can all think immediately of the students who have been helped, of college careers that have begun with a basic writing course. Good work has been done under the name of basic writing by both students and professionals. I cannot get over, however, my sense of the arbitrariness, the surrealism, of the choices represented by the sorting of students in actual basic and mainstream classes. Looking at the faces, working with the writing—the division never makes anything but institutional sense. There are cases to prove that the idea is a good one. There are cases to prove that the idea is all wrong.

And there are problems of error—of controlling the features of a written text—that stand outside of any theorizing about basic writing as a form of resistance. It seems to me finally stupid to say that every nonstandard feature of a student's prose is a sign of opposition, can stand as "unsolicited oppositional discourse." If I think back to Quentin Peirce's essay, some of the "errors" could be read as oppositional, but not all of them and not all of them for the same reasons. At the same time, the profession has not been able to think beyond an either/or formulation either academic discourse or the discourse of the community; either argument or narrative; either imitation or expression. Part of the failure, I think, is rooted in our inability to imagine protocols for revision, for example, that would negotiate rather than preserve the differing interests of students and the academy. We do not, for example, read "basic writing" the way we read Patricia Williams' prose, where the surprising texture of the prose stands as evidence of an attempt to negotiate the problems of language. I want to be clear about this. Williams is a skillful, well-educated writer. The unconventional nature of her prose can be spoken of as an achievement. She is trying to do something that can't be conventionally done. To say that our basic writers are less intentional, less skilled, is to say the obvious. But we would say the same thing of the "mainstream" writers whose prose approximates that of Shelby Steele. Their prose, too, is less skilled, less intentional than his. It is possible, it seems to me, to develop a theory of error that makes the contact between conventional and unconventional discourses the most interesting and productive moment for a writer or for a writing course. It is possible to use the Steele/Williams pair to argue that when we define Williams-like student writing as less developed or less finished than Steele-like student writing, we are letting metaphors of development or process hide value-laden assumptions about thought, form, the writer, and the social world.

Let me think back to Quentin Pierce. Do I believe in the course represented in *Facts, Artifacts, Counterfacts*—do I believe it is a reasonable way to manage his work as a reader and writer? Yes. I believe deeply in that course. At my school, it changes every time it is taught—with different readings, better writing assignments. But in principle, I believe in the course. Someone else will have to produce its critique. I can't. At the same time, I should add that a similar course is being taught at a variety of levels of our curriculum at the University of Pittsburgh. It is also the mainstream composition course and an introductory course for majors. There are differences that could be called differences of "level" (for the students more accustomed to reading and writing, we choose assigned readings differently; the course moves at a different pace; sentence level error is treated differently). It is, however, the same course. And the students who are well-prepared could easily be said to need extra time and guidance in learning to see the limits of the procedures, protocols, and formats they take for granted—the topic sentence, reading for gist, the authority of the conclusion. The point is that while I believe in the course, I am not sure I believe in its institutional position as a course that is necessarily prior to or lesser than the mainstream course. Do I believe Quentin is served by being called a basic writer and positioned in the curriculum in these terms? I'm not sure I do.

I don't think we can ignore the role of the introductory writing course in preparing students to negotiate the full range of expectations in the university (as it reproduces the expectations of the dominant culture), including linguistic convention, correction, etc. Does this mean a separate course? No. Does it mean we identify and sort students in useful, even thoughtful ways? No.

There was much talk at the Maryland conference about abolishing basic writing and folding its students into the mainstream curriculum, providing other forms of support (tutorials, additional time, a different form of final evaluation). Karen Greenberg and I argued this point at the open session. I am suspicious, as I said then, of the desire to preserve "basic writing" as a key term simply because it is the one we have learned to think with or because it has allowed us our jobs or professional identities. I think it would be useful, if only as an exercise, to imagine a way of talking that called the term "basic writing" into question (even, as an exercise, to treat it as suspect). Would I advocate the elimination of courses titled "basic writing" for all postsecondary curricula beginning next fall? No. I fear what would happen to the students who are protected, served in its name. I don't, in other words, trust the institution to take this as an intellectual exercise, a challenge to rethink old ways. I know that the institution would be equally quick to rely upon an established and corrupt discourse (of "boneheads," of "true college material," of "remediation"); it would allow the return of a way of speaking that was made suspect by the hard work and diligence of those associated with basic writing. As Shaughnessy told us, the first thing we would need to do to change the curriculum would be to change the way the profession talked about the students who didn't fit. Will I begin to formally question the status of basic writing at my own institution? Yes. In a sense, this was already begun several years ago by graduate students in our department, and by my colleague, Joe Harris.

I suppose what concerns me most is the degree to which a provisional position has become fixed, naturalized. "Basic writing," the term, once served a strategic function. It was part of an attempt to change the way we talked about students and the curriculum. We have lost our sense of its strategic value. "Basic writing," it seems to me, can best name a contested area in the university community, a contact zone, a place of competing positions and interests. I don't want to stand in support of a course designed to make those differences disappear or to hide contestation or to enforce divisions between high and low. It seems to me that the introductory curriculum can profitably be a place where professionals and students think through their differences in productive ways. I'm not sure more talk about basic writing will make that happen.

Works Cited

Britton, James. *The Development of Writing Abilities.* London: Macmillan Education, 1975. 11-18.
Pratt, Mary Louise. "Linguistic Utopias." *The Linguistics of Writing.* Eds. Nigel Fabb, et al. Manchester: Manchester UP, 1987.
_____ . "The Arts of the Contact Zone." *Profession 91.* New York: MLA, 1991.
Spivak, Gayatri Chakravorty. "Can the Subaltern Speak?" *Marxism and the Interpretation of Culture.* Eds. Cary Nelson and Lawrence Grossberg. Champaign: U of Illinois P, 1988.
_____ . "Gayatri Spivak on the Politics of the Subaltern." Interview by Howard Winant. *Socialist Review* 20.3 (July-Sept. 1990): 81-87.
Steedman, Carolyn. *Past Tenses: Essays on Writing, Autobiography and History.* London: Rivers Oram Press, 1992.
_____ . *The Tidy House.* London: Virago, 1982.
Steele, Shelby. *The Content of Our Character.* New York: St. Martin's, 1990.
Williams, Patricia J. *The Alchemy of Race and Rights.* Cambridge: Harvard UP, 1991.

Resisting Privilege: Basic Writing and Foucault's Author Function
by Gail Stygall

Trying to define "basic writing" perplexes us, as shot through as the term is with local contexts, different approaches, and standardized grammar tests. Any article or research report on basic writing has to be read carefully for how its author describes basic writing. "Basic writers" are equally elusive. Sometimes they are called "remedial," implying that they are retaking courses in material that already should have been mastered. Sometimes they are called "developmental," suggesting a cognitive or psychological problem. At other times and in other places, they may be called "Educational Opportunity Students," suggesting division by access to education. Or they are just "basic," requiring foundational or fundamental instruction in writing. As a case in point, several years ago, I wrote an article, on the basic writing program at Indiana University—Indianapolis, published in the *Journal of Basic Writing*. Impossibly, it seemed to me, I found an article on Harvard University's basic writers in the same issue in which my own article appeared. Surely, we weren't talking about the same students, nor the same writing. And, indeed, we were not. While the students I wrote about were having trouble producing any text, even text with attendant problems in organization and mechanics, the Harvard students were instead having problems with originality, creativity, and elaborating arguments (Armstrong 70-72).

Yet the presence of "basic" is tenacious in English departments and we might want to ask ourselves why the term—which seems only to give some vague indication of a deficiency—continues to signify something important to us. The signification of the term is often masked by the way "basic" is held to be something temporary, contingent, requiring emergency methods, quick fixes, "bandaid" solutions. Most explanations fit under some sort of "wave" theory, near invasions of our universities by unexpected, unanticipated populations: the GIs after World War II, economic opportunity students in the late sixties and seventies, returning adults dis-

Stygall, Gail. "Resisting Privilege: Basic Writing and Foucault's Author Function." *College Composition and Communication* 45.3 (October 1994): 320-341. Copyright (1994) by the National Council of Teachers of English. Reprinted with permission.

placed by the economy in the eighties. The "waves" seem to keep coming, for whatever reasons offered, and consequently, basic writing becomes required by the educational system, at the same time we continue to speak of it in terms of the temporary. Teachers of composition may have moved far away from deficit theories of language as an explanation for the presence of basic writing in college classrooms, learning as we have the effects of race, class, gender, and ethnicity on academic performance. But we have moved very little toward eradicating the perceived need for basic writing classrooms.

Michel Foucault's "What Is an Author?" shows how the concept of the author constitutes and regulates French academic and literary discourse. The "author function" is equally applicable to Anglo-American academic and literary discourse, and serves, I would argue, to organize the curriculum in English studies and define its proper object of study. It is a commonplace for a scholar to identify herself as, for example, a Wharton critic, or for one to say about himself that he "does Milton." And even though theorists using deconstructive, new historical, Marxist, psychoanalytical, feminist, and cultural studies approaches to literature may dispute who counts as an author, what they approach is often still the author—perhaps an unknown, noncanonical one, but still an author with most of the precepts of the author function intact. A brief glance at the index of Gerald Graff's *Professing Literature* affirms this orientation toward the author: The index is only briefly disturbed by references to theories and approaches, dominated as it is by the names of authors and critics, both regulated by the author function. If literature and its related author function remains opposed to non-literature, non-literary writers will always fall short of the English department's highest value. A master discourse that reveres one kind of authorship and dismisses all others is bound to affect those kinds of authorship counted among the "all others" category.

Specifically, I want to argue that the institutional practice of basic writing is constructed and inscribed by the notion of the author function, and that the teaching of basic writing is formulated around the *educational discursive practices* necessary to keep the author function dominant. What I mean by educational discursive practices are those activities and talk about education that we experience as natural, normal, inevitable, and unremarkable. These are practices that we take for granted: one teacher for each classroom; the existence of classrooms and buildings made expressly to be filled with large numbers of students and correspondingly few teachers; grading and sorting students; separating students by age and grade level; dividing time into semesters and quarters, days into class periods; homework and all those other aspects of the daily life of education that we rarely question.

Linda Brodkey found these discursive practices maintaining asymmetrical power relations in a variety of ways, when she analyzed a series of letters exchanged between a graduate class she was teaching and an Adult Basic Education (ABE) class. In the letters they traded, Brodkey's professionally oriented middle-class graduate students controlled the "conversation" with the ABE students through either silencing obvious class and experience differences or by transforming the ABE writer's experience into a middle-class version. For instance, the tensions and ambiguities that one ABE student felt in the aftermath of a murder of someone she knew was transformed into "that problem" in the graduate student's reply. In another exchange, an ABE student tells of having to move because the home she rents is being sold, while the graduate student responds with questions about what sort of house she will buy and comments on the current mortgage rates—a middle class reality wholly outside the experience of the ABE correspondent.

My own project, following Brodkey, was to examine the discursive practices evoked in a slightly different configuration of letters and comments on drafts between teachers and students. Unlike the combination in Brodkey's project, all these students—at all three universities involved—had some investment in a college education and in the academy. Instead of using class as a unifying principle, the graduate students' first loyalty related to the profession of English, not surprising considering that they and I were involved in a graduate seminar in an English department. The basic plan of the project worked in two parts. First, in the graduate seminar I was teaching at Miami University on the topic of basic writing, my students responded to papers written for a Temple University basic writing course taught by Frank Sullivan. Sullivan's urban Philadelphia students were conducting an educational ethnography of their own experiences, and his students were living worlds apart from bucolic Oxford, Ohio, the site of Miami's main campus, where my graduate seminar was held. Second, my students corresponded with students enrolled in a basic writing course taught by Betty Anderson at Indiana University—Indianapolis (IUPUI). My hope for the students in the graduate seminar seemed simple enough: reading and analyzing the dynamics of the project would convert to immediate differences in our practices. I thought that my students and I could resist reconstructing our correspondents as "basic writers" by becoming conscious of the discursive practices involved in doing so. But this proved difficult for all of us, in spite of our best intentions.[1]

In examining the operation of the author function in these exchanges I will begin by reviewing what Foucault says about the notion of the author, and then turn to the seminar participants' comments and letters to the basic writers for representations of the notion of author in English teachers' practice. These representations appear in several ways: First, in the substantial differences in the amount of text written in the letters—the graduate students writing lengthy letters, the basic writing students composing brief ones—and the stance of interrogator taken by the graduate students—asking numerous questions—serve to reconstruct differences covertly, that is without explicit comment. Second, in the graduate students' claims for the neutrality of educational discursive practices, a neutrality that can only maintain the dominance of the author function. Third, in the graduate students' constructions of an educational identity for themselves and for the basic writers with whom they corresponded—constructions which were radically different and serve to maintain difference at the same time they proclaim the unimportance of difference. I will draw from the letters and the comments made on the basic writers' papers for illustrations of these practices. Finally, I will conclude with a discussion of the hazards and hopes of such bridging projects, the attempts to resist privilege.

If This Is an Author, What Is a Basic Writer?

As Foucault writes in "What Is an Author?," in literary criticism,

> The author provides the basis for explaining not only the presence of certain events in a work, but also their transformations, distortions, and diverse modifications (through his biography, the determination of his individual perspective, the analysis of his social position, and the revelation of his basic design). The author is also the principle of a certain unity of writing—all differences having to be resolved, at least in part, by the principles of evolution, maturation, or influence. (111)

This idea of the author permeates much of what goes on in the teaching of literature, if not also in literary scholarship. Foucault suggests that novelists are not likely candidates to be "founders of diversity," using Marx and Freud instead as exemplars of those authors whose works created "the possibilities and the rules for the formation of other texts" (114). However, it is often those exemplars who provide the foundation of particular practices within literary criticism. Founders of discursivity are not just writers of their own particular texts; they are founders of schools of thought, creating entire discourses patterned on their work. Both versions of author function—author in the literary sense, and author in the sense of discursive initiation—regulate the work that goes on in English departments.

The author function, as Foucault develops it, has four characteristics: First, when writing or authorship became property and thus operant within the law of property, writing offered the possibility of transgression, especially in "the form of an imperative peculiar to literature" (108). Second, the author function can vary from discourse to discourse. For instance, while authorship is important in literature, it is less so in scientific writing. Third, the pairing of an author to a particular discourse is not a simple matching; it is rather the social construction of a "certain rational being" (110). Finally, the author function allows readings that acknowledge several selves of the same author, framed by processes of "evolution, maturation, or influence" (111).

What would these characteristics mean when applied to the teaching of basic writing? Certainly the right to transgress conventions is reserved for authors—whose works comprise the canons of literature or those who are published—and not to those apprentice writers who do "pseudo-writing." I would point to studies of teachers imposing student standards on professional texts, denying supposed nonauthors the right to transgress—as Joseph Williams demonstrates in "The Phenomenology of Error" in which he plays on our acceptance of his *CCC* authorship to lead us to ignore his "errors." Denial of the right to transgress has consequences in what teachers write on student papers. In examining a broad range of his colleagues' responses, Donald Daiker found nearly 90% of their responses to be negative. The dominance of the negative suggests that it is only pedestrian transgression that we find in the writing of students and that we reject it. Moreover, the primary means by which we designate a student as a basic writer is as transgression, typically by a placement test in which the students' writing is deemed deficient. The ownership of student texts is also in doubt—as suggested in the works of Nancy

Sommers, and Lil Brannon and Cy Knoblauch—who show teacher commentary often appropriates and redirects the student's texts. These aspects of transgression and ownership are intensified when applied to basic writers whose transgressions are always assumed to be less than artful and whose ownership of their texts is seen as unwarranted for their lack of value.

Foucault's second characteristic—the relative prominence a discourse gives authorship—places apprentice writers in an academic setting in which the author function has prominence. This prominence results in a principle of limitation operating for nonauthors. The positive value of a piece of writing is enhanced in literature by the recognition and confirmation of its individual achievement. As a consequence, plagiarism has a high negative value. For someone whose writing has been judged "basic" in quality, the principle limits the possibility of change, a quality reserved for authors. A significant development in a student's writing may mean she is greeted with cries of "who helped you with this paper?" or "whose work have you left uncited?" To further regulate this aspect, the teachers of writing classes, who are also often themselves scholars of literature, are also subject to the author function, and, as a consequence, have an interest in maintaining it. Finding and keeping a "good" job—that is, one on a tenure line—means publishing. Tenure decisions often mean the application of the author function to scholarly writing. Accordingly, the basic writer in an English department faces not only an object of study regulated by the author function but also teachers who are similarly regulated.

The third characteristic, the construction of a "certain rational being," also has implications for basic writers. If an author writes a passage that is unclear or that is not obviously related to what came before it, then readers assume there is a reason for it, embedded in the author's intent or milieu. If a basic writer does so, then teacher-readers often construct a nonliterate, non-logical writer (as in Thomas Farrell's argument that speakers of dialects without the copula lack abstract reasoning ability), or construct a less sophisticated, pre-conceptual thinker, (as in Andrea Lunsford's early work with basic writers), or even construct a mysterious Other (as in Mina Shaughnessy's description of her reactions to reading the work of basic writers).

Finally, though some composition scholars have recently examined the notion of the "authentic self," or the unified voice in relation to ideology, the dominant approach has been to silence multivocality and to unify self-presentation in students' texts. Richard Ohmann's political analysis of voice and unity as precepts of teaching composition suggest their value for a late capitalist society. These textual "qualities" also have value in maintaining the author function. Valorizing multivocality in works of literature has the effect of denying or banning its presence in works by non-authors. In fact, given the tensions and issues at stake in the basic writing classroom, one scholar, Ann Murphy, sees value in providing an explanation for the sense of division experienced by basic writers, but cautions that "a process which seeks further to decenter them strikes me as dangerous" (180). Thomas Recchio's recent *CCC* article on Bahktinian approaches to a student's writing suggests the strength of our disciplinary requirement that student texts be unified. Though Recchio recognizes and affirms the presence of multivocality in student texts, he concludes by saying recognition of multiple voices by the student is the way to "provide the coherence and continuity that the paper presently lacks" (453), but his is a minority voice. A glance at contemporary textbooks would hardly allow us to believe that the idea of unity was in danger of being abandoned.

None of the three groups of students involved in my letters project could begin to maintain authority within the academy without doing work that was valued by the academy, especially within English departments. Being declared a marginal writer as a first year college student is public and institutionally sanctioned. Being declared marginal in a graduate English program—as a consequence of a declared interest in composition, an interest in the non-authors, as it were—is less public, less officially sanctioned, yet is just as powerful. Its effects are evident in the comments and letters of the graduate students enrolled in the seminar. Like Brodkey's students, my students' best intention toward basic writers—to resist privilege—could not overcome the discursive practice of the author function, the fundamental ideological apparatus of English, the very affirmation of which could prove their "true" nonmarginal status.

Differences Inscribed in Letter Form

Graduate students, even those in composition and rhetoric, typically learn how to teach basic writers in one of two ways: by trial and error in their own classrooms or in a graduate classroom in which they are being trained to teach composition. Neither of these approaches raises the questions of differential educational practices, nor do these approaches ask the would be teacher of basic writers to examine her own role in reproducing a stratified system of conceptualizing and teaching writing. In order to pursue my goal of making educational discursive practices visible to teachers preparing to teach basic writers, I wanted to know whether being self-conscious about differences and their implications would result in less reinscription of status. Would the letters acknowledge difference and resist masking it? Broadly speaking, the research and theoretical literature on basic writing does not challenge the existence of the labeling of some writers as basic, but instead concentrates on the types of students to whom the label is applied or provides methods for teaching them. Nor does this literature typically challenge would-be teachers of basic waters to examine how the labeling or inscription takes place or to examine who is served by such labeling. I would argue that this occurs because our discursive practice is a master discourse and it assumes that we have an unconstrained right to divide and stratify our students as writers, dividing authors from nonauthors.

Each of my ten graduate students was writing to three of the IUPUI basic writing students and the letters analyzed for this essay include 46 actual exchanges. Nearly 70% of Anderson's students were male, while 75% of my graduate students were female. Some effects of gender were apparent, though gender was not the focus of my analysis. In addition, approximately 25% of Anderson's students were African American. The topic of race was absolutely missing from all discussion, both in the graduate student's basic writers' letters exchange and in the graduate students' responses to the Temple basic writers' essays, Temple being a site where gender was more balanced but African American students more visible. Anderson's students initiated the exchange, and she chose initially not to disclose that they were writing to graduate students in English. She feared that they would simply freeze and not write at all. By the second round of letters exchanged, both groups had revealed and discussed the status of the Miami students. My hope in having the basic writers initiate the exchange was to disturb the normal conversational assumption that the one who initiates the exchange and its topic sets the agenda for the conversation. My students knew that part of their task was to try to understand what being labeled "basic" meant to Anderson's students and what their lives were like at a large urban university. These initial exchanges are characterized by a formality typical of educational enterprises.

On both sides, the letter writers carefully answered each and every question raised by the correspondent, with one exception. Fully half of the basic writing students refused to answer direct queries about what they were doing in their writing course and what they thought about being there. Of the half responding to these queries about being labeled a basic writer, two types of answers dominate. As we might expect from the power of the institutional discourse to label, one response is to acknowledge their subjectivity, accepting the label, and take the blame for being a basic writer. Responses in this category included "my writing is not up to par," "I kinda flunked out," "I have to take refresher courses and not having good grades in high school," and "this course is mostly for people who had low SAT scores like me." The second category of responses is one in which the recipients of the labeling don't even have consciousness of some sort of subjectivity but instead see it as a natural fact of the world, as in "I wish I wasn't placed in the lowest class, but that's the way it happens, I guess." Also in this second category are the responses that characterize the Access Center, the name of the home of the basic writing course at IUPUI, as a kind of prison, as suggested by comments like "I can't wait to get out of Access Center," and "I'm still in the Access Center." Paradoxically, the Access Center restricts and regulates access to the university.

Yet it is the sheer difference in length that most constructs the graduate students into the author category, leaving the basic writers behind. With the exception of two pairings, the graduate students wrote letters three and four times as long as those of the basic writers. Consider the following exchange.

Dee

My name is James Jefferson Jones. I was born in Biloxi Mississippi in September 5, 1970. I am interested in sports, weight lifting, fishing and wood working. I am a freshman at IUPUI. I take 12 hours of classes, I am a full time student.

I work as a service worker at the Officers Club at Fort Benjamin Harrison. Indianapolis Indiana. I am planning on being a Dietician or an engineer.

Well Dee that is all that I have to say. I would like for you to write to me and tell me about yourself too. I really would like to know about you.

Sincerely yours

James Jones

Dear James.

Thanks for writing to me. I look forward to getting to know you. You must be busy being a full time student and working at the Officer's Club at Fort Benjamin Harrison. I admire you a lot for doing both. I work at the university, too, and go to school. You'll have to write and tell me more about the classes you are taking and what kinds of things you do at your job. (Is the food any good at the Club? Do you sample the cooking?)

You'll also have to tell me more about your weightlifting. A few weeks ago I bought my first pair of ankle and hand weights and an exercise videotape. My doctor recommended upper body exercise with weights to help a heart condition I have. I've been feeling wimpy! Even so, I work out every other day. I also try to walk two miles at our gym three times a week. Hopefully, I'll be in better shape soon. Unfortunately, my knees have been bothering me. Maybe I've been exercising too much? Do weights hurt your joints? Do you work out with machines? I've been thinking about looking into that too.

You said that you were born in Mississippi. How long did you live there? Why did you come to Indianapolis? Mississippi is one state I've never visited so I'd like to learn about it. I grew up in a small town near Indianapolis.

Of course, being a Hoosier means I'm an I.U. basketball fan. Actually, I like all the Big 10 teams. My favorite time of year is the NCAA playoffs in March-April. Do you have a team you want to win?

I'm looking forward to hearing from you again. I'm beginning to feel the crunch of having lots of work to do—papers to write, books to read, and projects to finish. Writing to you is a nice break from all that!

Sincerely,

Dee

This initial exchange between Dee, the graduate student, and James, the first year basic writing student, appears innocuous, without reminding James that he is a basic writer. But a closer examination reveals some interesting characteristics. James' opening letter is 109 words long, while Dee's response is 321. Clearly, Dee feels comfortable writing, even to someone she does not know. Further, James asked no questions, while Dee feels it appropriate to ask eight questions. Dee felt that she was simply responding to James by echoing back his declared interests, but how she did that was to elaborate beyond what he had managed painfully to write (the handwriting is tortured in the original). Moreover, her final paragraph subtly etches her proficiency as a writer in contrast to James, with her "papers to write, books to read, and projects to finish." For James, who doesn't think of writing as a pleasure, Dee declares "writing to you is a nice break from all that!"

So what, a reader might ask, is problematic about Dee's response and the others like it? That there is a difference in the length of the letters is no surprise, given that Dee is a graduate student and James a first-year student. And, after all, Dee was under my watchful eye. Dee in some ways intentionally wrote more so as to honor her correspondent, whom, she believed, may not have received lengthy responses from his teachers. But notice that Dee is responding *as a teacher*. Dee, like all the students in the seminar, could choose a role in these letters and several were available to them: learner, student, pen pal, or teacher. Nonetheless, she, and all the others, chose the role of teacher, their reactions to the correspondence guided by disciplinary knowledge about basic writers. Dee consciously intends to do nothing more than show interest in her correspondent, but she announces that she is an author of sorts, while James is not.

Eventually for some pairings, the length of the letters evened out. These were the more successful pairings and usually occurred between two women, though two crossgender pairings also achieved an evening of length during the course of the project. What is remarkable is that we did not notice the magnitude of the difference in length until well after the close of the letters project. We did discuss in class the interrogative stance that the graduate students took, but it was nearly a year later before we began to recognize the length as an important factor in reinscribing the basic writers' positions.

The Discursive Practices of Education, or the Obvious Benefits of Getting an Education

If these graduate students were unconscious of how structured their responses are when prompted to describe their personal selves, we can expect even less conscious control over their educational discursive practices. Here I am drawing from my students' responses to Sullivan's students, who wrote about their observations as students at Temple University. An early assignment in the seminar was for my graduate students to write a teacher's response to these papers. Though I told my students that these were final products, most insisted that the papers were drafts and they responded accordingly, telling the students what they found interesting and what they thought could be improved. What was striking about their responses was the absolute refusal to comment on the realities depicted in some of the Temple students' written observations. Not one of my students reacted directly to the critiques of classroom practices developed by the Temple students. Let me offer an example from one of the student papers from Temple. The student, an African American male, makes the claim that "where students sit does affect the class behavior." In the next-to-last paragraph of the paper, he makes the following statements:

> My last pattern is that no blacks sit in the front of the class and as I was thinking I came up with this hypothesis, for years whites were always in the front liked and liked to kiss up to people, in this case, teachers and blacks they just want to come to class, get the work done and do what they got to do . . . An when your in back like all the blacks are they tends to get lost and not get good grades.

While it is fairly common teacher lore that those who sit up front tend to get better grades, the racialization of the pattern asserted here received no comments. I've joked about the general pattern of "good" and "bad" student seatings with my large lecture classes, commenting on the impossibility of everyone sitting up front.

Every student in the graduate seminar had heard of this pattern and neither I nor they had ever applied it beyond "good" and "bad" students. Yet this Temple student was telling us that race was a factor as well and that white, "good" student behavior was considered "kiss up" in his community. Not one of us suggested that he or she had noticed anything similar. No one commented on the issue of race. Instead, we were silent on the educational practice and on the subject of race. Several of the graduate students chose to comment on the sentence structure or on developing what it meant to "get the work done and do what they got to do." We seemed to be saying that students sit where they sit; they know who "counts" as "good" students and so do we. They choose, we affirm the rightness of their choice, and that seems to be fair. So response moved to the form of the paper. Though my students did not make a large issue of grammar in these papers, they consistently invoked form—development, detail, logical progression—rather than respond to the actual observations of the Temple students.

In the letters exchange, the Miami students illustrated the discursive practices of education in their rhetoric of the "natural" benefits of education. The Miami students were well aware that the term "basic" was politically charged and applied to those least powerful in an educational system. Coursework included examinations of the practices of labeling; the relation of labels to race, class, gender, and ethnicity; and close analyses of a broad range of basic writing textbooks, including the all too common workbook "remediation" texts. My students recognized these practices as malignant and consciously sought change. But at the same time, all of us had the teaching of writing bracketed, somehow not affected by the rest of the practices that are so much a part of education. Teaching writing, so it seemed, was not culpable in maintaining these practices; after all, it, too, was marginal. But education, writing in particular, and the letters exchange itself were portrayed in the letters as benevolent processes.

The following series of comments represent some of the aggregate data from the study. Though I recognize that it might be more comfortable to read lengthy exchanges from selective pairings, I believe that it is the aggregate data that makes it clear that we are dealing with a shared practice, a discursive practice about education. The graduate students in my class were a diverse lot: a current high school teacher, a community college admissions officer, three former high school teachers now opting for the academy, a former creative writer, and two traditionally tracked literature students. Some had gone to prestigious undergraduate institutions; some had attended schools very much like IUPUI. That their ideas about educational practice should be so similar is remarkable; hence, my insistence on presenting the data as aggregated. All of the following comments were written by Miami graduate students. The first series displays for eight pairings how the graduate students wrote with the assumption that education is empowering for everyone; the second series shows them making the same sort of assumption about the value of the letters exchange.

Talking About Education and Its "Natural" Benefits

Katy to Dell: I think it's pretty brave of you to go back to school and work towards a career change, especially since you already have a good job at General Motors. I think a lot of people become complacent or just feel stuck in a job if they've had it for a while, especially if it s a good job.

Roger to Wini: You know how teachers are always asking you to do one thing or the other.

Katy to Eric: You said that you're not a "genius," but you never know—I know a lot of people who really flowered in college. Besides, you don't have to be a genius to do well in college; I'm living proof. It really makes a big difference when you have a lot of support from your family and friends and the school itself. All of those things helped me a lot.

Chris to Ron: I'm sorry that you have to deal with the challenges of dyslexia. It sounds as if you have learned to deal with it very well. I appreciate the tip on deciphering your letter. Actually I'm used to reading phonetically; my husband can't spell worth a damn!

Katy to Dell: Just out of curiosity, what does your family think and what do your children think about having a parent in college? Has it given you more things in common, more things to talk about? Are your school experiences different or pretty much the same?

Dee to James: I really admire you for working part time and taking classes—and especially for hanging in there after a bad first semester. I can tell from your letter that you are really trying to keep up with everything this semester. I know all that hard work will pay off for you in the end. Just don't give up on yourself.

Karen to Quentin: I think it's great that you love being in school. I'm excited about it, too—I'm 34 and I've been away from books and classes for a long time, so it feels especially good to be back.

Marge to Keith: You didn't tell me you were a karate *teacher.* Wow! How do you teach selflessness? (I think it might help me to learn some of that.)

Warren to Terry: Do you like your writing class? I like to write but it seems like I only have time to write what I have to for class, but that is ok for now, I guess. Do you write outside of schoolwork? Do you get the chance to write "for fun"? Do you carry writing outside of class? I don't do as much as I would like to, but sometimes I'll sit down and just freewrite a lot to get some feelings or thoughts or dreams out. It helps me clear my head sometimes.

That education is viewed as having unquestioned "natural" benefits is clear from these comments. Katy insists that seeking change through education is good and brave; Dee applauds James' struggle to go to work and school simultaneously; Karen tells Quentin that school feels good; and Marge reacts with pleasure upon finding out that Keith teaches something, even if it is not academic in nature. The discursive practice here privileges schooling and assumes that everyone receives benefits equally from it. What is surprising about this stance is that these teachers all know that education does not necessarily pay off for all students.

Justifying Educational Practice: The Letters Exchange

Katy to Eric: The letter exchange is something I get to do in one of my classes, but it's not like a chore or an inconvenience to me. I love to write letters, but I don't always have the time, so writing to you is kind of like a creative outlet for me. I like to write, even school papers, but I think letter writing for me is like fiction or poetry to a creative writer—I still put a lot of thought into my letters, but I can say what I say, and I don't feel too limited by subjects or themes. I feel free to pursue all kinds of subjects and ideas.

Chris to Ron: I wasn't sure if I should tell you I was a graduate student. I was afraid I would intimidate you and I didn't want to put any additional pressure on myself. It's hard enough to try to write an interesting letter to a stranger, particularly when two English professors get a copy of it for evaluation purposes. I figured that if you knew I was a grad student you would expect a very profound letter.

Laurie to Marg: Why are our teachers having us do this? We're interesting people! We write differently, go to different schools, have different lives—all that'll show up one way or another. Then they can write about us! I don't mind, either. It's really fun to meet another person—even through the mail—and I'll take my paragraph of fame if this winds up going somewhere for my teacher.

Rob to Erica: I guess my professor's goal in having us write to one another is for you to tell me what your writing course is like, what you learn from it, and things like that. In the meantime, I'll tell you what I learn. Maybe we will teach each other something.

Chris to Ron: I'm sorry we were both coerced into writing to strangers but I'm also convinced that of all the writing assignments I've had in college, this one could be the most fun. One or two letters from now we won't be strangers.

Laurie to Erin: My English class involves studying teaching methods and theories of teaching for classes like the one you're in. It looks at questions of what "competency" is and who determines it. I know I've re-read some of my rough drafts of papers and thought "wait—this is all mixed up." But what's okay for a draft isn't for another situation. Sometimes, too, I've looked back on a paper that I thought was food and thought "Did I write this?" It intrigues me—was I really a different person the moment I wrote that—maybe more involved, or caught up in the subject—and so a better writer. It's like another person wrote that paper.

Katy to Eric: By the way, I understand your doubts about me being a real person. This is an unusual class project, not to mention an unusual way to start writing to someone you don't know. If I had to pick a name off the chalkboard, I think I'd have my doubts too. In a way, I think you had the harder or riskier part in this—you had to take the initiative and get things started. Well, let me reassure you, I am definitely a "real person."

When graduate students turn to justifying the letters exchange, they also invoke the discourse of educational practice, Katy assumes writing is good, that individual creativity and freedom result from its practice. Rob and Laurie clothe the writing context in a learning experience—obviously good on the face of it. Katy interestingly has to respond to a male IUPUI student who doubts that she is a real person. Eric wrote in his first letter:

Anyway we were assigned in this class of mine to pick out a name of a chalkboard—I picked your name since it sounded the prettiest. To be honest, I do not really know if you are a real person, but if you are then I am sorry for douting you and my teacher.

Katy responds that indeed she is real and that she understands why he may have doubts, though she never expresses the actual reason he has doubts. Katy's correspondent seems to know that the person who stands in a classroom is a self constructed in an educational context, not a "real person," even if he can't say why that is true. None of the graduate students describe the debate about who basic writers are supposed to be or what their writing is supposed to say about their abilities.

The tone of the discourse is cheerful—difference is positive; learning is good for you—even though each writer knows the potential damage in being labeled. Katy, for example, writes Eric in her next letter to say how valuable she finds letter writing: it is on the same plane as creative writing. Laurie tells Marg that it's just that they're different, implying, with clear hope that there's nothing wrong with that, even though the literal difference—graduate students in English, and basic writers at an urban campus—is immense. Only Chris, a first semester graduate student admits that the writing feels uncomfortable. In one letter she says:

> I don't want to dishearten you but I don't think students, undergraduate or graduate, ever feel comfortable about their background or skills. Now that I am a graduate student I'm supposed to have achieved a certain level of success in writing. I feel intimidated every time I turn in an assignment. So don't feel like you are at a disadvantage.

Chris resists some part of educational ideology in the expression of her own doubts about her performance in writing, but she is nonetheless a graduate student in English, performing on cue for her classes. That ability to perform on demand and its inexpressibility—"so don't feel like you are at a disadvantage"—allows the reinscription of difference at the same time Chris offers solidarity with her correspondent.

Constructing an Academic Self

In order for the author function to be reproduced, apprentices in English departments must be inducted into thinking of themselves as author-scholars. Though these graduate students represent a range of standings—from second semester M.A. students to Ph.D. students nearing qualifying exams—they all identify themselves with institutional programs: Katy's an "English literature major," Dee's taking a course in "British 19th century autobiography," Roger's "working on a master's degree in composition and rhetoric," and on through the entire group. Throughout their letters, these students articulate the organization of the discipline, replicating its structural forms for their basic writing-correspondents. Moreover, these students write about writing, about authorship, about its centrality to what they do. Katy talks of her journal writing and diaries, even "freewrites" as "fun," while Warren juxtaposes his desire and satisfaction in writing with his like of "'trashy late night television.'" They take courses in writing, ask questions about writing, and see differences in writing. It is Katy who best expresses the demands of the discipline when she writes:

Sometimes when school work and 'real life' concerns really pile up, I feel like things are getting out of control, but somehow I manage to get done what needs to be done. I think one of the things you learn in school is how to establish priorities, which for me means deciding what absolutely must get done now and what can wait.

And what must be done now is writing, writing that will lead to being the author-scholar. Laurie's remark to Marge is telling: "I'll take my paragraph of fame if this winds up going somewhere for my teacher." Writing is the game and they intend to be players.

Why are graduate students in an English department seemingly so transparent in reinscribing the author function on these basic writers? That question deserves our consideration because it is so often our graduate students who teach basic writers. And even more than basic writers, graduate students in English departments are subjects of the master discourse, the apprentices who must subscribe to reigning educational discursive practices if they intend to remain in the academy.

Resisting Privilege

Yet it is these graduate students who also suggest the means of resisting the author function at the same time they appear to actively reinscribe it on to their basic writing correspondents. This move toward resistance slips in with their presentation of teaching narratives in the letters, almost as if to say that it is as teachers, not as author-scholars, that they are capable of scrutinizing their roles. In writing to Wini, Cincinnati public school teacher Roger comments on his first year of teaching in the following way:

> Teaching for me has become much easier. My first year was fairly difficult because the school is fairly big, about 2500 students, urban, and predominantly black, nearly 85% black. The students gave me a very rough time when I first started teaching. I actually had things thrown at my back the first couple of weeks of teaching.

Roger seems uncomfortable with the role of disciplinarian and surprised and upset by his students' denial of his authority to teach. That he acknowledges it at all is a kind of slippage in discursive practice. We are always supposed to be in control. And there is a second slippage as well in Roger's narrative. Roger comments on race, the single occasion in the letters in which race was explicitly mentioned, and thus he violates the practice of never mentioning racial difference in student populations.

Dee also slips away from educational ideology when she relates the following events to Greg, her correspondent:

> I had a great weekend! My sister and her family (husband, nephew—18 yrs old, niece—14 yrs old) came to visit. My one bedroom apartment is really small, so it seemed like wall-to-wall sleeping bags and people when we bunked down for the night! My nephew Rod is thinking about coming here to college next year. I called a

student from last semester and asked if he'd show Rod around campus. I was kind of nervous about Rod having a good time. I guess I wanted him to like it here. Anyway, Rod told me later that Ken (my student) is still mad at me because he got a B instead of an A in his class. I really like Ken and his being mad at me about a grade is just one of those unpleasant things about being a teacher.

The dismay Dee feels over the consequences of evaluation—a part of accepted educational ideology—was not part of "a great weekend." Dee is uncomfortable with the fact that she liked and trusted the student well enough to send him off with her nephew and that he complained to her nephew. Educational ideology intervenes. It seems impossible to keep them separate. That she characterizes her reaction as merely "unpleasant" suggests just how powerfully the educational discourse guides any discussion about its practices. Yet her telling of the incident also suggests her desire to go beyond a mere reproduction of existing practices. She is beginning to resist and beginning to be able to discuss her resistance. Why such resistance would appear in the form of teaching *narratives* is an interesting political question in itself. Perhaps because teaching lore is typically not a canonical form of the expression of authorship in English departments, such vignettes of classrooms are less subject to "discipline" and thus more available as a venue for resistance.

How we go about resisting deserves considerable rethinking on our part. Let me close with some observations on this project. As I said, I had hoped that we could become conscious of how we all participate in the process of constructing basic writers. I expected that process to occur through the course readings and activities which included critical discourse analysis of basic writing textbooks and course guides, as well as the reading of Brodkey's "'Literacy Letters'" at the beginning of the course. I also expected—and I hoped I was demonstrating—reflective practice. In short, I expected to use education to critique *and* change educational practice, a difficult paradox at best, but one that is a common project in much of contemporary graduate education in the humanities and social sciences. Liberal educational ideology assume, that knowing *about* a situation is enough to change practices. My training in composition and sociolinguistics left me predisposed to assume that teaching *about* the subtle labeling and structuring of English department practices would be enough to change those practices in the next generation of teacher-scholars, even as I knew that critical analysis would predict a different outcome. I had, in fact, probably undermined my own project by locating it in a graduate seminar. Where but in the graduate seminar does the panopticon discipline so well? I read, and my students knew I read, letters going both directions. I knew, and they knew, that I would be commenting on those letters by analyzing the practice. It made little difference that I invited my graduate students to participate in the project as peers; their being in my classroom was enough to tell them that we were anything but peers. Moreover, I, with my students, readily adopted the trope of the Other, setting off to other institutions to bring back exotic knowledge *about* the basic writer.[2] And "knowledge about"—rather than changed practices—is what we brought back.

From the standpoint of the letters alone, we were not successful and I was responsible. But this is only to offer the evidence of a single course, in a single semester. When I look to see what that group of graduate students is doing now, I see a group committed to change, and most are still engaged in some way in work with basic writers. The high school teacher has become a proponent of portfolios, allowing his students the opportunity to revise and present their best possible writing. Three of the students helped me examine gender differences in writing groups and hypothesized connections with class, race, and ethnicity as well. One of those students worked hard to reform an early opportunity program that clearly reinscribed minority students into a less privileged status at the same time it was inviting them into the academy. Another chose to teach at a branch campus of Miami so that she could begin to work with basic writers honorably. Yet another has taken on the principles of standardized testing, for its masking of reification of social differences. Only time could provide evidence of their commitments. Are these commitments based solely on the basis of this course? I would be foolish to make such a claim. But in this course, these students had the opportunity to rethink what was "natural" about basic writers and beginning that process of rethinking had later consequences.

And there are also things I would change in the actual mechanics of the class. The two groups of students—graduate students from Miami and basic writers from IUPUI—met at the end of that semester on the Indianapolis campus. Students on both sides had the opportunity to meet, talk, lunch, explore, and reorient perspectives. If I were to do the project again, I would make sure that the groups met earlier, perhaps exchanging days in which they shadowed one another. What would my students have thought about an employer who was suspicious of his or her employee bringing a "shadow" to work, a practice less remarkable in an academic setting? What would my students have thought about the sort of dead-end, minimum wage jobs that many of the basic writers were enduring? What would they have thought of the various administrative hurdle jumping that the basic writers had to negotiate in the Access Center? Surely the various disciplines to which basic writers are subject would be more apparent. If my purpose was to help my students understand how basic writers lived, letters alone could not provide enough context. The basic writers were as proficient in creating a rhetorical self on paper as the graduate students were, masking some of the very experiences that I most wanted my students to know about. And I would take greater advantage of the opening that the teaching narratives seemed to provide—moments when the graduate students dropped their professional personae and acknowledged their own insecurities within the master discourse.

Susan Miller, in the conclusion of *Textual Carnivals*, argues that composition scholars are in a unique position to use their marginal status as the means to understand practices in English departments and to become a "designated place for counterhegemonic intellectual politics" (187). As she suggests,

> These often-stated but persistently unpoliticized practices and insights in the field have positioned [composition] to transform its ancillary identity by engaging intellectual as well as practical political actions. As the institutional site designated as a passive enclosure for 'unauthorized' discourse, composition has simultaneously been designated as a marginalizing power. But this enormous power to contain the discourse of the majority can be, if its professionals claim it, the strength that represents the field's identity. (187)

The idea of authorship in English departments is constructed by the people who populate them. We do not have to simply accept current practices, especially when those practices make it impossible for some student writers to escape the imposition of negative status. By challenging the principles on which the author function rests, by exploring the lived experiences of our basic writing students, by agreeing to re-think our own positions, we can begin to resist the reinscription of power and col-laboratively redefine the author.

Specifically, several changes in basic writing pedagogy seem both warranted and necessary from this project. First, we should make the historicity of the basic writing "problem" visible to our colleagues and administrators. It is not temporary and our responses should not be based on its alleged momentary appearance. Only by continuing to see basic writers as temporary problems can administrators justify creating temporary faculty positions to answer the needs of these students. Who needs a tenure-line, permanent position for instructing basic writers when the prob-lem will evaporate as soon as the current crisis is over? Second, as composition fac-ulty, we should be rethinking the identity politics of labeling ability levels of writers. Who, we should be asking, is served by maintaining the labeling? We can and should acknowledge that at least one group well served by maintaining the abil-ity divisions is the faculty who teach both "regular" and "basic" writing, allowing us to celebrate supposedly homogenous classrooms, claiming that the homogenous classroom is to be preferred for its ease. Yet, as those of us who have taught basic writing can attest, homogenous basic classrooms are hardly the typical case. If we conclude at the local level that the politics of labeling must remain in place because of institutional constraints, then we should vigorously oppose the practice at many institutions of sending our least experienced teachers into the basic writing class-room. The vulnerability of graduate students and part-time instructors to institu-tional forces makes them the groups most likely to construct basic writers as the institution demands.

For some readers, the endpoint of a Foucauldian analysis seems to be despair, immobility, and hopelessness. Is it hopeless? I think not if resistance is foregrounded in our training of new teachers of composition and our own practice as teachers and administrators. It is to resistance that I would guide those who train teachers of basic writing, and it is what Foucault means when he discusses resis-tance:

> There are no relations of power without resistances; the latter are all the more real and effective because they are formed right at the point where relations of power are exer-cised; resistance to power does not have to come from elsewhere to be real, nor is it in-exorably frustrated through being the compatriot of power. It exists all the more by being in the same place as power. (*Power and Knowledge* 142)

Foucauldian analysis is only a beginning, not surrender to the inevitable. Like Da-vid Shumway, I believe that the power of Foucauldian analysis is best used in reconceptualizing contemporary politics and resisting disciplinary power. But we must act from the analysis. The letters described and reported in this essay are not anomalous. They are representative of the language we use in our commentary on students' papers, our talk in student-teacher conferences, and our modeling of talk appropriate for peer responses. In examining the role of the author function in creating and regulating the positioning of basic writing in English departments, I hope to point us to the path of resistance, one in which we examine our representations of educational discursive practices.

Acknowledgments

I would like to thank Miami University's Department of English for its support in the initiation of this project, and also thank project participants Betty Anderson of IU-Indianapolis, Frank Sullivan of Temple University, Maggy Lindgren of Miami University, and Linda Brodkey of the University of California-San Diego, and my collaborators and co-researchers, the graduate students in Composition and Rhetoric at Miami University. I would also like to thank my colleague George Dillon for several insightful readings and the *CCC* reviewers, Richard E. Miller and Kurt Spellmeyer, for their comments and their willingness to engage in "talk" about the subject.

Notes

1. All of the students, graduate and "basic" discussed in this article have been given coded names. In doing so, I am hoping to honor them for their honesty and their willingness to pursue self-reflection on their own roles.
2. I should make clear here that Miami University insisted that it had no basic writers, and thus had no basic writers for us to correspond with on the Oxford campus, even though the classroom experiences of some indicated otherwise. To be sure, Miami was selective in its admissions process, and most of its students came to first year composition with considerable competence. But at least two of the graduate students enrolled in the seminar had worked or were working in the Writing Center where the unacknowledged basic writers were often sent.

Works Cited

Armstrong, Cheryl. "Reexamining Basic Writing: Lessons from Harvard's Basic Writers." *Journal of Basic Writing* 7.2 (1988): 68-80.

Brannon, Lil, and C. H. Knoblauch. "On Students' Rights to Their Own Texts: A Model of Teacher Response." *CCC* 33 (1982): 157-166.

Brodkey, Linda. "On the Subjects of Class and Gender in the 'Literacy Letters.'" *College English* 51 (1989): 125-141.

Daiker, Donald. "Learning to Praise." *Writing and Response: Theory, Practice, and Research*. Ed. Chris Anson. Urbana, IL: NCTE, 1989. 103-113.

Farrell, Thomas. "IQ and Standard English." *CCC* 34 (1983): 470-484.

Foucault, Michel. "Powers and Strategies." *Power/Knowledge: Selected Interviews & Other Writings, 1972-1977*. Ed. Colin Gordon. Trans. by Colin Gordon, Leo Marshall, John Mepham, and Kate Soper. New York: Pantheon, 1980. 134-145.

_____. "What Is an Author?" *The Foucault Reader.* Ed. Paul Rabinow. Trans. by Joseu V. Harari. New York: Pantheon, 1984. 101-120.

Graff, Gerald. *Professing Literature: An Institutional History.* Chicago: University of' Chicago P, 1987.

Lunsford, Andrea. "Cognitive Development and the Basic Writer." *A Sourcebook for Basic Writing Teachers.* Ed. Theresa Enos. Manchester, MO: McGraw, 1987. 449-459.

Miller, Susan, *Textual Carnivals: The Politics of Composition.* Carbondale, IL: Southern Illinois UP, 1991.

Murphy, Ann. "Transference and Resistance in Basic Writing." *CCC* 40 (1989): 175-187.

Ohmann, Richard. *English in America.* New York: Oxford, 1976.

Recchio, Thomas E. "A Bakhtinian Reading of Student Writing." *CCC* 42 (1991): 446-454.

Shaughnessey, Mina. *Errors and Expectations.* New York: Oxford UP, 1983.

Shumway, David. *Michel Foucault.* Charlottesville, VA: University of Virginia P, 1989.

Sommers, Nancy. "Revision Strategies of Student Writers and Experienced Adult Writers." *A Sourcebook for Basic Writing Teachers.* Ed. Theresa Enos. Manchester, MO: McGraw, 1987. 535-544.

Stygall, Gail. "Politics and Proof in Basic Writing." *Journal of Basic Writing* 7.2 (1988): 28-41.

Williams, Joseph. "The Phenomenology of Error." *CCC* 32 (1981): 152-168.

Literacies and Deficits Revisited
by Jerrie Cobb Scott

Why do we continue to revisit the issue of deficit pedagogy, particularly in programs designed for what Rose calls "students on the boundary?" It is reasonable to assume that we have either failed to get to the root of the problem or refused to accept the explanations offered. In this discussion, I identify two factors that contribute to the recycling of deficit pedagogy in basic writing and other programs targeted for marginalized students. The first factor is traditional, technocratic definitions of literacy, viewed here as a mechanism for importing deficit theories into the content of instructional programs, resulting in the "missed education" of marginalized students. The second factor has to do with attitudes that pervasively but persistently resist change, notably in the delivery of instruction. To explore attitudinal effects on pedagogy, I offer the concept of "uncritical dysconsciousness," defined as the acceptance, sometimes unconsciously, of culturally sanctioned beliefs that, regardless of good intentions, defend the advantages of insiders and the disadvantages of outsiders. Throughout the second part of the paper, I present "think abouts" to challenge professionals working in basic writing programs to move to a higher level of critical consciousness and toward nondeficit approaches to programs targeted for marginalized students.

Definitions of Literacy

One clear linguistic indicator of an important societal problem is the redefinition of terms. Certainly "literacy" has been redefined often enough over the last two decades to give us pause. Do we need yet another definition? What does the term literacy really mean? And, have the various definitions moved us to a point of meaninglessness rather than meaningfulness? This discussion is less concerned with the precise definitions of literacy than with their effects on our approaches to instruction.

Scott, Jerrie Cobb. "Literacies and Deficits Revisited." *Journal of Basic Writing 21.1* (1993): 46-56. Copyright (1993) by the *Journal of Basic Writing*, Office of Academic Affairs, The City University of New York. Reprinted by permission.

Narrow definitions of literacy, or even the perception of only one kind of literacy, account in part for deficit approaches to instructional programs designed for students who either fail in schools or are failed by the schools. For example, remedial or developmental programs, including basic writing programs, often identify their target population in relation to the narrow definition of literacy, the ability to read or write. At the outset, then, such programs assume that the learner has deficiencies that must be remediated. Based on the logic that these deficiencies can be precisely diagnosed, the next logical step is to prescribe methods for correcting the deficiencies. We now know that it is merely wishful thinking that allows us to assume that learning processes are so neatly packaged, or that we have reached a level of understanding of learning that allows us to pinpoint discrete skills and a sequence for learning that has psychological reality for any one learner, much less a whole group of learners.

The notion of "unpackaging literacy" (Scribner and Cole) can be found in evolving definitions of literacy, some of which support and others that reject deficit approaches to instruction. In support of deficit approaches to instruction for nonmainstream groups is the view that explains literacy in terms of membership in advanced, high-tech cultures, particularly those that use an alphabetic writing system (Ong; Goody and Watt). This way of defining literacy leads us to a division among the cultures of the world—literate vs. oral cultures; it is inherently biased against oral literacy. Culture is also discussed in relation to the term "cultural literacy," the Hirschian model (Hirsch, 1987). While expanding the definition of literacy to include knowledge, the Hirschian viewpoint is biased toward the shared knowledge base of the dominant group or, more accurately, information and facts that the dominant group stores. If this viewpoint is carried into pedagogy, it can easily import the baggage of a deficit pedagogy, precisely because it makes unimportant the knowledge base of different subcultures within a diverse society.

Rapidly gaining attention among language educators are definitions of literacy that are not inherently biased against certain groups and that support nondeficit approaches to instruction. One such term is critical literacy, defined as neither a skill nor membership in a particular group, but an act—the act of socially transforming oneself to the level of active participation in and creation of a culture. Emphasis is placed on the use of creative and critical sensibilities of the general culture as well as its subcultures, to include nonmainstream groups. From the Freireian perspective, the importance of literacy rests with the ways we use reading, writing, and speaking skills so that our understanding of the world is progressively enlarged (Freire).

Work in anthropological studies, note Bloome and Green, argues for "reconsideration and redefinition of what counts as literacy in the broad sense, and literacy learning and pedagogy more specifically" (2). Similar views are held by scholars of this persuasion.

> [They] share a rejection of technocratic views of literacy and education. They reject the view that literacy consists of decontextualized cognitive and linguistics skills and that becoming literate is defined by the acquisition of skills. Instead, literacy and education are viewed as social and cultural practices and actions that vary across cultures,

communities, and across situations even within the same setting. Thus, there are multiple literacies rather than a single literacy and individuals may be literate in multiple ways. (2)

A point not to be overlooked about these various ways of defining literacy is that each definition varies according to purposes for defining. Bloome suggests an instructionally motivated purpose for anthropological studies: "The promise and substance of anthropologically based research on teaching the English language arts lie, in large part, in the possibilities and vision it yields for social equality in and through educational settings" (2).

I believe that instructionally motivated definitions of literacy are best conceptualized in ways that include the do's and can do's of the population to be served, rather than their weaknesses or differences from other groups deemed successful. Concerned that narrow definitions of literacy, e.g., the ability to read or write, yield instructional models often targeted toward problems associated with ways that nonmainstream groups differ linguistically and culturally from mainstream groups, I set out to define literacy broadly enough to be inclusive of multiple literacies and diverse ways of using literacies by different groups.

Thus, I define literacy as ways of knowing, accessing, creating, and using information. Literacy is neither a product nor a finite state, but a process that changes in response to different contexts. From this perspective, reading and writing are two important tools of literacy, particularly in a print-oriented society such as ours. There are, however, other tools of literacy, including oral and visual skills that can be represented in both print and nonprint forms.

This view of literacy has worked well in my own work, yielding a variety of models that seek to enhance multiple sensibilities through multisensory perceptions. One example is the Visual-Print Literacy model (Scott, Davis, and Walker). Developed in collaboration with an artist, Willis Davis, this instructional program encourages students to access information from both visual and verbal texts, to create meaning—multiple meanings—and to use those meanings to read the different messages in their personal, social, and academic worlds. It is important that the visual-print literacy program, as well as others, evolve from a definition of literacy that rejects deficit approaches to instruction.

In short, my definition of literacy, along with those that basically reject the technocratic orientation mentioned by Bloome, guards against importing the negative baggage of deficits into instruction, thereby allowing for instructional content that might otherwise be reserved for the so-called gifted or normative group. Narrowly defined definitions constrain content to what is perceived as simple, but is experienced as boring, insignificant, irrelevant, and nonchallenging to all, including basic writers.

Attitudes and Uncritical Dysconsciousness

Widely acknowledged is the pervasive manner in which attitudes affect instruction. From self-fulfilling prophecies, a recurring theme of the 1960s and 1970s, to their behavioral manifestations in student-teacher interactions discussed widely in applied anthropological linguistics of the 1980s and the early 1990s, attitudes may be seen as a mechanism for resisting change. As we approach the twenty-first century with a more rigorous agenda for change, we are challenged toward greater understanding of how attitudes affect teaching and learning.

Clearly, the research on linguistic and cultural diversity has played a significant role in the restructuring of curricula, including the integration of information about language differences into language instruction for ethnically and socially diverse students and the infusion of multicultural content across disciplines. Nevertheless, many questions regarding attitudes as mechanisms for resisting change remain unanswered, leaving the problem of deficit approaches to instruction for marginalized groups unresolved.

Without reviewing the literature on attitudes, suffice it here to say that we know more about what the negative attitudes are than about how to change them. Noting the importance of the "will to educate all children" to effective education in a pluralistic society, Hilliard calls for deep restructuring:

> Deep restructuring is a matter of drawing up an appropriate vision of human potential, of the design of human institutions, of the creation of a professional work environment, of the linkage of school activities and community directions, of creating human bonds in the operation of appropriate socialization activities, and of aiming for the stars for the children and for ourselves academically and socially. . . . The beauty and promise of true restructuring is that it will provide us with the opportunity to create educational systems that never have existed before, not because they were hard to create but because we have not yet made manifest the vision or tried to create them. (35)

The vision of creating educational systems that never existed is widely sought after, as evidenced in the New American Schools program's (1991) call for break-the-mold innovations in educational programs, presumably changes that will address the needs of a diverse student population. However, as Hilliard's explanation of deep restructuring suggests, restructuring is needed not only at the level of content, but also at the level of attitudes that ultimately determine how the content will be delivered.

The three examples below illustrate what can happen if we limit restructuring efforts to surface level changes in the curriculum: (1) linguistic differences, cast in the traditional delivery mold, treat differences as deficits (Scott, 1992); (2) literature-based reading programs, delivered in the same manner as basal programs—popularly referred to as the basalization of whole language approaches, import the same pedagogical problems that the literature-based programs sought to resolve; and (3) a reductionist approach to multicultural education lends itself to a devaluing, rather than an appreciation and understanding, of the richness and potential unifying dimensions of diversity. The challenge, I submit, is to find ways to bring about deep restructuring to accompany the surface-level restructuring of curricula. And this will require a fuller understanding of various forms of marginalization.

There is now a growing body of literature in the areas of racism, sexism, and classism that has implications for the more general problem of marginalization. Moreover, it appears that this work could be of use to teachers. I offer here some notions about "uncritical dysconsciousness," not as models but as "think abouts." Think first about the term uncritical dysconsciousness, a phrase coined from critical consciousness and dysconciousness. "Critical consciousness," notes King, "involves an ethical judgment about the social order," whereas dysconsciousness is "an uncritical habit of mind that justifies inequity and exploitation by accepting the existing order of things as given" (154). Broadening the two terms to cover various forms of marginalization, I use uncritical dysconsciousness to refer to the acceptance, sometimes unconsciously, of culturally sanctioned beliefs that, regardless of intent, defend the advantages of insiders and the disadvantages of outsiders. As teachers, we tend to operate without questioning the extent to which practices deviate from the ideal, socially sanctioned ideologies of society or how our individual processes of self-identity interplay with the self-identity of students. To fail to critically examine the practiced vs. the preached ideologies of society or the student vs. the teacher's self-identity is to support, through uncritical dysconsciousness, the recycling of attitudes that resist changes that benefit those marginalized in school systems.

What can be gleaned from discussions of ideology and self-identity is that we have largely focused on one side of the marginalization coin—the problems, ideologies, and identity of outsiders, resulting in a pattern of defining problems in relation to inequities experienced by the disadvantaged but finding solutions in the ways and means of the advantaged. On the other side of the coin, there also exist problems, ideologies, identities among insiders. We might think about exposing both sides of the coin, thereby providing a more balanced picture of what needs to be changed and a fuller understanding of resistances to change, or more specifically, the staying power of deficit pedagogy for marginalized students.

In the article "Dysconscious Racism: Ideology, Identity and the Mis-education of Teachers," King illustrates how a group of preservice teachers, accustomed to accepting the ideals of the democratic ethic, may readily accept what Tatum calls the myth of meritocracy: the belief in a just society where individual efforts are fairly rewarded. Focusing on ethnically based marginalization, King found that her students tended to link racism to either the distant past—slavery, individual cases of denial, or lack of equal opportunity—or to normative patterns of discrimination. King concludes that these responses show the general failure to recognize structural inequities built into the social order. Of importance to this discussion, the responses point to the ease with which one can ignore the differences between the practiced and the preached ideologies of society. Teachers can easily move toward a sense of hopelessness because of their inability to change the past, their understanding of the problem as individual cases of discrimination for which they are not responsible, and their social distance from the problem. Further, if attention is focused on only the experiences of outsiders, in this case African Americans, it becomes easy to provide a rationale for deficiencies. Despite the 1970s and 1980s preachings and teachings about differences, rather than deficits, Hull, Rose, Fraser, and Castellano explain that, "We struggle within a discourse that yearns for difference, and differ-

ence, in our culture, slides readily toward judgments of better-or-worse, dominance, Otherness" (24).

To rectify the problem of conflicts between practiced and ideal ideologies, King
suggests the use of counterknowledge strategies that allows teachers to consciously
examine their ideologies about "otherness." I am suggesting that one way to hurdle
the difference- transformed-to-deficit obstacle and the self-fulfilling-prophecy pattern is by providing a context for examining the democratic ethic of social equality
from the point of view of both the advantaged and disadvantaged, looking particularly at who benefits and who suffers from structural inequities that are built into the
social order and allowed to have a practical existence that contradicts the culturally
sanctioned ideals of society. By examining societal ideologies from both perspectives, it should be possible to diffuse the thinking that confuses differences with deficits, a confusion that serves to justify the recycling of deficit pedagogy.

We also have an imbalance in the focus on self-identity. A good deal of attention
has been given to the development of self-identity among nonmainstream
groups—how for example, identity influences resistances to change toward the
norms of the dominant group, including language (Ogbu). Looking at only the student side of the identity issue, it is easy to overlook the teacher side. Regardless of
the qualifying basis for marginalization—ethnic group, gender, religion, income, or
membership in developmental or remedial programs—self-identity will vary
among individuals within a group as well as across groups. Moreover, we each
move in and out of marginalized status, teachers and students alike. Teachers in basic writing programs, for example, often share their students' sense of
marginalization. Having linked self-identity to attitudes that affect student-teacher
interactions, I suggest that exposure to various ways that individuals develop
self-identity would provide a more balanced and useful way of understanding interactions among people in general and between teachers and students in particular.

Focusing on ethnically based marginalization, Tatum's discussion of the
development of self-identity illustrates the importance of viewing self-identity
from the dual perspectives of outsiders and insiders. In her analysis of stages in
the development of White and Black racial identity, she uses a journal entry of a
White male to illustrate the first stage of White racial identity development, the
Contact stage. This stage is characterized by the lack of awareness of cultural and
institutional racism and of White privileges, and "includes curiosity about or fear
of people of color, based on stereotypes learned from friends, family, or the media" (13). She uses the journal entry of an African American female to illustrate
the first stage of Black racial identity, the Pre-encounter stage. In this stage the African American absorbs many of the beliefs and values of the dominant group.
Both journal entries were produced in a psychology course that treats issues of
racism, classism, and sexism:

> As a white person, I realized I had been taught about racism as something which puts
> others at a disadvantage, but had been taught not to see one of its corollary aspects,
> white privilege, which puts me at an advantage. . . . I was taught to see racism only in
> individual acts of meanness, not in invisible systems conferring dominance on my
> group. (Tatum, 13)

> For a long time it seemed as if I didn't remember my background, and I guess in some ways I didn't. I was never taught to be proud of my African heritage. . . . I went through a very long stage of identifying with my oppressors. Wanting to be like, live like, and be accepted by them. Even to the point of hating my own race and myself for being a part of it. Now I am ashamed that I ever was ashamed. I lost so much of myself in my denial of and refusal to accept my people. (10)

The final stage of each group represents a comfort zone that facilitates interactions across groups. For African Americans, the internalization/commitment stage is characterized by a positive sense of racial identity, sustained over time, allowing the individual to practically perceive and transcend racism and to develop and execute a plan of action. For White Americans, autonomy, the final stage, is marked by racial self-actualization, an ongoing process that leads continually to new ways of thinking and behaving regarding racism.

Three points are of special interest to this discussion: first, Taylor's discussion shows the problem of attitudes to be so deeply rooted that students resist talking about them; second, a process is involved for both mainstream and nonmainstream students, ending with behaviors that are more accepting of differences; and third, variations in identity development may be seen as potential sources of conflicts between members of different ethnic groups, and implicationally between students and teachers, as each brings different sets of self-qualifiers to the classroom setting. In essence, the questions of, "Who am I?" and, "Who are you?" affect interactions between teachers and students.

Tatum suggests that resistances can be reduced and development promoted by creating a safe classroom atmosphere and opportunities for self-generated knowledge, and by providing a model to enhance understanding of one's own processes and that utilizes strategies that empower one to act as change agents. I am suggesting that more attention be given to discovering how self-identity of teachers and students affects the context for learning. If treated as tendencies that people follow when their status is viewed as marginalized or nonmarginalized, the developmental stages may serve as a heuristic device for exploring deeply rooted attitudes that allow the resurfacing of deficit approaches. To "think about" is the question of how different ways of defining oneself affect student-teacher interaction in the classroom and therefore the delivery of educational programs. Drawing on different sources of information, e.g., racism, sexism, classism, it is possible to generalize findings to the broader issues of marginalization, student-teacher interaction, and the kinds of changes needed to produce learning environments where students and teachers of diverse backgrounds confront the problems of resistance that negatively affect student-teacher interactions. No matter how the surface structures of the curriculum are restructured, without deep restructuring we can expect problems in the delivery of instruction.

In this era of new democracies and transformed curricula, it will be important to move toward a balanced treatment of attitudes, one that actually allows us to see both sides of the marginalization coin. To fail to do so is to continue to struggle with the ills of uncritical dysconsciousness. In no way can we expect educational reforms in curriculum to bring about educational changes, without also addressing the attitudes that shape the context for learning. We need, as Hilliard notes, "deep restructuring," and that involves the restructuring of frames for thinking about marginalization and changing practices that recycle deficits.

Why do we continue to revisit the issue of deficit pedagogy, particularly in relation to programs designed for students on the boundary? This presentation suggests not an answer, but different ways of thinking about the roots of the problem. Evolving definitions of literacy allow us to think differently about how definitions affect pedagogy. The notion of uncritical dysconsciousness challenges us to think about attitudes that are embedded in a complex matrix of societal ideologies and individual stages in the development of self-identity, two of the areas that can affect the effectiveness with which we deliver restructured instructional programs. The bottom line is that both knowledge and the care we take in delivering knowledge are important. Simply, very simply, students don't care what we know unless they know we care.

Works Cited

Bloome, D. "Anthropology and Research on Teaching the English Language Arts." Eds. J. Flood, J. Jensen, D. Lapp, and J. Squire. *Handbook of Research in Teaching the English Language Arts.* New York: Macmillan, 1991.

Bloome, D. and J. Green. "Educational Contexts of Literacy." *Annual Review of Applied Linguistics*, 1991.

Freire, P. "The Adult Literacy Process as Cultural Action for Freedom." *Harvard Educational Review* 40 (1970): 205-25.

Goody, J. and I. Watt. "The Consequences of Literacy." *Comparative Studies of Language in Society and History* 5 (1963): 304-45.

Hilliard, A. "Do We Have the Will to Educate All Children?" *Educational Leadership* 48 (Sept. 1991): 31-36.

Hirsch, E. D. *Cultural Literacy: What Every American Needs to Know.* Boston: Houghton, 1987.

Hull, G., M. Rose, K. Fraser, and M. Castellano. *Remediation as Social Construct: Perspectives from an Analysis of Classroom Discourse.* (Tech. Report No. 44). Berkeley: U of California, Center for the Study of Literacy and Writing, 1991.

King, J. "Dysconscious Racism: Ideology, Identity, and Mis-education of Teachers." *Journal of Negro Education* 60.2 (1991): 133-45.

Ogbu, J. "Minority Education in Comparative Perspective." *Journal of Negro Education* 59.1 (1990): 45-57.

Ong, W. "Literacy and Orality in Our Times." *Journal of Communication* 30 (1980): 197-204.

Rose, M. *Lives on the Boundary.* New York: Penguin, 1989.

Scott, J. "Deficit Theories, Ethnic Dialects, and Literacy Research: When and Why Recycling Is Not Cost Efficient." *Literacy Research, Theory, and Practice: Views from Many Perspectives.* Forty-first Yearbook of the National Reading Conference. Chicago: National Reading Conference, Inc., 1992.

Scott, J., W. Davis, and A. Walker. "A Picture Is Worth a Thousand Words: The Visual-Print Connection." *Dialogue: Arts in the Midwest* (Nov/Dec 1989).33-40.

Scribner, S. and M. Cole. "Unpackaging Literacy." *Social Science Information* 17 (1982): 19-40.

Tatum, B. "Talking about Race, Learning about Racism: The Application of Racial Identity Development Theory in the Classroom." *Harvard Educational Review* 62.1 (Spring 1992): 1-24.

Constructing Teacher Identity
in the Basic Writing Classroom
by Jacqueline Jones Royster
and Rebecca Greenberg Taylor

A high moment in the workshop occurred when Jacqueline Jones Royster and Rebecca Greenberg Taylor directed participants to focus on ourselves and colleagues as basic writing teachers. After Royster explained how they had come to believe that too much attention had been concentrated on defining and categorizing our students, she led us in an informal survey to help us examine our own institutions for racial, gender, and class differences. We then wrote about our self-perceptions and aspirations and shared some of these. Next, Taylor powerfully presented a paper on a year in her life as a graduate student in the Rhetoric and Composition Program in the English Department at the Ohio State University and as a basic writing teacher during the 1996-1997 in the OSU Basic Writing Program. Her teaching directly related to her interests in authority, identity, genre, and the teaching of writing. Jacqueline Jones Royster, the Vice Chair for Rhetoric and Composition in the English Department, is Taylor's dissertation advisor and has complementary interests in issue of identity, classroom culture, and the development of literacy.

Our focus is on the implications of identity in the construction of classroom culture. Our imperative was to emphasize that "identity" in the classroom is a person-driven enterprise, i.e., that such a term becomes most salient by referencing the unique characteristics of the actual people in the room and not through definitions that abstract general traits and push teacher/researchers toward the construction of identities in generic terms. All too often teacher/researchers in our discipline have centered attention on only one set of the people in the room, the students, with only peripheral attention being directed toward the other set, the teacher.

While articles such as Lu (1994), Johnson (1994), Gunner (1993) and Dean (1989) have raised awareness of the extent to which as professionals, we are all racialized, gendered, and political subjects in classroom space, the interrogative gaze in both theory and practice has generally been unifocally determined (i.e., defined by the negotiations of students) rather than multifocally determined (i.e., defined by the negotiations of both students and the teacher).

In being multifocal in our gaze, we shift attention from the students to the teacher and then examine the implications of this viewpoint, not only for the students, but for the creation of the classroom culture to which students are adjusting. Discounting the teacher as an active agent in the classroom wrongly positions students as subjectable primarily to disembodied systems and overly constrained by outcomes rather than converging processes. By focusing on teacher identity, we re-shuffle these relationships and re-make the balances in order to make recognizable the notion that the negotiation of classroom identity involves an interaction of all parties, sometimes with competing agendas.

General Background

The project that became the springboard for this way of thinking emerged from interactions between Royster and Taylor that came about through a set of graduate courses that Taylor took and two quarters of basic writing courses in the Ohio State University Basic Writing Program that Taylor taught. These experiences enabled Taylor and Royster, her graduate advisor, to have sustained conversation about a collective of issues. Working together, we realized that there are advantages in shifting both the location from which we were envisioning our mutual concerns and the analytical paradigm by which we were operating.

In terms of our own location as workshop leaders in the CCCC workshop, our questions remained cognizant of student experiences in classrooms. The shift, however, was to foreground the multiple ways in which issues of identity become more slippery and compelling when we refine this view to notice more directly the race, gender, class, age, culture, institutional position, etc. of the teacher as classroom subject. Our intent was: to acknowledge both sets of people in the room, students and the teacher; to shift the paradigm so that students are not perceived simplistically as the site and/or source of pathology and so that teachers are perceived as the primary site and/or source of power, privilege, and culture-making; and to recognize, as Keith Gilyard (1996) and Jerrie Cobb Scott (1993) suggest, the need to flip "the script" and "the marginalization coin."

In effect, we had become impatient with the discussion of identity, most especially in basic writing classrooms, as the students' problem, rather than also as the teacher's problem, and we wanted the dialogue to take into direct account the culpability of teacher location in the creation of learning space. In our work, we have been instructed by a conscious interrogation of our assumptions about who is likely to occur in basic writing classrooms on both sides of the desk, especially in public institutions. Recognizing how much classroom constituencies actually vary from institutional site to institutional site, what we have affirmed is how consistently characteristics of writing performance become conflated in research and scholarship with issues of identity (race, class, gender, age) and with issues of good character or ethos.

In addition to interrogating our own assumptions, we have also been informed by demographic projections for the United States to the year 2020 (Campbell 1994) that indicate shifts in who is likely to occupy classrooms in the next century. By all indications, regardless of how students in the classroom may be constituted in terms of identities, what is likely is that the teacher will probably not share particular identities with the students, including the possibility of race, ethnicity, class, age, gender, etc., but also including factors such as histories of academic success, institutional status, and "cultural" sense of being. All of these factors relate to issues of "location" in the classroom that we assert will indeed become increasingly important in all of our classrooms, but clearly in basic writing classrooms. At the levels at which students are most insecure about writing performance i.e., in basic writing courses, "location" becomes exacerbated by the pressures of multiply defined experiences of marginality based not only on personal identity but also on social and institutional identity—or non-identity.

Our primary goal for the workshop was to debunk the myth of the conflation of race, class, culture, and character in the basic writing classroom, and to begin acknowledging the teaching self. The goals of the workshop were:

To blend self-critique and institutional "location" in creating a leverage point from which to shift paradigms for theory and practice in basic writing classrooms.

To generate strategies for interrogating the multiple relationships encoded in:
how we represent ourselves in the basic writing classroom;
how we represent our students in the basic writing classroom;
how these representations shape and direct what we teach, how we teach it, and how we assess progress and performance.

In order to carry out this agenda, we chose activities that were designed to be hands-on.

At the beginning of the workshop, we conducted an informal survey (See Appendix 1) in order for participants to notice the differences among their institutional sites, their material environments, as well as their student populations. The results of the survey served to remind us in quite direct ways that material conditions do indeed vary. We found that while as a group we might talk about our institutions in generic terms, they were actually quite distinctive in several ways (e.g., in terms of regional location, size, age of the student body, diversity among the faculty along gender, age, and ethnic lines, mission of the institution, etc.).

With the survey as general backdrop, we engaged in short writing activities (See Appendix 2) to make use of the memory work that enriches discussions of classroom theory and practice. These activities included the participants thinking about perceptions of themselves in the classroom, about particular moments in their classroom during which questions of identity might be raised, and about possible gaps between how they represent themselves and how students might represent them. Having primed these memories, we structured applications (See Appendix 3) that were designed to help participants concretize perceptions, draw forth classroom-based challenges, and share strategies and solutions to contentious problems and issues. The applications were based on incidents that had arisen from Taylor's experiences in her classroom, covering a range of issues: the selection of reading materials; the use of collaborative activities; assessment issues; issues related to technology; issues related to gender, authority, ethnicity, and so on.

The heart of our session, however, and the part that in the end seemed to yield the most was the sharing of Taylor's classroom experiences as she, a white woman raised in a Jewish household in Richmond, Virginia, entered a "multicultural" classroom filled with students whose success as writers and whose success with negotiating their academic and institutional identities varied considerably.

Expectations, Alliances, and Identities: A Case in Point

> As teachers, we tend to operate without questioning the extent to which practices deviate from the ideal, socially sanctioned ideologies of society or how our individual processes of self-identity interplay with the self-identity of students. To fail to critically examine the practiced vs. the preached ideologies of society or the student vs. the teacher's self-identity is to support, through uncritical dysconsciousness, the recycling of attitudes that resist changes that benefit those marginalized in school systems. (Jerrie Cobb Scott, "Literacies and Deficits Revisited")

I remember reading Jerrie Cobb Scott's "Literacies and Deficits Revisited" for the first time in the Spring of 1996. As a graduate student in a seminar designed to introduce us to the field of basic writing and to prepare us to teach in my university's own basic writing program, I was asked to draft a bibliographic essay focused upon the field's most recent (1990's) scholarship. I knew right away what I wanted to investigate: how notions of identity—gender, class, race, region, ethnicity—shape contemporary basic writing scholarship. All of my work as a student of rhetoric and composition had previously addressed the relationship between identity, authority, and the teaching and valuing of student writing and I expected these issues to prove especially crucial to the field of basic writing, where (for highly problematic reasons) students often represent a variety of cultural, racial, and economic categories of difference. But I was unprepared for what my brief bibliographical study of the *Journal of Basic Writing* and other composition journals would yield. While the issue of *student* identity permeated every facet of the scholarship, explorations of *teacher* identity seemed almost absent. I began to feel as if ghost writers were at work—quite literally. Who were these teachers, these researchers, representing the words and lives of their students? How did they figure into their own discussions?

Even now, nearly one year after reading "Literacies and Deficits Revisited," Scott's essay resonates quite powerfully for me. It points toward the tendency in basic writing scholarship to define basic writers. Whether defining these students in terms of their membership (or lack thereof) within academic discourse communities, or in terms of their cognitive "skills," the drive to define, and I would argue, objectify, students persists. Sometimes teachers and researchers focus the definitional act on the students' written products as metonymic stand-ins for the writers themselves. Perhaps most disturbingly, as William Jones reminds us in "Basic Writing: Pushing Against Racism," sometimes they utilize the term *basic writer* to serve as "euphemism and code for minority students" (74). As a white teacher I am perhaps most troubled by Jones' argument, but I will not respond to that argument by forwarding yet another definition of basic writers. Instead, like Jerrie Cobb Scott, I argue that basic writing scholars must cease to concentrate so intensely upon the act of defining these communicative "others," objectifying them and claiming all of the power that comes with the act of naming itself. I suggest that basic writing teachers and researchers must begin instead to question our own identities, examining critically the relation between who we are and the work we make possible for our students. This work is necessary for all teachers, but for white, middle class teachers of basic writing, who may find themselves, as Royster reminds us, feeling different from those who occupy the other side of the desk, the work is especially crucial. If Scott is right about the dangers of seemingly dysconscious (albeit well-intentioned) attitudes that reproduce the status quo, we must ask what it means for composition researchers and teachers not to address their own identities, to assume that multiple literacy practices can take place in a single classroom without the kind of "violence" that J. Elspeth Stuckey describes (1991). The challenge to teachers and researchers of basic writers is to "flip" what Scott so aptly calls the "marginalization coin" (51) in order to allow themselves to be described, discussed, defined, or named.

This challenge drove my research in the graduate seminar last year. I remember the end of the quarter looming along with my appointment to serve as a TA for the basic writing program the following autumn. I knew that my own identity would radically impact my teaching of the course, that my ways of valuing student texts, of determining what I would consider meaningful had everything to do with who I was and where I came from. Before I stepped into that basic writing classroom in the fall, I needed to stop and ask: What am I doing here? What drives me to work in the context of a basic writing classroom? What do I expect of my students and how did I construct those expectations?

But scholars like Jerrie Cobb Scott remind me that making a quick reference to my own race/class/gender at the beginning of my own scholarship is not enough. I must answer the questions I raise above, but such questions should not act as ends in themselves; instead, I use such questions as a means to interrogate my own teaching practices *in order to imagine new kinds of questions*. Naming who we are does not let us off the ethical hook. Actually, I am not really looking to my race, class, and culture as individually distinguishable factors that impact my teaching. Instead, I consider my race and class as two examples of the multiple sites that constitute what I name my culture(s). Thus a host of other factors, including age, regional affiliations, educational history, and institutional location are also part of what shapes who I am as a teacher in my classroom, a distinction which does not negate the need for white teachers to critique their racial and socio-economic identities. Rather, the distinction helps me to broaden that critique so that it encompasses other identities in helping me to realize how race and class are always implicitly a part of other sites of identity formation. In broadening the view, the goal is to historicize and critique the sites of identity formation and the sources of my own knowledge about basic writers. Thus I can articulate *how* and *why* I "am" in the basic writing classroom.

Voicing Identities in the Basic Writing Classroom

While teaching basic writing in the Fall of 1996, I undertook an independent study of teacher identity with my mentor and advisor, Jacqueline Jones Royster. What started as a bibliographical exploration for a graduate seminar became a more tangible project. I kept a teaching journal to help me study my own identity, as it was constructed by me and by my students. At the same time, I continued my review of basic writing scholarship, problematizing the ways in which teachers and researchers of basic writing represent their students without naming or critiquing themselves. My daily teaching journals reflected my own concerns regarding my position as a new teacher/scholar of basic writing, and by examining those concerns alongside others' approaches to teacher identity in basic writing scholarship, I explored potential sites for my own acts of uncritical dysconsciousness. As illustrated below, what became most informative in transforming this project into a CCCC Workshop presentation was the process of juxtaposing my voice with the voices of my students in order to study, reflect upon, and generate questions about the process of teacher identity-formation in the basic writing classroom.

Some of the characters in these journal entries are my students, but most of the characters are me: the TA struggling to stay theoretically grounded, the new teacher at the Writing Workshop trying to negotiate membership with colleagues, a white instructor worrying about her relationships with students of color, a woman troubled by gendered alliances among her students, and a suburbanite facing her own representations of rural students and their values. My competing identities, the characters here, don't always get along; and the setting has an awful lot to do with the plot. Within my journal entries, I represent student voices as they spoke during classroom conversations, via e-mail or personal conferences with me, and through their written responses to classroom assignments. Troubling for me in representing my students in writing, even when I use their own words, is that the nature of any written representation of "real" events is always just that—a linguistic representation, not an "actual" transcription capable of conveying totally what was said and what was communicated. I feel compelled to say that these stories are, of course, products of my own shaping and not intended to be set forth as unmediated "truth."

The Pre-Quarter Orientation: TA or Not TA?

The staff of the Workshop seemed so dedicated, enthused, and it was great to be among colleagues who love to talk about teaching again. But I definitely felt like the junior colleague, the student among professionals, and I resisted some of those activities. When we practiced hypothetical placement test reading, no matter how many sample essays I saw, I couldn't quite determine how to "place" an essay into one of our department's courses. When I asked what I thought made a student text successful, I said "it's communicative in context." I remember the other workshop staffers smiling at me politely.

It strikes me now how desperately I seemed to want to define myself as a graduate student visiting the Basic Writing program—not as a permanent resident. How many others find themselves, like me, expecting merely to "pass through" their basic writing teaching appointments? At my own institution, questions concerning the professionalization, scholarly commitment, and even work ethics of our basic writing teachers seem to arise frequently. How do such institutionally driven doubts affect basic writing scholarship and pedagogy?

After a particularly difficult October staff meeting at the Workshop, I write: *Last week, while we were discussing our observations of one another's classes, the highest compliment seemed to be, "I visited x's class and he was practically invisible." I will never be invisible in my classroom. Invisibility for a TA means powerlessness, lack of authority. But I'm afraid to speak up in these staff meetings because I'm a beginner. I'm worried that I'm starting to define myself as some sort of rebel here. That's not who I want to be.*

I'm not sure that I overcame that rebellious streak; rather, I reconceptualized it as the year wore on, working hard to balance my need to ask questions of my colleagues with the recognition that I was, in fact, inexperienced. Interestingly enough, I think my colleagues, too, reconceptualized me as they saw how my questions were helping me to bring the parts of myself—student, teacher, scholar—together in my work as a teacher at the Workshop.

Once the quarter began, my journal addressed my expectations about who these basic writers would be—and how I would find ways to make connections with them.

September 25: Great Expectations

I got my roster before I taught class today. The first thing I noticed was ethnicity. Or should I say, I noticed my own attempts to guess the ethnicities of my students, and then to pretend that I wasn't noticing. Was Juan Carlos a native speaker of Spanish? Where was he from? How many of the Asian names on my roster belonged to ESL students, and how many of them named students born and raised in the Ohio suburbs? Did I really only have two women in the class? How would they deal with Kingston's The Woman Warrior? *Once I matched names to faces, I found out that "T.L." was actually a Tiffanie—thank God! She seemed really interested—her writing sample suggests she's given a great deal of thought to the challenges she faces as a Black woman at the university. She's a sophomore, though. What happened last year? Did she take the course once? I never even took Freshman Comp. What experiences, if any, will my students and I share? Do we have to share experiences in order to work together successfully?*

As the quarter progressed, I found that spending time in two buildings, one which houses the basic writing program and the other the English Department, caused me to lose track of more than just my gradebook and coffee mug. Sometimes I felt like I lost a little bit of myself—the part of me I most clearly defined as Graduate Student—each time I made the trek from the English department to the basic writing program facility. But something else gradually replaced the part I had lost: a questioning, engaged, and often troubled teacher.

September 29: The Outsiders

The other TAs in the English department don't really understand why I'm interested in teaching basic writing five days a week, and after the basic writing staff meetings I feel as though my colleagues there think I am "questioning" them and their pedagogy. I suppose I do question the program—but not its pedagogy or its right to funding. I'm really questioning the institutional structures that put such a course in place. I mostly worry about how I handled my students' questions about 052. I think I let them know that I, too, am frustrated by the placement system. I suspect that they'll continue to say, "show me the difference between my paper and a 110 student's paper." Then who will I turn to? Bartholomae's work? Mike Rose's books? How should I answer such a question?

Interestingly, once my students began sharing their drafts in mid-October, I became the cultural outsider. It's an experience I highly recommend.

October 15: "Yet Do I Marvel"

I'm noticing that my own responses to student papers are somehow engaging the question of culture—even if I choose not to articulate that to the students themselves. For instance, Demetrius' first response log batch came in, and I noticed that when describing the protagonist in The Chocolate War, *Demetrius began to use a stylistic device that I could only describe as sermonic. He spoke in his journal about Jerry (the character) and his ability to "restoreth" the spirits of his teammates and friends. Such moments are fascinating for me—markers of a rhetorical tradition outside my own tend to make me want to stop, admire, ask questions. But would it be appropriate to share such moments with students? To talk to them about the intersections of culture and rhetoric ? Or, does my response simply imply that I'm too willing to generalize about African American students' discourse because I've read Smitherman or Gates? What's the best way to talk about community literacies and not fall into a kind of generalizing?*

Late October: Invisible Man

Jason, who moved here from China as a high school student, continues to worry me. The other night he wrote me via e-mail, expressing his disappointment that his classmates were not writing to him as often as he liked. "I wait for the rooster," he wrote, referring to the Eudora icon, "but he never come." Jason's quietness in class and his eagerness to speak over e-mail have contributed to my students' marking of him as Other. Sometimes I even forget he's in the room. What role should I play in helping Jason to assimilate? Should he assimilate at all?

What strikes me now as I read my journal responses to both Demetrius and Jason is how two facets of my own identity, my race and my own research agenda, colored my pedagogical instincts. As a graduate student enmeshed in discussions of contrastive rhetorics (Shen 1989) and critiques of assimilationist projects (Lu 1992, Giroux 1992), I seemed incapable of considering Demetrius' rhetoric and Jason's desire for acceptance from any other perspectives. As a white instructor I might have been engaged in dysconscious acts of transgressive voyeurism (Royster 1995), reading Demetrius in terms of "nonmainstream" rhetorical traditions and attributing Jason's difficulties only to cultural difference. I found myself moved not to action, but simply to further contemplation. What might I have done instead to make Demetrius' text a part of a larger classroom discussion? How might I have asked other students to respond to Jason's request for e-mail?

In November, frustrated with classroom interaction, lack of student preparation, and low morale, I turn to my workshop colleagues for support. "It's mid-term," they remind me. But I knew more was at stake. I was terrified that my lack of experience had been translated to my students, who knew, after all, what "TA" meant in their other classes: TA's were graders, proctors, apprentices "stuck" working with first-year students while secretly (or not-so-secretly) longing to escape to their laboratories. Worse, perhaps they suspected what I often worried about myself—that their classroom was the laboratory and I was merely learning how to teach.

Mid-term Reflections: "I felt a funeral in my brain"

Even as the writing in my class seems to be improving, attendance is falling off. Rosa has missed eleven class days—Tiffanie eight, though many were excused absences. When Dylan comes, he doesn't bring his materials. Gordon is increasingly withdrawn committed to his fraternity and just sort of scraping by in my class. Mike threatened me with a 6:30 a.m. wake-up call on the first day of Winter Quarter ("Your husband will think I'm your boyfriend"), and followed that comment with a pornographic e-mail to me this week—muppets doing pretty unspeakable stuff. Apparently, he believes I am the kind of person who would find humor in Web Porn. As Elizabeth Ellsworth would say, this does not feel empowering. Boundaries are being crossed by Black students and white ones, by women and men, by "good students" and forgetful ones. And where is the article of research that helps me deal with this?

I feel like I've spent the last two weeks trying to let students know that I realize I am complicit in all of this, but some boundaries can't be crossed if I am to be an effective teacher. I am becoming increasingly aware that any discussion of teacher identity in the basic writing classroom needs to take into account multiple facets of identity. My institutional identity, my age, my gender, my place in the department, my tenuous place within the Writing Workshop, and, of course, my race and class need to be considered.

All of these crucial shapers of identity came to the forefront for me when my students took the floor as presenters and discussion leaders, and I became one of the participants.

December's Presentations: The Sound and the Fury

Today the three women, Casey, Tiffanie, and Rosa presented on "sexism in 052."
Rosa read from her paper about her mother's ovarian cancer. She then told us what
it was like for her to be one of three women in a class of men, describing how she al-
tered the language of her paper so that she wouldn't upset male members of the
class, particularly her peer group. That backfired. Gordon blew up, disgusted that
Rosa thought he was "too dumb" to understand her. I tried to step in, explaining
that she wasn't calling them dumb, but that Rosa felt uncomfortable discussing
some issues with them. Was I placating Gordon or defending Rosa? When Tiffanie
spoke, all hell broke loose. She claimed that all of the men who preferred Kingston's
book were "Mama's Boys," while the ones who preferred Cormier's book were sex-
ists. I watched the men on the left side of the room (students from rural areas) suck in
their cheeks and count to ten. Others shut down completely. When Casey, the third
woman, spoke, she prefaced her comments by saying that she had never felt dis-
criminated against as a woman in our class. How was I to respond? Whose position
was I to validate? I felt hurt and betrayed. I've certainly never been accused of not
fostering feminist texts/values in my classroom. But I know I was hyper-aware of the
number of men in my course, and I didn't push them to discuss gender on a daily ba-
sis. I had bitten my tongue on several occasions, worried that my male students
might perceive my feminism as threatening. But I didn't want the women to be put on
the spot all the time as the "representatives" of womankind.

Our reading of Maxine Hong Kingston's *The Woman Warrior* even further complicated my own understanding of my role within the classroom. When should I
speak, and when should I remain silent?

"No Name Woman" meets Dick Vitale

I have assigned my students, in groups of five, to lead discussion once over the
course of the quarter. The first two groups are talking about *The Woman Warrior.*
Today's group (three white men from rural areas, Mike, Mike, and Mark, one white
woman from Cleveland named Casey, and Shirish, a newly-made American citizen
originally from India) "presented" by subjecting my class to thirty excruciating
minutes of Dick Vitale on tape. The tie, they argued, was that Vitale motivates his
players through story-telling the same way that Kingston's mother motivates her
daughter by telling her the story of the "No Name Woman." All eyes, save mine and
Tiffanie's, glazed over in worshipful abandon! These students bought Vitale's
cliches and generalizations about the power of sports. "A boy, a ball, a dream," he
repeated like a mantra. And I thought, what about the girls? And what does it mean
to tell generations of boys that the ball is the dream? I raised these questions, but all
of my students shot me down pretty quickly. Talk about culture shock. All of my
students extolled the virtues of Vitale's way of seeing the world. Tiffanie and I just
shook our heads and sighed.

The Grapes of Rap

The second group, comprised by all of the African American students (Tiffanie, Dylan, and Demetrius) and Rosa, a bilingual student from Mexico, presented the class with a video today, a 25 minute MTV special memorializing rapper Tupac Shakur, an artist whose films I admired and whose music I knew very little about. I have such mixed feelings about this group's alliance. I want so badly for students of color, many of whom speak to me about racism in their dorms, to find networks of support. But my class is dividing rapidly along racial/ethnic lines. Do I assume heterogeneous groups are more effective educationally? I think as a high school teacher in Virginia I did. But now I'm not so sure. Maybe heterogeneous groups make me, not my students, feel safe. This group argued that like Kingston, Shakur uses personal experience to shape his texts. They wanted us to consider Shakur's life and death from this perspective, and then discuss our responses to the video.

The class was polite (a few eyes rolled and the boy next to me, Nathan, winced visibly as he heard of Shakur's sodomy charges). I took notes on the video. Shakur spoke powerfully and made it clear that he had to speak from and for his community. He also explained why, even though he had made a great deal of money as a rapper, he continued to live in South Central. "Where are the neighborhoods where I can be both safe and among my own people?" he asked. I felt the white student next to me bristle, but he continued to watch, tapping his foot in impatience.

The group asked us all to share our quick responses to the video. "I liked," Jason replied. He offered no further explanation. Several of the white students from rural communities muttered their responses, but one student completely surprised me by launching into a thorough discussion of Shakur and his work. I don't think the group expected Gordon to be a Tupac fan, and neither did I. I welcomed the surprise. Nathan asked about Shakur's violence. "After prison, did he keep beating people up?" Demetrius and Tiffanie fielded the question, but didn't really satisfy Nathan.

Later in the quarter, Mike told us why he had been so uncharacteristically silent after the video. "How many of us from farms even have cable TV? Do you really think we had all heard of Tupac Shakur? I only got MTV for the first time this year, in the dorm." A response like this easily gets forgotten in the midst of all of the scholarship about CUNY, SEEK, and Open Admissions programs in what Mike and Nathan call "the big city."

Final Portfolios: Grim Fairy Tales

While sharing their portfolios today, the classroom became a Dale Carnegie meeting as students vowed to submit their work to the evil Writing Workshop Committee and skip right over 053. After nine weeks of hard work, we were back to the question of placement. Nobody celebrated the improved writing as an accomplishment; rather, the improvement they saw in one another's work was important only if it granted direct access to English 110. Even as I told my students that courses like 052 are the reason they are admitted to the university that if these courses were eliminated, so, too would the university eliminate them—they continued to script

*the Writing Workshop staff as the "bad guys" preventing them from reaching their
"true potential" in 110—only I could champion them to the rest of the Workshop.
They seemed unable to understand that I, too, was a part of that system.*

I suspect now that my students sensed my own contradictory feelings about the
work I did as their teacher. The issue of placement was so powerful for Mike, whose
mother is an English teacher and whose father is the vice-principal of the town middle school, that he uses it to structure the cover letter for his final 052 portfolio. In
that letter, he figures the Writing Workshop as an "Evil Stepmother" preventing this
"Cinderella Class" from going to the "Ball"—English 110.

Conclusion: Grim Fairytales Revised

Perhaps the most eloquent storyteller of the quarter was Casey, a young white
woman from a large city whose silence throughout the quarter is reflected in my
journal; her name appears less often than anyone else's. She struggled quietly, and
her final essay, an allegory written in response to the prompt, "Tell the story of 052,"
moved all of us. What it suggests about the identities our students themselves find
most meaningful is quite provocative. Casey's paper reads as follows:

* * *

"The City of 052"

*Many, many miles below the ocean stood an enchanting city with the identification
number 052. This city was trapped infinitely on the floor of the ocean in a large glass
bubble . . . The members of the city were an unusual group of individuals. Not one person carried the same personality trait or the same physical feature. Although the
members seemed to be nothing alike, each one of them bonded together by the simple
fact that they were unhappy to be stuck in a city confined to the bottom of the ocean.*

*The members of the city 052 were placed there by the government because they were
considered to be slightly behind the rest of the world in intelligence . . . [their] work
was not much fun, but was there to educate them and to better enable them for the real
world . . . The first few days were a little uncomfortable or even confusing for every
member of the city. Being in a city that was underwater was a little bit different then
the way they were used to living. . . .*

*There was one member of the city that was ahead of everybody else, and her name was
Becky. Becky had been in this city for many, many years but was only there to guide
those with assumed less intelligence. They were all a little surprised by Becky, because they had expected someone a little stricter and less happy . . . The whole group
seemed to be bonding, at least that's what most of them thought. They seldom had contact with the real world but when they did, they learned that the work that was getting
done in the underwater city was as complicated, and took more work than the work
that was getting done in the real world. Many of the members of this interesting group
became frustrated by this fact. "This is so unfair that the education we are getting
down here will not count towards credit in the real world," said Nathan. Nathan al-*

ways seemed to be bringing up this point every time the group met. Tiffanie and Mike
agreed with Nathan. That is why the group probably bonded so well, even if only a few
people spoke up, everybody felt the same. . . .

Casey believed that a kind of "bonding" took place despite cultural, gender, racial, and regional differences. And I smile even now at Caseys depiction of me as a "laughing, happy individual"—that certainly isn't how I represent myself in my journals. Her reading of me as someone with experience, someone who has been in the city "a long, long, time" gives me pause. How do we negotiate our constructions of our own identities with our students' depictions of us? When I reread those journals, I noticed how I wrestled with notions of authority, defined variously in several instances. When students were absent, I attributed those absences to my status as a TA who couldn't "make them" come to class; I questioned my institutional authority. When I refused to push students to critique Dick Vitale's ideological stance, I denied myself a chance for feminist advocacy, perhaps subverting my own political authority, but privileging my students'. When I resisted engaging the question of multicultural rhetorics while reading Demetrius' work, I subjugated my identity as a white reader to my expertise as a rhetorician, creating a lack of professional authority, but perhaps recognizing a student's cultural authority.

What I wish to emphasize now is not a sort of "revelation." I won't argue that, yes, I had authority all along and that Casey's text helped me see that. Instead, I want to suggest that the keeping of a teaching journal—which required me not only to reconstruct classroom experiences, but to pay attention to the act of construction itself, to come to terms with how who I am prevents and/or enables me to reevaluate classroom practice—helped me to understand classroom authority in more dialogic terms. That journal allows me to ask the new kinds of questions I imagined at the outset of this essay: How did my own expectations of having to negotiate racial difference first and foremost affect the pedagogical decisions I made throughout the quarter? Was that difference, in fact, the difference my students most perceived? What other factors constitute teacher/student cultures and identities? What kinds of mechanisms shape the relationships between those factors in the classroom, determining which factors are most powerful in any given moment? Perhaps most importantly, how can interrogation of teacher/scholar identities alter the landscape of existing basic writing pedagogies?

Implications for Teaching and Research

From this collective of workshop activities, we walk away with direct challenges for what identity means in terms of classroom transformation. Our starter questions for analyzing scenarios from the basic writing classroom have acquired new life in that they have become the places where our rendering of challenges begin.

What issues emerge from a shifting of our view of identity and culture formation in basic writing classrooms to include the merging of teacher and student locations in classroom space?

How do teacher "location," student "location," and institution matter in the ways that each of us might center the gaze in the classroom and articulate the nature of the teaching/learning engagement?

How can we use our conscious awareness of self, students, place, and enterprise in making the basic writing classroom a richer (i.e., more positive, productive, intellectually invigorated) literacy development arena?

What advice or "cautionary tales" do we need to remember?

Clearly, we do not have prescriptions for these questions. The first three certainly constitute a rather complex agenda for research, scholarship, and classroom practices. The fourth question also brings with it ill-formed responses. However, as our experiences resonated during the workshop with the experiences of the participants, we realized that we are indeed not starting from scratch in being both warned and well-instructed by the experiences and expertise that we have developed in basic writing classrooms over the last thirty years especially.

Implications for Research and Scholarship.   The scholarship in basic writing, as we discussed earlier, does not focus on teacher identity. When teacher identity is considered, scholars often provide only brief statements at the beginning of essays (e.g., "I am a white-middleclass-woman-at-a-large-state-university"), rather than sustaining self-critique throughout the piece. How might we better imagine ways to enact our identities, to question them, to consider how these identities impact our classrooms? Can a teaching journal, such as the one demonstrated here by Taylor, be considered worthy as a research tool or as a rhetorical form worthy of study? What forms would/should scholarship that is more attuned to teacher identity take?

As evidenced by the form of this article, even when we try to concentrate on teacher identities and their construction, we face challenges of ethics and representation. For one thing, student voices creep into the center of our concerns and are often the most compelling voices that we hear. How can we make room for those voices and skill sustain a dialogic balance—us, them, the systems around us all? Is it possible, for example, to focus on teacher identity without engaging the voices of our students? If it isn't possible, how do we incorporate their points of view? How do we ethically represent their experiences? Can we begin to talk about teacher and student identities as mutually constitutive? What are productive ways to do so? What can this kind of reconceptualization offer the field of rhetoric and composition in terms of methodologies in research and scholarship?

In one way, this article is yet another call to story as a very useful methodology for sharing classroom experiences—this time with the gaze on the teacher. Our call, however, is also for a critical step back from our narratives to make them reach out more inclusively and more meaningfully for the general landscape of our work. At this point, our view is that we need to think, not only about ourselves in classroom space, but also about the art of storytelling in terms of its theoretical and political implications. What have we learned about the telling of stories? How do we assign meaning and draw value for the classroom cultures from which our telling comes?

Implications for Teacher Training and Classroom Pedagogy. Re-imagining the work of basic writing programs in the twenty-first century demands that we break the cycle of classroom representations that permit our own locations as teachers to go unnoticed and uninterrogated. Who we are and how we are as human beings impact upon our pedagogical choices. Being aware of this reality permits us to see success and failure in our classrooms with different eyes, with a different sort of critical questioning. We can become more sensitive to the possibility that what in the past we may have attributed to issues related to student identity may also be a function of issues related to our own identities. Is a "problem" a matter of ill-literacy or multiple literacies? Is a "problem" a function of student ignorance and inexperience or teacher ignorance and inexperience? Can a given usage be explained within institutional contexts or home contexts? Is the "problem" tied to performance or to the nature of engagements that we ourselves forge between ourselves and our students, or between ourselves and our institutions, or between those of us inside the classrooms and the systems that operate around us? What do we as teachers really know about the literate possibilities maximally available to us in a classroom? How have we learned to make good use of what we know? How have we learned to discover what else we might need to know and make use of?

In large part, the demographics of students in writing classrooms are shifting significantly, but the demographics of teachers entering writing classrooms don't seem to be keeping a comparable pace. Writing teachers, and especially basic writing teachers, tend to be white women. Given the differences in these demographic factors, the obvious probability, as indicated previously, is a variety of mismatches between teacher and students. Whatever a teacher's personal, social, or institutional identity, however, whether that person conforms to the norm for teacher demographics in basic writing classrooms or not, what is clear is that we need to re-think teacher training and to rethink classroom pedagogies with these factors in mind.

Obviously, we are not at all suggesting that only insiders in a particular discourse community have the capacity to teach other members of that community. We are not interested in even belaboring this point. We are suggesting that teachers think more consciously and reflectively about the implications of difference in the classroom. How can we utilize knowledge of differences across personal, social, and institutional lines to respond better to student needs or to adjust our own needs when we encounter students who seem unfamiliar to us? What do we do when the identities that we hold most dear are not the features with which our students are connecting? In Taylor's case, for example, her sense of herself as a white female instructor was less important to her than her sense of herself as a teaching assistant who was forging a professional/institutional identity for herself.

This article suggests, then, that teachers might benefit from taking into account ways to engage in dialogue with students about how they are seeing us and not just about how we are seeing them. A critical question, therefore, is how do we develop habits as teachers, and especially as teachers in training, that support: the explorations of difference in classrooms including the ways in which our own locations contribute to this complexity; the accumulation of specific knowledge about students and student performance as a multiliterate enterprise; or about the use of that knowledge in developing the flexibility to match variable strategies with variable classroom needs and to construct classroom cultures that are positive and productive?

In terms of basic writing classrooms as a specific site of engagement, are we being systematic in training people for the particular needs of students at this level? How many teachers are simply "passing through," as in Taylor's case, i.e., learning from the site but not necessarily planning to make careers there? Should we be moving as a profession to draw more colleagues to basic writing as an area to which one is professionally devoted and not just generally interested? In other words, who are we thinking of when we think of "basic writing teachers" for the twenty-first century? What are the pedagogical implications of our answers? What are the implications for teacher training?

Implications for Re-considering Invisible Literacies.   In the contemporary scholarship in which "basic writer" is often conflated with minority students, many kinds of literacies remain hidden. Issues such as how regionalisms and geographical alliances affect writing instruction seem to get left out of consideration. The concept of literacy as shaped by specific contexts inside and outside of the university is not always used to greatest advantage. The dominance of "open admissions" at particular colleges and universities sometimes dominates our views of what literacy is or is not in ways that prevent us from seeing the strengths of our own students. For example, as teachers who work often with rural students rather than urban and suburban students, we have had to re-think some basic assumptions, such as how the presence or absence of cable television affects resources for writing. Our experiences with this project have led us to take into much fuller account the ways in which conflating race or ethnicity with lack of membership in academic discourse communities actually deflects attention away from other kinds of issues. Looming large among these issues is how writing professionals at all levels might productively critique the "gatekeeping" roles of first year writing that seem to be built automatically into the very fiber of our academic system.

One Last Word

At the end of this article, we feel compelled to make one last statement. While caution in all that we do seems well-advised given how complicated classroom challenges inevitably are, the commitment to more sustaining theories of classroom engagement and more generative and respectful classroom and scholarly practices is a challenge worth accepting. Affirmed by our experiences in the workshop, watching and listening as other teachers from across the nation saw ways in which their views of issues and challenges merged with ours, we were incredibly inspired to re-commit ourselves to this work in the company of others who were doing likewise: Taylor to her work toward her dissertation; Royster as she continues to investigate issues of identity, agency, and authority in multiple environments. In the meantime, in recognition that the task of debunking mythologies demands the sharing of counter viewpoints, we submit to the discourse on classrooms this view of teachers, not just students, in extending the call to others to make a different, more inclusive, more interactive case for how attention might be brought to bear on issues of classroom identity.

Selected Bibliography:
Teacher Identity and Basic Writing Research

Bizzell, Patricia. "What Happens When Basic Writers Come to College?" *College Composition and Communication* 37.3 (1986): 294-301.

Campbell, Paul R. *Current Population Reports: Population Projections for States by Age, Sex, Race, and Hispanic Origin, 1993 to 2020.* Washington, D.C.: U.S. Department of Commerce, 1994.

Dean, Terry. "Multicultural Classrooms, Monocultural Teachers." *College Composition and Communication* 40.1 (1989): 23-37.

Gilyard, Keith. *Let's Flip the Script: An African American Discourse on Language, Literature, and Learning.* Detroit: Wayne State UP, 1996.

Gunner, Jeanne. "The Status of Basic Writing Teachers: Do We Need a 'Maryland Resolution?'" *Journal of Basic Writing* 12.1 (1993): 57-63.

Hindman, Jane. "Reinventing the University: Finding the Place for Basic Writers." *Journal of Basic Writing* 12.2 (1993): 55-76.

Hourigan, Maureen M. *Literacy as Social Exchange: Intersections of Class, Gender, and Race.* New York: SUNY, 1994.

Hull, Glynda, Mike Rose, Kay Losey Fraser, and Marisa Castellano. "Remediation as Social Construct: Perspectives from an Analysis of Classroom Discourse." *College Composition and Communication* 42.3 (1991): 299-329.

Johnson, Cheryl L. "Participatory Rhetoric and the Teacher as Racial/ Gendered Subject." *College English* 56.4 (1994): 409-419.

Jones, William. "Basic Writing: Pushing Against Racism." *Journal of Basic Writing* 12.1 (1993): 72-80.

Laurence, Patricia. "The Vanishing Site of Mina Shaughnessy's Errors and Expectations. *Journal of Basic Writing* 12.2 (1993): 1827.

Lu, Min-zhan. "Conflict and Struggle: The Enemies or Preconditions of Basic Writing?" *College English* 54.8 (1992): 887-913.

_____ . "Professing Multiculturalism: The Politics of Style in the Contact Zone." *College Composition and Communication* 45.4 (1994): 442-458.

McCarthy, Cameron and Warren Crichlow, eds. *Race, Identity, and Representation in Education.* New York: Routledge, 1993.

Mutnick, Deborah. *Writing in an Alien World.* Portsmouth: Boynton/ Cook, 1996.

Neuleib, Janice. "The Friendly Stranger: Twenty-Five Years as 'Other.'" *College Composition and Communication* 43.2 (1992): 231-243.

Patthey-Chavez, G. Genevieve, and Constance Gergen. "Culture as an Instructional Resource in the Multi-ethnic Composition Classroom." *Journal of Basic Writing* 11.1 (1992): 75-95.

Reagan, Sally Barr. "Warning: Basic Writers at Risk—The Case of Javier." *Journal of Basic Writing* 10.2 (1991): 99-115.

Rondinone, Peter. "Teacher Background and Student Needs." Journal of Basic Writing 10.1 (1991): 41-53.

Schor, Sandra. "The Short, Happy Life of Ms. Mystery." *Journal of Basic Writing* 10.1 (1991): 16-25.

Scott, Jerrie Cobb. "Literacies and Deficits Revisited." *Journal of Basic Writing* 12.1 (1993): 46-56.

Severino, Carol. "Where the Cultures of Basic Writers and Academia Intersect: Cultivating the Common Ground." *Journal of Basic Writing* 11.1 (1992) 4-15.

Shen, Fan. "The Classroom and the Wider Culture: Identity as a Key to Learning English Composition." *College Composition and Communication* 40.4 (1989): 459-466.

Tobin, Lad. "Reading Students, Reading Ourselves: Revising the Teacher's Role in the Writing Class." *College English* 53.3 (1991): 333-348.

Appendix 1: Informal Survey for
Basic Writing Workshop Participants

1. For what kind of institution do you work?
   —two-year college
   —four-year college
   —two-year technical college
   —technological college/university
   —research university
2. Are you:
   —a writing/other skills teacher in a basic writing program
   —an administrator of a basic writing program
   —other
3. How many years have you worked with students in basic writing classrooms?
   —1-3 years
   —4-9 years
   —10 years or more
4. How much diversity is evident among your teaching faculty?
   —25% people of color
   —25% men
   —50% or more people of color
   —50% or more men
   —majority white
   —majority women
5. How many of you work in programs that are:
   —separate administratively from freshman writing
   —included administratively with freshman writing
   —a majority of teachers that are tenure track
   —a majority of the teachers that are non-tenure track
6. What are the percentages of people of color in the program?
   —under 5%
   —under 10%
   —about 25%
   —about 50%
   —about 75%
   —about 90%
7. How many of you are associated with programs in which the correlations between the basic writing students and the general college/university are in balance
in terms of:
   —race
   —gender
   —age
   —cultural belief system
   —majors
   —urban vs. rural
   —private vs. public schooling

Appendix 2

Let's begin with some short writing. I'd like you to generate three lists just to get the juices flowing. Think about a specific class—preferably a writing class that you're currently doing, or might have quite recently completed.

—List 3 adjectives that you think that your students would use to describe you now that the course is over or about over.

—List 3 adjectives that you think that these same students would probably have used on the very first day of class.

—List 3 adjectives that you would use to describe yourself in the classroom and specify whether your choices are closer to how you really are or how you hope that you are.

Spend a couple of minutes reviewing your lists and jot down a sentence or two specifying whether you see differences in the lists and how you might account for there being or not being discrepancies.

Now, I'd like you to write a short, short story about a real incident. Choose one moment from your teaching that involved a question of identity or image. Explain what happened, how you felt, whether this issue is ongoing or resolved for you.

Save your story until later, but turn now to two people who happen to be seated near you. Talk about the adjectives that you generated. See if you can come up with a list of issues to share with the full group that seem to show themselves in your conversation.

Share the list of issues.

Appendix 3: Scenarios: Constructing Teacher Identity in the Basic Writing Classroom

1. Reading Materials

You are teaching Robert Cormier's *The Chocolate War,* a novel classified as "young adult" and one that prompts discussion of peer pressure, teacher authority, gendered behaviors, individuals and communities (feel free to substitute the young adult novel of your choice here). Several students in your basic writing course are writing in their journals that they are enjoying the experience of engaged reading for the first time in their academic careers. Yet in classroom discussion, other students are claiming that the text is "too easy," that it is a text appropriate for "middle schoolers."

—How do you speak to both groups' of students' concerns?

—How do you select reading materials for a basic writing classroom?

2. Collaboration

You are teaching basic writing in a multiethnic classroom. You decide to assign peer groups for the quarter that are heterogeneous, and you pay particular attention to issues of race, culture, class, and writing strengths. Your African American students request to work together, thereby offsetting the "balance" you had worked to achieve. Suddenly, the peer groups seem to be structured along racial lines.

—How do you respond to the request?

—How do you determine the structure of peer response groups in your basic writing classroom?

3. *Structure*

Your basic writing pedagogy privileges a process-oriented, holistic approach to drafting and revising. You encourage your students to enlist a variety of prewriting strategies, but you do not prescribe them; likewise, you talk to students about "focus ideas" or an "implied thesis," but you do not ask students to begin their prewriting by drafting a thesis statement. One of your students, an Asian American enrolled in his first sociology course, pulls you aside after class. "I have a complaint," he says. "Today in Sociology 101, my teacher asked me to turn in my thesis statement and topic outline for my research paper. When I turned my stuff in, she said I didn't know what a thesis or an outline even was."

—How do you answer your student?

—How do you balance an emphasis on writing conventions with other possible emphases in the classroom?

4. *Gender*

Two white students, one from a rural community and the other from a suburban area, are presenting their findings concerning sexual harassment and the "P.C." movement to a multiethnic basic writing class. Only one of the ten students is female. As you listen, you become aware that the presenters are speaking about sexual harassment issues in highly problematic ways. However, these two students have expressed their frustrations regarding their own discomfort with your "multicultural curriculum" throughout the quarter.

—How do you respond to the presentation?

—How do you facilitate the ensuing discussion?

—How do you determine an appropriate focus or set of values for your own course?

5. *Assessment*

Upon completing a quarter of your basic writing course, you feel that one of your students should, in fact, bypass the second quarter of the basic writing sequence. You tell this student that he can submit a portfolio of his work to you, and that you will write an accompanying letter of recommendation to the coordinator of the Basic Writing program advocating this action. Your other students hear it is possible to "bypass" the rest of the sequence.

—How do you speak to the group about the process?

—How do you explain who "belongs" in a basic writing program and who doesn't?

6. *Technology*

Your basic writing class meets in a computer-assisted classroom where you often utilize an on-line discussion program. You have set up two discussions or "chat rooms" for your students to participate in; the two discussions center around the "English Only" debate. As is often the case, the students divide themselves along ethnic lines; all of the Hispanic students choose to enter one chat room, while the white students enter the other. You, the teacher, are able to "float" between the chat rooms. You notice that the white students have begun a discussion of Mexican migrant workers and issues of class that is highly problematic, but the Hispanic students on the other side of the room are not aware of the discussion.

—How do you participate in the troubling discussion?

—How do you encourage cross-talk?

7. *Experience*

You are teaching Mike Rose's *Lives on the Boundary* to your multiethnic basic writing class. Your Latino and African American students are excited by the book, but your white, rural students connect with the text on only one point. They argue that they, like Mike Rose, have been victims of testing mix-ups.

—How do you encourage both groups to think critically and creatively about the book?

—How do you account for differences in personal history and experience in your classroom pedagogy?

8. *Agency and Authority*

You are a teacher of basic writing in a multiethnic classroom, and your class is working on collaborative projects involving contemporary language issues: Ebonics, bilingualism, the "English Only" debate, and the "P.C." movement on college campuses. A group of African American students presents their thoughts on Ebonics to their classmates. One of the speakers contradicts herself several times as she reads from the Oakland City Amendment; she cites the amendment, then "translates" to her classmates in highly problematic ways. To complicate matters further, when the presentation is over, the students pose all of their questions to you, not to the group.

—What role should you play in negotiating the discussion?

—How do you simultaneously: encourage critical questioning; hold students accountable for accuracy, clarity and precision when they lead discussion; and require respect for others in the basic writing classroom?

Bibliography
by Nels P. Highberg

This bibliography is meant to augment the extensive bibliography that Theresa Enos offers in *A Sourcebook for Basic Writing Teachers.* In other words, this bibliography offers a representative sample of texts that have been published since 1987. In that time, there has been a great expansion of interest in the field of basic writing, and many scholarly trends have evolved and grown. Trends that emerged when basic writing just began developing as a field remain evident, such as how to define "basic writer." Still, other research questions continue to arise, such as clarifying the role that changing technologies will hold for basic writing pedagogies. By no means complete, this bibliography, along with those listed along with each individual article in *Landmark Essays in Basic Writing,* will points towards key issues, authors, and ideas that continue to shape basic writing scholarship.

Adams, Peter Dow. "Basic Writing Reconsidered." *Journal of Basic Writing* 12.1 (1993): 22-36.

Adler-Kassner, Linda, and Thomas Reynolds. "Computers, Reading, and Basic Writers: Online Strategies for Helping Students with Academic Texts." *Teaching English in the Two-Year College* 23.3 (1996): 170-8.

Armstrong, Cheryl. "Reexamining Basic Writing: Lessons from Harvard's Basic Writers." *Journal of Basic Writing* 7.2 (1988): 68-80.

Bernstein, Susan Naomi. "Life Writing and Basic Writing." *Teaching English in the Two-Year College* 25.2 (1998): 122-5.

Bishop, Wendy. "We're All Basic Writers: Tutors Talking about Writing Apprehension." *The Writing Center Journal* 9.2: 31-42.

Creed, John, and Susan B. Andrews. "Publication Project in Alaska Offers Ways to Open New Worlds to Basic Writing Students." *Journal of Basic Writing* 13.1 (1994): 3-13.

Cross, Geoffrey. "Left to Their Own Devices: Three Basic Writers Using Word Processing." *Computers and Composition* 7 (April 1990): 47-58.

Dean, Terry. "Multicultural Classrooms, Monocultural Teachers." *College Composition and Communication* 40.1 (1989): 23-37.

Deem, James M., and Sandra A. Engel. "Developing Literacy through Transcription." *Journal of Basic Writing* 7.2 (1988): 99-107.

_____ . "The Educational Oral History: An Approach to Teaching Basic English." *Teaching English in the Two-Year College* 15.2 (1988): 105-9.

Di Matteo, Anthony. "Under Erasure: A Theory for Interactive Writing in Real Time." *Computers and Composition* 7 (April 1990): 71-84.

DiPardo, Anne. *A Kind of Passport: A Basic Writing Adjunct Program and the Challenge of Student Diversity.* Urbana, IL: NCTE, 1993.

_____ . "Narrative Discourse in the Basic Writing Class: Meeting the Challenge of Cultural Diversity." *Teaching English in the Two-Year College* 17.1 (1990): 45-53.

Dixon, Kathleen G. "Intellectual Development and the Place of Narrative in Basic and Freshman Composition." *Journal of Basic Writing* 8.1 (1989): 3-20.

Gay, Pamela. "Questions and Issues in Basic Writing and Computing." *Computers and Composition* 8 (1991): 63-81.

_____ . "Rereading Shaughnessy from a Postcolonial Perspective." *Journal of Basic Writing* 12.2 (1993): 29-40.

Gould, Christopher. "Literature in the Basic Writing Course: A Bibliographic Survey." *College English* 49.5 (1987): 558-74.

_____ . "Teaching Literature to Basic Writers." *Journal of Basic Writing* 8.1 (1989): 57-66.

Greene, Brenda. "Empowerment and the Problem Identification and Resolution Strategies of Basic Writers." *Journal of Basic Writing* 11.2 (1992): 4-27.

Gunner, Jeanne. "The Status of Basic Writing Teachers: Do We Need a 'Maryland Resolution'?" *Journal of Basic Writing* 12.1 (1993): 57-63.

Hashimoto, Irvin. "Pain and Suffering: Apostrophes and Academic Life." *Journal of Basic Writing* 7.2 (1988): 91-8.

Henning, Barbara. "The World Was Stone Cold: Basic Writing in an Urban University." *College English* 53.6 (1991): 674-85.

Hindman, Jane. "Reinventing the University: Finding the Place for Basic Writers." *Journal of Basic Writing* 12.2 (1993): 55-76.

Horner, Bruce. "Discoursing Basic Writing." *College Composition and Communication* 47.2 (1996): 199-222.

Houston, Linda. "Knowing Learning Styles Can Improve Self-Confidence of Developmental Writers." *Teaching English in the Two-Year College* 24.3 (1997): 212-5.

Hull, Glynda, Mike Rose, Kay Losey Fraser, and Marisa Castellano. "Remediation as Social Construct: Perspectives from an Analysis of Classroom Discourse." *College Composition and Communication* 42.3 (1991): 299-329.

Huot, Brian. "Reading-Writing Connections on the College Level." *Teaching English at the Two-Year College* 15.2 (1988): 90-8.

Hunter, Paul, and Nadine Pearce. "Basic Writers: The Writing Process and Written Products." *Teaching English in the Two Year College* 14.4 (1987): 252-64.

Jones, William. "Basic Writing: Pushing Against Racism." *Journal of Basic Writing* 12.1 (1993): 72-80

Laurence, Patricia. "The Vanishing Site of Mina Shaughnessy's *Errors and Expectations.*" *Journal of Basic Writing* 12.2 (1993): 18-27.

Liebman, JoAnne. "Contrastive Rhetorics: Students as Ethnographers." *Journal of Basic Writing* 7.2 (1988): 6-27.

Lu, Min-zhan. "Professing Multiculturalism: The Politics of Style in the Contact Zone." *College Composition and Communication* 45.4 (1994): 442-58.

Martinez, Joseph G.R., and Nancy C. Martinez. "Who is Alien in the Developmental Classroom?: A Comparison of Some Student-Teacher Values." *Journal of Basic Writing* 8.2 (1989): 99-112.

McAllister, Carole, and Richard Louth. "The Effect of Word Processing on the Quality of Basic Writers' Revisions." *Reasearch in the Teaching of English* 22.4 (1988): 417-27.

McDonald, James C. "Student Metaphors for Themselves as Writers." *English Journal* 81.4 (1992): 60-4.

McLaughlin, Margaret A., Patricia T. Price, and Mildred Pate. "Using Whole Language to Incorporate African American Literature into Developmental Reading/Writing Classes." *Teaching English in the Two-Year College* 22.3 (1995): 173-8.

Meeker, Linda Hanson. "Pragmatic Politics: Using Assessment Tools to (Re)Shape a Curriculum." *Journal of Basic Writing* 9.1 (1990): 3-19.

Middendorf, Marilyn. "Bakhtin and the Dialogic Writing Class." *Journal of Basic Writing* 11.1 (1992): 34-46.

Murphy, Ann. "Transference and Resistance in the Basic Writing Classroom: Problematics and Praxis." *College Composition and Communication* 40.2 (1989): 175-87.

Mutnick, Deborah. *Writing in an Alien World: Basic Writing and the Struggle for Equality in Higher Education*. Portsmouth, NH: Boynton/Cook, 1996.

Nelson, Marie Ponsot. *At the Point of Need: Teaching Basic and ESL Writers*. Portsmouth, NH: Boynton/Cook, 1990.

Reagan, Sally Barr. "Warning: Basic Writers at Risk—The Case of Javier." *Journal of Basic Writing* 10.2 (1991): 99-115.

Robertson, Elizabeth. "Moving from Expressive Writing to Academic Discourse." *The Writing Center Journal* 9 (Fall-Winter 1988): 21-8.

Rondinone, Peter. "Teacher Background and Student Needs." *Journal of Basic Writing* 10.1 (1991): 41-53.

Roskelly, Hephzibah, ed. "Survival of the Fittest: Ten Years in a Basic Writing Program." *Journal of Basic Writing* 7.1 (1988): 13-29.

Royster, Jacqueline Jones and Jean C. Williams. "History in the Spaces Left: African American Presence and Narratives of Composition Studies." *College Composition and Communication* 50.4 (1999): 563-84.

Rubin, Lois. "Combining the Personal and Analytical: Assignments for Basic Writing." *Teaching English in the Two-Year College* 19.2 (1992): 141-7.

Schor, Sandra. "The Short, Happy Life of Ms. Mystery." *Journal of Basic Writing* 10.1 (1991): 16-25.

Scott, Jerrie Cobb. "Literacies and Deficits Revisited." *Journal of Basic Writing* 12.1 (1993): 46-56.

Severino, Carol. "Where the Cultures of Basic Writers and Academia Intersect: Cultivating the Common Ground." *Journal of Basic Writing* 11.1 (1992): 4-15.

Shor, Ira. "Our Apartheid: Writing Instruction and Inequality." *Journal of Basic Writing* 16.1 (1997): 91-104.

Soliday, Mary. "From the Margins to the Mainstream: Reconceiving Remediation." *College Composition and Communication* 47.1 (1996): 85-100.

Spigelman, Candace. "Taboo Topics in the Rhetoric of Silence: Discussing *Lives on the Boundary* in a Basic Writing Class." *Journal of Basic Writing* 17.1 (1998): 42-55

Sternglass, Marilyn S. "The Need for Conceptualizing at All Levels of Writing Instruction." *Journal of Basic Writing* 8.2 (1989): 87-98.

Stygall, Gail. "Politics and Proof in Basic Writing." *Journal of Basic Writing* 7.2 (1988): 28-41.

Thorne, Shelia. "Prewriting: A Basic Skill for Basic Writers." *Teaching English in the Two-Year College* 20.1 (1993): 31-5.

Tinberg, Howard. "Teaching in the Spaces Between: What Basic Writing Students Can Teach Us." *Journal of Basic Writing* 17.2 (1998): 76-90

Wiener, Harvey S. "Inference: Perspectives on Literacy for Basic Skills Students." *Journal of Basic Writing* 11.1 (1992): 16-33.

Young, Morris. "Narratives of Identity: Theorizing and the Nation." *Journal of Basic Writing* 15.2 (1996): 50-75.

Index

A

abstract(ion), 40
   knowledge, 73
   thought, 44, 114
abstraction(s), 24, 37, 51
academic
   community, 17, 137, 142–143
   culture, 123, 133, 147, 150
   discourse, xv, xvii, 58, 63–66, 108, 112,
      137, 151–153, 160, 182, 186,
      187
   discourse communities, 109–110,
      114–115, 159, 216, 228
   language, 123, 132
   world view, 20–21
academy, 144
accommodation, 137, 146, 148, 150,
      152–153, 155, 174–175
   defined, 146
acculturation, xviii, 137, 139–142, 148, 152,
      155, 161
Adkins, Arthur, W.H.
   quoted, 44
Adler, Jonathan, 38
administrators, 201
admission requirements, 121, 126
adolescence, 36
adult basic education, 186
Against Our Will (Brownmiller), 78
age, 215, 221
agency, 223
agonism, xviii, xix
Alaska Land Claims Settlement Act, 99
Albuquerque, University of, xvi, 69
Alchemy of Race and Rights, The (Williams),
   175
Alice in Wonderland (Carroll), 5
alienation, 152
alphabetic literacy, 41, 43–44
American Reading Instruction (Smith), ix
American Scholar, 154
analysis, 24, 30, 47, 108, 110, 113–114, 116,
      118, 126, 201
   political, 6
analytic thinking, 35, 41, 143

Anderson, Betty, 187, 190–191
Anglo
   teachers, 111
   writing tradition, 112
Animal Farm (Orwell), 113, 115
anthropological studies, 41, 44–45, 206–207
Anzaldua, Gloria, 151
   quoted, 135–136, 144, 146
aphasia, 31
Applebee, Arthur, x
   quoted, ix
argument, 78
articulated vs. global perception, 26
artificial intelligence, 39, 48
assessment, 28, 30, 216, 232
assimilation, 161
audience, 47, 80, 91, 98, 109, 112, 124
Austen, Jane, 6
authentic self, 189
author, xx, 109, 189–190, 197, 201
   function, 186–190, 198, 201–202
      defined, 188
authoritarian, 132
authority, 91–93, 111, 127–128, 140, 143,
      155, 182–183, 198, 213, 216, 219,
      225, 233
autonomy, 127, 211

B

back-to-basics movement, 121–122
Bahamas, College of, xvi, 69, 71
Bahamian
   men, 79–82
   women, 72, 80
Bakhtin circle, 104, 106, 107
Bakhtinian approaches, 189
   dialogue, xviii
   reading, 106
Baldwin, James, 1, 5, 149–150
Baltimore, xvi
Bambara, Toni Cade, 2
banking concept of education, 105
Bartholomae, David, 16, 59, 220
   quoted, xix–xx, xxii, 16, 59
basal programs, 208

and race, 18, 60, 62, 66, 190
    and class, xii–xiii, 177, 194, 213
and racism, 49–50, 217
and racist and xenophobic ideology, 104
    see also: students
and recreational life, 57
and religious life, 57
and rhetorical
    forms, 78
    patterns, 113
    power, 152
and the rod and frame test, 25
and SEEK, xiv, 1, 147, 223
    see also: City College of New
        York
and sexism, 49–50
and spatial-orientation discrimination,
    31
and speech
    inner, 70–71
and Standard English, 15,21
    absolutes, 19
    commitments, 19,–20
    mastery, 20
    and cognitivism, 23
and style, 28
and technocratic definitions of literacy,
    xx
and *Journal of Basic Writing, The* xiii
and tracking, 179
and uncritical dysconsciousness, xx,
    205, 209, 212
and voice, 136
and Vygotsky, Leo
    see: curriculum
and wave theory, 185
and Western Literature, 5
and women
and work, 57
and written English, 65
and Virginia Woolf
as borderlands, xviii, 146
see also: contact zone
as remedial, remediation 69, 89, 184,
    185, 194
at CUNY
see: City College of New York
at College of the Bahamas, the, 69, 71
at Harvard University, ix
at Indiana University, 185
at Michigan, the University of, ix
at Pennsylvania, the University of, ix
at Pittsburgh, the University of, 174

at Wellesley College, ix
at Wisconsin, the University of, ix
audience, 47, 112
borders, 135
    see also: contact, margin
boundary, 136
controlling idea, 177
curriculum, ix, xii, 103, 108
    and Bakhtin, 104, 106
    and literacy, 107
    and Friere, 104–105, 107, 109, 130,
        133
    and the inner-city, 104
    and Vygotsky, 104, 108, 170–172
    changes, 208
critical consciousness, 209
    see also: uncritical
        dysconsciousness
deficient model, xii, 137
definitions of, 174, 184, 185, 228
diversity
    linguistic and cultural, 208
    see also: discursive
educators
    see: teachers
ideology, 210
in Albuquerque, 70
in *College Composition and Communi-
    cation*, xiii
in *College English*, xiii, 123, 164
in New Mexico, 70
in Women's Studies, xxii
metaphors, 104–105
    of growth, 160
    of initiation, 160–161
myths of, 15
paragraphs, 77
pedagogy,
    and popular magazines, 74
    deficit, 205–206
    of Bruffee and Farrell, 143
    liberatory, xvii, 132
    post-critical, xix
    process-oriented approach, 85
    skills-oriented approach, 85
    student-centered, 104
    student-generated, xvi
    vs. skills debate, xvi
skills, 137, 216
students
    African-American and/or Black,
        83–86, 190–191
    and racism, 209